Empire and Co-operation

Empire and Co-operation

How the British Empire used Co-operatives in its Development Strategies 1900–1970

RITA RHODES

To Pam,

Warmest Greetings,

Rita (Rhodes)

First published in Great Britain in 2012 by
John Donald, an imprint of Birlinn Ltd

West Newington House
10 Newington Road
Edinburgh
EH9 1QS

www.birlinn.co.uk

ISBN: 978 1 906566 56 2

The publishers gratefully acknowledge the support of the Plunkett Foundation, the International Co-operative Alliance Committee on Co-operative Research, the Co-operatives Research Unit, Open University, and the UK Society for Co-operative Studies towards the publication of this book

British Library Cataloguing-in-Publication Data
A catalogue record for this book is available on request from the British Library

Typeset by IDSUK (DataConnection) Ltd.
Printed and bound in Britain by Bell and Bain Ltd, Glasgow

For Bernard Rhodes and Robert Marshall
Each was a 'verray, parfit gentil knyght' (Chaucer)

Contents

Preface

There is much contemporary interest in various forms of mutuality, with attempts to reduce the state but increase collective and voluntary efforts in the Big Society.

In the process there is often re-invention of the wheel and a lack of recognition that history throws up many earlier examples of successful mutuality. They occurred in terms of mass participation and wealth creation and frequently among the poor who owned few factors of production other than their labour.

Co-operatives have the longest and most successful history among the different forms of mutuality, constituting the most clear-cut form of business organisation with social objectives. Throughout the world in diverse cultures, religions and climatic conditions they showed themselves to be building blocks of civic society, becoming wealth creators and educators who instilled democratic, business and organisational skills among their members.

The history of co-operatives therefore offers many lessons to current debates including that on the environment, as the recent Rio Declaration acknowledged. However, a part of their history little studied is that of their development within empires. This book seeks to redress that imbalance by studying how and why the British Empire came to use co-operatives as part of its development strategies.

Imperialism and co-operation seemed to be an unlikely partnership; their underlying ideologies were incompatible. That a productive synergy emerged points to qualities in both. It suggests that some features of the British Empire could be seen in a positive light: it was pluralistic, it permitted different elements and had an ability to adapt. It also shows that co-operatives proved a valuable tool for development being versatile, ubiquitous and universal. They offered an alternative business form to that of the investor-owned enterprise and of their own volition may well have spread throughout the world. As this study shows, however, the British Empire became a valuable vehicle for their expansion.

As the first of its kind this book is not exhaustive. Hopefully it will encourage others to explore aspects such as post-colonial co-operative development and the extent to which other empires also developed co-operatives. *Empire and Co-operation* is a narrative history based on sources which suggested that the focus should be on the government promotion of co-operatives; in other words, a top-down process. However, co-operatives are bottom-up organisations. That suggests that complementary studies from that perspective could also be productive. Even before parliamentary reform and full adult suffrage British co-operatives gave equal voting rights to their men and women members. Hopefully gender issues within co-operatives in the British Empire might also be explored as well as legal frameworks. In Britain co-operatives came under the Industrial and Provident Societies Acts. For many reasons these could not be easily replicated in other parts of the Empire. India's early co-operative legislation, however, proved far more relevant. In some territories inappropriate co-operative legislation hampered effective development and could perhaps prompt subsequent research.

A work on the British Empire means that names of countries during the imperial period often changed when independence was granted. Consequently modern names are given in brackets after the pre-independence name at first mention in the text, with pre-independence names only being used from then on.

Please note also that the Plunkett Diaries are now with the Irish Co-operative Organisation Society, and the Plunkett Archive remains with the Plunkett Foundation. The Co-operative Union's Archive is now named the National Co-operative Archive.

Throughout this study the aim has been to describe, analyse and interpret developments. The sources quoted have been extensively footnoted and it is hoped that they will act as signposts for those who wish to study further the issues raised. A further hope is that this study will contribute to the contemporary re-evaluation of the British Empire.

Acknowledgements

I should like to thank the many who have helped me in this study. The sponsoring organisations which have supported and encouraged throughout – the Plunkett Foundation, the International Co-operative Alliance Committee on Co-operative Research, the UK Co-operative Society for Co-operative Studies and the Co-operative Research Unit, Open University – are due special thanks, as is Professor Roger Spear of the Co-operative Research Unit of the Open University. He has been a constant source of support and comment. I am also grateful to Emeritus Professor Ian Donnachie (Open University) and Professor Johnston Birchall (Stirling University) for their comments on different chapters. Dr Mike Aiken, visiting research fellow, Co-operatives Research Unit, Open University, proved a tower of strength in helping prepare the manuscript for publication.

I should also like to record my thanks to my husband, Bernard Rhodes, to whom this book is jointly dedicated. Sadly he died while it was being written but for his help in this and other works I will always be grateful. I recall others who have also died during the book's long preparation. They include Dr Robert Marshall, past principal of the UK Co-operative College to whom this book is also dedicated, Basil Loveridge, David Lazell and Archie Macintosh. Each contributed through taped interviews and subsequent comments on chapters.

Thanks to the living include those to Jim Craigen, ex MP for Maryhill, Glasgow, Trevor Bottomley, retired co-operative registrar and Edgar Parnell, past director of the Plunkett Foundation. They generously gave their views throughout. I am also indebted to a number of archives including those at Durham University Library, the International Co-operative Alliance, the National Co-operative Archive and the Plunkett Foundation. Warm thanks are extended to them and their helpful staffs.

I gratefully acknowledge the help of various individuals and organisations who supplied photographs for reproduction in the plate section, and gave permission for their use. The photographs of Grey, Wolff and Watkins are reproduced courtesy of the Archive of the International Co-operative Alliance; the photographs of Plunkett and Digby are reproduced courtesy of the Archive of the Plunkett Foundation; the photograph of Macintosh is reproduced courtesy of the National Co-operative Archive; and the photographs of Marshall, Youngjohns and Bottomley are family photographs.

Final thanks are due to my publisher and their editor, Nicola Wood.

PART ONE: 1900–1918

1. The British Empire in 1900

INTRODUCTION

Imperialism, like nationalism, has become outdated and not popular in the modern world. In Britain many feel uncomfortable with her imperial past. After a gap of some fifty years or so since the end of Empire it may now be easier to revisit and review some aspects of it. The Empire was not wholly evil. Nor was it homogeneous in ideology or centralised in administration. One of its more enlightened elements was the role it played in development. True that was originally in support of imperial objectives such as trade or security and so roads, transport and communications facilities became important. Later, however, development widened to include more humane aspects such as health and education in support of economic development and it was in these that co-operatives of many different kinds were found to have a role to play.

Co-operatives, though, were based on an ideology which was influenced to a considerable extent by the ideas of Robert Owen (1771–1858) a common thread of which sought for greater morality in economic and social relations. It was an ideology greatly different from that pervading imperialism, which sought foreign domination, the exploitation of local populations and natural resources, and imposed government at odds with indigenous forms. Co-operation, as it grew in Britain from the ideas of Owen and others, encouraged self-management and economic and social democracy. From the mid-nineteenth century onwards co-operatives were a new form of business where all rights and privileges rested with members rather than shareholders. They were businesses in which capital was created from members' contributions but received only a fixed and limited rewards. Service to the members rather than return on capital invested was their raison d'être. They were quite different from the massive trading companies of the Empire such as the East India Company and Cecil Rhodes's British South Africa Company. Although existing by Royal Charters such companies were based on private and public investors. A slogan of the Empire was that the 'Flag followed trade'. It meant that British army and naval, police and administrative forces followed the trading openings these companies created, which then needed to be secured.

Founding empires was not a purely British activity but followed the earlier examples of Spain and Portugal. In time the British Empire would compete with those of France and Holland and with Germany in the late nineteenth century. The term 'the Scramble for Africa' sums up the competition of major empires for the one remaining area of the world still to be developed. Britain had already triumphed in India, Canada, Australia and New Zealand.

It seems pretty remarkable that a geographical entity as small as Britain should come to dominate these countries. Many reasons can be found for this in her navy, her commercial dynamism including founding of the Bank of England in 1694 and political traditions that shaped her governmental systems and which could be broadly labelled Tory and Whig.

Britain was not monolithic or homogeneous. Her empire would be similarly diverse. Its administration varied between dominions, colonies, protectorates and mandated territories and ideas had the freedom to compete, to be accepted or rejected.

Co-operatives began to be considered as a means of development in the early twentieth century. Discussions about their potential, however, had begun several decades earlier and were shaped by co-operative developments in Britain and Ireland in the second half of the nineteenth century.

To trace how co-operatives became a tool of development in the British Empire we first need to examine the extent and nature of the Empire and then that of the British Co-operative Movement in 1900.

THE NATURE AND EXTENT OF THE BRITISH EMPIRE IN 1900

The British Empire developed over some 400 years. By the time Queen Victoria celebrated her Diamond Jubilee in 1897, it comprised some 372 million people in 11 million square miles.[1] This meant that it occupied roughly a quarter of the earth's surface, and governed around a quarter of the world's population.

Historians tend to divide the Empire's time-span into two periods, despite there being obvious continuities such as the growth of companies like the East India Company. The first period dated roughly from John Cabot's claim to 'New Found Land' in 1497, until the culmination of the American War of Independence in 1783, with the second from then until the two World Wars of the twentieth century. The main characteristic of the latter was the Empire's massive geographical expansion into the Far East and Africa in the late nineteenth century. It came to be labelled 'new imperialism', although it was sometimes termed 'jingo imperialism' because of the popular sentiment and support it aroused. By 1897 Queen Victoria ruled the largest empire the world had ever seen.

Moreover, as Jan Morris noted in her book *Pax Britannica*, 'The Roman Empire was self-contained. The Spanish Empire was concentrated. The Russian Empire was continental. The British Empire was broadcast across the earth . . .'[2] Popular British support for empire in the last two decades of the nineteenth century overturned Sir John Seeley's earlier assertion that the British Empire had been acquired 'in a fit of absence of mind' because Britons were so indifferent to 'the mighty phenomenon of the diffusion of our race and the expansion of our State'.[3] By 1900 Britons were no longer indifferent to their empire.

Besides changes resulting from the Empire's geographical expansion, Britain itself underwent a transformation during the nineteenth century. Accelerating industrialisation and urbanisation brought greater class fluidity, a widening electoral franchise under the Reform Acts of 1832, 1867 and 1884, and improved education. The last meant that more people were capable of reading and so able to benefit from the mass circulation newspapers now being published. These kept them up to date with events in the Empire which became ever more newsworthy. Gone were the days when knowledge and experience of British colonies were limited to those directly involved.

The numbers of those directly involved had increased during the nineteenth century. By its end many Britons were engaged in the Empire's administration through the Colonial and Indian Civil Services. Many others were enrolled in its imperial armies and navies, and others were involved in imperial trade. Trade within the Empire had increased dramatically, making Britain's merchant navy by far the largest in the world. The advent of the steam engine had revolutionised transport by making possible railways and steamships. Together with the invention of the telegraph, they greatly facilitated increased international trade.

From the mid-nineteenth century such developments marked what has been termed 'the imperialism of free trade'.[4] Willie Thompson, in *Global Expansion – Britain and its Empire* 1870–1914, summed up thus:

> . . . what had been for over a century a global economy in terms of trade networks, became an enormously more tightly articulated and

> productive one . . . Dominating the entire structure were British production, British commerce and British financial services . . .[5]

HOW THE EMPIRE WAS GOVERNED

By 1900 the British Empire's arterial blood could be said to be its trade that moved along its extensive transport routes. Within this vast imperial structure various forms of suzerainty applied. Such diversity would distinguish it from the more centralised systems of other empires, notably the French. It would also later affect how co-operative legislation would be introduced and implemented in its different parts.

Three broad types of government applied. White dominated territories such as Canada, Australia and New Zealand had become, or were about to become self-governing dominions, although their governor-generals were still representatives of the British Crown. The bulk of the Empire, however, comprised its colonies. These had colonial governments largely made up of British officials and administered by colonial civil servants. A smaller, and less formal part of the Empire comprised protectorates, mandated territories, trucial and controlled states.

Whatever form of government applied its apex was the British monarch. Until her death in 1901, Queen Victoria was Empress of India, and sovereign of Britain's dominions and colonies. After the Glorious Revolution of 1688, and the eighteenth-century Hanoverian accession, the British monarchy had begun to evolve into a constitutional monarchy. This process had been accelerated by nineteenth-century Reform Acts. By 1900, the queen in Parliament had become the supreme imperial authority. As we have seen, Parliament, or rather its increasingly dominant lower house, was subject to a widening electorate. As a result, its make-up, and its views on imperial issues, could change from one general election to another. Although greater consciousness of empire and the new imperialism began to alter this, members of Parliament appeared content to leave imperial matters to the executive. This meant that Parliament devolved its legislative authority on imperial matters to the Secretaries of State for India and the Colonies, both of whom were parliamentarians sitting in one of the two Houses of Parliament.

Given the above, it is somewhat surprising that it was an effective apex of empire. Having said that, from the mid-nineteenth century onwards, its control and administration were assisted by the establishment of the Colonial Office in 1854 and the Indian Civil Service four years later. Each gave formal support to the secretaries of state administering the Empire on behalf of the queen in Parliament.

The India Office had evolved from the East India Company which had been granted its first charter by Elizabeth I in 1600. It appeared to be a 'semi-privatised imperial wing of the Hanoverian state'[6] and was markedly different from the Colonial Office in a number of respects. Its offices in Whitehall were more grand and stately. It also concentrated on one, albeit very large, area of the Empire. The Indian government, with the viceroy at its head, was based in Calcutta. Its departments were largely mirrored by those of the India Office. In effect, it was an agency of the Indian government and was, indeed, financed from Indian revenues. Its officials were advised by the Council of India which comprised appointees, mainly retired generals and administrators, who had been previously based in India.[7]

This symbiotic relationship between the Indian government and the India Office has led to the suggestion that the latter 'knew more about India than any office of government, anywhere, had ever known about another country'.[8] The India Office also acted as a focal point for visitors from India; as well as for those who had previously worked there but had retired in London. Together they made up the 'India of London' who could be lobbied on Indian questions and were, in fact, on proposals for India's first co-operative legislation.[9]

On the other hand, the Colonial Office, prior to its establishment in 1854, had come under the Offices of the Secretary of State for War and the Colonies. Two measures had preceded its becoming a separate identity. First was Parliament's provision for Crown Agents (1833). Second, four years later, was the introduction of Crown Regulations. These represented an attempt to consolidate 'standing regulations' so as to introduce 'a better method, and . . . greater certainty in the despatch of the duties of the Governors, and other Public Officers in the Colonial possessions of the Crown'.[10]

The Colonial Office was also less specialist. Because it covered the whole of the Empire, apart from India, it was necessarily more diverse. Its departments were therefore unable to act as counterparts to those in any colony, making it more of an embassy for colonies rather than an agency like the India Office.

The two great offices of the Empire were somewhat different from each other. Generally speaking, that of the Colonial Office was to act as 'a trustee for the underdogs of Empire'. During its formative years of 1836–47 its under-secretary had been Sir James Stephen who had taken leading roles in campaigns to outlaw slavery. During his time at the Colonial Office it was considered that 'the bias of the Office had generally been towards a liberal generosity'.[11] It will later be argued that such a tendency played a part in the Colonial Office's subsequent receptiveness to ideas about co-operatives.

Besides being the Empire's legislature and executive, the British Parliament also headed its wide variety of legal systems. We should now move to consider these.

LEGAL SYSTEMS

We speak in the plural because the British respected indigenous laws. Where they made sense, or where they were in line with local customs and natural justice, they allowed them to remain, at least until they were specifically superseded. The main exception were those local laws that permitted practices outlawed throughout the rest of the Empire, such as slavery. Moreover, once a territory had become a colony of the British Crown, legislation could only apply to it if it was expressly stated that it should.

Another reason for a lack of uniformity in the Empire's legal systems was the difficulty of transposing English legal traditions, particularly that of English Common Law. It became desirable to supplement or modify it to bring it into line with local traditions. Occasionally, local laws were actually thought to be an improvement on the British original, British India's Penal Code being one example.

For one reason or another, there was no uniform legal system throughout the British Empire. Remnants of older systems intruded, thus:

> The French Canadians kept their archaic version of French law, as it had been before the Revolution, while Mauritius and the Seychelles had the Napoleonic Code. Sicilian law applied in Malta, Roman Dutch in Ceylon and Cape Colony, Ottoman in Cyprus. Traces of Spanish law still applied in Trinidad, and faint remnants of the old Breton laws in Ireland.[12]

Future colonial co-operative legislation would be grafted onto this variety, with all kinds of consequences, not least in the appellate stages of cases, where the Empire's highest Court of Appeal remained the Judicial Committee of the Sovereign's Privy Council. It was more of a committee than a court. Its function was to hear appeals and then to advise the sovereign on whether they should be upheld or dismissed. Moreover, because it would have been unseemly to have delivered dissenting judgements, it pronounced no verdicts. It always comprised six leading British jurists, and met in a chamber in Downing Street rather than in a court of law. Its members did not wear the gowns and wigs of the English judiciary.

For all this, the judicial committee of the Privy Council was the apex of the Empire's legal system, requiring to adjudicate according to the British imperial legal system but keeping in mind the legal traditions of the territories bringing appeals.

The committee acted as a final court of appeal to a quarter of the world's population; it is appropriate to look at those peoples.

DIVERSITY OF PEOPLES

The sheer geographical extent of the Empire meant that it was necessarily multi-racial. It also prompted large movements of population: that of Britons to administer the Empire or to develop its farms, mines, plantations and other enterprises; and that of native populations, particularly Indian, to provide labour. The need for the latter increased not only with the development of colonies but with the abolition of slavery.

The ability of Britons to move within the Empire helped to ease potential population pressures at home. Britain's population rose dramatically during the nineteenth century. The first official population census (1801) revealed a population of around 10,500,000. By 1900 it exceeded 38 million.[13] A declining death rate contributed to that increase. In turn that had been assisted by improvements in home agriculture which sustained a rising population. Another factor had been improvements in housing, sanitation and health regulations. Each had become necessary to counter the worst effects of urbanisation prompted by the massive expansion of the British economy under industrialisation. Those living longer enjoyed the availability of a greater amount and variety of food made possible by the expansion of the Empire in the later 1800s. By then, wheat, meat, fruit and cereals could be imported from Australia and New Zealand. Tea, coffee and cocoa arrived from India and Africa and with increasing supplies, their prices became lower and thus affordable to the middle and lower classes.

Although Britain became better able to sustain a larger population in the nineteenth century, it could have experienced population pressures had its people not been able to move into other parts of the Empire. By the later years of that century more formal encouragement was being given to emigration. Before then convicts had been transported to the penal colonies, mainly Australia, and other people had been driven out by famine in Ireland or recurring depressions at home. This type of migration was essentially manual; similarly workers attracted to those colonies that experienced booms or gold rushes. The timing of, and the number involved in such exoduses, necessarily fluctuated whereas the migration of business and professional people remained more steady. Altogether, though, it has been estimated that by the mid-1800s some 10 million Britons had already migrated to the colonies, for whatever reasons.

Such movements were largely unplanned. By 1890, however, an officially financed Emigrants' Information Office had been set up, and several government departments had begun concerning themselves with emigration. Similarly, a number of charitable bodies. A view widely held was that people were not so much moving from one country to another, but rather participating in a 'redistribution of population within the nation'.[14]

Those moving to territories within the Empire could be broadly divided into those who were doing so temporarily, such as Colonial and Indian civil servants, and those who moved to settle. The latter increased significantly in the second half of the nineteenth century as trade within the Empire grew and generated large-scale employment. The development of railways and steamships assisted even greater trade increases. Together with the telegraph, they enabled the transporting of bulk supplies of mineral and agricultural products from the colonies to Britain. This increased trade also encouraged greater large-scale British investment in colonies. Not only did Britain export the railways and their rolling stock, but often the capital with which to buy them. British built, and British financed railways, helped to make viable the development of mines, ranches and plantations. In turn, these encouraged a further wave of British investment, as well as the emigration of administrators and managers.

However, it was not only Britons who were on the move. Sometimes the insufficient supply of local workers encouraged migrations from one part of the Empire to another. The most significant one in terms of size was that of Indians. They helped to fill the labour shortages arising from the outlawing of slavery. As indentured labourers they offered obvious advantages. Not only were they populous, but they were capable of working in the hot climes of many parts of the Empire. Soon their movement out of India was officially encouraged and arranged by agents of the Colonial Office in Calcutta. Indian labour became essential to the success of white colonists in areas such as East Africa.

A consequence of such movement was the development of racial tensions between the descendants of indentured workers and the host populations. The second half of the nineteenth century witnessed examples in the West and East Indies, East Africa and Sri Lanka.

By 1900 the British Empire had moved not only millions of Britons around the globe, but had also shifted millions of its subjects.

BRITISH ATTITUDES TO EMPIRE

At the beginning of the twentieth century, compared with only fifty years earlier, Britons were now far more conscious of the size and nature of the Empire; also of their being at its very centre. Such a change in consciousness had come about for a variety of reasons

Not only had Britain's population grown massively, it was also no longer mainly rural. Industrialisation, whose acceleration had been assisted by the expansion of the Empire, had helped Britain to become 'the workshop of the world'. The process had brought people into towns where their living styles, culture, education and communications had changed. More people could read and had access to mass circulation newspapers. These contained news items about issues and events within the Empire and so helped to make the Empire more tangible to Britons.

Compulsory primary education further deepened knowledge of the Empire. When schools taught geography they showed maps marking British possessions in pink or red that covered a quarter of the world. School children also took prominent part in the celebrations and pageants on the annual Empire Day. A love of, and pride in, the Empire were thus encouraged from an early age; it became the natural order of things that Britain was at the centre of a vast, good and noble empire.

Britain was also becoming a mass society in the sense that many events were now large-scale occasions, football matches being an obvious example. Then there was the growth of mass member organisations such as consumer co-operative societies and building societies, although, like football teams, they had specific locales. Entertainment could offer mass events helped by the building of large halls. Music halls celebrated military victories and park bandstands sounded Elgar's imperial marches. Such 'jingo imperialism' reached its zenith with Queen Victoria's Diamond Jubilee in 1897. Massive crowds in London saw the queen's procession in which representatives from all parts of the Empire joined. Britons outside London could enjoy the event through newspapers and the music written to commemorate it.

All these factors helped to increase consciousness of the Empire which, in turn, contributed to changes in attitudes both among ordinary people and political leaders. The latter were undoubtedly influenced by the rapid geographical expansion of the Empire illustrated by the estimate that in the last quarter of the nineteenth century Great Britain added over 4,750,000 square miles and almost 90 million more people to its Empire.[15] Part of this increase occurred among South Pacific islands, Malay states and Upper Burma. The greatest spread of British power, though, came in Africa.

Until the 1880s Britain's African possessions had been few. Then, the development of the railways, and the use of quinine to control malaria, made it easier for Europeans to work there. Rapid British expansion followed and replaced the earlier relatively low key policy which had largely consisted of making trading agreements with local leaders, and backing these by gunboat diplomacy if necessary. From the 1880s Britain began acquiring territory and then instituting political control. For example, in 1882 she occupied Egypt in what was a supposedly limited intervention to restore order in an area where Ottoman rule was breaking down. Two years later British protectorates were declared in Somaliland in East Africa, and Bechuanaland (Botswana) in the South. Elsewhere political control tended to follow in the wake of trading companies. For example, in 1899, two Nigerian protectorates were declared. They were based on the area covered by Sir George Goldie's Niger Company which had received its royal charter some thirteen years earlier. Similarly, in 1889 Cecil Rhodes's British South Africa company was given powers to extend British influence northwards from Bechuanaland into what would become Northern and Southern Rhodesia. In 1894–5 Uganda became a British possession while the Imperial British East Africa Company took control of Kenya. By conquering the Sudan in 1898, Britain became predominant in the region of the Upper Nile. A number of reasons have been advanced for this rapid expansion of the Empire. Some writers, such as J. A. Hobson, have focused on economic arguments. Hobson suggested that Britain's domestic market had contracted because of the unequal distribution of industrial profit. This made it more attractive to financiers to invest their surplus capital abroad where, although the risks might be higher, the rewards could also be greater.[16] Hobson's views were influential among contemporary British Co-operators, including some who were later involved in imperial co-operative development. Other writers saw Britain's part in the 'scramble for Africa' as part of the intensification of European rivalries, particularly after Germany's unification in 1870 and the rise of her imperial ambitions. Yet others interpreted Britain's African expansion in terms of strategic factors, while some saw it resulting from the interaction between the decisions taken in London and those taken locally. They believed that the latter was influenced by administrators, commercial and other pressure groups, as well as by indigenous leaders and local cultures. Such influences could result in initiatives that had quite unintentional consequences for London. One example can be found in the actions of Cecil Rhodes, (1853–1902) who became one of the Empire's most fervent and visionary imperialists. Managing director of the British South African Company, and later prime minister of the Cape Colony, he had to resign the latter position when implicated in the Jameson Raid, the failed attempt to overthrow the Transvaal government. The raid did, however, become one of the main disputes leading to the South African, or Boer War of 1899–1902.

A statement by Lord Salisbury lends weight to the view that imperial developments could outrun the ability of politicians in London to understand their nature, or to control them, observing: 'I do not exactly know the causes of this sudden revolution [Britain's rapid expansion in the Empire]. But there it is.'[17]

The two Houses of the British Parliament had been content mostly to leave the running of the Empire to the secretaries of state for India and the Colonies and their departments. By the third quarter of the nineteenth century, however, political leaders were becoming more actively engaged as imperial affairs loomed more largely within Britain's foreign policy. Benjamin Disraeli (1804–1881), Tory leader and prime minister briefly in 1868 and then between 1874 and 1880, had, in 1876, been the one to suggest that Queen Victoria assume the title of Empress of India. A year earlier he had made Britain half owner of the Suez Canal.[18] His main political rival, Liberal leader William Gladstone (1808–1898), was prime minister between 1868 and 1874, from 1880 to 1885, February to July 1886, and 1892 to 1894, and presided over Britain's moves into Egypt and the Sudan. He was, however, a more cautious imperialist than Disraeli. For example, he had been anxious to extricate Britain from her increasing rivalry with the Boers in South Africa but had failed to do so.[19]

The British prime minister most closely identified with the 'new imperialism' of the last decades of the nineteenth century, was Robert Cecil, third Marquis of Salisbury (1830–1903). He was Disraeli's foreign secretary between 1878 and 1880 but went on to become prime minister (1885 and 1886, 1886–92 and finally 1890–2). Salisbury, the last British prime minster to sit in the House of Lords, was a member of the Cecil family whose members had held high office since the time of Elizabeth I. It is perhaps not surprising, therefore, that his imperial philosophy has been summed up as being 'pragmatic, sceptical and always profoundly aristocratic. . .'[20] He appeared to weigh events in the Empire against the background of his main concerns which were the security of British routes to the East and the balance of power in Europe.

Salisbury's pragmatic, sceptical and aristocratic approach was in sharp contrast to that of Joseph Chamberlain. Their backgrounds also differed sharply. Whereas Salisbury was aristocratic, Chamberlain was a self-made man. Joseph Chamberlain (1836–1914) had been born in London but went to work at Nettleford's screw factory in Birmingham and retired in 1874 with a fortune. Six years earlier he had become a Birmingham town councillor and went on to become mayor between 1873 and 1876. He then entered Parliament where he became identified with schemes for the regeneration of the masses and was appointed president of the Local Government Board in 1886. Such British preoccupations shifted when he became Secretary for the Colonies in 1895. Whereas Salisbury was a Tory, Chamberlain became leader of the Liberal Unionists in 1891.[21] He joined the coalition Conservative Unionist Government of 1895 after a massive defeat of the Liberals.

The unlikely combination of Salisbury and Chamberlain headed the new imperialism at the turn of the century. Of the two, Chamberlain came to embody its style and pace with statements such as 'England without an Empire! Can you conceive it? England in that case would not be the England we love.' And, 'Let us do all in our power by improving our communications, by developing our commercial relations, by co-operating in mutual defence, and none of us will ever feel isolated.' It was he who had coined the phrase 'trade follows the flag',[22] although the reverse could equally be said to apply. Such strident patriotism chimed with mass sentiment.

Chamberlain claimed that it was the task of the Foreign and Colonial Offices to 'find new markets and to defend old ones', while the War Office and the Admiralty should protect the flow of commerce. Such demands added burdens to government. These prompted William Gladstone to remonstrate with Cecil Rhodes, 'Our burden is too great . . . We have too much, Mr. Rhodes, to do. Apart from increasing our obligations in every part of the world, what advantage do you see to the English race in acquisition of new territory?'[23] Rhodes's reply summed up well the nature and rationale of the new imperialism:

> Great Britain is a very small island . . . [her] position depends on her trade, and if we do not open up the dependencies . . . we shall shut out the world's trade . . . That is why you must deal with these questions of expansion and retention of the world.[24]

People who supported Gladstone also had reservations. His political prominence stemmed from his ability to get the various factions of the Victorian Liberal Party to work together. These included the aristocratic

Whigs, with their long traditions of executive leadership, and Liberal members from the commercial and industrial middle classes. The latters' political views were often more radical and frequently shaped by the non-conformist churches they attended. They were attracted by Gladstone's Christian and moral approach to politics.[25]

A later contention of this study will be that it was from these Liberals, whether members of the Liberal Party, or liberal in outlook, that co-operative initiatives in the Empire stemmed. Certainly, in the late 1800s, members of British consumer co-operatives were closely associated with the non-conformist churches and were also frequently Liberal Party supporters.

Some of the excesses of new imperialism, however, shocked the moral liberal element in British society. The exploitation not only of natural resources but also of people led to increased Christian missionary work; also to a growing literature epitomised by Joseph Conrad's allegorical novel, *Heart of Darkness*.

Moral issues, though, were always likely to be overshadowed by the imperatives of trade. British and colonial co-operatives might have different structures and rationale from other businesses, but businesses they were and, as such, they were engaged in trade. Thus they were to become part of the Empire's trading system.

CONCLUSIONS

In this chapter we have looked at the origins of the Empire and noted the point it had reached in 1900 both in terms of how it was governed and the diversity of its legal systems together with the final Court of Appeal in the Judicial Committee of the Privy Council. Arising from the Empire's geographical spread we observed the range of its peoples, noting in particular the strong population growth in Britain itself during the nineteenth century. Finally, we looked at British attitudes towards the Empire among both ordinary people and politicians and noted moral concerns about the excesses of new imperialism. In the main, such concern was to be found among the more liberal of British society. It was also from among these that the impetus came for co-operative activity both in Britain and in the colonies. This will be examined in greater detail in our next chapter which will deal with British co-operation in 1900. It is intended to be a companion chapter to this which has attempted to describe, analyse and interpret the British Empire in 1900.

2. British Co-operation 1900

INTRODUCTION

We should now turn to the second element in this study, namely co-operation. In particular, we should note how far it had developed in the mother country by 1900. By that date it had become quite a force in which consumer societies formed the largest part.

Their growth had been rapid. In 1862 there had been 450 retail co-operatives with an aggregate membership of 91,502, a share capital of £573,582 and a total trade of £2,349,055, producing a profit of £166,302. By the end of the century, their number had risen to 1,820 with a total membership of 1,596,726, a share capital of £19,856,945 and a total trade of £65,270,640 producing a profit of £6,834,689.[1]

British consumer societies, therefore, had not only increased rapidly in number and strength, but they had also proved profitable. They had distinctive attitudes to profit that stemmed from their early history and emerging philosophy. Thus, early British consumer co-operatives would, at the end of a trading period, allocate part of their profit to reserves to facilitate their future growth, while another part would be allocated to fund members' collective benefits such as education, cultural events or funeral grants. The remainder was then paid to members as their individual benefits, being equitably divided according to how much each had traded with the society. It was measured as so much in the £ of that trade so that if a member had spent £50, and the dividend was 1s (5p) in the £, he or she would receive a 'dividend' of £2 10s (£2.50).

Unlike private enterprise businesses, co-operatives operated not for profit but as mutual trading businesses. They were distinguished from them in other ways. Besides abhorring the term 'profit', the dividend they offered was quite different from that in private companies where it was still the division of profits but based on the number of shares held. In co-operatives dividend represented a reward of loyalty or solidarity, prized attributes in co-operatives. As we shall see later, co-operatives also held distinct attitudes to capital. It was needed as a factor of production but was only ever to receive a limited reward that reflected utility and not speculation. From the beginning, co-operatives' emphasis was on the return to labour. We need to see how such ideas, novel for their time, had come about.

Some of co-operatives' elements had a long history, such as the medieval concept of a just price. Another was the seventeenth-century English ideal of 'commonwealth' or 'commonweal' while a more recent influence had been the French Revolution and its calls for liberty, equality and fraternity. A more immediate catalyst had been Britain's industrialisation. Co-operative ideas can be interpreted as an attempted palliative to the exploitative competition it encouraged.

While co-operation was one response to industrialisation, another was the redefinition of economic theories or the proposition of new ones. Influential during the period was Adam Smith's (1723–1790) *Inquiry into the Nature and Causes of the Wealth of Nations*. Published in 1776, it examined the effects of economic freedom on the division of labour, the functions of markets, and the means of exchange. Smith's ideas not only contested earlier economic theories but also heralded the doctrine of laissez-faire that would underpin much of nineteenth-century British political and economic practice.

Not all economists agreed with Smith's analyses. For example, David Ricardo (1772–1823) differed from him over the extent to which labour determined economic value. While both agreed that labour had been its main determinant in early societies, Smith argued that in later ones, in which the landlord and capitalist had emerged, labour's wages had to be shared with rent and profits on capital. Ricardo, on the other hand, held that too sharp a distinction should not be drawn because the capital goods used in production necessarily embodied past labour. He therefore continued to argue a labour theory of value to which early co-operators subscribed.

However, they took it further by linking it to the medieval concept of a just price. They used both to criticise the worsening of labourers' conditions as British industrialisation accelerated, and sought practical ways of applying a labour theory of value. One of the first and most notable figures to do this was Robert Owen (1771–1858) who, in the early nineteenth century, tried to found a number of co-operative communities within which labour became the chief determinant of price. Owen also encouraged the setting up of labour exchanges, or bazaars, in which only labour notes were used as a medium of exchange, their value based on the amount of labour used in producing those goods on sale. Co-operators' attempts to apply a fair or just price for labour continued during that century: the Christian Socialists encouraged the setting up of producers' co-operatives; and early retail co-operatives paid a dividend, or bonus, on their workers' wages.

These, and related ideas, provided the motive force for much of nineteenth-century British co-operation and shaped the movement that we find in 1900.

EARLY CO-OPERATIVE IDEAS

Robert Owen

Important, indeed pre-eminent among early co-operators, was Robert Owen. His ideas were essentially moral and amounted to a condemnation of early industrialisation which he believed prevented people from achieving their full moral stature. Owen observed that the contemporary massive increase in productive power was held largely in the hands of a new form of enterprise that was more ruthless and competitive than that preceding it. In the early nineteenth century a national capital market had still to emerge and ways for entrepreneurs to accumulate capital were relatively unstructured and lacking regulation. One quick and direct way of maximising capital, and thus the means of funding new production, was limiting workers' wages. At that time many workers were already in a weakened position having become redundant from their crafts or rural occupations. As a result they were forced to move to the new towns and their factories to seek employment. These invariably offered harsh conditions but workers found it hard to resist them particularly after the Combination Laws, passed in 1799, severely restricted collective action. Factory owners, keen to prevent workers joining together to press for higher wages, had lobbied for this, but the readiness of the British government, fearing spread of revolution from France, should also be noted. Thereafter, for much of the nineteenth century, British governments abstained from interference in much of British industry and commerce, adopting strong laissez-faire attitudes which permitted a period of rampant and untrammelled capitalism to unfold. Co-operators were in the vanguard of opposition to this. The conditions it gave rise to are well caught in the quotation below:

> all ties between employers and employed are frittered down to the consideration of what immediate gain each can derive from the other. The employer regards the employed as mere instruments of gain, while these acquire a gross ferocity of character, which, if

> legislative measure shall not be judiciously devised to prevent its increase, and ameliorate the condition of this class, will sooner or later plunge the country into a formidable and perhaps inextricable state of danger . . .[2]

It has been suggested that it was during this period that a new class consciousness emerged in Britain. Moreover, that Robert Owen was perhaps the first to use the term 'working class' to describe the greatly increased labour force manning the new factories.[3]

To help people achieve their full moral potential, Owen proposed a system of co-operation that would replace capitalist competition. Besides being a man of ideas Owen was also a practical man.

Although a successful entrepreneur himself, he campaigned for the first Factory Act, but was disappointed when he found that it did not go far enough. As an employer, though, Owen was able to improve the conditions of his own workers.

His main opportunity to do this came in Scotland having earlier established himself as a successful manager and businessman in Manchester. In 1799 Owen married Caroline Dale whose father owned cotton mills at New Lanark. Owen became the manager of these and later a partner in the business. At New Lanark he created better working conditions as well as improving workers' housing. Most revolutionary of all, he set about educating workers and their children not only in the three 'Rs' (reading, (w)riting and (a)rithmetic), but in subjects aimed at improving pupils' moral fibre.[4]

Owen was subsequently to influence both British education and trades unionism but his influence on British co-operation was the most marked. It was achieved in a number of ways. One was his writings, particularly the four essays he published under the title of *New View of Society, Essays on the Formation of Character* between 1813 and 1816, in which Owen argued that to become more moral people had to live in environments that were themselves moral. To create these he proposed the establishment of co-operative communities whose members could be cut off from the pressures of acquisitive industrial society. He led a number of experiments at Orbiston (1825–7), Ralahine (1831–3), Queenwood (1839–45) and New Harmony in the United States (1825–7). For various reasons none survived long and Owen himself became a casualty when the co-operative community at New Harmony swallowed much of his private fortune. Writing later of its failure, he said that his object had been, 'to improve the character and condition of its own members and to prepare them to become associates . . . having common property'. Owen acknowledged that the attempt was premature because community members were not yet ready to live together 'as a common family'.[5]

Nevertheless, Owenite communities remained a goal among early co-operators who were also strongly influenced by Owen's economic ideas. When campaigning for factory reform, Owen had published in 1815 an essay under the title of *Observations on the Effects of the Manufacturing System*. In this he suggested that Britain's changing economy was creating imbalances. For example, he contended that before machinery had been introduced, supply equalled demand but this balance changed when machinery displaced labour and increased output. Consequently, wages were reduced and with them workers' purchasing power which led to workers being unable to buy, or to benefit from, the increased production of goods. New overseas markets were opening up but Owen believed that increasing exports could only be a short-term solution.

In his *Report to the County of Lanark* (1820) Owen argued that money created artificial and false standards of value and that the true standard of value was a unit of labour power. He further suggested that profits resulting from prices could be eliminated if commodities were exchanged at their natural value, which he believed to be the amount of labour taken to produce them. Such ideas were not completely original. They had some similarity with those of David Ricardo, mentioned earlier, and they also bore some resemblance to the theories propagated by a group known as the 'Early English Socialists'.[6]

Owen also influenced early co-operators in unintended ways. While many of his views could be labelled unconventional, or even utopian, his practical work at New Lanark nonetheless attracted attention and eminent visitors, including royalty. However, much of this interest disappeared when, in 1817, Owen denounced all organised religions. Even some Owenites, including co-operators, felt the need to distance themselves from such views. As a result, the Rochdale Pioneers Equitable Society (formed in 1844) declared itself religiously and politically neutral, as did the retail co-operatives that followed based on the Rochdale model. This gave rise to two co-operative principles, namely those of religious and political neutrality and of open membership, which meant that co-operatives were open to people whatever their beliefs.

Owen was undoubtedly a paternalistic figure, as illustrated in his approach to the setting up of New Harmony. However, the co-operatives inspired into existence by his teachings exhibited a strong degree of independence and democratic self-control. Indeed, they introduced a democracy that was quite extreme for the times. It was based on one member, one vote and operated among people who had never had the vote in parliamentary elections. In this the early British co-operatives were exhibiting the influence of Chartism rather than that of Owenism. Nevertheless, their practice of one member, one vote evolved into a third co-operative principle.

How co-operatives had moved away from dependence on philanthropists such as Owen to becoming independent and self-governing is an interesting transition and one that we should now examine.

Dr William King

An obvious reason for the shift was that co-operators were necessarily open to a variety of contemporary influences, including those of the American and French Revolutions, Chartism and Methodism. A more direct and major influence was that of Dr William King (1786–1865). Whereas Owen had provided moral inspiration, Dr King gave practical ideas on how co-operatives could be set up. While agreeing with Owen's analysis of society, and the idea of setting up co-operative communities, King argued that working people could fund their establishment themselves rather than rely on external help. He believed they could raise the necessary capital by extending the functions of provident or mutual benefit clubs to trade mutually with each other. The profits resulting from such trade could then be accumulated to form co-operative communities' initial capital.

This was a practical idea in many ways. It built on a practice that was already familiar to many workers. Provident and mutual benefit clubs, which had developed from the late eighteenth century, had become an important means through which workers could protect themselves against sickness and death. Their members paid in small regular sums which they, or their families, could redeem at times of sickness and death. King believed that such clubs could be extended to engage in a low level of trade to provide basic foodstuffs to their members. The resulting profits could then be used to found co-operative communities. Besides being practical, this idea marked the beginning of an important co-operative concept, namely that of union or unity by which a number of people coming together, or co-operating, could achieve collectively what they could not have achieved individually.[7]

Whereas Owen was a self-made entrepreneur, William King came from a middle-class and academic background. After marrying in 1821 he moved to Brighton where he remained in medical practice for the rest of his life.[8] Like Owen he was influenced by contemporary radical thinkers including Elizabeth Fry (1780–1845) the Quaker and prison reformer, and Dr Birkbeck (1776–1841), the founder of the educational Mechanics' Institutes. King helped Elizabeth Fry to form the Brighton Provident and District Society, and he joined with Birkbeck in setting up a Mechanics' Institute in Brighton in 1825. Both activities brought him into close touch with workers and their conditions.

King's involvement with the Brighton Provident and District Society had evolved from his earlier engagement with the Brighton Provident Institution whose object had been to replace the begging of the poor with organised relief. Together with Elizabeth Fry in 1824, he helped to change this organisation into the Brighton Provident and District Society. This had an additional object, that 'of collecting, by house-to-house visitation, weekly subscriptions in the summer, which were returned together with a small bonus of 6d. per 4/- (met with the contributions of the rich) in the form of coal, blankets and food in the winter'.[9] The Society was philanthropic in the sense that about half its contributions were made by the wealthy. It nonetheless encouraged thrift and self-help among the poor and helped to shape King's co-operative ideas.

These crystallised in his publication of the *Co-operator*, a series of monthly essays which appeared between 1828 and 1830. King's main arguments here could be summarised as follows. By co-operating, workers could find the remedy for their plight in their own hands. 'But before many can work they must join hand in hand; they must know their object and feel a common interest and a common tie.' Owen had said much the same thing but *after* the failure of New Harmony. In part King argued a labour theory of value when he held that workers' poor conditions stemmed from the fact that they worked for others rather than for themselves. If they were to enjoy the whole product of their labour they needed to work for themselves.

To do this by setting up co-operative communities required capital. Believing that they could provide this collectively, King pointed to the large accumulations of workers' savings in friendly societies and savings banks to show what could be achieved. He argued, however, that co-operatively saved capital should not lie idle, or be lent to others to use for their own profit. Instead, he suggested that workers could accelerate their capital accumulation if they opened a small shop and traded mutually with each other. This would require only a small initial outlay and little experience to run. If members bought only in money, were loyal and shopped nowhere else, the experiment should succeed. Its profits would supplement the members' continuing weekly contributions. As the shop's capital increased, it could widen its range of commodities and perhaps later employ one of the society's members to make shoes or clothes for other members. The profits from this new operation should also be placed to the common capital thus making it possible in time to employ an ever-growing number of the society's members. Eventually, the society would be able to manufacture the goods consumed by its members. Through such relationships King believed that it would be possible for members to enjoy the whole product of their labour and, at the same time, continue to increase their collective capital to purchase land to grow their own foodstuffs, build their own houses, provide their own schools, maintain their sick and aged members. In other words, they would have evolved into a co-operative community.

It is interesting to note the dynamic present in King's proposals. Although the end would be the same as envisaged by Owen the process would have been quite different. Instead of a co-operative community being created through a paternalistic initiative, one would result from an organic and evolutionary process that would always be in the control of the members who began it. They might be poor but King had suggested a way through mutual savings and trade that they could achieve a collective improvement in their conditions.

Another important difference between King and Owen was that King did not spurn organised religion. Indeed, Christianity was a motivating force in his proposals. In the first issue of the *Co-operator* he stated:

> it is self-evident that the fundamental basis of such a Society, is to 'love your neighbour as yourself'. This is the great social Commandment of our Saviour, and it is equally the great main spring of the actions of such a Community.[10]

Like Owen, King recognised the importance of education, as his work with the Brighton Mechanics' Institute and his links with Birkbeck illustrate. In the co-operative field, however, King evolved more practical educational ideas than Owen. Whereas Owen's educational ideas were broadly linked to the betterment of human character, King's co-operative educational ideas were more closely linked to what emerged from co-operative operations. He saw that as soon as people were gathered together to discuss how they might better their conditions they became subject to new forces. Their desire for knowledge would be increased; they would need to exercise judgements to probably a greater degree than they had before; they would also need to develop skills in weighing and balancing probabilities, and assessing human nature, particularly that of the members of their co-operative.

King believed that an operating co-operative became an educational force in itself, a view taken by subsequent generations of co-operators and one that would later commend itself to colonial administrators. Because co-operatives were businesses, their members had to acquire knowledge of the commodities they bought and traded with their members. Just as they learned how to accumulate capital, so too would they need to understand how prices were determined and the variations to which they could be subjected. As co-operatives employed members to begin producing and possibly farming, they would have to upgrade their investment and pricing skills. More basically, they would need to understand that benefits arose from maintaining a quick turnover of stock, buying and selling for cash and keeping accurate accounts. Literacy and numeracy were essential to understand accounts and to keep control of a co-operative and make it truly self-governing. For all these reasons, King believed that operational co-operatives became an educational force in themselves. Education would later become a co-operative principle.

Yet another co-operative principle to be articulated later was that co-operatives should be independent and autonomous. This was also shaped by King's ideas. Because co-operation enabled people to better themselves through their own action, King believed that it was evolutionary rather than revolutionary. It should therefore be a stabilising force in society, particularly as it was not a combination of the poor against the rich. Of all early co-operators, King was the one who most clearly envisaged the dynamics that would come into play through co-operative action. It was a power that derived from people to whom the benefits of mutual action would be returned directly and almost immediately. King held therefore that:

> Co-operation is a voluntary act and all the power in the World cannot make it compulsory, nor is it desirable that it should depend on any power but its own – the interference of governments would only cramp its energies and misdirect them[11]

Such ideas became a powerful force in co-operation, and the basis of British co-operators' subsequent reservations about government-promoted co-operatives within the Empire. King's ideas of independence from the state, however, were quite in keeping for this time in which the doctrine of laissez faire held sway in British political and commercial circles. Having said that, King had perceived the dynamics inherent in co-operative action and had rightly anticipated the power that co-operatives could generate. His journal, the *Co-operator*, became very influential despite its short life. It extended King's ideas far beyond Brighton and, indeed, the period in which it was written.

Robert Owen and William King should be accounted among the most influential early co-operative thinkers. Many of their ideas, but particularly those of Owen, were taken up in co-operative experiments in the 1820s and 1830s. However, none of these formed the basis of a new cohesive and dynamic movement in the way that the Rochdale society would after its establishment in 1844. A number of these earlier experiments ignored King's advice that profits should be allowed to accumulate and not be divided, and that credit should not be given. Moreover, early co-operatives' accounts were often not well kept or their members' meetings well run. They also lacked legal protection. King's proposal that they should extend the functions of mutual benefit societies might have been good practical advice but it did not come within the law. Consequently, embryonic societies had to appoint trustees who, rather than their members, had ultimate control of them. In addition, early societies had no redress in law regarding dishonest officials.

It has been observed that co-operatives in their formative stages have to overcome two crises. One is that of credibility while the other is that of management.[12] Neither had been overcome in the 1820s and 1830s but stronger steps became possible with the launching of Rochdale co-operation. Rochdale's co-operators would also bring together the main ideas of Owen and King and add some of their own.

The Rochdale Pioneers

Later in the study we will find it important to place the start of new co-operative movements within their economic, political and social backgrounds because these inevitably shaped them. We need to do the same in connection with the establishment of the Rochdale Society of Equitable Pioneers. The importance of such a process has been emphasised by earlier co-operative historians such as G. D. H. Cole and Arnold Bonner. We should therefore note that Rochdale, and its surrounding areas, were fundamentally changed by industrialisation. Their long-established flannel manufacture had faced changes in its methods of production. Factory-based power looms were displacing individual home-based handloom weavers. In addition, exports were being adversely affected by American tariffs. Rochdale's other main industry, hat-making, was in outright decline.

Such restructuring led to civil unrest in Rochdale and the nearby West Riding of Yorkshire. Some strikes and disturbances even led to the military being called in to restore order. A number of radical elements began calling for factory and political reforms. Contemporary historians such as Brett Fairburn and Peter Gurney have also pointed to the significance of the cultural and social movements that resulted from such upheavals. For example, using a sociological approach, Brett Fairburn suggests that:

> Rather than stressing that Rochdale was started by 28 weavers (a sociological-economic category) who were poor (lacking economic resources), we should perhaps stress that it was started by ideologically motivated Owenite activists (a cultural-political category) who were rich in 'social capital' – the ideas, networks and practical experiences that enabled them to get things done. Perhaps we should look at what factors, in the Rochdale environment, favoured their success . . .[13]

The Rochdale Society's founders were Owenites who were also familiar with King's ideas. As we know, many Owenites felt it necessary to distance themselves from his views on religion. To do this they formed the Universal Community Society of Rational Religionists, which became a forum for their studies and discussions. Its title enabled it to hold missionary meetings on Sundays and from such meetings a number of branches were formed. One was No. 24 in Rochdale and, in April 1838, this gained the use of an annex to the Weavers' Arms in Yorkshire Street and named itself the New Social Institution.[14] This became an Owenite meeting place for a number of years and also the first headquarters of the Rochdale Pioneers.

A failed weavers' strike, and subsequent attempts to start a flannel weavers' productive society led to some teetotallers, Chartists and Owenites of Branch 24 to become the main movers in starting a store co-operative. Set up along the lines proposed by King, this had an intermediate aim of providing self-employment for its members and a long-term one of founding a co-operative community. The society was formally established in August 1844 and opened its store on 21 December that year.

The Pioneers' first store opened only on Saturday and Monday evenings to start with, but within three months was opening every evening except Tuesdays. Its stock range was limited: 28 lb butter, 56 lb sugar, 6 cwt flour, a sack of oatmeal and tallow candles. The total cost of this amounted to £16 11s 11d. Bonner observes that 'This first stock was speculative neither in nature or quantity. This was well for men who had no experience in selling groceries or buying them wholesale.'[15] G. D. H. Cole reckoned that those initially involved in the Society numbered around thirty-four including four arbitrators who were not members.[16] By the end of their first year the Rochdale Society's membership had risen to seventy-four, its sales to £720, its capital to £181 and its profits to £22.[17]

The eventual success of the Society probably owed much to this cautious beginning which contrasted sharply with its rules and objects. Its objects, as stated in its 'Law the First' were:

> . . . to form arrangements for the pecuniary benefit, and improvement of the social and domestic condition of its members, by raising a sufficient amount of capital in shares of one pound each, to bring into operation the following plans and arrangements.
>
> The establishment of a store for the sale of provisions, clothing etc.
>
> The building, purchasing or erecting of a number of houses, in which those members desiring to assist each other in improving their domestic and social conditions may reside.
>
> To commence the manufacture of such articles as the Society may determine upon, for the employment of such members as may be without employment or who may be suffering in consequence of repeated reductions in their wages.
>
> As a further benefit and security to the members of the Society, the Society shall purchase or rent an estate or estates of land, which shall be cultivated by the members who may be out of employment, or whose labour may be badly remunerated.
>
> That as soon as practicable the Society shall proceed to arrange the powers of production, distribution, education and government, or in other words, to establish a self-supporting colony of united interests, or assist other societies in establishing such colonies.
>
> That for the promotion of sobriety, a temperance hotel may be opened in one of the society's houses as soon as convenient.[18]

The influences of both Robert Owen and William King can be seen in these objects. Likewise in the Society's early practices which were summarised in a statement made by the Society in its almanac of 1860:

> The present Co-operative Movement does not intend to meddle with the various religious or political differences which now exist in society, but by a common bond, namely that of self-interest, to join together the means, the energies, and the talents of all for the common benefit of each.

1. That capital should be of their own providing and bear a fixed rate of interest.
2. That only the purest provisions procurable should be supplied to members.
3. That full weight and measure should be given.
4. That market prices should be charged and no credit given nor asked.
5. That profits should be divided *pro rata* upon the amount of purchases made by each member.
6. That the principle of 'one member one vote' should obtain in government and the equality of the sexes in membership.
7. That the management should be in the hands of officers and committee elected periodically.
8. That a definite percentage of profits should be allotted to education.
9. That frequent statements and balance sheets should be presented to members.

One hundred or more years later, students at the British Co-operative College summarised these practices with the acronym of Rochdale:

Religious and political neutrality
Open membership and one member one vote
Cash trading
Homogeneous market prices
Dividend on purchases, and democratic control
Adulteration of food forbidden
Limited Interest on capital
Education promoted

In the 1930s, a more formal codification by the International Co-operative Alliance resulted in the following being recognised as basic co-operative principles:

Open membership
Democratic control
Dividend on purchases
Limited interest on capital
Political and religious neutrality
Cash trading
Promotion of education

These 'principles' or 'practices' may sound prosaic but they reflect an underlying philosophy that represented an advance on Owen and King. Two aspects of this, equity and democracy, were particularly important in shaping future co-operative forms. Equity, equitability or equality had been present in the ideas of Owen and King, but the Rochdale Pioneers made it central to their initiative and applied it in quite specific ways. One of these was the equitable distribution of the dividend at the end of each trading period. Rochdale had also introduced the co-operative practice of selling at current market prices. As much as anything, this was a defensive mechanism intended to prevent local traders from claiming that they were being undercut and from raising possible retaliatory measures against the Society. However, selling at current market prices resulted in a 'surplus', equivalent to a private traders' profit. With co-operators' traditional abhorrence of profit, the Pioneers introduced the dividend so as to dispose of this equitably. As we have seen, the concept of a bonus had been known in King's Brighton Provident and District Society although that had been largely funded by benefactors. Some early co-operative experiments had also introduced forms of dividend, but the unique contribution of Rochdale was that their dividend was directly linked to the trade each member did with the Society. That part of the 'surplus' which remained after contributing to reserves and providing members with collective benefits such as reading rooms and educational classes, was distributed as a percentage of each £ of that trade.

This was an ideologically driven practice but it was one from which practical benefits flowed. It helped assure the Society's future by strengthening its sense of unity through the encouragement of members' loyalty and sense of identity with the co-operative. It also gave practical expression to the Pioneers' 1860 description of their practices, namely that they shared 'a common bond, namely that of *self-interest*'. It was in members' self-interest to co-operate to improve their conditions. Any self-centredness was redeemed by mutual trade and the equitable sharing of its rewards.

The importance that the Pioneers attached to equity or equality can also be seen in their attitudes to capital. As stated in their 'Law the First', this was to be a 'capital in shares of one pound each'. In the 1860 description of their practices the Pioneers stated 'That capital should be of their [members'] own providing and bear a fixed rate of interest'. Thus capital was for use and not speculation as private shareholders would intend when trading their shares. The Pioneers' sense of equity led them to state in their rules that members' share capital would be rewarded only by a low and pre-determined rate of interest.

This egalitarian impulse also shaped the strong forms of democracy that Rochdale introduced, taking them far beyond the ideas of either Owen or King. They ran directly counter to Owen's paternalism, although they may have been anticipated in King's ideas of mutuality and self-help. Moreover, as the 1860 statement of practices stated, 'the principle of 'one member one vote' would 'obtain in government and the equality of the sexes in membership'. This was at a time when no Rochdale member was likely to have a parliamentary vote and the Chartists went no further than calling for universal male suffrage. Rochdale's radicalism went further when it stated in its practices 'That the management should be in the hands of officers and committee elected periodically'. In practice members with one vote each periodically elected a committee whose officers managed the society according to its rules.

This led to a dynamic situation. Although membership fluctuated according to trading and employment vagaries, it was on a general upward trend. One reason for this was the principle of open and voluntary membership. This was linked to early co-operators' and the Pioneers' principle of religious and political neutrality. Quite soon this gave rise to the question of whether there might be an optimum number of members for a co-operative. Initially based around one store, the Pioneers debated long and hard whether to advise those seeking to join them from nearby areas to form their own co-operatives or whether to allow them to become members of the Rochdale Society which then developed branches to cater for them. The latter course was eventually agreed thus endorsing the policy of open membership.

POST-ROCHDALE

It can be argued that Rochdale concluded the initial evolution of co-operative ideas. The Society's success represented the point where ideas were put into practice. It was also the point from which an identifiable movement developed. The subsequent exponential growth of co-operatives using the model created by the Rochdale Pioneers led to their being called Rochdale co-operatives and the practices on which they were based to become known as the Rochdale, or co-operative, principles.

The massive growth of the new movement, and its dynamism, was indicated by the figures quoted at the beginning of this chapter. Local, or primary retail societies remained the basic unit but within twenty years of Rochdale, local and national federal co-operative organisations were also being established.

For a number of reasons the original goal of establishing co-operative communities was being replaced. Within the urban living that resulted from industrialisation co-operatives found that they could become in effect a community within a community. Not only did they provide a wide range of goods, catering for their members from 'cradle to grave', but they also sponsored educational, cultural and social activities. In addition, their members created a number of auxiliary organisations, the most notable being the Co-operative Women's Guild, founded in 1883. Co-operatives also found, as King had predicted, that they could create jobs for their members by employing them in their shops, in producing goods and services, and in building houses for co-operative members and employees.

Societies put down deep roots in urban communities in other ways. The name of the town or area in which a society was situated was invariably included in its registered title. Moreover, because members provided its capital and had ultimate democratic control, no external interests could close or move it from its community.

However, the main reason why earlier visions of self-supporting and independent co-operative communities faded was the sheer success of consumer co-operatives, which were now becoming an end in themselves rather than the means to an end. Not only were they appropriate in newly industrialised and urbanised communities, they were also strongly innovative. Soon they learned how to gain economies of scale from vertical integration, and passed the benefits from this onto their members in the form of goods of assured quality sold at prevailing market prices, and rising dividends.

Co-operative vertical integration occurred at two levels. That at the local or regional level could be found when primary societies created secondary federal societies to undertake specialist activities such as bakeries, laundries and funerals. Larger co-operatives often contained such departments, but smaller ones did not. A group of them therefore needed to join with each other to organise a viable service.

Over and above such local or regional initiatives, co-operatives were also showing a readiness to join together at national level where the main interest was in wholesaling. Societies required steady supplies of goods of guaranteed quality at fair prices but were frequently at the mercy of unscrupulous private wholesalers. The Rochdale Society had attempted to provide a wholesaling service for itself and nearby co-operatives but without success. The idea of a national co-operative wholesale therefore remained active. Eventually, in 1863, the Co-operative Wholesale Society (CWS) was formed for England and Wales and a Scottish counterpart, the Scottish Co-operative Wholesale

Society (SCWS) was set up in 1868. Subsequently, both extended their wholesaling activities into secondary and primary production and later set up banking departments which became Co-operative Banks. The CWS also set up the Co-operative Insurance Company: co-operatives' expanding trade needed insurance cover.

The 1860s ended with the establishment of the Co-operative Union. This became the movement's 'parliament'. Its members were primary and secondary societies for whom it provided a national forum through its annual congresses. The Union also offered advisory services, initially mainly legal in drawing up model rules to assist new co-operatives to register with the Registrar of Friendly Societies, but later in providing labour and parliamentary advisory services and co-operative education. Shortly after the Union's establishment, the North of England Newspaper Company was set up in Manchester. Its main purpose was to print a national co-operative newspaper and the first edition of *The Co-operative News* appeared in 1871.

All these secondary co-operative organisations were set up, owned and controlled by primary societies. They nominated and elected their boards by virtue of the fact that they contributed their share capital. Primary societies had no difficulty in attracting sufficient share capital. Their membership was growing and these members, being less frequently unemployed, were enjoying relatively greater prosperity. Co-operatives' turnover therefore continued to rise and, because they adhered to Dr King and Rochdale's strictures on not allowing credit, they had few bad debt problems. Such a policy meant, however, that consumer co-operatives were not benefiting the poorest who were those most often out of work.

Mid-Victorian habits of thrift also assisted societies' capital to grow, as did the fact that co-operatives were now viewed as places where it was safe to lodge savings. The secondary societies that co-operatives developed were useful in themselves but they also became an important element in recycling and putting to productive use the growing co-operative system's funds. There was a general concern for capital to be employed productively.

Rochdale's influence remained strong in setting up the two Wholesales with a number of its leaders being prominent in these moves. For example, Abraham Greenwood, who had joined the Pioneers' Society in 1846 and became a member of its management committee, proposed the lines on which the CWS should be established, and in the subsequent campaign he was supported by an original Pioneer, William Cooper. Greenwood became the CWS's first president while other Rochdale members were elected to the Wholesale's board. These included two Pioneers, James Smithies and Charles Howarth.[19] Yet another Pioneer, Samuel Ashworth, became the CWS's buyer and manager.

In view of his importance in shaping the direction of British co-operation in the closing years of the nineteenth century, it is perhaps appropriate to mention at this point that another Rochdale figure, J. T. W. Mitchell became the Wholesale's chairman in 1874, a position he retained until his death in 1895. One effect of Mitchell's work was its shaping of British co-operators' later attitudes to colonial co-operatives, a question to which we will return.

By 1900 the British Consumer Co-operative movement was large both in terms of trade and membership. It had become a mass membership organisation with a large degree of active participation. In comparison with other late Victorian Friendly Societies its level of member participation was on par with that of trades unions but in excess of that of building societies. Each of the 1,820 co-operative societies had a board of management of eight to twelve members elected from society members. Most co-operatives also had similarly elected education committees. They might also have halls committees to administer the co-operative halls in a Society's area which were used for members' meetings and a wide range of co-operative educational and cultural activities. Many societies also ran brass bands, choirs and orchestras, which used these halls along with branches of the Co-operative Guilds and Youth Groups. Co-operative auxiliaries, particularly the Co-operative Women's Guild, became important constituencies in societies' elections.

Before they were large or successful enough to appoint staff, co-operatives were managed by their management mommittees. Some societies rotated the membership of these so as to give members experience in running their society. Staff, however, became necessary once a society had grown beyond a certain point. They were usually recruited from among a society's membership who, at their general meetings, ratified the appointment of at least senior staff members. As usual, the practice of one member one vote operated, women voting equally with men.

PATERNALISM IN BRITISH CO-OPERATION

For all its success the young British co-operative movement was not entirely self-sufficient. It owed something to what we might term paternalism, that is certain roles and functions were undertaken on its behalf by others because it could not yet take them on for itself. Of particular significance in this respect were the Christian Socialists who, between

1848 and 1854 were a formal group, and individuals who later could also be described as Christian Socialists. The former, comprising largely clergymen and lawyers, included J. M. Ludlow (1821–1911), a young barrister who first brought the group together, Rev. F. D. Maurice (1805–1872), Professor of Theology, the Rev. Charles Kingsley (1819–1875), poet and novelist, and Thomas Hughes (1822–1896) and Edward Vansittart Neale (1810–1892), who were both lawyers.[20] The latter included eminent co-operators such as Edward Owen Greening (1836–1923), Hodgson Pratt (1824–1907) and the fourth Earl Grey (1851–1917). All were attracted to co-operation through their Christian beliefs and concerns about the effects of industrialisation. All were also upper or upper middle class and so were not of the class that most co-operators came from, namely the working class. For all that, they were not paternalistic as Owen had been. Where he had been largely dismissive of the 'store' movement, they sought to encourage it. They also strongly upheld a labour theory of value which led them to support largely unsuccessful experiments with producer co-operatives.

Christian Socialists brought ideas, administration and legal skills to the British Co-operative movement. Ludlow had been educated in France where he became familiar with French producer co-operative ideas and tried to introduce these into Britain. He was actively involved in the establishment of the Co-operative Union, having helped to convene the 1869 Co-operative Congress which established it. In 1874 he was the secretary to the Royal Commission on Friendly and Building Societies and a year later became the Registrar of Friendly Societies under which co-operative societies registered.

Thomas Hughes, author of *Tom Brown's Schooldays*, was also a lawyer and, like Ludlow, was active in the setting up of the Co-operative Union, He actually presided at the 1869 congress and gave its inaugural address. With his close friend Edward Vansittart Neale he wrote *A Manual for Co-operators* and championed the cause of producer co-operation during the 1870s and 1880s.

Neale was the Christian Socialist most closely and longest involved with the young British Co-operative movement. He worked with Ludlow to secure the Industrial and Provident Societies Act of 1852, the first legislation to apply to British co-operatives, and in the drawing up of model rules after Ludlow had become Registrar of Friendly Societies. Neale generated many ideas, including those of a Central Co-operative Agency, a Co-operative Insurance Company, a Co-operative Newspaper Society and the Co-operative Productive Federation. He was also at the heart of the debate about producer versus consumer co-operation during the 1870s and 1880s. Perhaps most significantly of all he acted as the Co-operative Union's unpaid general secretary from 1873 until his death in 1892.[21]

The Co-operative Union gradually developed a sectional structure with seven sectional boards. These were geographical sections and together they formed a central board. The executive, known as the united board, comprised one representative from each section.[22] Different sections undertook different responsibilities for the whole of the Union. For example, that of the Southern Section kept an eye on parliamentary matters. Hodgson Pratt acted as its honorary secretary for a number of years.[23]

The British Co-operative Movement was to become well organised and sturdily independent. Before it reached this happy state it had undoubtedly benefited from paternalistic and altruistic help. This is relevant for two reasons. One is that British co-operation would have advanced more slowly without it. The other is that we will find paternalism present in colonial co-operative movements, but to a far greater extent.

OTHER KINDS OF BRITISH CO-OPERATIVE

Consumer co-operation was by far the most developed form in Britain by 1900. It was helping the new working classes to emancipate themselves through mutual trade and self help. This was occurring at a time when industrialisation and urbanisation was increasing the significance of consumption within the British economy, a trend that was accentuated by Empire and the availability of colonial and dominion products.

The two other main forms of co-operation in Britain by the end of the nineteenth century were the worker or producer societies and agricultural co-operatives. Both operated in areas that needed mutual action to offset their existing poor conditions but neither brought forward a formula for success as Rochdale had done for consumer co-operation.

In general, this was a period of co-operative experimentation in which people were sometimes involved in more than one type of co-operative. For example, J. M. Ludlow and Edward Vansittart Neale, together with Edward Owen Greening, were active in the producer and consumer co-operative movements. Greening was also a pioneer of agricultural and horticultural co-operation.

Producer co-operation had its roots in Owenism and in the question of what should be a proper reward to labour. Grafted onto these were the French co-operative ideas of Saint Simon (1760–1824), Philip Buchez (1796–1865), Charles Fourier (1772–1837) and Louis Blanc (1811–1882). Ludlow had become familiar with these and went on to popularise them in Britain, though they did not have the success that they had in France. Their problems were summarised by a manager who attributed his society's difficulties to a lack of co-operative knowledge, purpose and will. In the good times members:

> called each others brothers, sang songs about 'labour's social chivalry' and did wonders in the way of work and profit ... But the slack season came, for which we had not provided and brought with it those terrible evils, jealousy and disunion ... I believe all of us talked too much about rights, and thought too little about duties.[24]

The Christian Socialists were prime movers in setting up the Society for Promoting Working Men's Associations. This noted in its report of 1851 that many of the problems of producer co-operatives stemmed from their members being unready for association. Consequently, the Society had to discourage the formation of some societies and refuse to give financial assistance to others unless their potential members showed a willingness to work co-operatively and to subscribe part of their funds.

Even recognition of these weaknesses failed to bring solutions and by 1880 only fifteen producer co-operatives remained in existence. Thereafter, their position weakened still further, particularly in their trade with consumer societies. The two Wholesales began to manufacture goods for primary societies and effectively became competitors of the producer societies. Some degree of rapprochement took place when consumer and producer co-operatives developed the co-partnership form of co-operative in the 1880s, in which retail societies provided much of the capital and the markets for producer societies. Even so, workers' co-operatives never represented more than 2.61 per cent of retail societies' trade.[25]

Agricultural co-operation found it even more difficult to establish successfully. In 1900 it was quite insignificant. Reasons for its difficulties lay in the traditionally conservative attitude of British farmers, the fact that British agriculture was being blighted by a growing volume of cheap imports and the resulting declining land values. Edward Owen Greening, who was active in both the consumer and producer co-operative movements, was a notable early figure in British agricultural co-operation. In 1868, with help from other Christian Socialists, he set up the Agricultural and Horticultural Association. Its object 'was to combat high prices and especially the adulteration of feed and fertilizers which was common before the passing of the Fertilizers and

Feeding Stuffs Act of 1893'.[26] As in retail societies, an early aim was the elimination of adulterated goods. There had been previous isolated attempts to strengthen farmers through co-operative action but Greening's initiative provided a pattern for a number of future ones.

A far more notable pioneer of agricultural co-operation was Sir Horace Plunkett (1854–1932), another paternalistic figure. From an Irish aristocratic family, he was elected to the British Parliament for the South County Dublin seat in 1892 as a Unionist member. To promote and support Irish agricultural co-operatives, particularly creameries, he set up the Irish Agricultural Society in 1894. Counterparts along similar lines were established in England in 1901 and in Scotland in 1905. In comparison with the consumer co-operative movement the British agricultural movement remained small.

LAWS UNDER WHICH BRITISH CO-OPERATIVES DEVELOPED

It can been seen that British consumer co-operatives were voluntary and self-generated. They owed nothing to the state. Nevertheless, the state, or British government impinged on them in matters of law and taxation. Suitable legislation quickly became urgent and several Christian Socialists helped to lobby for this and then prepare draft legislation.

Later, colonial co-operative movements were initiated with legislation. Invariably including 'Co-operative' in its title, such legislation laid down the scope of co-operatives' activities, their structure and how they were to be financed, which state authority would supervise them, how they would report to this and their members, and at what frequency. That legislation was specifically for co-operatives and began a distinct type of legislation. By contrast British co-operative legislation evolved from earlier legal traditions. Because British co-operatives had had tenuous beginnings and their form gradually evolved over some half century, it was not initially or readily apparent under which legislation they should come. Moreover, early co-operatives did not themselves press for legislation: their early concerns were organisational and later trading. As they took root, however, they realised the need for legal protection against dishonest officials and traders who supplied them. It was not until after the establishment of the Rochdale Society that co-operative pressure for protective legislation emerged. Before that, and from a government point of view, early co-operatives were seen has having features in common with Friendly Societies whose own legal protection derived from a series of Acts dating from 1793. Co-operatives were not allowed to register under these because they were also perceived to be similar to Corresponding Societies which, in the wake of the French Revolution, were prohibited. It was not until the Friendly Societies' Acts of 1834 and 1846 that co-operatives were allowed to register under this type of legislation. Even then they had to have no purpose 'contrary to the law' but were allowed to be trading societies 'for the frugal investment of the savings of members for better enabling them to purchase food, clothes and other necessaries, or the tools or implements of their trade or calling, or to provide for the education of their children or kindred'.[27] However, they were not allowed to trade with those who were not their members, thus preventing producer societies from registering. This also meant that consumer societies could not trade with each other or create federal bodies to carry out specific functions such as wholesaling.

It is a moot point as to how far such inappropriate legislation hampered early co-operatives. Probably to no great extent because they were in an experimental phase and would later benefit from identifying what they needed from legislation and then campaigning for it. Colonial co-operatives, as distinct from dominion and British societies, were unable to pass through a similar phase. Their experimentation would always be bounded by the laws under which they operated.

More suitable British co-operative legislation required the help of friends with connections in high places. As we have seen, the Christian Socialists brought much to British co-operation in terms of ideas and administration. It is perhaps in legislation that they proved most useful in providing a link between a working-class movement that did not yet have parliamentary representation and government.

With the support of the noted liberal economist John Stuart Mill, the Christian Socialists successfully campaigned for the setting up of a committee of the House of Commons to consider how obstacles to the encouragement of the safe savings of the middle and working classes could be removed. The committee concluded that legislation was needed and J. M. Ludlow and Edward Vansittart Neale set about drafting it.

Co-operatives appeared to have the support of both the main political parties. Although the Liberal government that had received the committee's report and had begun the enactment of legislation fell in 1851, the Conservative government that replaced it restarted the process and eventually passed the first legislation. It did not have 'Co-operative' in its title, a tradition that continued into the twentieth century with only a few exceptions, and these not applying to consumer societies that came to form the major co-operative sector in Britain. The first legislation (1852) had the strange title of Industrial and Provident Societies

Act. This was 'intended to intimate . . . that such societies should be industrial as making their profits by the mutual personal exertions of the members and provident as distributing their profits by way of a provision for the future'.[28]

This legislation permitted the 'carrying on or exercising in common of any labour, trade or handicraft, or several labours, trades or handicrafts, except the working of mines, minerals or quarries beyond the limits of the United Kingdom and except the business of banking, whether within the United Kingdom or not'. The Act also laid down a limit of £100 of shares that a member might hold. Such shares should be withdrawable and the interest on them not exceed 6 per cent. Moreover, the total amount a society borrowed should not exceed four times the value of its paid-up shares. Although co-operatives could own land not exceeding an acre in size, they could do so only through trustees.

For all the advances it brought, the first Industrial and Provident Societies Act had limitations. For example it did not provide protection against fraud; that still remained with the Friendly Societies' legislation. Moreover, the Act did not confer corporate status or limited liability, issues of increasing importance to co-operatives. However, these were given in a second Industrial and Provident Societies Act (1862). This added 'whether wholesale or retail' to the list of possible activities of co-operatives, thus making way for the formation of federal societies. These were also facilitated by the provision that one society could invest up to £200 in another society. Minor amending Acts were passed in 1867 and 1871 but a major consolidating Act was passed in 1876 which some believed gave industrial and provident societies 'an independent and almost self-contained code of law'. Apart from provisions for the appointment of the chief and other registrars, Industrial and Provident societies no longer came under the Friendly Societies Acts. A further consolidating Act was passed in 1893 and minor amendments were made in Acts of 1894 and 1895.[29]

It had taken almost fifty years for British co-operatives to achieve legislation with which they were reasonably satisfied. That legislation, however, was labelled 'Industrial and Provident' rather than 'Co-operative', reflecting a period in British history in which personal industry and providence were much valued, particularly for the working classes. British co-operatives had had to seek this legislation, which came in the wake of their early development. As we shall find in later chapters, legislation preceded the development of co-operatives in the colonies which therefore reduced or precluded experimentation in advance of legislation. By comparison with British co-operatives, their dependence on initial legislation meant that they were less voluntary in nature.

CONCLUSIONS

In concluding this chapter we can summarise the main features of the British Co-operative movement in 1900.

By that year it had grown hugely, with a popular mass membership of almost 1,600,000 who were organised in over 1,800 societies. Aggregate members' share capital had risen to almost £20 million and their annual trade of over £65 million was profitable. Such levels of trade offered private traders strong competition to which they responded in a variety of ways including politically. Generally speaking, however, British co-operatives were acceptable to both of the main political parties, the Liberals and the Conservatives, in ways that contemporary trades unions were not.

Consumer co-operatives were the most successful form of co-operative to have developed by 1900. The growth of producer co-operatives had proved both more problematic and contentious. They never rivalled retailing societies in terms of membership or trade. While attempts had been made to initiate agricultural co-operatives, these were still quite insignificant by 1900.

We have also seen that British consumer co-operatives established a formula for success after much experimentation. They represented spontaneous and voluntary growths. Their relationship with government had been coloured by the views of Dr William King that Co-operation must be voluntary and independent of the state. By 1900 their interface with government had been largely limited to questions of legislation and taxation.

During the nineteenth century the philosophy and rhetoric of British co-operatives had gradually emerged. By 1900 both could be summed up in the following statement by Professor Charles Gide, the eminent French co-operative leader and thinker:

> The programme of the consumers' societies admits capitalism to a certain extent as they are societies with shares, and as they demand from the members contributions to capital and pay them an interest and it does not admit the expropriation, properly so called of the possessing class or at least it desires a different expropriation from that which would be brought about by the play of free competition if some day the co-operative enterprises show themselves superior to capital enterprises and get rid of them by their

> successful development. But these are not the characteristics of collectivist expropriation and, above all, there is this difference, that the essential article of the Socialist programme, which is the class conflict, cannot be included in the co-operative programme for the obvious reason that the consumer does not represent any class; he has neither difference of class nor difference of sex; everybody is a consumer . . . everybody, Socialist or otherwise, has the right of admission to the association and that is a feature which suffices to give the co-operative movement its right of autonomy.[30]

In years to come, much would be made of the claim that British consumer co-operatives reflected an association of labour in consumption rather than the more struggling association represented through trades unions in production. Elsewhere in the Empire, though, more co-operatives would be associated with production and relatively few in consumption for production. This will be one of the first and major differences we shall find between co-operatives in the mother country and those in her empire.

3. Developments, Attitudes and Personalities

INTRODUCTION

Our last chapter was concerned with the growth of the British Co-operative movement and largely concentrated on its external features. This chapter will delve more deeply into aspects of the movement's evolving philosophy, particularly those parts which would shape its attitudes to co-operatives in British colonies and dominions.

THE SHAPING OF BRITISH CO-OPERATIVE ATTITUDES TO COLONIAL AND DOMINION CO-OPERATIVES

The Triumph of the Consumer Theory of Co-operation over the Producer Theory of Co-operation

By 1900 British co-operation was essentially a consumer co-operative movement. Other types of co-operative had either not yet developed or, like producer societies, were comparatively insignificant. Moreover, an intellectual bandwagon was gaining momentum in support of what could be termed a consumer theory of co-operation. Luminaries such as Beatrice Webb (née Potter) were adding weight to the arguments of Charles Gide. To a certain degree consumer co-operation had become politically acceptable, as seen in the passing of the industrial and provident societies legislation, and now it was also gaining intellectual endorsement.

It can be argued, though, that the success of consumer co-operation detracted attention from the potential of other types of co-operative. Increasingly, British co-operators saw consumer co-operation as the most legitimate form of co-operation with other kinds being less so because they were sectional rather than universal. The 1870s and 1880s therefore saw a debate about the future direction of British co-operation. Should this lie through all-embracing consumer co-operatives whose multiple activities came under unified ownership and democratic control?

Or was the way forward through a looser system in which different kinds of co-operatives traded with each other?

The trouble was that other kinds of co-operatives, other than retail societies, were not yet successful. They had not found a formula for success like that the consumer co-operatives had gained from the Rochdale Pioneers. Moreover, they had difficulties in raising their initial share capital because their smaller memberships limited those contributing to it. They were also at a disadvantage in trade. Whereas retail societies were increasingly able to obtain advantageous terms through their well-organised bulk buying, producer co-operatives were more vulnerable to their markets because their sales were necessarily specialist and fragmented. Had they been assured of retail societies' orders that vulnerability would have been reduced. The retail societies' creation of two Wholesales, and the competition these provided, prevented such co-operative inter-trading.

Despite the problems producer co-operatives faced, some co-operative theorists still believed them to be the best means of securing for the worker a just reward for his labour. Producer co-operation therefore retained some influential support notably among the Christian Socialists and particularly with Edward Vansittart Neale (1810–1892) and J. M. Ludlow (1821–1911). Ludlow had been the original promoting force[1] but Neale would ultimately prove to have the longest and closest relationship with the young British Co-operative movement. He not only became involved in the formation of each of its national federal organisations but also spent his own money in a number of co-operative ventures. For example, he was the prime mover in the establishment of the Central Co-operative Agency in the 1850s which he believed could be 'a legal and financial institution for aiding the formation of stores and associations, for buying and selling on their behalf and ultimately for organising credit and exchange between them.'[2] At this time it was still possible to envisage an inter-related and inter-trading co-operative movement and Neale believed that the Agency could help ensure its organic development. However, the Agency proved too costly and had to close. During the 1860s the need for it was obviated by the creation of the two Wholesales and the Co-operative Union. Neale became general secretary of the Co-operative Union and in that position tried to ensure that it was the Union of all co-operatives and not just of retail societies. However, the latter's increasing number and the weight of the Wholesales shifted the balance and the movement settled ever more firmly in the direction of consumer co-operation.

It is worth examining the reasons for this in a little detail because they illustrate a dynamic of co-operative development. One obvious reason was the apparent failure of producer societies to become as successful as their retail counterparts. Another reason was the rate at which the movement was building up funds requiring reinvestment. Through successful trade, and though the growing membership that this encouraged, retail societies had rising memberships which brought with them increasing loan and share capital. Co-operative societies were being seen as safe places for their members' savings which might be small individually but when aggregated became significant.

These rising savings nevertheless posed problems for their recipient societies. One was that under the industrial and provident society rules, members' share and loan capital was withdrawable at short notice. Societies therefore hesitated to reinvest it in their own businesses. Instead, they made long-term investments in what were considered safe investments such as government stocks and railways, and shorter-term ones with the Wholesales. To accommodate the increasing funds being placed with it the CWS, in 1872, set up a loan and deposit department. When amendments were made to the Industrial and Provident Societies Act in 1876 it became possible for the CWS to make this into a banking department.

At first this was welcomed, with Neale and others expecting that a co-operative bank would help finance workers' co-operatives. Counter views soon began to be heard. The poor record of producer societies led some to argue that the CWS banking department would be better advised to fund future CWS development, including production. Thus, in 1873 the CWS began biscuit production at Crumpsall in Manchester and that of boots and shoes at Leicester. Other productive ventures followed and similar ones occurred through the SCWS in Scotland. Thus the position of independent producer societies was threatened by competition from the Wholesales. It also soon became apparent that the CWS had increased its significance in the movement by virtue of its becoming its banker.

Certainly the need to put co-operative capital to remunerative use had been one reason why the Wholesales entered production but other benefits soon became obvious. It enabled the Wholesales better to secure supplies to their member retail societies with which some suppliers refused to trade. Production by the Wholesales also constituted vertical integration creating economies of scale that benefited their retail society members. These were better able to raise, or at least sustain, the levels of dividend they paid to their members. In turn this encouraged greater member loyalty and the continuing success of a society. It was also believed that production by the Wholesales provided better standards of employment than prevailed in much of British production at that time.

For all these benefits there was a downside represented by the sharpened divide in British co-operation. Producer co-operative theorists became more strident in their arguments that factories or other places of manufacture should be owned and controlled by their workers. They believed that there was an inevitable clash between the interests of employers and those they employed and that this prevented an adequate and just return being made to labour.

Against this consumer co-operative theorists argued that co-operatives based on production necessarily fostered sectional interests while failing to lessen the tensions between buyers and sellers or reduce what they considered to be the waste inherent in the buyer–seller relations. The question at the heart of the debate was whether production should be under the ownership and control of producers through their co-operatives or under that of consumers through their retail societies. Supporters of the latter view believed that workers could still benefit from co-operative membership if they joined their local retail society. Employees of the Wholesales and retail societies were thus encouraged.

Linked to the main debate was a subsidiary one about whether the profits of Wholesales' factories should be partly shared with their workers or wholly returned to the retail societies that owned them. In 1875 the CWS decided in favour of the latter and abandoned profit-sharing. The run-up to this decision brought forth eloquent arguments from the Christian Socialists. Ludlow attacked the idea of consumer sovereignty, recalling that,

> consideration for the producer was the first stepping stone in the path of English Co-operation . . . the main question was not whether consumers should get goods cheaper, but whether the men who spend themselves on the production of that article, shall or shall not have the primary claim to the fruits of their labours. The question is not whether producers are to have better masters, but whether they are to be their own masters.[3]

The entry of the CWS into production, and its abandonment of profit-sharing with its employees led Backstrom to observe:

> Two things were evident to all observers: firstly that the Wholesale was the unrivalled and almost unquestioned business centre of the Co-operative Movement; and secondly, that its conduct in the sphere of production would determine the future course of Co-operation.[4]

In one way it is possible to interpret the conclusion of this long and often acrimonious debate as the point at which the British Co-operative movement became fully self-governing. Before that, and while constituent parts such as the Wholesales and the Co-operative Union were forming, strict delegation had not always been possible. For example, when referring to conference committees which pre-dated the geographical sections of the Co-operative Union, Bonner notes that a provisional one in the South was appointed to act with similar committees in the North and in Scotland to organise the 1870 congress. He remarks that only one of the Southern Committee's members, namely E. O. Greening, was delegated by a co-operative society. The rest comprised 'friendly Members of Parliament, some prominent reformers, co-operative propagandists such as Holyoake and Lloyd Jones, and two trade union leaders . . .'[5] The time of the debate on producer versus consumer co-operation largely coincided with that during which national co-operative federal organisations became firmly established and threw up their own working-class leaders. As a result the delegating and mandating of delegates to federal meetings became regular features of co-operative democracy and the need for well-meaning outsiders declined. Many, like Edward Owen Greening, became retail society delegates and Edward Vansittart Neale became general secretary of the Co-operative Union in 1873[6] and held that position until he retired in 1891.

In contrast, the CWS was led by its chairman J. T. W. Mitchell (1828–1895) who was of a working-class background. He had risen to this eminence through the Rochdale Society and open elections to the Wholesale. It is interesting to compare the family backgrounds of these two protagonists in the debate on consumer versus producer co-operation.

Neale has been called a 'Gentleman turned Socialist'.[7] His ancestors included William Wilberforce, the anti-slavery campaigner, and Nicholas Vansittart who was chancellor of the exchequer between 1812 and 1824. Neale was from the professional upper middle classes with some minor aristocratic connections.

Mitchell had a working-class background and had strong co-operative antecedents. His grandfather was associated with the earlier failed Rochdale Society and had also subscribed to the Owenite Queenwood Community. Mitchell himself had joined the Pioneers' Society in 1853 and was elected to its management committee in 1856. Although closely associated with the work of the Co-operative Union, to whose central board he was elected in 1872, he was chiefly identified with the CWS. He was elected to its board in 1869 and was its chairman from 1874 till his death in 1895.[8]

Mitchell proved a strong leader of the CWS and led the arguments in favour of the consumer theory of co-operation. Records of that debate lay mainly in the reports of proceedings of Co-operative Union congresses. A Wholesale Society was central to the effectiveness of consumer co-operation. Its position in the debate could therefore never be in doubt. Not surprisingly, then, little of the debate is reflected in CWS board minutes. These are interesting for their brevity, recording only the decisions reached, primarily on administration and trade. They suggest little of Mitchell's supposed forceful character but are perhaps indicative of behind-the-scenes decision-making. However, many accounts of Mitchell exist and while he may have been an active temperance campaigner and Sunday School worker[9] he was also described as a person of strong words and strong action who could rise 'like a lion' at CWS general meetings.[10]

Both Neale and Mitchell died in the 1890s by which time working-class leaders had emerged locally and nationally in the British Co-operative movement. It needed to rely less on paternalistic helpers such as the Christian Socialists in drafting parliamentary legislation. It had set up its own parliamentary committee and office to keep a watch on issues before Parliament and to report on how these might impact on the movement. Through this committee it also began to develop its lobbying and representational skills with civil servants and politicians. At the Co-operative Union Neale had drawn up sets of model rules for co-operatives to use to register with the Registrar of Friendly Societies and to organise their businesses within the provisions of the industrial and provident societies' legislation. Succeeding general secretaries of the Co-operative Union came to that position through the movement, and were able to continue its legal work.

Despite the movement's growing self-reliance, it retained close links with upper-class, and even aristocratic well-wishers. One of these was the fourth Earl Grey (1851–1917). Besides being an active co-operative advocate he also held high positions within the British Empire, serving as governor of Rhodesia and later governor-general of Canada. Although Grey was not among the original Christian Socialists, he was nonetheless Christian Socialist in outlook and an enthusiast for co-operative production and profit-sharing.

Earlier we noted that the Wholesale had become 'the unrivalled and almost unquestioned business centre of the Co-operative Movement'. Correspondence between Grey and Edward Owen Greening reflects Grey's close interest in the movement and also suggests that the CWS board was becoming a working-class élite.[11]

The debate between the protagonists and antagonists of consumer co-operation aroused strong feelings and had ramifications for other co-operative developments including the establishment of the International Co-operative Alliance (ICA). Some like Neale envisaged it as an alliance of the 'friends of co-operative production' while others argued that it should be open to all that were 'genuinely co-operative'. The latter view eventually prevailed.[12] Earl Grey presided over the Alliance's inaugural congress in London in August 1895.

In Chapter 4 we will trace the roles of Henry Wolff, Plunkett and Earl Grey in spreading the idea of co-operative development within the British Empire. For now we should note that a factor in the success of British consumer co-operation in the late nineteenth century was the favourable interaction of the contemporary British economy, including its colonial trade, and the co-operative form. We earlier noted that Professor Charles Gide was one of the earliest economists to argue the significance and importance of the consumer in the modern economy. He also believed that consumers' power could be enhanced by joining consumer co-operatives because these enabled them to gain economies of scale through both co-operatives' horizontal and vertical integration. The former occurred where societies established a number of branch stores, and the latter derived from their creation of secondary, and even tertiary co-operatives. These latter economies are well described in a lecture given by William Maxwell, president of the SCWS in 1888, when he described how co-operatives were changing.

The two Wholesales had formed a joint committee which later entered primary tea production by purchasing tea estates in India, Ceylon (now Sri Lanka) and East Africa. At a theoretical level the implications were profound. Charles Gide argued that consumer sovereignty could obviate the class war, he held that consumer co-operation changed the emphasis from the supply and the cost of production to demand and the economic satisfaction of needs. In this way it eliminated, or greatly reduced, waste. Co-operative societies aggregated an ascertainable demand. The production organised to meet demand was therefore not speculative as would be the case in capitalistic production. As a result the consumer benefited from the economies achieved and because all people were consumers the Co-operative movement could enjoy infinite expansion.[13]

Within this new system Gide relegated labour to the position that the Rochdale Pioneers had given to capital: it was necessary but should receive only a just but limited reward. Consumer co-operative theorists believed this not to be unfair because employees could still access the benefits of consumer co-operation by becoming members of their local retail societies. Consumer co-operation had thus shifted co-operative theory from its Owenite and Christian Socialist roots. The biggest change was that the prime reward no longer went to labour but to the consumer. This subsequently shaped British co-operators' attitudes to rewards paid to producers in the British Empire whose supplies of tea, cocoa, meat, wheat, dairy products and other staples were transported to the UK by the Wholesales in their steamships with co-operative names such as the *Liberty, Equity, Federation, Pioneer and Progress.*[14] British consumer co-operators hardly reflected on the fact that British agricultural co-operatives were hindered from developing in an agricultural sector hard hit by cheaper imports. In the heyday of new imperialism, they could perhaps also have been excused from believing that such trading arrangements, like the British Empire, were in the natural order of things.

For decades to come many British co-operators would consider that consumer co-operation was the best form of co-operation. By the 1930s, however, such views had begun to be challenged. At its congress in Vienna in 1930, the International Co-operative Alliance accepted a French proposal that co-operative principles, adumbrated almost a century earlier, should be reviewed. However, the resulting review had to be undertaken in two stages. The report of the first stage was rejected because, under British influence, it had been too consumer oriented. Consequently, the ICA decided that a second review was necessary so that the variety of co-operative forms that then existed could be taken into account.[15]

British Co-operatives' View of the State

Not only did British co-operators have distinct views on the primacy of consumer co-operation, they also had views about co-operatives' independence from the state. These had been shaped by the views of William King and the sturdy independence of the Rochdale Pioneers. By contrast, colonial co-operative movements came into being by government action and were later supervised and directed by government. In British co-operative eyes, therefore, they were not true co-operatives. Dominion co-operatives were usually more independent of government but sometimes even their birth was preceded by a government commission or some other kind of government action.

Despite being strongly internationalist, and playing a large part in the ICA, the British Co-operative movement did not really become interested in colonial co-operatives until after the Second World War. Before then links tended to be at a personal, rather than at an organisational level. There were a number of reasons for this distance but important among them was British co-operators' view that true co-operatives were voluntarily started by their members, who subscribed their initial share capital and continued thereafter as autonomous entities independent from the state.

Shortly we will refer to the rise of agricultural co-operatives in central and eastern Europe which had a different view of their relationship with the state. Some governments, such as the Prussian, attempted to restructure agriculture and were prepared to assist agricultural co-operatives in their early days with state subsidies. Such needs had not arisen in British consumer societies because they had been able to match their growth with the capital their members could subscribe. Consequently, it was easier for them to heed King's dictum that co-operation should be voluntary and that 'all the power in the world cannot make it compulsory, nor is it desirable that it should depend on any power but its own – the interference of Governments would only cramp its energies and misdirect them'. Moreover, the Rochdale Pioneers had disassociated themselves from politics, if not from government, when they said in their almanac of 1860, that 'The present Co-operative Movement does not intend to meddle with the various religious or political differences which now exist in society, but, by a common bond, namely that of self-interest, to join together the means, the energies, and the talents of all for the benefit of each.'

However, British co-operatives could not long remain indifferent to Parliament. They needed to have appropriate legislation so as to provide legal security and permit co-operative evolution. They also required a tax regime that would take account of co-operatives' different business structures and treat them differently from privately-owned businesses. Yet another reason was that societies were becoming employers of labour to the extent that they needed to take account of parliamentary action on labour matters.

The movement also developed positions on trade. Through congress resolutions it adopted a free trade policy, and thus opposed Joseph Chamberlain (1836–1914) when he advocated tariff reform designed to give preferential treatment to colonial imports and protect British manufacturers.

By the late 1800s the British Co-operative movement was conscious of how Parliament could affect its workings. Initially it asked the members of the Southern Sectional Board, comprising representatives of societies in and near London, to keep a watching brief on Parliament and to warn them of measures likely to affect co-operatives. It soon became apparent, however, that because 'many of the questions dealt with by Parliament affect societies as traders and manufacturers more than in any other direction . . .'[16] more formal arrangements were required. The Co-operative Union Congress of 1900, therefore set up a joint parliamentary committee. Comprising representatives of the Co-operative Union and the two Wholesales, this committee and its officials kept watch on Parliament and advised the movement on proposed legislation or taxation changes; it also began to channel the movement's views on issues that affected it to government ministers and civil servants.

That lobbying was initially directed to Liberal MPs because it was with their party that the movement had the closest links. The Liberal Party was then the main political outlet for working-class voters and many co-operative leaders were Liberals. For example, Mitchell stood, unsuccessfully, as a Liberal candidate in the Rochdale municipal elections of 1893 and 1894.[17] Moreover, one of the Christian Socialists, Thomas Hughes (1822–1896), was also Liberal MP between 1865 and 1874.[18] Co-operatives, in fact, had good relations with Liberals at the highest level. William Gladstone (1809–98), British chancellor of the exchequer and prime minister, so appreciated the support that early members of the Royal Arsenal Co-operative Society (RACS) gave him in his Greenwich seat that he gave them a portrait of himself and his wife taking tea.[19]

The arrival of the Labour Party, and co-operatives' growing relations with it, eroded earlier co-op/Liberal links. In trying to resist these, some co-operators argued that the movement should work through 'all friends of co-operation in Parliament'.

This view was well summed up by Edward Owen Greening at the Co-operative congress in 1917. Although an active member of RACS, he attended the congress as a delegate of the London Co-operative Bookbinders. Greening urged the congress to instruct

> the Central Board of the Co-operative Union to invite the assistance, impartially, of all friends of Co-operation in Parliament, members of all political parties, to resist attempts to levy taxation on our Societies for which there is clearly no equitable justification.[20]

The debate in which Greening spoke was on the proposal that the British Co-operative movement create its own political party, the Co-operative Party. Such an idea went back to the 1890s when, for reasons including splits within the Liberal Party, previous links with Liberal MPs weakened. The view then grew among a significant number of co-operative leaders, and in the joint parliamentary committee, that the movement needed to have a direct say in Parliament. For example, at the Co-operative Union Congress at Perth in 1897, the congress president, William Maxwell, stated that while he did not seek to introduce politics into co-operation, he was 'most anxious to see Co-operation introduced more into politics'. However, factors precipitating the actual decision to set up a Co-operative Party arose from British co-operative grievances during the First World War. Co-operators had not been able to persuade the war-time government led by Lloyd George to redress what they saw as discriminations on issues such as food supplies, mobilisation and taxation.[21]

The decision to create a Co-operative Party had ramifications beyond the bounds of this study and only one will be noted. In protecting itself the movement could not ignore the state as represented through its elected government. To be able better to influence the government of the day it needed to engage directly in party politics. It was no longer sufficient to rely on lobbying by individual co-operative members or the joint parliamentary committee. This was a seismic shift in British co-operative tradition. Indeed, one later historical commentator went so far as interpreting the setting up of the Co-operative Party as a loss of confidence in co-operative voluntary action. In a judgement unusually harsh in co-operative literature, B. J. Youngjohns in his Co-operative College Paper of 1954 saw the move as being one that was designed to allow the movement to tap powers outside of itself. He concluded:

> . . . The forces which were to bring about the reversal of this attitude [non-political actions] were nevertheless hard at work. For 24 years they had been nagging and worrying. The Socialists were advancing within the Movement itself, instilling a consciousness that the Movement had left many things undone – unemployment, the extremes of riches and poverty – things which could be done only by capturing political power. Above all, the Movement had lost faith in itself . . .[22]

Such an unusually harsh critique deserves analysis and interpretation. Youngjohns, writing in the mid-1950s, obviously had the benefit of hindsight and his analysis may also have been coloured by more recent events. During the previous decade the movement had struggled to delineate and defend its boundaries against the state socialism of the 1945–50 and 1950–1 Labour governments. Co-operative insurance, in particular, had been under threat of being nationalised along with other mutual and private insurance companies. Moreover, Youngjohns's timing of the demise in the belief of unlimited co-operative expansion may be suspect. Gide continued to advance the view in the 1920s and few doubts of its continued expansion were openly expressed within the British Consumer Co-operative Movement until after the 1939–45 war. It is therefore doubtful how far a conscious factor it was in establishing the British Co-operative Party. Additionally, while Youngjohns is right about there having been a long debate about British consumer co-operation becoming more directly involved in politics, the immediate debate about the setting up of the Co-operative Party was primarily concerned with self-defence. It has to be admitted, though, that some, like Maxwell, had the long-time hope of seeing co-operation introduced more into politics.

Youngjohns is on firmer ground when he acknowledges that co-operation had not so far impacted successfully on the macro-level problems of unemployment and the extremes of riches and poverty; also that socialist ideas had grown among many, including some co-operators, that the state was the appropriate instrument through which these problems should be solved. There was also the recognition that although Rochdale co-operation had helped to improve the standards of living of millions of British workers and their families, it had not benefited the poorest in British society. Because these were the ones who most frequently suffered unemployment, they could not regularly buy their basic goods with cash. Consequently, they could not always shop at the co-op and so often fell victim to less scrupulous traders or money-lenders. They fell through the limited safety-net that co-operatives provided.

This was a recurring problem. While co-operatives would prove effective in raising the standard of living among those who had some capacity for helping themselves through collective action, they would prove less relevant to the needs of the really poor.

Youngjohns was also right in noting the changing relationship between socialists and co-operators. The failure of co-operatives to help the poorest had undoubtedly been one factor. In earlier times the terms 'co-operation' and 'socialism' had sometimes been synonomous. For example, Robert Owen interchanged them and the term 'Christian Socialism' defined the Christian Socialists' brand of co-operation. However, the terms diverged as the nineteenth century progressed and the works of Karl Marx (1818–1883) and Engels (1820–1895) became known. These highlighted the existence of classes and their emphasis on revolution contrasted starkly with the evolutionary workings of co-operation. By the early twentieth century a sharp distinction could be drawn between co-operation and socialism. Their divergence was well summed up by Charles Gide, of whom C. R. Fay said

> He saw in the Rochdale dividend the socialisation of profit without the constrictions of *etatisme*. He . . . found a substitute for competition; and he saw that in an autonomous co-operative movement there was a middle way between *laissez faire* and Marx.[23]

The above references to consumer co-operation should not distract us from the relevance of the underlying co-operative principles of open and voluntary membership and the socialisation of profit through the dividend which apply in all co-operatives. However, the decision to engage in politics directly by the setting up of the British Co-operative Party could be interpreted in three ways: a lack of confidence in co-operative action on its own; a readiness to take co-operative ideas into politics; and a breaching of the co-operative principle of religious and political neutrality. Strangely perhaps, what it did not do was to breach co-operators' traditional views of their independence from the state. They still made the important distinction between themselves and the state in that they were self-created and democratically owned and controlled. The state had no part in their establishment and they functioned as autonomous associations independent of it. They traded successfully and looked for no state subsidies.

Indeed, as can be seen from the reports of early congresses of the ICA, British co-operators were scornful of those European co-operatives that sought subsidies from their governments. The question was tied up with the relationship between the state and co-operatives. At its third congress in Delft in 1897 the ICA had acknowledged the power of the state to legislate; a series of papers illustrated the different systems under which early co-operatives were operating, and also how much successful co-operative development was dependent on an appropriate legislative framework. The conclusion reached by the Delft congress was that the state should enable, but not interfere with co-operatives.[24] The sixth ICA congress in Budapest in 1904 took further the debate on state/co-operative relations. Under a paper entitled 'The Duty of the State towards Co-operation: Should it Subsidise it or not?'[25] representatives of central European agricultural co-operatives tried to persuade the ICA to take a more lenient attitude towards the state. Arguing that it could be a positive element in co-operative development, they suggested that it should not necessarily prejudice the movement's characteristic features of self-help and mutual aid. However, they believed that any state assistance should be 'moderate and temporary' and that it should 'scrupulously respect' co-operative self-government.

This debate presaged central problems for future co-operative development: how to limit state subsidies to a temporary period only;

and how might recipient societies avoid infringement of their self-management as governments attempted to ensure the proper use of the subsidies they had granted.

The ICA'S Budapest congress of 1904 was held within the soon-to-be-dismantled Austro/Hungarian Empire and reminds us once again that the nature of states can change. Throughout the period of this study, 1900 to 1970, the British state evolved, as did the states within her empire as they responded to circumstances such as war and ideologies including those arising from independence movements or the influence of ethnic groups. In each case, co-operative movements within these states needed to respond to those changes.

We end this chapter by viewing the relations between British and Irish co-operatives in the closing years of the nineteenth century and the early years of the twentieth. These were complicated by Irish pressures to secede from the United Kingdom and so change the nature of both states, and by British co-operatives' adjusting their relations to other types of co-operative.

CO-OPERATIVES AND THE IMMEDIATE EMPIRE – BRITISH/IRISH CO-OPERATIVE RELATIONS

Ireland can perhaps be termed the 'immediate empire' as the western-most point of the British Isles and with long historical ties. These went back to Henry II (1133–1189) who had first sent troops there. Hundreds of thousands of other troops followed, as well as generations of British administrators, and, down the centuries, a class of Anglo-Irish gentry had evolved. Ireland's closeness to Britain was reinforced by an Act of Union in 1800. Until then there had been an Irish parliament with its own House of Lords and House of Commons although, indicative of the religious divide in Ireland, no Catholic had been eligible to sit in it since 1692. Similarly, after the Act of Union, no Catholic could sit in the UK parliament either.

Besides creating a united parliament, the 1800 Act of Union had a number of other objectives. One was ensuring the continuation of the Protestant ascendancy in Ireland, particularly in Ulster. Even by Irish standards that had had a troubled history. It lay in north-east Ireland and in the early seventeenth century its aristocracy had fought unsuccessfully against the English. In retaliation their lands were confiscated and redistributed among Anglican lowland Scots who were shipped in to settle the land. This was an early example of the British Empire transplanting populations. In Ireland, however, it accentuated religious divisions and stoked hatreds.

Another objective of the Act of Union was to secure Ireland's military and naval strategic importance. By binding her more closely within the Union it was hoped that she would be less open to Britain's enemies. In the past these had included France and Spain and during the First World War Germany would be the threat.

In addition to the Act of Union Ireland was tied into the United Kingdom in other ways, including the armed forces in which many Irish served. Once again these reflected religious divisions. Whereas the ranks usually comprised the Catholic rural poor escaping famine and poor land conditions, the officers tended to come from the Irish Protestant gentry. They included some notable British soldiers such as the Duke of Wellington; Sir Garnett Wolseley, commander-in-chief of the British army; Field Marshal Lord Roberts of Kandahar; and Field Marshal Lord Kitchener of Khartoum.[26]

Politically, as well as militarily, there was integration. For the main part Irish MPs settled well in the British Parliament. One observer noted that 'for much of the 19th century Irish Nationalist MPs at Westminster were generally conservative in their social and political outlooks, and not prepared to rock the ship of state in which they had found themselves for the most part so comfortably berthed'.[27]

The real divide came in matters of religion and of land. As far as religion was concerned, figures in the early twentieth century reveal that nearly 75 per cent of Ireland's population were Catholic; the Anglican Church of Ireland claimed 13 per cent; the Presbyterians 10.5 per cent and the Methodists 1.42 per cent.[28] The religious divide was compounded by a geographical one, with Protestants being most strongly represented in the North-East in Ulster and Catholics elsewhere in Ireland. Complicating this situation was the fact that Irish Catholicism touched many areas of life. 'In many ways it functioned as an alternative government in Ireland and had a huge political, social, cultural and educational influence on the lives of its congregation.'[29] Interestingly, though, while the Catholic Church supported calls for Home Rule, it opposed revolutionary forms of nationalism, because it feared that they could lead to anticlericalism, as they had elsewhere in Europe during the nineteenth century. However, it was not only Catholics who were calling for Home Rule. Some Protestants also joined the Irish nationalist movement and prominent among these were Charles Stewart Parnell (1846–1891) who became its leader, and John Redmond (1856–1918) who succeeded him.

The other main area of divide was the question of land and, like religion, it became caught up with growing calls for Home Rule. Despite its being one of the most fertile in Europe, the Irish countryside was unproductive and neglected and accelerated the decline in Ireland's population. The potato famine in the 1840s had prompted the first exodus from the land and migration from Ireland. Other migrations followed as problems such as lack of cash and bad agricultural practices were compounded by the emotive issue of absentee landlords. Rural Irish communities were becoming poorer and were further blighted by the rise of the 'gombeen-man'. He was 'the Irish species of dishonest shop-keeper, produce-buyer, money-lender and userer'.[30] Ireland's rural distress is perhaps best demonstrated in the country's population decline. In 1841 Ireland's population had been 8 million. By 1897 it had dropped to 5 million. This decline was in sharp contrast to the rising population elsewhere in the UK, influenced by a declining death-rate. In Ireland the death–rate had risen and that effect was exacerbated by people migrating.

The Westminster Parliament passed a series of ameliorative measures including security of tenure, and grants for agricultural improvements and for peasants to buy their land. Some interpreted these measures as 'killing Home Rule by kindness',[31] but demands for Home Rule continued. Two Gladstone administrations tried to legislate for this but in 1886 his proposals split Gladstone's party; his Bill was rejected and after an appeal to the country he was defeated at the polls. Returning to office in 1892, he reintroduced a Home Rule Bill in 1893. Although it was passed by the Commons this time, it was defeated by the Lords and Gladstone resigned for the last time in 1894.

Moves towards Home Rule were hampered by the opposition of those living in the more prosperous North-East. Ulster unionists were opposed to it, fearing that it would threaten their economic prosperity and allow the Catholic Church to become dominant. They wanted to remain within the UK and gained considerable support from the Conservative and Unionist Party. However, a third Home Rule Bill, when presented to the Westminster Parliament, was finally enacted in September 1914. Then, irony of ironies, its implementation was delayed for the duration of the war that had begun a month earlier.

The complexities of Irish nationalism form only a background in this study, but the struggle for Irish independence would inspire subsequent independence movements in the British Empire and thus become a reference point for them. Our main purpose in mentioning it here is to show the difficult framework within which early Irish co-operative experiments occurred. An important element of that was the low state of Ireland's agriculture.

A series of measures were passed to improve it, the first being Gladstone's Land Act of 1881. Its main aim was relief of the Irish tenant farmer through determining fair rents, granting security of tenure and allowing free sale. The Land Commission set up under the Act, with powers to fix judicial rents, soon ran into difficulties. Firstly, it was quickly swamped with thousands of cases. Secondly, the Act excluded more than half of Irish tenants who held more than an acre; these included 280,000 leaseholders and occupiers who were in arrears with their rent. The fact that further Land Acts were passed in 1891, 1896 and 1903 underline how difficult was the Irish land situation.[32] They also reflect a high degree of government concern and involvement.

It was during this period that the first steps were taken in Irish co-operation. The main mover and visionary was Horace Plunkett (1854–1932), later Sir Horace. Plunkett came from an Anglo/Irish aristocratic family and his forebears included a former deputy governor of Ireland and the Blessed Oliver Plunkett. Born in Gloucestershire, Plunkett was the third son and sixth child of Edward and Ann Constance Plunkett. His father was in the Royal Navy and would become an admiral. Plunkett's immediate family were 'Low Church' and it has been suggested that 'The terrors of a narrow and harsh religion oppressed Plunkett . . . accounting for his later agnosticism and his preference for oblivion rather than a life hereafter'.[33] The Plunketts were part of the Dunsany family and they moved to Dunsany in Co. Meath when Plunkett was seven. He spent the rest of his childhood there, apart from his education at Eton and Oxford.

The Dunsany family were benevolent landlords at a time when we have seen that most Irish landlords were not. It was also distinguished by having both Catholic and Protestant wings. The former handed over their property to the latter for safe keeping during penal times and had it returned when the difficulties had passed.[34] So large and eminent was the family that when Sir Horace died there was some uncertainty about which Plunkett he was.[35]

Plunkett's position on Irish Home Rule was not fixed and shifted over the years. Initially he believed that Ireland's union with Britain should continue because she was not economically ready for home rule. Moreover, he believed that the land question should be settled before independence and also feared that the nationalists were insufficiently sensitive to the complexities of the problems with Ulster. By the early years of the twentieth century his views appeared to be shifting in support of Home Rule. In 1904 he wrote a book, *Ireland in the New Century*, in which he suggested that 'Ireland must be recreated from within. The main work must be done in Ireland and the centre of interest must be Ireland.' He also wrote, 'Anglo-Irish history is for Englishmen to remember, for Irishmen to forget.'[36]

Plunkett's contribution to Irish regeneration lay in two main areas. The first was in the field of agricultural co-operation and rural social economy. W. G. S. Adams in his introduction to Margaret Digby's book *Horace Plunkett – an Anglo-American Irishman* placed Plunkett alongside 'the great pioneers like Grundtvig in Denmark and Raiffeisen in Germany'.[37] Plunkett's second main contribution was in the area of government administration. In particular, he introduced a new model of government in the field of agriculture and technical instruction.

In 1892 Plunkett had been elected the Unionist MP for Dublin South but eight years later was defeated by a narrow margin. It seems that members of his own party had become distrustful of him because of his shifting views on Home Rule, land reform and his support for a Catholic university. Plunkett toyed with the idea of standing for an Ulster seat but then unsuccessfully contested a by-election in Galway. His parliamentary career was over.

In 1895, while still an MP, Plunkett had written to the press with a proposal affecting the general welfare of Ireland. The background to this was that in a general election the previous month, the Unionists had been returned with 411 seats, the Liberals with 177, Nationalists with 70 and the Parnellites with 12. Plunkett believed that with such a Unionist majority, there was unlikely to be any movement on the question of Home Rule during that Parliament. In the interim he believed that the Irish should unite to promote legislation that would be useful to them and on which all parties could agree. He suggested that such legislation should include the establishment of a Board of Agriculture for Ireland and a Bill to promote technical education. Plunkett also proposed a committee comprising representatives of the main political parties to advance the proposals.

Their report in August 1896 was favourably received. It gained British support because it proposed taking an important Irish issue outside the British Parliament. Moreover, instead of the usual blanket demand for Home Rule, this represented a more subtle approach and that made it difficult to oppose. The report also gained considerable support within Ireland because it offered a means of gaining a measure of Irish control over a specific sector such as agriculture rather than leaving it with the British Parliament.

The report drew on the agricultural experiences of other countries. Like Owen and the Christian Socialists, particularly Neale, Plunkett was a wealthy man who was prepared to fund his ideas. On this occasion Plunkett paid for most of the work. Researchers visited a number of European countries to study their government agricultural departments, levels of technical instruction and the degree to which co-operatives had so far developed. Their findings were then compiled into a review of measures taken in Europe to promote agriculture, rural industries, fisheries and forestry.

The final report also surveyed Ireland's economy, noting that it had little manufacturing apart from linen and ship-building in the North and brewing and distilling in Dublin. The rest of the economy was based on an agricultural sector hampered by poor cultivation of a decreasing acreage, and a declining population that lacked both industrial habits and technical skills. The report went on to propose the adaptation of European practices to Irish conditions. Concerning agriculture it suggested that because the government was unable to deal directly with the individual, it was desirable that there be an organisation of the people themselves. Some state subsidy was proposed for voluntary organisations as long as they did not trade. In fisheries and industry, however, the report suggested that the government might have to take direct action.

From a co-operative point of view the report is interesting for the emphasis it placed on education and training. These two have been recurring features in this study. In the Irish context, however, they were seen to be within the purview of government, as distinct from the self-provision of Rochdale Co-operation. The report urged the improvement of technical or practical education which should extend from primary school to university. Moreover, the professional status of the agricultural technician and industrialist should be raised and there should also be travelling instructors. Plots should be set aside for model cultivation, and experimental stations and laboratories should be established. Co-operative banking should also be developed.

In addition to a consultative Council of Agriculture that should have some members elected and others appointed, there should also be a new Department of Agriculture. This would incorporate some existing government departments such the Fisheries and Veterinary Departments and some sections of the Board of Education. It should have in charge a minister who would be responsible to Parliament but who would be assisted by an Agricultural Board and advised by the proposed Consultative Council of Agriculture.

The Department of Agriculture and Technical Instruction (DATI) was established in 1896 and Plunkett became its vice-president. That meant, in effect, that he was its working head. The Council of Agriculture that advised him comprised representatives from each of the local authorities and it has been observed of this that 'This emphasis on local involvement in decision-making was a marked innovation in 1900.'[38]

Such pluralistic concerns were a distinct feature of Plunkett's approach. They had also been evident in the care that he took to ensure that the committee whose report had led to new government machinery for Irish agriculture should include representatives of all religious and political persuasions. Plunkett, however, ran into difficulties when he found himself no longer an MP, in 1900. His position as vice-president of the DATI was that of a minister. While the law allowed him to remain vice-president, his loss of a parliamentary seat meant that he was no longer able to report the Department's work in Parliament. However, high public regard for Plunkett, and the fact that the government were content for him to remain, led to his retaining that position.

His second main area of importance was the major part he played in the development of Irish rural co-operatives. Indeed, he has been held to have 'brought into being the Irish Agricultural Co-operative Movement'.[39] He saw agricultural societies as being an important plank in Ireland's rural regeneration.

Plunkett had begun his 'study of the co-operative principle under such leaders as Holyoake, Vansittart Neale, Tom Hughes and Alfred Marshall'.[40] His early co-operative interests seem to have been in consumer co-operation. He attended the Co-operative Union's Congress in 1889 where he met Beatrice Potter (1858–1943) and Sidney Webb (1859–1947). Potter, soon to be Mrs Sidney Webb, had written cogently in praise of British consumer co-operation. Plunkett's first co-operative efforts were to be in trying to establish store co-operatives along the Rochdale lines.

Long before that, in 1878, Plunkett had established on Plunkett land the Dunsany Co-operative Society. On returning from Oxford to act as agent and estate manager he had been distressed by his tenants' economic conditions. Whereas the better-off could shop in the larger towns, the rural poor had to shop where they lived. They suffered from poor standards of service and high prices. A few other retail co-operatives had also been established, the first at Inchicore in Dublin in 1859. They were, however, weakly growths which Plunkett thought could be strengthened by the setting up of a Co-operative Store Organisation Society to co-ordinate their efforts and foster new societies. Nevertheless, retail co-operatives never really took off in Ireland.

During this experimental phase of consumer co-operation in Ireland links were established with the British consumer co-operative movement. An Irish exhibition in London in 1888 provided the venue for contacts with the Southern Section of the Co-operative Union which agreed to organise a conference to discuss how the co-operative movement might be extended in Ireland. This was held 'with a sprinkling of Irish visitors' and under 'the chairmanship of Lord Aberdeen'. He was chief British administrator in Ireland in 1886 and again between 1905 and 1915. His wife, Lady Aberdeen, was a friend whom Plunkett sought to involve in the propagation of his co-operative plans. The conference proposed the formation of a 'propagandist association' for Ireland.[41]

However, around this time, Plunkett changed direction. He had realised that the type of retailing, wholesaling and manufacturing co-operative movement suitable in England, Wales and Scotland, was less relevant in an Ireland where the major part of the economy was based on peasant farming. As a result he focused increasingly on agricultural co-operatives. In attempting to organise these he gained the support of many of his aristocratic friends. These included the Honourable Alexis Roche, who had spent time with Plunkett ranching in the USA. Plunkett had shown early signs of developing tuberculosis, the disease from which his mother and eldest brother had died. Part of the treatment prescribed for him had been an outdoor life in a dry climate; so, Plunkett spent part of each of the next ten years ranching in Wyoming. Although he recovered, he never enjoyed robust health, but his time in Wyoming gave him insights into American agriculture that he tried to apply to Ireland.

Co-operative propaganda was seen as an important part of creating a favourable climate in which co-operatives could develop. It was delivered in a variety of ways. The Irish Co-operative Aid Association, which had been a result of the conference organised by the Southern Section of the Co-operative Union, 'made contact with everyone known to have influence in Ireland. Soon people in every parish in Ireland received literature by post, explaining the co-operative movement and its possibilities'.[42] Plunkett, on the other hand, was bending the ears of his friends. He spoke

> . . . to his 'sporting friends at the Horse Show and to bewildered dinner parties at the Castle', to Lord Yerburg, and Henry Wolff, to the Duchess of Hamilton, to Vaughan Nash, the future secretary to the Development Commission, to Lady Aberdeen, Lord Zetland and many others.[43]

while another of his supporters, Robert Anderson, had a much rougher time. He

> . . . travelled the length and breadth of Ireland by train, sidecar, horseback and bicycle, holding meetings in all kinds of buildings and addressing all manner of suspicious and sometimes hostile audiences . . . in one month he slept in thirty different places,

> sometimes on the seat of a night train with no covering but his frieze overcoat and no pillow but his wallet of papers.[44]

The future backbone of Irish co-operation would be the co-operative creamery which would buy farmers' milk and turn it into dairy products. A number were established on the estates of Plunkett's wealthy landowning supporters. Plunkett despatched Anderson to Sweden to study its modern dairy and creamery techniques carrying letters of accreditation written by the Duchess of Hamilton.[45]

As the number of creameries grew, Plunkett realised their need for a central organisation. At first he tried to develop this under the umbrellas of two existing organisations, the Royal Dublin Society and the British Co-operative Union. He found the former unlikely to be interested in the 'problems of five-cow tenant farmers in west Limerick', while he believed he detected in the latter a 'narrow selfishness'; he found it easier to develop a rapport 'with the Christian Socialists, Neale, Ludlow and Hughes'. He believed that what was needed was a specialist agency for the joint marketing of creamery products. In 1893, with some thirty creameries operating with a combined turnover of around £150,000, the Irish Co-operative Agency Society was established with a personal financial guarantee from Plunkett. He was elected its first president.[46]

Within its marketing remit the Agency proved successful. By the turn of the century it had become one of the largest shippers of butter in Ireland. However, it could not meet some of its members' other needs such as the supply of fertilisers, seeds and implements, and the marketing of barley; it soon hived them off to another organisation, the shortlived Irish Co-operative Agricultural Agency whose functions were taken over by the newly-formed Irish Agricultural Wholesale Society in 1897. Even then, Plunkett felt that Irish farmers, with their other problems, needed another organisation with a wider remit. He therefore proposed the creation of the Irish Agricultural Organisation Society (IAOS). Its objects were:

> To improve the condition of the agricultural population of Ireland by teaching the methods and principles of co-operation as applicable to farming and the allied industries; to promote industrial organisation for any purpose which may appear beneficial; and generally to counsel and advise those engaged in agricultural pursuits . . .[47]

By the late 1800s primary and secondary co-operatives had developed in Ireland as they had in Britain. However, there was an important difference deriving from their economies. Whereas the former were linked to production, the latter were geared to consumption. A point of similarity was the need to keep co-operative members out of the grasp of private moneylenders. In Britain, where co-operative activity was less immediately linked to production, that need was not so great as long as co-operative members enjoyed fairly regular employment. The co-operative principle of members trading with their societies only for cash had the double benefit of preserving the co-operative from running up bad debts and preventing its members incurring debts that they might not be able to pay. Moreover, consumer co-operatives encouraged their members' thrift by becoming savings institutions and opening small deposit accounts for their members. In Ireland, where co-operative activity was more closely linked to production, payment for that production, or farmers' income, was necessarily cyclical and therefore more widely spaced than that of British wage earners. Moneylending in various forms, but usually pernicious, had been endemic in rural Ireland for generations.[48]

The formation of the IAOS, with its wider remit, allowed examination of how Irish farmers's indebtedness could be eased. Another of Plunkett's close colleagues, Fr Finlay, had spent time in Germany where he had become familiar with the Raiffeisen banks. He argued that a similar system was needed in Ireland if the co-operative agricultural movement there was to succeed. Finlay therefore proposed that the IAOS committee should invite Henry Wolff to visit Ireland. He was a leader of the fledgling ICA but also an acknowledged expert on co-operative finance.

Wolff proved a seminal figure in the development of co-operatives throughout the British Empire. Born in Leeds, he had spent many years farming in Germany and, like Finlay, had become familiar with the Raiffeisen system. He was in a pivotal position to keep apace with co-operative developments outside Britain, and co-operative banking and thrift and credit co-operatives. In 1895, the year after IAOS had invited him to visit Ireland, he published *Agricultural Credit Societies*[49]. In Ireland, Wolff added weight to Finlay's view that the Raiffeisen system was the most appropriate.

To spearhead their promotion of Irish credit societies the IAOS recruited George William Russell (popularly known as AE). Plunkett had discovered him when he was working as a £60-a-year clerk in a Dublin drapery store and said of him, 'While he outdreams us all . . . none of us have as shrewd business judgement or as nice a sense of humour.'[50] AE did more than successfully organise village banks. He also proved to be an effective propagandist. The Irish Co-operative movement began producing its own weekly paper, *The Irish Homestead*, in 1895. In 1906 AE became its renowned editor.

Although the financial strand of Irish co-operative development proved more problematical[51] than the establishment of creameries and other co-operative provisions, it nevertheless became one of its notable features, providing another point of contrast with the British consumer co-operative movement. It also revealed a need for credit linked to agricultural co-operative development.

It can be said that before Irish independence the UK had two distinct co-operative movements: a consumer-based movement in England, Wales and Scotland, and an agricultural movement in Ireland comprising creameries, agricultural supplies, and thrift and credit. Before examining the relationship between these two movements, we should note some important differences between their origins, particularly in terms of their early development.

British co-operation was an economic and social movement that had grown out of Owenism and Chartism. It had a clear ideology, believing in co-operation as distinct from competition and initially supporting a labour theory of value. It was also strongly anti-capitalist and saw co-operation as a peaceful means of transforming a capitalist economy into one that was socially owned and democratically controlled. While it had had its paternal figures such as Owen, the Christian Socialists and, to a lesser extent, William King, it had become largely self-generating from the time of the Rochdale Pioneers who had married motive and capacity.

Irish co-operation had evolved differently. While there had been personal links with the Owenite and Chartist movements, these had not developed along Rochdale lines.

No popular co-operative movement emerged in Ireland as it had in Britain through the Rochdale Pioneers. Ideology was never to become as strong a motivator in Irish co-operation as it had elsewhere in the UK. While Plunkett had been attracted to Owen and co-operative ideas, his starting point had been empirical observations of Ireland's condition. He believed that co-operation could help solve Ireland's problems, but he also saw a role for government, as in his work leading to the setting-up of the Department of Agriculture and Technical Instruction.

In Ireland the driving force in initial co-operative development was not a social movement as in England and Scotland but Plunkett and the people he gathered around him. A large proportion of these were aristocratic although, as we have seen, Plunkett recruited from all classes and all religions. He built institutions designed to assist co-operative development: the Irish Co-operative Agency Society, the

Irish Co-operative Agricultural Agency and its successor the Irish Agricultural Wholesale Society, and the Irish Agricultural Organisation Society. By contrast, British co-operative institutions such as the Wholesales, Co-operative Union and Co-operative Press, were federal bodies created by primary societies.

The interaction between these two quite distinct co-operative movements within the British Isles occurred in a number of ways, the two main ones being through trade and through membership of the Co-operative Union.

In trade the relations were between Irish co-operative creameries and the English and Welsh Co-operative Wholesale Society Ltd (CWS). Those relations were not always easy. The difficulties that arose essentially reflected tensions between the interests of British co-operative consumers and Irish co-operative producers.

A feature of British consumer co-operation was the speed at which it had grown. Part of that success lay in the economies of scale that its two Wholesales had achieved by entering all the stages of the food chain: distribution, wholesaling, manufacturing and primary production. By the end of the nineteenth century the Wholesales owned large farms in Britain and Canada and these would soon be joined by tea estates in India and Ceylon. However, their production could not meet all the needs of the growing membership of retail societies and buying depots were also set up in France, Denmark, Canada, USA, Sweden, Spain and Australia. Often the goods channelled through these were transported to the UK by the Wholesales' steam ships. Within the UK, and for the purchase of dairy products, Irish depots were established in Tipperary (1866), Kilmallock (1868), Limerick (1869), Armagh (1873) and Tralee (1874).

The first actual dairy co-operative was established at Drumcollogher in West Limerick in 1889. Patrick Bolger in *The Irish Co-operative Movement – Its History and Development* and Percy Redfern in *The Story of the CWS* give good and detailed accounts of how this came about. They record how the Drumcollogher Society was initially promoted by W. L. Stokes, the CWS's butter buyer in Limerick and Robert Gibson, a butter merchant. The rules of Ireland's first dairy co-op were drafted by the Co-operative Union in Manchester and the CWS took out ten £1 shares in the society. After two years the society faltered, although Bolger observed that the CWS had 'co-operated admirably in the founding of Drumcollogher'.[52]

Elsewhere, however, such collaboration ran into difficulties. The CWS also took shares in another co-operative creamery, at Castlemahon, Limerick. After two years it also almost collapsed and Robert Anderson observed that the trouble with its members was their 'preferring politics to business'. Someone else attributed its difficulties to 'The parties being equally divided . . . when one side was managing the creamery the other side refused to send their milk, and vice versa.'[53] The CWS was anxious not to become more closely involved, but to save the enterprise took over the tenancy of Castlemahon for a year. It installed new equipment and managed the business successfully. After a year the CWS's offer to return the creamery to the Dairy Co-operative was declined. Matters came to a head when the dairy society's creditors pressed for payment. The bailiffs were then put in and the society was put on the market. At that point the CWS bought it for £850. Disagreements multiplied with subsequent developments. Redfern summed these up:

> The point of divergence was that the CWS went on to create an auxiliary to Castlemahon and also to erect a new creamery near Listowel. And this meant working out the federal co-operative principle of associated consumers controlling their sources of supply. But the principle of the new Irish Agricultural Organisation Society was control by Irish producers.[54]

The CWS's direct entry into Irish dairy production was raised at two Co-operative Union congresses. The first followed the announcement by J. T. W. Mitchell at Lincoln in 1891 that the CWS proposed to purchase land in Ireland, to stock it with cows and to erect and operate co-operative creameries. According to Bolger:

> Plunkett and Anderson were on their feet immediately, expressing amazement and indignation. Plunkett made an impassioned plea to be allowed to teach co-operation to the Irish farmer. Dairying was the one fruitful avenue open to him. Only through self-help and personal participation could the Irish farmer come to anything. He was an indifferent producer of home-made butter. Where there were proprietary creameries in Ireland, the farmer was a supplier of indifferent milk. Only by taking business and responsibility into his own hands and seeing the benefits of co-operation, could the Irish farmer acquire the qualities of mind and heart, the habits of thrift and industry that would raise him from serfdom. Paternalism, however, generous, could not uplift him now; as a policy, it would be no more successful than the coercive treatment which in the past had sought to make him a docile and useful slave.[55]

Tensions worsened again when the CWS broke an agreement not to operate creameries in areas where independent co-operative creameries already existed or there were plans to open one. At the 1895 Huddersfield congress Plunkett, again supported by Anderson, moved an addition to the report from the Irish Section of the Co-operative Union deprecating the CWS's action.[56]

Variations on these issues would recur in co-operative development elsewhere in the British Empire. At their heart lay the familiar co-operative dilemmas of equitably marrying fair rewards for consumer and producer co-operatives, and how to organise that convergence efficiently.

The CWS had other considerations. In the short-term it experienced a number of difficulties, including the fact that creamery buildings were sometimes ill-designed for Irish conditions. Machinery and equipment also often proved inadequate, and local managers did not have authority to install more appropriate items, were indifferent and were sometimes dishonest.[57] Plunkett castigated the CWS creameries 'as being practically proprietary instead of co-operative'.[58]

In the long-term the CWS had an overall objective to ensure the delivery of the best dairy produce to its retail society members. It also needed to note changes in the supply market. Earlier in its operations the CWS was limited to 'high prices each winter, and a great scarcity of all except very salt Irish butter'.[59] Gradually, by extending its sources of supply, it reduced the differences between summer and winter butter prices but the average of the latter remained higher. British co-operative consumers eventually benefited from the reorganisation of Scandinavian dairies and in particular from the fact that,'The Danish butter makers are organised as producers, and their admirably intelligent combinations give them the full advantage of the market.' Moreover, 'About 1880 the mild butter scientifically made by State-instructed dairymen of Denmark was ousting Irish salt butter at one end of the scale, while the new margarines or "butterines" attacked it from below.[60]

Another difficulty for the CWS was how to position itself in Ireland. Some felt that the awkward situations that had arisen might have been minimised had there been an Irish counterpart to the English and Welsh and Scottish Co-operative Wholesale Societies. This, however, had not materialised because Irish consumer societies had not set up in sufficient numbers. Although a large consumer society was established in Belfast, and a few others would follow elsewhere, they never comprised a sufficiently critical mass capable of supporting an Irish Wholesale Society that could produce its own supplies.

The CWS did not feel that the Irish Co-operative Agency Society was a reasonable alternative. It was critical of it for 'overlapping' its own activities, highlighted by the fact that its headquarters were nearby their own in Manchester. One CWS representative considered the Irish agency 'practically a syndicate'.[61]

Such acrimonious relations necessarily impinged on the Co-operative Union's relations in Ireland. Early in its history, the Union had organised itself into geographical sections. In 1889, in response to the growth of agricultural societies in Ireland it set up an Irish Section. This superseded the earlier Irish Co-operative Aid Association; Plunkett became its chair and Anderson its secretary.

Despite this leadership, events were to show that the new Irish Section of the Co-operative Union lacked cohesion. Consumer co-operatives were scattered and not yet firmly established. Agricultural societies were reluctant to affiliate to the Co-operative Union, seeing greater relevance in their own IAOS that formed in 1894. It had therefore not become particularly obvious to Irish co-operators that they needed an Irish Section of the Co-operative Union before the contentious 1895 Huddersfield Co-operative congress. In its aftermath the board of the Irish Section resigned and the Section itself collapsed. The Co-operative Union retained the affiliation of a few consumer societies and then brought these under its Scottish Section. Irish agricultural societies cleaved to the IAOS and effectual splits had arisen between Irish consumer and agricultural co-operation and between Irish and British co-operators.

They were not irrevocable divides. Anderson could still speak of Mitchell as 'a splendid type of whole-hog co-operator',[62] and co-operative relations continued through participation in the International Co-operative Alliance formed in 1895. Moreover, Irish farmers later had occasion to be grateful to the magnanimity of the CWS when it wrote off a sizeable part of the bad debts of the Irish Agricultural Wholesale Society (IAWS). This organisation was similar to the CWS in that it was a wholesale for the purchase of goods but these were agricultural goods for Irish farmers rather than the purchase of consumer goods for British co-operative members. Its progress was less sure than that of the CWS because of recurring slumps in Irish agriculture

The Irish Wholesale gradually recovered and co-operative solidarity was vindicated.

CONCLUSIONS

Relations between British and Irish co-operatives have been covered in some detail for a number of reasons. The first is that they illustrate how co-operative development occurs in different economies at different stages of development and give rise to different types of co-operative. In

Britain, consumer co-operatives were appropriate because of the degree to which industrialisation and urbanisation had occurred; also the rise of a working class. By comparison, Irish agriculture had been shaped by Ireland's subservient position to Britain, and a semi-feudal ownership of land. Peasant farming predominated and little industry or manufacturing had developed. In these circumstances consumer co-operatives would have little relevance whereas agricultural co-operatives would. Their growth coincided with reforms in land ownership and in the creation of government machinery. Both contributed to an environment more conducive to the growth of agricultural co-operatives. This meant, however, that Irish co-operative development was more closely linked to government than that of British consumer co-operatives. Consequently, it would be more in line with that which would occur quite shortly in other parts of the British Empire.

Another reason for tracing British/Irish co-operative relations has been to note the role of the CWS, which had exhibited a pragmatic approach to co-operative trading relations in which two considerations were uppermost: securing the best supplies for British retail societies and their members; and by fair trade with Irish farmers. The CWS did not go as far as Horace Plunkett would have wanted. It did not buy from farmers' co-operatives and thus give their members an experience in self-management that would help them learn to be good farmers and businessmen. The CWS subscribed to the view that the co-operative consumer, rather than the co-operative producer, was sovereign in its operations.

At one point, in the case of Castlemahon Society, it looked as if the CWS was prepared to go down the co-partnership route when it put shares into the business. When the Society failed, however, and the only means of saving the business was to buy it outright, the CWS did that. Although the CWS was to have relationships with suppliers and producer co-operatives elsewhere in the British Empire, it did not proceed down the co-partnership route. In this sense its relations with Irish producers pre-figured those it would have elsewhere.

The beginning of Irish co-operatives provided a sharp contrast to that of British co-operatives. In Ireland there was no popular movement from which a co-operative movement could spring as there had been in Britain. There had been Irish supporters of Owen and propagators of his ideas. However, because these had not given rise to actual movements, no social capital and experience had been created of the kind that helped to establish the Rochdale Pioneers. In Ireland initiatives came from outside of the people themselves, from Plunkett and his helpers, and they had to make considerable propaganda efforts to popularise the co-operative idea. This approach was repeated time and time again throughout the British Empire.

While Rochdale gave a co-operative form, ideology and inspiration, it would have only an indirect part to play in the promotion of co-operatives within the Empire. Instead, along with European thrift and credit societies, co-operative experience in Ireland would be quoted as an example relevant to the needs of colonial and dominion co-operatives. It was therefore one to be followed.

We may conclude that Britain gave rise to two quite distinctive co-operative movements. Just as the Roman Empire provided a framework in which Christianity could spread, so will we find that the British Empire provided similar opportunities for co-operation.

FURTHER READING

James Kinloch and John Butt, *History of the Scottish Co-operative Wholesale Society Limited*, Co-operative Wholesale Society Ltd, Manchester, 1981.

Stephen Yeo, *Who was J. T. W. Mitchell?*, Co-operative Wholesale Society Ltd, Manchester, 1995.

Yuichiro Nakagawa, 'Development of French Co-operative Thought in Britain: E.V. Neale and Community-based Well-being', *The Bulletin of the Institute of Social Sciences, Meiji University*, Vol. 22, No.4, 2000.

4. The Self-governing Colonies 1900–18

INTRODUCTION

Having traced the evolution of co-operative ideas in Britain, we now begin to trace how they were taken up within the British Empire. Our exploration divides into three main periods, which encompass natural periods in the Empire's history, that largely coincide with distinct phases in co-operative development: 1900–18, the inter-war years and 1945–70.

During the first of these periods self-governing dominions had emerged, or were emerging, within the Empire. At the same time, prominent among eminent figures arguing that co-operatives could assist imperial development were Henry Wolff, Sir Horace Plunkett and the fourth Earl Grey. The period 1900 to 1918 also saw a number of different co-operative forms emerge and, compared with the two later periods, it was one of relative imperial co-operative experimentation.

The second period, comprising the inter-war years, saw the development of a cadre of professional people involved with colonial co-operative development. It was a period of considerable change within an empire that had been economically weakened by war. The Empire also faced demands for self-government from a number of colonies. At the same time, new additions to the British Empire had been made from the post-war settlements. These consisted of mandated territories in East Africa and the Middle East, each requiring government and administration. Co-operative advances would be made within these as well as within dominions and colonies. Within colonies and mandated territories these developments were invariably initiated by government legislation which established departments of co-operatives, or co-operative development. Often placed within a ministry of agriculture, these departments were administered by colonial civil servants. Several notable co-operative registrars emerged who set the tone and pace of development, laying down a pattern that was followed for many years and, indeed, beyond the end of Empire.

The third period, 1945 to 1970, saw not only the effects of the aftermath of the 1939–45 war but also the transformation of the British Empire into the Commonwealth. Much of the Empire had gained independence by 1960 leaving only a few colonial outposts such as Hong Kong and the Falkland Islands. Until independence colonial administrations remained and, within them, departments of co-operatives or co-operative development.

At this time closer links were established between the British Co-operative movement and colonial co-operatives. Important among the reasons for this was the setting up of the United Nations. Its agencies were charged with helping to create a new world order in which a major aim was freedom from want. This aim was supported by the British Labour government elected in 1945. Traditionally, the British Co-operative movement was part of the wider Labour movement in Britain and joined the Labour Party and the Trades Union Congress in the National Council of Labour. It therefore had close links with this new government and became involved with a Labour-led Colonial Office in increasing co-operative development in three main ways. Firstly, in helping to shape the Colonial Office's post-war policy on colonial co-operatives, which is discussed in a later chapter. Secondly, through an increased number of British co-operators becoming employed by the Colonial Office as experts. Thirdly, through courses for colonial co-operative officials that were now offered at the British Co-operative College owned by the Co-operative Union Ltd.

THE EMPIRE'S CHANGING FRAMEWORK – THE EMERGENCE OF DOMINIONS

It is desirable to note the changing political frameworks within British territories because their prevailing class structures, political institutions, and their underlying ethos and culture would determine how co-operatives were perceived and to what extent they would be welcomed. The political framework of British territories would also shape the legislative and taxation systems within which co-operatives had to operate. The most notable thrust in imperial constitutional development during the second half of the nineteenth century was towards the self-government of its white settler colonies; the term 'dominion' was not coined until 1907. They were Canada, Australia, New Zealand and South Africa. Their settlers were not exclusively British, but Britons eventually became the dominant race in each case.

One effect of this was to strengthen ties with the mother country, and, as a result, its imprint would be clearly seen in their constitutional settlements, patterns of land ownership and social structures.

Canada

Canada set the pace towards self-government and also provided a model for others to follow, beginning the pressure on Westminster to create forms of devolved colonial government that would also remain under the British Crown. To some extent Canada's quest was shaped by the American Revolution. After it several thousand Empire loyalists, wishing to remain under British rule, left their American homes and settled in Ontario and the Maritime Provinces. They were later joined by Britons who left the mother country because of unemployment or famine. As economically dispossessed migrants, the latter had little love for Britain. Moreover, although the Empire loyalists might have left America because they wished to remain under the Crown, they did not necessarily accept the political status quo: in the American colonies they had already gained some constitutional experience and a sense of independence. Another factor influencing both groups, and other immigrants, was ensuring that they safeguarded the economic advances they made in their new territory. Securing political rights was an important way of doing this. Quite apart from such self-interest, their growing political consciousness was also shaped by the family links with the mother country through which they learned of British constitutional and economic developments.

Figuring high in these was the campaign for, and the eventual passing of, the 1832 Reform Act. Though this was limited in its extension of the franchise, some Canadian immigrants had been Chartists, or were sympathetic to their calls for the extension of male adult suffrage. Yet another significant development in Britain was her repeal of the Corn Laws in 1846 and, three years later, the repeal of her remaining Navigation Acts. Both sets of legislation had been central to Britain's policy of trade protection. The first protected British corn prices from the competition of lower priced imports; the second ensured that Britain's foreign trade was carried in British ships.

This shift in policy had been brought about by a number of factors. One was a series of recessions that had occurred after the Napoleonic Wars which had led to widespread unemployment and civil unrest. Another was British agriculture's increasing inability to feed a growing population. The abolition of protectionism and adoption of a policy of free trade ensured that it became possible to import cheaper American and European grain, helping to reduce prices but also increasing food supplies for the growing number of Britons. Moreover, under free trade, duties were abolished on imported raw materials, lowering their cost and thus enabling British exports to be cheaper and more competitive. This change heralded the long decline of British agriculture, but strengthened agriculture in the settler colonies by encouraging increased exports to the mother country. Thus, the trading patterns of Canada, Australia, New Zealand and South Africa became a factor in their constitutional development.

Canada's constitutional development began with fears that Empire loyalists could become a destabilising element because they were not prepared to accept less than what they had had in the American colonies. Even before independence, they had already gained some degree of autonomy as well as experience of embryonic representative institutions. To head off their demands Westminster passed the Canada Constitutional Act in 1791 which divided what had previously been known as British North America into two provinces: Upper Canada comprising Ontario and the Maritime Provinces; and Lower Canada which included Quebec with a French-speaking majority.

The 1791 Act was soon superseded by events. Tens of thousands of new immigrants, the majority from Britain, arrived in Canada in the early 1800s and gravitated to the English-speaking areas with only a few going to Quebec. As a result, the population balance swung heavily in favour of ex-Britons. Many of these were economic migrants who were already predisposed to liberal political reforms. Even the French-speaking immigrants had not remained unaffected by the uprising in France in 1830 which had led to a new constitution and a citizen king, Louis Philippe.

Canadian settlers soon found the 1791 Act out of date and inadequate; Westminster found it ineffectual in deflecting the tensions arising between newer immigrants and the longer established economic and social interest groups. A series of small-scale rebellions in 1837 helped push the British authorities towards further constitutional reform. They were anxious to head off Canadian separatism, mindful of the precedent set by the seceding American colonies in the previous century. There were also fears that an expansionist America might try to absorb Canada.

Britain's response to these mounting constitutional pressures was to appoint a small committee of enquiry charged with reporting on Canadian discontent and making recommendations. Its work and subsequent conclusions not only showed the way ahead for Canada but also helped to shape constitutional developments in Australia and New

Zealand. The committee was led by Lord Durham, a member of the British cabinet who was noted for his independent views; he was also part of the group of statesmen and theorists known as the 'radical imperialists'. His two colleagues were reckoned to be 'two of the most constructive and brilliant of contemporary colonial thinkers . . .':[1] Charles Buller and Edward Gibbon Wakefield. The latter's extensive writings became seminal in colonial constitutional development.

It has been said of the committee's final report that its 'confidence and sweep . . . made it appear a Magna Carta of colonial constitutional development, commanding respect and admiration for over a hundred years'.[2] Its main recommendation was that 'responsible government' should be extended to Canada. This differed from the 'representative government' that had been operating, under which a governor and executive council worked with a partly nominated and partly elected legislature; and from Westminster, where an executive, in the form of the cabinet, was responsible and accountable to the legislature. The Durham Committee proposed a similar form of 'responsible government' in Canada where an elected legislature would form an administration and then hold it accountable. However, the Canadian legislature and its executive would deal only with domestic affairs. Westminster would retain authority on imperial matters including constitutional amendments, foreign and commercial policy and the disposal of public lands. It would also appoint a governor who would represent the British monarch in Canada.

The report also recommended the constitutional union of Upper and Lower Canada, despite French Canadians' resistance. British Canadians now constituted a considerable majority thus making them more politically important than the French who, in any event, were appearing increasingly anachronistic. They remained heavily dependent on agriculture and accentuated their *ancien régime* heritage. Legislation joining the two Canadas was enacted in 1840 and was supplemented by measures later in the decade to strengthen 'responsible government'. In the late 1850s the new Canada was joined by the western seaboard colonies of British Columbia and Vancouver Island.

However, Canada's constitutional changes were not yet finished. Ideas of federation grew and were shaped by a number of questions, including, first, how to create a Canadian nation from a country of great diversity spanning more than three and a half thousand miles; and secondly, how to accommodate growing Canadian provincialism.

Changing patterns of trade also impacted on Canada's move towards a federal constitution. On this the British showed themselves capable of taking a longer-term view, even at the expense of shorter-term benefit.

For example, in 1859, the Canadian government decided to impose a tariff on its steel imports, the greater part of which came from Britain. The British might have been expected to veto this decision but they hung back. The Canadians argued that they needed the tariff so as to encourage the development of their own industries. They also threatened Britain that if she blocked the decision, she should then be prepared to resume direct rule, which would have to be imposed against the wishes of the Canadian people.

The British response showed some subtlety. Westminster concluded that it wished to retain its imperial connections and trade with Canada and believed that both could be assisted by the creation of a Canadian federal state. That, in turn, was more likely to come about if the various parts of the country were spanned by a Canadian trans-continental railway which would also encourage greater British Canadian trade. Britain was therefore prepared to introduce legislation to create a unified Canada under a federal constitution. She even went so far as to encourage Canadian acceptance by offering financial help to construct the trans-continental railway.

The British North America Act was passed in 1867, and Canada became the first federal self-governing colony in the British Empire. This process established a number of precedents for later self-governing colonies. One was that the British, rather than an American constitutional, model had been adopted. Even though Canada had a federal constitution, it was one that embodied 'responsible government' of the Westminster kind. This meant that at federal, or central government level, she had an upper and lower legislative house sited at the country's new capital, Ottawa. She also had an independent judiciary. The central government was complemented by provincial legislatures and administrations that had clearly defined powers. In remaining areas central government had the final word. Vestiges of British rule remained; in the governor-general who represented Britain's constitutional monarchy; and in the provision that future constitutional amendments remained the prerogative of the British Parliament.

Australia

Australia's route to dominion status had almost as long a history as that of Canada's but was of quite different origins. Britain's involvement in Australia was initially prompted by the loss of her American colonies and her need to find alternative sites for penal settlements. When Britain's First Fleet sailed into Botany Bay in 1788, New South Wales offered few prospects. Because of her distance from anywhere else, and her sparse aboriginal population, she provided no alternative markets to compensate Britain for the loss of her American ones. What she did offer, though, were vast tracts of land on which penal settlements could be built. British convicts were soon being transported to New South Wales and this continued until 1840. Penal colonies were also begun in Western Australia and lasted until 1867. Although convicts were free to return to Britain when they had served their sentences, very few were able to do so because of the distance involved. The majority therefore settled in Australia.

Not all of these ex-convicts had been hardened criminals. In the eighteenth and nineteenth centuries British penal laws were harsh: those caught poaching, or stealing food, could be transported, as could political prisoners. The last included Chartists, early trades unionists such as the Tolpuddle Martyrs, and Irishmen who threatened rebellion or seditious political activities. After serving their time they became the nuclei around which many new communities began. Their harsh treatment, however, made it unlikely that they would be readily sympathetic to the British authorities. In fact, they became a leavening in early Australian political life.

By the 1840s British officials were suggesting that there should be a more ordered approach to the settlement of white immigrants in the colonies. It was proposed that large areas of Australia should become Crown lands and then sold to finance an orderly and appropriate colonisation.

The approach was clear but its implementation proved to be less straightforward. Firstly, the vast distance between Britain and Australia made it difficult for Westminster to control developments. Carrier pigeons could not be used and ships took months travelling to and from the Antipodes, although the development of the telegraph did help. Secondly, the British government's continuing adherence to a policy of laissez-faire, tended to inhibit attempts at long-distance control of Australian progress. As elsewhere, these were delegated to a trading company, in this case the South Australia Company. However, it was not all that successful in operating an orderly approach to the linked questions of colonial settlers and land utilisation. The Crown failed to pursue a consistent policy on land prices with resulting confusion. Moreover, many immigrants were simply determined to follow their own ideas rather than those of the trading company or a far removed Westminster government.

At least the Company assisted British hegemony, as did the fact that the majority of immigrants entering Australia were British. By 1842 the population of New South Wales had grown to some 160,000.

A decade later there were also well-established settlements in Victoria and Tasmania (Van Diemen's Land). Population elsewhere in Australia was sparse: developments in South and Western Australia were negligible while the Northern Territory was still largely an uncharted wilderness.

As in the case of Canada, Australia's constitutional development was inextricably linked to a rising population and its economic growth. Two main thrusts appeared in the latter. The first was the successful development of sheep farming. Australia not only had immense lands on which to rear sheep but also the staple wool of most of her flocks proved suitable for Britain's woollen industry. Its take-up of this raw material rose exponentially: in 1821 only some 175,000 lbs of Australian wool was exported to Britain; by 1850 that figure had risen to 39,000,000 pounds.[3] Then came land development, which soon became attractive, with private companies, government agencies and even the City of London becoming involved in development schemes and in emigration to Australia. In turn, such schemes encouraged large-scale investments of British capital and the setting-up of British banks in Australia.

The second important boost to the Australian economy was the discovery of gold near Bathurst in New South Wales in 1851. This not only encouraged ancillary developments but also a new rush of immigrants. From the early 1850s, when Australia began exporting gold as well as wool, her economic expansion accelerated. Between 1850 and 1890, except for occasional minor setbacks, her economy grew at the rate of 5 per cent per year. In fact, Australia's rate of economic expansion proved to be higher than that of the mother country. However, the link between the two economies remained strong: as late as 1912, Britain took 40 per cent of Australia's exports while supplying Australia with half her imports.[4]

Although impressive, this progress did not bring social and political harmony. Despite Australia's vast area, there were many disputes about the price and ownership of land. Some of these arose from sheepmen running their flocks onto Crown land. When they were challenged, disputes arose over the land price, and often the sheepmen were prepared to defy the imperial authorities by squatting there. Land squatters became a recognisable group in the Australian economy. In the final analysis they were difficult to dislodge because of their economic power.

Exports to Britain increased as the demand for wool soared. The economic muscle of the Australian sheep farmers was shown by their readiness to lobby British woollen manufacturers and their bankers to bring pressure on the British government to intervene on their behalf when they fell into dispute with the Australian authorities. Similarly, Australian gold mining did not remain free from disputes between colonists and the British authorities. Indeed, one of these led to an armed confrontation at Ballarat in 1854 in which twenty-two died.

The eventual triumph of the sheepmen, squatters or not, and the gold miners, had implications for Australian political development. In due course, the squatters became substantial and wealthy landowners. Down the generations, they also became conservative pillars of Australian society. However, they did not mirror the English landed gentry with its aristocratic, Anglican and Tory tendencies. As we have already noted, many Australians had ancestors who had been convicts, and these included 'Catholics, Dissenters, Irish and radicals'.[5] Their attitudes to government were shaped by their ancestors' struggles with the imperial authorities, and their current wealth did not necessarily mean that they would side with the authorities in maintaining the political status quo.

Another factor shaping Australian politics was that the transportation of convicts was gradually phased out and replaced by other forms of immigration. In 1835 and 1836, non-convict colonies were established in Victoria and South Australia respectively. This shift in immigration, linked to vibrant economic growth, encouraged Australian settlements to become not only self-governing but also quite democratic.

Generally speaking, even with the growth of interest groups and the occasional violent dispute, Australian constitutional institutions evolved smoothly. They were no doubt guided by Canadian precedents. During the 1820s powers were transferred from the originally appointed and autocratic governors to appointed councils. In time these councils became elected on a property franchise and were later replaced by parliaments whose lower houses were 'elected by all men who were neither mad nor bad enough to be incarcerated'.[6]

In 1850 the Australian Colonies Government Act was passed giving Australians responsible government similar to that in Canada. Thereafter, 'Governors learnt to limit themselves to advisory roles, civil servants reinforced continuity, and a core of conservative politicians organized factions to ensure passage of legislation.'[7] Australia's size predisposed her towards federal development. It was also a natural evolution from the growth of her political institutions. Pressures for a federal constitution were answered when, in 1900, Westminster passed the Australian Commonwealth Constitution Act. As in Canada, Australia had a federal constitution but one based on the Westminster model of 'responsible government'.

New Zealand

New Zealand's constitutional development was closely linked to that of Australia's. The opening-up of her territory began with Captain James Cook's arrival in 1769 although Britain did not immediately lay claim to New Zealand. The subsequent arrival of British sailors, traders, missionaries and officials, however, brought her within the British orbit which was also strengthened by her geographic closeness to Australia. Strategically and economically, New Zealand came to be seen as coming within the British sphere of influence although Britain followed a policy of minimal intervention until the 1830s. It then became less easy to maintain and, in 1840, Great Britain annexed New Zealand. Of this event it has been suggested that, 'Coming within the Empire at a moment of liberal humanitarianism, New Zealand experienced a colonialism and colonization less brutal than some.'[8]

The well-tried method of initially governing through a trading company was repeated with the establishment of the New Zealand Company. Its overall aim was to further British interests. A British consul was also appointed, initially to negotiate for British sovereignty in areas of British interest and to offer British protection to the remaining parts of the country. Subsequently, British sovereignty was extended to the rest of New Zealand and the consul then effectively became a buffer between the indigenous Maori and the increasing number of settlers. The Treaty of Waitangi (1840) confirmed Britain's annexation of New Zealand, and also provided for the country to become a bi-cultural society. Whereas the Maori took the treaty to be binding, some British politicians did not, and it came to be ignored by the majority of settlers and the New Zealand courts.

Moreover, the British authorities delayed its implementation until the white population had a clear majority over the Maori, who had been difficult to ignore during the treaty negotiations, because they numbered probably between 70,000 to 90,000, whereas the early European population in which the British had the majority was only around 2,000;[9] and the Maori also had strong and well-developed local structures.

After six years the British and white settlers outnumbered the Maori. As in Canada and Australia, British settlers accounted for much of the changed balance of population. Another factor was an absolute decline in the Maori population through decreasing fertility and a rising death rate. Eighteen years after the signing of the treaty, the Maori numbered around 56,000 while the white population had grown to near 59,000. There followed an even faster growth of white settlers and a 1896 census revealed that the European population was now 701,000 whereas the Maori had declined to a mere 42,000. New Zealand's constitutional evolution was closely linked to this changing balance between the two populations.

European immigration had taken two main forms. The first had been financially assisted and organised through the New Zealand Company which offered immigrants the prospects of low land prices, jobs and high wages. The second was unsponsored and largely prompted by the discovery of gold in the 1860s. As in Australia, this encouraged the creation of new jobs in financial services. Demand also increased for domestic servants and labourers to build the railways and roads needed to link New Zealand's growing gold and pastoral communities.

Under the Treaty of Waitangi the colony was divided into two. Each had a lieutenant governor representing the Crown, and a two-chamber assembly which appointed representatives to a general assembly whose remit was to administer common issues. Only men literate in English were entitled to vote in assembly elections. That meant that the vast majority of Maori males could not vote.

While there had been pragmatic reasons for delaying the implementation of the treaty, a number of colonists had been angered by it. One response was to boycott the assemblies. Another was to form constitutional associations through which they campaigned for self-government, including lobbying for it in London. Such pressures led to a Constitution Act in 1852 which moved away from the earlier division of New Zealand into two parts. Six provinces were based on settler towns with each administered by an elected superintendent and a council. At national level was a two-house general assembly which handled most internal matters. The legislation it passed required the Crown's assent. External relations, as well as the control of Maori policy, remained in the hands of the British government and its appointed governor. Voting rights were now linked to property rather than to literacy in English. A limited number of property-owning Maoris were therefore qualified to vote as long as their property was held under English tenurial conditions.

The 1852 constitution was intended to give the greater power to New Zealand's central government but it effectively created a quasi-federal system. Over time adjustments were made as New Zealand's political institutions evolved. Against a background of increasing immigration, early tensions between regional and central powers were gradually resolved by parliamentarians who agreed on a central policy, creating an environment in which settler societies could develop and prosper. While this brought cohesion among Europeans, it impacted adversely on the Maori and tensions between them and the settlers worsened.

The latter claimed that much New Zealand land was unproductive but that they could remedy this by clearance and cultivation. Maori displacement followed. This, and the fact that little had been done to bring them into government, led to proposals in 1853 and 1854 that the Maori should have parallel political institutions; they even considered appointing one of their leaders as their king. However, strife was not avoided and concerned competing land claims. Unrest led to the imposition of martial law in 1860.

This led to uncertainty over what should be the role of British troops. At that time, the British government was attempting to transfer the cost of their maintenance onto colonial governments. Such a policy was complicated in New Zealand where the British government, through the New Zealand governor, was still responsible for Maori policy. Eventually, the British government persuaded the New Zealand authorities that they also needed to become self-reliant and agreement on this in 1864 led to all but one regiment of imperial troops being withdrawn during the next two years.

Maori wars continued throughout the 1860s but increasingly the settlers became dominant. Fighting Maori were labelled rebels and some 3.25 million acres of their land was confiscated. Subsequently, about half of this land was returned but the initial land-grab long remained a major grievance between the Maori and white New Zealanders. Displaced from land, the Maori also became politically marginalised. In 1867 four Maori seats were created in the lower house of New Zealand's parliament. However, those elected to them, and others later appointed to the upper house, appeared to be little more than political pawns and proved incapable of adequately protecting Maori interests.

We can see from this process that to a far greater extent than in Canada or Australia, New Zealand's indigenous population actively resisted the policies of land ownership, economic activity and political representation that would eventually confirm their marginalisation as New Zealand became a white settler colony.

South Africa

The Union of South Africa's route to self-government was the most turbulent of processes. New Zealand's domination of its native populations paled by comparison with what happened to Africa's indigenous tribes. The opening-up of Africa was accelerated by the discovery and exploitation of its vast mineral resources, and the competition between European powers for its vast lands, much of which, in the late 1800s, was still unmapped. There was a particularly significant struggle in the most southerly parts of the continent between British immigrants and the Dutch Boers, sharpened by Britain's 'new imperialism'.

Cecil Rhodes (1853–1902) was the catalyst of much of Britain's expansion in Africa. One of his close associates was the fourth Earl Grey (1851–1917). Incongruously, he was a leading co-operator, a strong supporter of producer co-operation, actively involved in the British consumer co-operative movement, and the president of early congresses of the International Co-operative Alliance. Yet he was at the heart of the British Empire. In 1896 and 1897 he was administrator of Rhodesia and between 1904 and 1911 governor-general of Canada. After his Rhodesian appointment he became a director of the British South Africa Company which became the main vehicle for Rhodes's imperial and African ambitions.

He was an unusual character. Like Horace Plunkett, he had suffered from TB and was recommended to move to a dry climate. Plunkett went ranching in Wyoming and Rhodes went to Natal to help his brother grow cotton, where he flourished, becoming a multi-millionaire in his early twenties. Ironically, this resulted from the first great slump at the Kimberley diamond mines in 1875, prompted by a world-wide fall in the price of diamonds and a simultaneous strike by diggers at Kimberley working what appeared to be worthless blue clay soil as the diamond-producing yellow lode ran out. These two developments led to many diggers giving up and Rhodes and his partner bought up many of their abandoned claims. When the blue clay soil proved unexpectedly rich in diamonds, Rhodes and his partner became immensely wealthy. In 1881 they merged their interests with the De Beers Mining Company and, through the new company, De Beers Consolidated Mines Company, Rhodes eventually controlled the African mining industry. He subsequently became a major player in its gold industry when gold was discovered on the Rand in the Transvaal in 1886.

With his wealth Rhodes set up the British South Africa Company and was its managing director until 1896. The Company received its royal charter in 1889. Like the East India Company in India, it created its own police and military forces. Thus Rhodes was able to bring new areas of Africa under the British Crown.

Besides being controversial, Rhodes seems also to have been somewhat unbalanced. His rabid imperialism is well illustrated by his first will and testament which charged his executors to set up a secret society whose aim would be:

> to bring the entire continent of Africa under British rule, to populate South America, the Holy Land, the seaboards of China and

Japan, the Malay Archipelago, the islands of Cyprus and Candia and any islands in the Pacific not already possessed by Britain, with British settlers . . .

They were also instructed to recover the United States for the British Empire, work to consolidate the Empire as a whole, and to introduce a system of colonial representation in the British Parliament to bring about the establishment of so great a power as to hereafter render wars impossible and promote the best interests of humanity.[10]

British interest in South Africa dated back to the end of the eighteenth and the beginning of the nineteenth century when troops occupied the Cape Colony, capturing it from the Dutch East India Company. The British considered the Cape to be of strategic importance in helping to keep open the sea routes to India. This remained the view even after the opening of the Suez Canal. Along with Singapore, Alexandria, Gibralta and Dover, it was considered one of the 'Five strategic keys [which] lock up the world'.[11]

The Treaty of Paris in 1814 confirmed Britain's rule of the Cape Colony and British settlers began to arrive in the 1820s. Among the Europeans already there, the Boers were the dominant race. Of Dutch descent, they had first come to Cape Town in 1652. They practised a primitive form of Calvinistic theology which led them to believe that God had chosen them to be masters in their new land. This view took on increased force when the Dutch East India Company gave them a largely free hand to manage their own affairs. That included the enslavement of the indigenous population to work for them.

The Boers' relative autonomy was disrupted when the British arrived. They disliked their more intrusive liberal and humanitarian rule. The year after the British abolished slavery in 1833,the Boers began their Great Trek.

Taking place over several years, the Great Trek into the African hinterland brought the Boers into conflict with the native Ndebele and Zulu states whom they eventually defeated in a series of wars in the late 1830s. They went on to set up the Transvaal and Orange Free State republics. In all this, Britain's over-riding objective was to maintain local stability. She eventually concluded that the Boer republics assisted this but was uneasy at the Boers' redrawing of the South African map. Britain felt the need to act as a buffer between the Boers and natives. She therefore annexed Natalia, another newly created Boer republic, and renamed it Natal. Britain finally acknowledged the

Boer republics in 1854, but only after they had agreed to acknowledge British sovereignty and to remain within the Empire.

This new accord was short-lived. When diamonds were discovered in Griqualand, Britain annexed the province. The find encouraged a further wave of immigrants in the late 1860s and new economic activity. Inward investment increased with the rapid construction of the railways required to give access to the mines. Both the digging for diamonds, and the laying of railway lines created huge demands for unskilled labour and led to the rapid recruitment of black South Africans. At this point the development of South Africa diverged from those of Canada, Australia and New Zealand. Although in Canada the surviving and dispossessed original natives seldom became part of the labour market, in Australia the aboriginal labour became a significant element in the running of the sheep stations although on low wages. In New Zealand the Maori were quite quickly integrated into the labour market where they also constituted a pool of cheap labour. They were employed on farms, in construction, in the docks and on the railways.

South Africa's need for a plentiful supply of cheap labour led to far harsher conditions. The mining corporations found it more economical to separate black workers from their families. Two benefits arose for employers: because their workers had no families to support they could be paid lower wages; and they could be accorded only the status of migrant workers which meant that they had no residency rights in mining areas.[12]

Security reasons entered into the calculation. Some black workers had used their wages to buy guns which were then used in support of the Zulu uprisings. Low wages restricted such opportunities. Nevertheless, uprisings continued throughout the 1870s, and cost the British army almost £5 million before they were finally subdued.[13]

There were also political reasons why employers repressed black workers. During the 1870s Britain planned for the creation of a South African Federation comprising the Cape Colony, Natal and the two Boer republics. It was hoped that such a federation would become a self-supporting political unit that would be capable of providing a stable framework within which South Africa's mineral resources could be exploited. The Boers, however, did not like the idea, fearing that they would be disadvantaged. Ultimate British success in subduing the Zulus and her later occupation of the Transvaal only served to alarm them more. They decided to rebel before Britain could establish the federation and embarked upon what has become known as the first Boer War (1880–1). Their defeat of a small British force at Majuba Hill in northern Natal led to Britain's restoration of the Transvaal's independence. However, the situation remained volatile and discovery of gold on the Witwatersrand in 1886 had a further destablising effect.

This discovery not only transformed the Transvaal economy but also heightened Rhodes's eagerness to restore British control over the territory. This was necessary, in any event, if he were to achieve his long-term dream of linking Cape Town and Cairo by rail and expanding British influence in between. Rhodes, with the troops of his British South Africa Company, began a series of moves to create a British counter-balance to the Boer republics. First, he sought the annexation of Bechuanaland. Then, in a northward push, the British South Africa Company's troops crossed the Limpopo river and opened up the land that was to become Rhodesia, so named after its virtual founder. Rhodes's link with the territory was strengthened when his friend and collaborator, Earl Grey, was appointed its administrator.

Rhodes also took political initiatives. He recognised that if a South African federation was to be created under British sovereignty, the co-operation of Afrikaners was required. He therefore sought rapprochement and a political alliance between the English-speaking Progressive Party in Cape Colony and Afrikaner moderates. He was successful and became premier of the self-governing colony. However, he held the position for only a short time, being forced to resign after his suspected involvement in the abortive Jameson Raid in 1895. Although Rhodes was not directly involved in the raid, he was generally thought to be the moving spirit behind it. Its leader, Dr L. Storr Jameson (1853–1917) was a close ally of Rhodes and an administrator in the British South Africa Company. The aim of the raid was to topple the Transvaal government whose president was Paul Kruger (1825–1904). Steeped in the South African struggles, he had been born into a strict Puritan family and at the age of eleven had joined the Great Trek with his parents. They settled in the Transvaal where Kruger became a leading Boer politician. Two years after the success of the Boers at Majuba Hill in 1881, and the restoration of Boer independence, Kruger became president of the Transvaal. It was this regime that Rhodes sought to replace.

Towards this end Jameson led a force of 470 mounted men from Bechuanaland into the Transvaal where it was planned that they would join up with non-Boer Europeans and advance the 180 miles to Johannesburg. The non-Boer European revolt did not materialise and Jameson's force was captured four days after crossing the frontier. Jameson was sentenced to prison but served his time in a British prison. After his return to the Cape he became its premier (1904–8). Three years later he was made a baronet.[14]

The failure of the Jameson Raid had far-ranging consequences. Rhodes had to relinquish his premiership of the Cape Colony with the rupturing of his alliance with non-Boers. Throughout South Africa, Afrikaner opinion became more pro-Kruger and the more moderate and anti-Kruger factions within the Transvaal became quieter.

Within Europe the raid became notorious. In a provocative move, but one that was indicative of wider European interests in Africa, the German Kaiser, Wilhelm II, sent a telegram of congratulation to Kruger for his success in repelling the raid. In Britain there was embarrassment and Liberal opinion was horrified. A House of Commons select committee report was generally considered to be a whitewash. Liberal members of the committee were thought to have pulled their punches in attempts to disguise how far leading Liberals were implicated. Moreover, although Joseph Chamberlain, colonial secretary in Salisbury's Conservative–Unionist government, denied all knowledge of the raid, he did admit knowing of the possible non-Boer uprising in the Transvaal. Another reason for suspecting a whitewash was that Chamberlain and Rhodes were not asked to produce incriminating telegrams which had conveniently gone missing. It has been said:

> Realistically, it is easy to see why neither Rhodes nor Chamberlain was brought to book over the Jameson Raid. Each could so seriously harm the career and reputation of the other that both were as a consequence entirely safe: Rhodes could reveal evidence of Chamberlain's complicity; for his part, the Colonial Secretary could seriously undermine Rhodes' imperial mission by stripping his British South Africa Company of its Royal Charter, the effective authorisation for its continuing rule of the Rhodesias.[15]

Chamberlain, apparently 'Unbowed by the attacks on his integrity and by the embarrassment of the official enquiry . . . set about restructuring British policy in South Africa.'[16]

That policy, which included continuing subversive support for non-Boers in the Transvaal, ultimately led to the second Boer War (1899–1902). Unrealistic and harsh concessions were demanded of the Transvaal government. Moreover, the Kruger government felt it could take a firm stand because of the support it was receiving from the Orange Free State and from Cape Afrikaners; also in its belief that it had gained European sympathies, particularly those of Germany.

In October 1899, after the spring grass essential for feeding the horses of Boer commandos had grown, the Boers made a series of raids that left the British army 'outmanoeuvred, outfought and outwitted'.[17] They then besieged the British garrisons at Ladysmith, Mafeking and Kimberley. A British counter-offensive brought their eventual relief. The British then went on to occupy the Boer capital of Pretoria. After that there was a period of guerilla warfare in which the British army struggled to prevent the Boer commandos from raiding isolated British units. Its response was to erect blockhouses and to move some civilian Boers into concentration camps. The war ended with ostensible British victory in 1902. By the Treaty of Vereeniging, the Transvaal and the Orange Free State were incorporated into the British Empire. Each was promised eventual self-government which was granted in 1907. Moreover, a financial grant of £3 million was made to assist the recovery of Boer lands after their devastation in the final stages of the war.

In 1903 a customs union was formed comprising the British-dominated colonies in South Africa and Rhodesia. Six years later the British Parliament passed the South Africa Act. This approved a constitution drafted by a convention of representatives from Cape Colony, Natal, the Transvaal and the Orange River Colony. It provided for a Union of South Africa which would be a dominion within the British Empire. The Act also granted equal status for people of British and Dutch descent.

By this time, however, Cecil Rhodes, the architect of British interests in Southern Africa, had been dead seven years. Initial impressions might suggest that he had succeeded in achieving British supremacy in the region. Closer examination suggests otherwise. Although British control of South African industries and economic activities had been achieved, as well as the Simonstown naval base to enhance security, British culture did not eclipse that of the Afrikaner. Afrikaans language remained on par with English and, if anything, Afrikaner nationalism was strengthened by the Boer Wars. Every prime minister of the Union of South Africa between 1910 and 1961 was an Afrikaner. Of the four self-governing colonies, or dominions, to emerge within the British Empire in the latter half of the nineteenth century and the early years of the twentieth century, that of South Africa was the most turbulent in its creation.

We should perhaps recall the salient features of these British dominions. Although Canada, Australia and South Africa had gained federal constitutions, and that of New Zealand quasi federal, they nevertheless followed the Westminster model of government where the executive was responsible to an elected legislature. Within the new constitutions the British government retained certain prerogatives: that of appointing a Crown representative, the right of veto over future constitutional changes and ultimate control over a dominion's foreign policy. Overall, the dominions' constitutions were liberal and democratic.

We have studied at length the political evolution of the dominions because they provided the political and state framework within which dominion co-operatives would grow. Important also were the people who would create the social structures within them and we should now examine these and the ramifications of emigrants' ties with Britain. The dominions' constitutional development was inextricably linked to the type of immigrants they attracted, how these prospered economically and what attitudes they had to the mother country.

Immigrants' arrival in white colonies was either planned or unplanned. The former included those transported to Australia's penal settlements, as well as those voluntarily emigrating through official bodies set up to encourage them through offered employment or land. The latter and unplanned form occurred when emigrants sought to escape famine and unemployment at home or were attracted by discoveries of mineral wealth. Whether planned or unplanned, the nineteenth century saw the transfer of millions from Britain to her colonies. It has been estimated that between 1840 and 1872, which saw famine in Ireland and recurring depression elsewhere in the UK, some six and a half million Britons emigrated. Although the pressure slackened somewhat during the 1880s and '90s, some 200,000 still left each year. By the end of the nineteenth century probably some 10 million Britons had moved to British colonies.[18]

In some quarters, particularly among the new imperialists, this movement of people was seen as 'a redistribution of population within the nation'.[19] It undoubtedly constituted a major factor in securing the expansion of the British Empire. It also helped to transplant British culture and values throughout the world; and a British sense of class and hierarchy. In time, at least within the dominions, more home-grown cultures evolved but from 1900 to 1918, these were still pervaded by a sense of British-style gentility and hierarchy. These grew because early settlers who had grown rich in their new countries bought property. Those in country areas bought large estates and became a new landed gentry, aping the style of the gentry back home and seeking to strengthen their positions through marriage. Within towns the new gentry provided the social leadership as well as becoming noted for their conspicuous consumption. Such tendencies were perhaps to be expected. It was always likely that in their new environments settlers would recreate the familiar. This was even more likely if their territories were sparsely populated with immigrants scattered over vast areas. Social intercourse, marriages and a settled way of transferring land rights through generations then became even more important.

Another factor predisposing British immigrants to recreate the social patterns they had known back home was the fact that they had been joined by a fair measure of Britain's minor aristocracy. Its members were prompted to relocate by Britain's depressed agriculture during the last half of the nineteenth century, as well as by the fact that the economies of the white colonies were primarily agricultural. The availability of land and labour, and the ability to farm in temperate climates, were added attractions. The colonial minor aristocracy gravitated to the leading positions in society. They built country houses, and became part of the colonial legal system when appointed justices of the peace.

Such tendencies led to a divergence between Canada and her immediate neighbour, the United States. In the former, while the constitution remained democratic and liberal, society favoured the more traditional hierarchical structures associated with British life. These contrasted sharply with those in the USA which remained in line with the American constitution and were egalitarian, democratic and republican. Canadians not only looked back to British society but also to the ideas of conservative empire loyalists who had left the American colonies to settle in Canada in order to remain within the British Empire. Although they had evolved with the constitutional changes, they still tended to have an excessive regard for the British Crown, and valued their imperial ties and British traditions.

Classes emerged in dominion populations but they proved less fixed than those of the mother country. There was more social mobility within them and they were also shaped by local factors. British dominions and colonies offered scope for all kinds of workers, business and professional people and labouring. It was among these lower orders that dominion co-operatives would grow. To a far greater extent than in Britain, they would also develop among farmers. It was in the agricultural sector in particular that the role of co-operatives vis-à-vis a dominion, or colony's, development could be seen most clearly.

THE EMPIRE AS A DEVELOPMENT AGENCY AND THE ROLE OF CO-OPERATIVES WITHIN IT

A central argument of this study is that development in its many forms was an important aspect of the British Empire. Moreover, that within it, co-operatives played a significant part. To examine this assertion it would be helpful to establish what we mean by 'development'.

Obvious activities come to mind. These include mapping, irrigation, the building of roads and railways, and the provision of medicine, education and communications. The Empire was concerned to build its territories' infrastructures for a number of reasons. One was to assist a colony's good government. Another was strategic: how best to secure sea routes to important parts of the Empire, particularly India. Ceylon's importance, for example, lay in her being a staging post from India to British territories in SE Asia. Other objectives were met when engaging in medical and education provisions. One was a concern that local populations were fit and capable of playing subordinate roles in colonial administration and also of providing a qualified workforce for local economic activities.

Until the 1890s, however, colonial administration did not become engaged in economic development in any kind of systematic way. That policy shifted somewhat when Joseph Chamberlain became colonial secretary for two main reasons, firstly to try to head off social discontent where this arose from economic decline. An example of such intervention occurred in the British West Indies where the region's economic decline led to the British government setting up the Norman Commission to examine its social consequences. Its report in 1897, led to the government making loans and grants to the area totalling almost £600,000.

The second reason for a more interventionist policy stemmed from a growing acceptance of Chamberlain's view that the Empire was like a country estate. If it were to be profitable, its assets had to be developed. Thus, the Colonial Office under Chamberlain, began to encourage improvements to colonial agriculture, veterinary practices, husbandry, the control of tropical diseases and social welfare. This more systematic approach to development replaced earlier laissez faire attitudes and the belief that, almost through the process of osmosis, the mother country would assist her colonies' development by transmitting her technological and scientific knowledge to them. In any event, it was felt that this process was being hastened by the increasing number of British emigrants moving to the colonies.

This new policy undoubtedly increased productivity but it could also disturb earlier patterns of agriculture. Often these were linked to traditional indigenous support systems and these were also broken. In any event, traditional methods were proving insufficient for colonies' rising populations and were inferior to the new methods being introduced. Such disregard for what had gone before was frequently shaped by white settlers' attitudes to native populations and their methods of production. The 'natives' were often seen as 'savages', particularly in Africa, and it was felt that they should be grateful for having 'civilisation' brought to them.

CONCLUSIONS

In 1900 co-operatives were still to become a discernible strand within dominion and colonial development. The development spectrum ranged from heavy industry at one end which was involved in building canals, railway lines and roads, to the dealing with health, social and micro-economic issues at the other end. Co-operatives would emerge in activities in the latter end of the spectrum. We will give examples of such activities in a variety of locations and circumstances during each period studied.

5. Three Influential Figures in Early British Imperial Co-operative Development

INTRODUCTION

The years between 1900 and 1918 were a take-off period for co-operative development within the British Empire during which theories and structures were experimental. Nevertheless, co-operative solutions were being proposed in widely different settings and for widely different purposes, including sugar production in the West Indies, agricultural reconstruction after the Boer War in South Africa, and rural regeneration and debt reform in India.

It was also a period in which individuals could influence imperial co-operative development and this chapter notes three. They are Henry Wolff (1840–1930), Sir Horace Plunkett (1854–1932) and the fourth Earl Grey (1851–1917). Grey was an earl and Plunkett, although knighted for his own endeavours, came from a prominent aristocratic Anglo-Irish family. Wolff was of the upper middle classes but appears to have had private income. All three therefore had the means to spend considerable time and effort on their co-operative enthusiasms. Each had specific co-operative interests. For Grey it was producer co-operation; for Plunkett, agricultural co-operation; and for Wolff, thrift and credit societies. Moreover, Grey and Plunkett were occasional politicians. Grey was the Liberal MP for the Tyneside Division in 1885 and later joined the Unionists after the Liberal Party split on the issue of Irish Home Rule. In 1894 he succeeded the third Earl Grey and then sat in the House of Lords. Grey's parliamentary career was broken between 1896 and 1898 when he became administrator of Rhodesia and again between 1904 and 1911 when he was governor-general of Canada. Plunkett had also sat in the British House of Commons as the Unionist MP for South Dublin in 1892. Seven years later a Department of Agriculture and Other Industries and Technical Instruction in Ireland was established and in becoming its vice-president, Plunkett achieved ministerial status. However, this was short-lived when he lost his South Dublin seat the following year and left Parliament for good.

Wolff, Plunkett and Grey might not have been close friends but they certainly frequently communicated with each other on mutual co-operative interests, such as the early International Co-operative Alliance (ICA). Between its inception in 1895 and 1904 Wolff chaired its executive while Grey was its president, and Plunkett also took part in a number of early congresses.

The three men were from Britain's liberal tradition which had been one source of co-operative ideas. Britain's liberal elite broadly came from this tradition and exercised political power and influence. They were frequently aristocratic. A number of such people had helped establish the credibility of early British co-operatives within the upper reaches of British society and would later spearhead the development of co-operatives throughout the British Empire. Britain's liberal tradition had a wider imperial significance. It has been suggested that:

> what is very striking about the history of the [British] Empire is that whenever the British were behaving despotically, there was almost always a liberal critique of that behaviour within British society. Indeed, so powerful and consistent was this tendency to judge Britain's imperial conduct by the yardstick of liberty that it gave the British Empire something of a self-liquidating character. Once a colonized society had sufficiently adopted the other institutions the British brought with them, it became very hard for the British to prohibit that political liberty to which they attached so much significance for themselves.[1]

An interesting question for this study is to what degree colonial and dominion co-operatives aided the 'self-liquidating character' of the British Empire.

HENRY WOLFF (1840–1930)

Little is known of Henry Wolff's early life other than that he was born in Leeds and was educated at Bonn and Heidelberg Universities.[2] In Germany he became well acquainted with Prussian agricultural reforms and early thrift and credit societies. A 'polyglot', 'he had had years of farming experience in Germany'.[3] One of his close friends was Edward Owen Greening with whom he helped to set up the Agricultural and Horticultural Association. A close associate of Greening was Edward Vansittart Neale (1810–1892), who was a Christian Socialist, a staunch advocate of producer co-operation and general secretary of the British Co-operative Union. Together with Greening, Neale was a prime mover in establishing the ICA, but died in 1892 before its inaugural congress in 1895. His death was a blow for the fledgling alliance because he had considerable linguistic skills and extensive links with European co-operative leaders. Wolff was similarly qualified but initially rejected proposals that he take Neale's place because he thought the proposed alliance too narrowly based if limited to one of 'co-operative production'. Wolff believed that it should be widened to include all kinds of co-operative, a view supported by Horace Plunkett. Wolff finally accepted and became the chairman of the committee appointed to organise the Alliance's inaugural congress and later chairman of its executive committee after the Alliance was established in 1895. Earl Grey presided at the inaugural congress and remained the ICA's president until 1907.[4] This brought him into contact with Wolff on ICA matters and both frequently spoke on behalf of the organisation with state officials in Britain and abroad. Wolff, in particular, became a reference point for people and government departments seeking information on the growing number and types of co-operative movements.

Wolff's contribution to the young ICA suggests that he was a good organiser. He also appears to have been effective in dealing with politicians and other people of influence, as we shall see later in this study. He became a central figure in a large but amorphous network of co-operative enthusiasts, politicians and civil servants. Perhaps Wolff's main contribution was his propagation of theories about thrift and credit co-operatives. His farming experiences in Germany had brought him into contact with their pioneers, Franz-Hermann Schulze-Delitzsch (1808–1883) and Friedrich Wilhelm Raiffeisen (1818–1888). Wolff later corresponded with Alphonse Desjardins (1854–1920) and his wife Dorimene (1858–1932), the pioneers of co-operative credit in the Quebec region.

Besides maintaining an extensive correspondence with leading co-operators, Wolff wrote many books on co-operative subjects.[5] These confirmed his status as an authority on co-operatives, particularly thrift and credit societies. One effect of his books was to codify existing co-operative practices. Another was to popularise the co-operative form of organisation.

Wolff was also receptive to ideas of co-operatives assisting colonial development. Through him and Greening we glimpse an early attempt at imperial co-operative development. At the Co-operative Union's congress of 1890, Wolff as a delegate from the Epsom Co-operative Society and Greening as one from the Agricultural and Horticultural

Association, moved and seconded a resolution on co-operation in the West Indies. Although pious, it anticipated some of the problems that would arise with imperial co-operative development, particularly the form that co-operative legislation should take. The resolution read:

> That this Congress urges upon the Legislative and Executive Councils of British Colonies in the West Indies the great desirableness of bringing local legislation, with respect to Industrial and Provident Societies, and the gratuitous registration of said societies, as soon as possible into complete unison with the legislation and practice as to registration now prevailing in the United Kingdom, in order to give the labouring population of those colonies the same opportunities for improving their social and economic position which are now enjoyed, with such excellent results by the working classes of the home country.

In moving the resolution, Wolff referred to a government Blue Book which revealed the extent of distress and poverty in the West Indies. He suggested that co-operatives could help relieve this but were hindered from doing so by the lack of appropriate legislation:

> In the first place the people had no corporate laws like they do in the United Kingdom, nor was the Industrial and Provident Societies Act known in the West Indies. In British Guiana and in Grenada, however, the Friendly Societies Act and the Industrial and Provident Societies Act were rolled into one. For the principal colonies there was only a Friendly Societies Act, and the people could not form co-operative societies. The second hindrance was that the fees of registration were exorbitantly high . . . In addition, they were severely oppressed with taxation

Friendly Society Acts had proved inadequate for early British co-operatives because they did not allow friendly societies' members to trade with each other. With the help of the Christian Socialists, early co-operatives had successfully lobbied for new legislation which arrived in a series of Industrial and Provident Societies Acts. It seemed that a similar development was required in the West Indies, as well as a modification of tax structures and a reduction in the cost of co-operative registration.

In seconding the motion, Greening urged:

> Congress to take its stand on the principle that the right of free association, like the right of free speech, free printing, and free

> assembly, should not be the subject of taxation . . . it was for the nation to pay the expense when it attempted to put taxes on people seeking to redeem themselves by this principle of free association.[6]

We can see from this that Wolff and Greening expected imperial co-operative legislation to follow the British pattern but this later proved not to be feasible and different forms of legislation emerged. The first piece of British imperial co-operative legislation was passed as early as 1890 in Barbados. The Co-operative Sugar Factories Act was intended to encourage the setting up of factories and permitted contracts, not exceeding forty years, under which raw sugar could be delivered to co-operative factories for manufacture. The Act also exempted the first of these factories from duty on imported machinery and tramways. Other Acts relating to the sugar industry followed.[7] However, they lacked the significance of later co-operative legislation, particularly that in India, because they provided no model for use in other parts of the Empire. The resolution that Wolff and Greening proposed to the 1890 Co-operative Union congress was passed. It is significant inasmuch as it provides an indication that co-operatives were being envisioned within the Empire.

For all that, Wolff was alert to co-operative possibilities nearer home. He provided an interesting example at the 1901 Co-operative Union congress where he moved a resolution suggesting that the experience of Co-operative and Savings Banks in 'France, Germany and Belgium' showed that they could finance 'Comfortable, cheap, sanitary dwellings' for the working classes.[8] Wolff regretted the fact that there were not similar possibilities in Britain because legislation required that 'every penny of . . . deposits must go into Consols, to lie dead and unproductive'. They therefore represented 'money withdrawn from productive employment'. Wolff argued when moving his resolution that:

> The experience of France, Belgium, and on the largest scale, Germany, has shown that out and out the best bodies to be entrusted with public money for the purpose of setting up working men's dwellings are co-operative societies. They produce a better and also a cheaper article. The experience of Germany shows that an advance of two-thirds of the value of a house corresponds, in fact, in the case of co-operative societies, to three-fourths of the actual cost. And dwellings set up by co-operative societies are always occupied. And Co-operative societies also are found to provide so much better security that actually 97 per cent of the

value of buildings have been advanced to them and never a loss has been made.

The resolution was passed unanimously although it represented a potential departure from the practice of British retail societies. They were quickly becoming universal providers of goods and services, including savings facilities and building of housing estates. To some extent the latter was a nostalgic obeisance to the earlier ideas of co-operative communities. At a practical level it became a means of profitably employing surpluses generated by co-operative trade. Such activities were internal to the movement. Wolff, however, was proposing the co-operative use of non-co-operative savings and suggested three grounds for doing so. One was that such savings were likely to include workers' deposits. Another was that in their present form under British legislation, these reserves were unproductive. Thirdly, the experience of European co-operatives had shown that societies could use savings banks' deposits efficiently and productively to build good quality homes for workers. Nevertheless, Wolff's proposals represented a departure from tradition. British consumer co-operatives remained self-contained and independent and held themselves aloof from receiving grants, subsidies and any form of public monies. By necessity, Irish co-operators were more open to various forms of public support as we now see as we follow Henry Wolff to Ireland.

In 1894 the Irish Agricultural Organisation Society (IAOS) sought his advice. It had found that although creameries and secondary co-operative organisations had been successfully established, they had only partially lessened rural poverty. Rural indebtedness remained high and thus undermined the effectiveness of the creameries.

Wolff concluded that the problems of Ireland's rural poverty and indebtedness were similar to those found elsewhere in the British Empire. Farmers needed capital to grow crops or rear animals but then had to wait until these matured and could be sold before any income could be received. At best this was deferred income. At worst it was deferred and uncertain income: adverse weather conditions, animal illnesses and fluctuating prices could reduce it. Farmers therefore had little encouragement to borrow and invest but without this they were unlikely to improve their farms or farm more intensively.

Wolff believed another factor weakening Irish agriculture was that most farmers were tenant farmers which meant that they had little or no security to offer even if they did wish to borrow. Moreover, their access to rural credit was limited because branches of joint stock banks were few. These inhibiting factors indirectly threatened the co-operative creameries. Not only were their members hindered from borrowing but even where they did, they had to pay high rates of interest for the traditional forms of rural credit. If they then fell into debt, it was more likely that they would sell their produce to private merchants at reduced prices so as to gain at least some income. Such sales were at the expense of the co-operative creameries. They also perpetuated the cycle of indebtedness among Irish farmers.

Another feature of Ireland's rural economy shared with other parts of the British Empire was its dependence on money lenders. Their loans were taken not only for farm production but also for funerals, marriages and family settlements which were important features of Ireland's social and cultural life. Irish moneylenders charged excessive rates of interest and were of two main types. One only lent money. The other, known as 'gombeen' men, made loans but also required those who borrowed from them to buy goods from their shops. There were other indigenous alternative systems but none radical enough to improve the financial position of Irish farmers.

Wolff urged Irish co-operators to consider the two distinct forms of thrift and credit co-operatives that had emerged in Germany. One pioneered by Franz-Hermann Schulze-Delitzsch had much in common with Rochdale co-operation in that its societies were based on one member one vote, provided limited liability, gave limited interest on capital and divided surpluses in proportion to members' transactions. These co-operatives attracted some farmers but the majority of their members were small businessmen and wage earners.

The other type of German credit co-operative had been introduced by Friedrich Wilhem Raiffeisen and differed from the Schulze-Delitzsch and Rochdale-type co-operatives in an important way by not granting their members limited liability, that is their members' liability was unlimited.

Consequently, members were jointly and severally liable for all the debts of their society. Moreover, these societies had no share capital and their membership and activities were limited to a local area in order that lending decisions might rest on members' knowledge of each other. These co-operatives paid no dividends to their members, and any surplus made was put to reserves. It was this latter type of co-operative that Wolff thought most appropriate to Ireland's conditions. IAOS agreed and began promoting what came to be called 'village banks', which kept closely to the Raiffeisen model. They operated in distinct and limited geographical areas because this enabled members to have a good knowledge of each other which became important when loans were being made. Their members were jointly and severally liable for the debts of their society whose rules laid down that loans could be made only for productive purposes. Loans for social purposes such as weddings and funerals were excluded. Applicants for membership had to be 'sober, honest and industrious' and when they wished to borrow, they required two sureties.[9]

The Irish 'village banks' made an important departure from their German counterparts. Whereas German thrift and credit societies were funded solely from their members' deposits, levels of Irish rural poverty made this difficult. Sir Horace Plunkett had long recognised this reality and saw in it a possible role for government. He successfully sought this and in 1898 the Congested Districts Board started to provide limited loans at favourable rates to societies within its areas. When the Department of Agriculture was later established it followed suit. It meant a departure from the practice of German societies and from British consumer co-operatives which remained independent of any government support and its accompanying oversight.

The first Irish Agricultural Credit Society, or village bank, was opened at Doneraile in County Cork in November 1894.[10] By 1900 seventy-six such societies existed with a combined membership of 3,138[11] and in 1913 there were 235 societies with a total membership of 20,211.[12] The First World War brought a decline and by 1930 there were only fifty-two village banks with a combined membership of 3,672.[13] A small number of credit societies continued until the early 1950s but by now they were insignificant and no longer an example to be held up to others.

This, however, had not been the case during the take-off period of imperial co-operative development. Then, along with other European thrift and credit co-operative movements, the apparent success of the Irish Agricultural Credit Societies was quoted when efforts were made to encourage imperial policy makers and administrators to consider co-operatives as a means of economic development. Through his involvement with the Irish village banks, Henry Wolff had an indirect role in this.

SIR HORACE PLUNKETT

Considerable reference has already been made to Plunkett in Chapter 3 and more will be made in Chapter 9. His contribution to British imperial co-operative development extended over a longer period than either those of Wolff or Grey and continued indirectly after his death through the work of the Plunkett Foundation established in 1919. At this point we merely note his pivotal influence.

THE FOURTH EARL GREY (1851–1917)

Albert, fourth Earl Grey is an ambiguous figure who is mentioned in co-operative and imperial literature but only on the fringes of each. In this study, however, he personifies the imperial–co-operative divide.

He was a genuine co-operative supporter, who also served on the board of the British South Africa Company, the agency through which Cecil Rhodes spearheaded his advances into southern Africa. He shared Rhodes's dream of the British Empire becoming a federation of white self-governing dominions.

Grey was a devout and practising Christian. Yet all these moral instincts seemed limited to the poor at home and white settlers in the British Empire. They did not extend to Africans whom he viewed as 'savages' who should be prepared to pay the annual hut tax of £1 for having the privilege of civilisation being taken to them.

It is difficult for the modern mind to comprehend Grey's mentality, but he was a product of his times. Not only was the late nineteenth century the high point of British imperialism, it was also a period in which the wealthy and the privileged engaged in charity and good deeds. Besides his support for co-operation, particularly co-operative production, Grey was active in movements espousing temperance, electoral and Church reform, university extension and garden cities.

We do not know how and when he became a co-operative enthusiast but he was one of a number of British aristocrats who encouraged the setting-up of retail societies on their family estates. Plunkett's initiative at Dunsany has previously been mentioned. Other examples include Lord Wenlock at Escrick in Yorkshire[14] and Earl Manvers at Edwinstowe in Nottinghamshire[15] Grey was the prime mover in the starting of a retail society at his estate at Howick, Northumberland. Such actions were undoubtedly paternalistic and some were later discredited.

Grey was a prominent and active member of the Labour Association, and was elected its president for 1900.[16] Other aristocratic members included the Duke of Westminster, the Earl of Stamford and Lord Wantage. The clergy were present in the persons of the Bishop of Durham and the Bishop of Ripon and several MPs were also members. Their support for co-operation can be attributed to a desire to avoid economic and social conflict, support for the in-vogue ideas of thrift and self-help among the working classes, and a strong impulse to do good works. However, Earl Grey's motivation seems well summed up in the address he gave to the Church congress in Bradford in 1898. His subject was 'The Relation of the Church to Co-operation' and in it he extolled the virtues of consumer co-operation. He told his audience that before a retail society could affiliate to the Co-operative Union, it needed to show that:

> It is guided by the desire:-
>
> 1. To promote the practice of truthfulness and economy in production and exchange
> 2. To abolish all false dealings
> 3. To conciliate the conflicting interests of the capitalist, the worker, and the purchasers, by an equitable division among them of the fund commonly called profit.[17]

The greater part of Grey's address, however, stressed the virtues of co-operative production and ended with thoughts on how the Church might assist its development.[18]

Earl Grey, in both the British Co-operative movement and the ICA, was well informed of the strides that late-nineteeth-century co-operation was making in Western Europe among the poorer sections of society. More to the point, he was in a position to act on that knowledge in the wider reaches of the British Empire through the positions he would hold. Between 1896 and 1898 he was administrator of Rhodesia. We catch an interesting vignette of him in this position.

> The social centre of the colony was Government House, a pleasant rambling bungalow in the Indian manner, with an iron roof and a wide veranda, and servants' huts around a yard. There lived Lord Grey, described by his predecessor Jameson as 'a nice old lady', with his wife and daughter Lady Victoria. The grandson of a British Prime Minister, Grey was a director of the [British South Africa] Company, a fervent disciple of Rhodes and an ardent imperialist. 'The Empire is my Country,' he used to write in autograph books, 'England is my Home.'[19]

We catch other glimpses of Earl Grey in Rhodesia. Apparently he rode an all-red bicycle which 'had a coronet on its back mudguard, and a municipal coat of arms'.[20] It seems that 'Grey, the gentle and high-minded Administrator', disapproved of English settlers refusing to do the physical work that they could leave to native servants. He tried to set an example by planting a tree in commemoration of a Festival of Empire. His example was not followed and 'When Jubilee Day came round, the only tree planted in homage to Queen Victoria was the Administrator's gum-tree.'[21]

Grey's association with Cecil Rhodes came through his position as an MP. He had been returned as a Liberal MP for the Tyneside Division in 1885 but when the Liberal Party split over the question of Irish Home Rule, Grey became an Unionist. While in the House of Commons before succeeding to his earldom in 1894, he became a member of the South Africa Committee of the House and it was in that capacity when Rhodes's British South Africa Company was awarded its royal charter in 1889 that Grey was invited to join its board. In the aftermath of the abortive Jameson Raid Jameson had resigned as administrator of the British South Africa Company and Grey succeeded him.[22] This was presumably his springboard to becoming administrator of Rhodesia.

Grey's links with Rhodes and Africa are obviously controversial. Yet he seems to have retained great affection for all things African. On his appointment as governor-general of Canada, he wrote to a friend:

> It will probably be announced before you receive this that I am going to Canada as Governor General. I have not sought the position in any way, but on the contrary have expressed my wish to the Authorities to remain at home as my heart is in Rhodesia and I have many interests in England, which make me desire to divide my life between Africa and England. The request, however, has come to me in a way which it is impossible for me to refuse and I shall start in November for a five years term in Canada. If I am alive at the end of this term I hope the experience which I shall obtain in Canada will be of use in Rhodesia.[23]

Grey maintained his African associations while in Canada. In May 1905 he received a letter which referred to 'Jameson's wonderful influence' and to a gift of apples Jameson received from a Natal 'Boer politician'. Replying from Government House, Ottawa on 30 May 1905, Grey spoke of his delight at hearing of 'Jameson's wonderful influence ironing out the wrinkles of racial antagonism'. He added that Jameson had sent him thirty-two cases of Cape wine 'in the hope that it may agree with Canadian stomachs'.[24]

While in Canada Grey encouraged trade between Canada and Africa, including the importation of African fruit, wines and tobaccos often offered at official functions.[25] In return he urged South African railways to buy Canadian sleepers for their building and maintenance programmes.

Grey delivered a speech while Canadian governor-general, for which only his draft notes remain, revealing his imperial credo. In it he spoke of his hope for the 'self-governing Dominions being incorporated . . . in some sort of organic union with the Motherland'. Within such an 'organic federation', Grey was keen to encourage British emigration to Canada.[26]

If we were considering Grey solely as an imperial figure, we might not wish to study him much further. However, because he championed co-operative advances in Africa and Canada, and because he was eminent in British and international co-operative circles, he becomes an important figure in this study. He had direct and indirect influence. It is possible that he used some of the latter with other aristocratic imperial leaders. These included his brother-in-law, Earl Minto (1847–1914) who preceded him as governor-general of Canada and who, between 1905 and 1910, was the governor-general of India. In terms of imperial co-operative development this was an important period. During it India's first co-operative legislation, the Co-operative Credit Societies Act of 1904, was implemented and consideration was being given to widening its provisions in a second Act which was passed in 1912.

Grey was proud of the way that the British South Africa Company had opened up Africa without a charge on the British taxpayer. As far as Rhodesia was concerned, Grey wrote to a friend:

> I do not think it possible for any honourable man to deny that the country which has been conquered, settled, opened out, and railwayed by the shareholders of the Chartered Company is under a moral obligation to repay its shareholders a large part of the money which they have found for this purpose.
>
> It is true that the Chartered shareholder has taken the place of the British taxpayer, and that the settler in Rhodesia may say that the services which have been rendered by the shareholders of the Chartered Company ought to have been rendered by the taxpayers of the United Kingdom. That is an argument which does not justify them in repudiating their debt to the shareholders of the Chartered Company, but which may be made use of by the settlers in dealing with the Imperial Govt.

Grey recalled how he had raised questions in the House of Lords:

> With the object of showing that Rhodesia is the one part of the British Empire which has cost the British taxpayer nothing, I moved for a Return in the House of Lords to show what has been the cost to the British taxpayer of the various portions of Greater Britain [Grey is referring to his proposed British white imperial

> federation]. You will see my remarks in 'South Africa' of August 13th. When you compare the white population and the trade of Rhodesia with the white population and trade of Uganda, British Central Africa, British East Africa, Nigeria &c., all of which provinces are costing the British taxpayer large sums of money annually, the case which you, the People of Rhodesia, will have for demanding . . . assistance from the British Govt. appears to me to be very strong.[27]

In the same letter he objects to a man who 'was strongly opposed to any increase in the Native Hut tax'.[28] His support for this tax was controversial and aroused the criticism of some British co-operators. Grey's reported response in the *Co-operative News* was harsh:

> In replying, the Earl referred to his position with the imposition of taxes on the natives in South Africa to compel these savages to go into the open market. He did not think there was any hardship in it, and sure if his critics were in that country they would go further than he did. These natives were now living in security, and he did not think it was too much to ask a small tax for this privilege.[29]

The *Co-operative News*'s coverage of this issue and its later publication of two articles on 'The Growth of the British Empire in the Nineteenth Century'[30] reflect British co-operators' interest in the Empire and perhaps counter the view of Bernard Porter that while the British had created the greatest empire the world had ever seen they took little interest in it.[31]

CONCLUSIONS

Wolff, Plunkett and Grey were co-operative enthusiasts and dedicated to promoting co-operative development from their different positions in society. As a senior aristocrat, Grey had access to prominent policy-makers in the British Parliament and Empire. He appears to have believed that they could help reconcile the tensions between labour and capital. However, his idealism did not extend beyond the white co-operator in Britain or the dominions.

Plunkett was a minor member of an Anglo-Irish aristocratic family. Nevertheless, he had entrée to its senior members and through them to the upper reaches of British and imperial society. He used such contacts assiduously over many years in the co-operative cause. Plunkett was not called upon to hold imperial positions in the way that Grey had been.

However, just as Grey was drawn to Africa, Plunkett developed strong links with America. For over a decade he farmed in Wyoming, returning home for several months each year. This period undoubtedly shaped his agricultural ideas and brought him long-lasting friendships including that with Theodore Roosevelt. Plunkett's American experiences seem to have strengthened his pragmatism which is reflected in the slogans he coined. Perhaps his most famous was 'Better farming, better business, better living', which he proposed to Roosevelt when he was promoting his rural life policy.[32] This slogan also became the clarion cry of Irish co-operatives.[33]

Wolff was influenced by the years he had spent farming in Prussia. These had introduced him to agricultural innovations and to the pioneering of thrift and credit co-operation. It seems significant that all three were shaped by experiences beyond Britain. Such experiences are likely to have given them international perspectives which built on those that they gained through their work in the early ICA.

Wolff was not aristocratic but seems to have been a man of private means. In any event, he was able to support himself while writing his many books, chairing the ICA executive and lobbying for co-operatives in Britain or the Empire. Of the three men he seems to have been the only one who envisaged the development of co-operatives among non-whites in the British Empire. He was actively engaged in encouraging India's first co-operative legislation, the Co-operative Credit Societies Act of 1904 which was primarily for Indians. Grey no doubt welcomed this Act and was undoubtedly interested in it as documents relating to it exist in his archive. Grey was interested in co-operatives in Africa but primarily as a means of helping white settlers establish themselves economically. There are no clear indications as to whether Plunkett racially discriminated.

6. Early Examples of British Imperial Co-operative Development: India

INTRODUCTION

This and the two following chapters complete Part One of this study. They are concerned with the practical implementation in the British Empire of co-operative ideas developed in Britain and Europe in the second half of the nineteenth century. Each is likely to prompt comparisons with early co-operatives in the mother country.

BRITISH RULE IN INDIA

British rule in India had evolved over three centuries, beginning with the arrival of the East India Company which had received its royal charter from Elizabeth I in 1600. India differed from other British imperial territories in that it was an empire in itself comprising a collection of princely states. The East India Company secured trading treaties with some of these. To safeguard these and to expand its interests, it developed its own army and police force. Its political and economic influence in London and India grew to such an extent that it has been suggested that by the eighteenth century it constituted 'the semi-privatised and imperial wing of the Hanoverian state'.[1] Let us remember, however, the view of Adam Smith (1723–1790), that 'The government of an exclusive company of merchants is perhaps, the worst of all government for any country whatever.'[2] Smith was the Scottish economist and philosopher whose book, *Wealth of Nations*, is held by many to be the first masterpiece in political economy. Such stature adds weight to his view but it was an eighteenth-century view. However, British rule in India was to last a further two centuries and changed over time.

Initial British development was piecemeal with the British competing with the French and Portuguese. By the middle of the 1700s, however, they had gained ascendancy for a number of reasons such as political fragmentation in northern India, the rise of regional war-lords and

Robert Clive's victory at Plassey in 1757.[3] Late in the century, the East India Company gained virtual control of the whole sub-continent and some degree of mutual co-existence between the British and Indian hierarchies emerged. How one such relationship worked out is beautifully described by William Dalrymple in his book *White Mughals*[4] while *The Journals of Fanny Parkes* first published in 1850 but recently re-published[5] lend credence to the belief that there was closeness and relative ease between leading Indians and Britons.

This harmony fractured as new factors came into play. They included the arrival of evangelical Christian missionaries, the emergence of divisive theories of racial hierarchy, and improved shipping services which allowed a greater number of British wives to join their husbands serving in India. Such influences were compounded by a more pervasive factor:

> After 1815 the old Company live-and-let-live approach to the governing of India was replaced by one which set great store by remoulding the country along Western lines. India became a sort of laboratory for current British liberal, evangelical, and utilitarian theorists who sought, in various ways, to regenerate all mankind.[6]

Prominent among the utilitarian theorists were James Mill (1773–1836) and his son John Stuart Mill (1806–1873). Mill the younger supported the growing co-operative movement in Britain and thus helped to enhance its credibility.[7] Both were also employees of the East India Company in London, a fact that throws into sharper relief the views of the father on native Indian religions. He believed that they hindered the spread of Western enlightenment and that to overcome such hindrance it was necessary for 'humane British officials' to sweep away 'these supernatural encumbrances'.

The views of Thomas Macaulay (1800–1859) also impinged on the growing British/Indian divide. He was another prominent liberal who had close Indian connections. Poet, historian and Liberal MP, in 1833 he chaired a committee set up to consider educational policy in India. Macaulay urged that all teaching in India should be in English and based on English texts. He had the foresight to recognise, however, that such practices could help to create an élite which might eventually press for Indian self-government.[8]

The spread of European values in India was hindered by Indian resistance and also by the fact that there was no uniform system of government. The East India Company had established presidencies in Bengal, Madras and Bombay, through which it delegated authority. Elsewhere, native princes ruled under the guidance of British representatives.

Throughout, the taxation system remained unfair. Land revenues were heavily dependent on the small surpluses made by peasant farmers and, as we shall find in other of its territories, the British Empire used local taxation to fund its development agency functions. Thus, local taxation in India contributed heavily to the provision of schools and hospitals, the building of roads and later railways and other means of communication. Indians were not always convinced of the benefits accruing from these and, in any event, resented how the pace of change affected them.

Who benefits most from an imperial situation is a large question and there are many who are critical of British rule in India. They include Dr Ake Eden, the Swedish historian who has studied the East India Company in depth. He suggests that early English industrialisation was financed not so much by the earlier agricultural revolution but by the 'de-industrialisation' of India.[9] Eden quotes experiences in the Bengal textile industry which he believes was deliberately weakened by heavy British taxes and the importation of cheaper British textiles. Bengali textiles were further weakened by 'drastic and macabre actions'. Eden records that, 'It is said that high British Officers chopped off thumbs of many artisans to protect the British textile product and create a colonial manufacture industry in the Bengal following the English pattern.'[10]

Eden asserts that the income of Indian taxpayers was barely sufficient to feed their families yet their tax burden was probably greater than that of taxpayers in Britain and Ireland. He quotes Frederick John Shore of the Bengal Civil Service who wrote in 1837 that 'The British Government has created an impoverishment unparalleled in the history of the world.'

We shall see later that India suffered from recurring famines and persistent rural indebtedness and that the idea of introducing co-operatives was part of a strategy to improve both situations. Eden, however, believes that late-nineteenth-century Indian famines were 'manmade famines' resulting from Britain's mismanagement of India's rivers and canals and suggests that 'there is no evidence for famine catastrophes during the Mogul time . . .' He opines that British rule damaged traditional forms of Indian rural finance and quotes Sir William Wedderburn (1838–1918) a judge of the Bombay High Court:

> . . . the ryot's [peasant's] original relationship with the money-lender was highly beneficial to both parties and . . . these relationships had become disorganised, mainly through the introduction of unsuitable English laws . . . the British government established the the civil courts in the rural districts and thus placed a new and powerful weapon in the hands of the creditor. The power and

> activity of these courts was gradually increased and the Civil Procedure Code of 1859 made everything the ryot possessed liable to seizure and sale of execution. He was further liable to be arrested in default of payment and imprisoned in a debtors jail. It is easy to understand how this change completely reversed the old order of things.[11]

Running counter to Eden's criticisms of the British management of Indian rivers and canals are the claims of Jan Morris in *Pax Britannica*. In this she speaks approvingly of a massive irrigation scheme in the Indus Basin which transformed the Punjab from a 'dun gloomy waste-land, with a rainfall so sparse that when it showered, so they said, one horn of a buffalo got wet, but not the other', into a potential 'granary for the whole of the Empire'.[12]

Writing about the 'colossal' scale of imperial works in India she states:

> the whole British-built irrigation system included some 40,000 miles of canals, irrigating nearly 20 million acres – much the greatest system of waterworks in history. The dam at Tansa, near Bombay, was claimed to be the largest piece of masonry erected in modern times: two miles long, 118 feet high, with a road along the top. In the west of India an astonishing tunnel under the rocky mountains called the Ghats conveyed water from the Periyar River, on the coastal plain, to the Flatlands on the eastern side of the mountains. In the central plain almost the whole flow of the Ganges was, in winter and spring, diverted into a canal, cutting across the grain of the Himalayan drainage so boldly that for miles it leapt over or burrowed under a series of torrents and river beds in one of the most spectacular displays of Victorian technique.[13]

Whichever interpretation is made of events it is undoubtedly true that British rule changed many indigenous systems in India. Dissatisfactions with these played a large part in the Indian Mutiny of 1857 which almost overthrew British rule in northern India.

THE INDIAN MUTINY AND ITS AFTERMATH

The Mutiny's flash point came in the army where a number of fears had grown, including those of forced religious conversion; and of the dubious animal fat with which cartridges of the new Enfield rifles were greased. Moreover, new military regulations that had been introduced supposedly to increase efficiency in fact increased the sense that Indian social structures based on caste, status and function were being eroded. Reforms elsewhere, such as those introduced by Lord Dalhousie, the governor-general, and the Indian government, also caused unease. The pace of change, disturbance of Indian susceptibilities, and the sometimes coercive nature of reforms caused feelings of revolt, coalescing in the army where the Mutiny began in 1857.

It lasted only six weeks or so but was particularly bloody, causing long-lasting bitterness on both sides. The Mutiny did not fail because of superior British might. Indeed, the British were almost toppled from power in northern India. Rather, it lost direction probably because the numerous and diverse dissatisfactions it encompassed resulted in an overall lack of purpose and leadership.

Besides rupturing Indo/British relations, the Mutiny had two important consequences. It heralded Indian nationalism and the numerous campaigns in India and Britain that would culminate in Indian independence in 1947.[14] It became an example to nationalists elsewhere in the British Empire, particularly in Ireland. A second effect of the Mutiny was the way it changed how India was governed.

It needed to be a form of government which secured India firmly within the British Empire. The two main reasons for this were trade and India's strategic importance. In trading terms she was the gateway to south-east Asia. As far as security was concerned she was a buffer zone preventing Russian expansion into Asia. Consequently, the Mutiny prompted changes in British foreign policy. Britain strengthened her presence in Cape Town in South Africa so as to protect her Indian Ocean routes. She also took greater control in Egypt in order to safeguard her interests in the Suez Canal.

In London the debate about how India should be governed fell broadly into three. There were those who felt that Britain was superior because of her 'purer religion . . . sterner energies . . . subtler intellect . . . more creative faculties . . . and indomitable will' and these qualities gave her the right to rule firmly. Others believed that Indians were 'fellow citizens' of the Empire and should be tutored in the arts of government and prepared for eventual self-rule. These proponents probably had in mind developments at home where, after the 1832 Reform Act, it was increasingly recognised that it was more politic to educate the working classes rather than to alienate them. Yet others took an even more cautious approach. They noted that Indians had 'governed a continent for three thousand years . . . filled it with beautiful cities . . . erected buildings which Europeans regarded with longing admiration . . . covered provinces with works of irrigation . . . organised armies, carried out policies, invented arts' and consequently they were unlikely to be contented with 'permanent degradation'.[15]

In 1858 Westminster passed the India Act which reflected that the option for firm rule had been taken. Under the Act, Westminster assumed the prerogatives previously enjoyed by the East India Company and instituted direct rule. The Act pledged to 'safeguard property, uphold established traditions, protect native faiths and honour treaties'. It also created two sources of executive power. One was the newly created secretary of state for India, a British MP, who became answerable to Parliament on all Indian matters. The other source was vested in the viceroy or governor-general whose powers were increased. Based in Calcutta, he oversaw everyday administration and legislation. Ceremonially, he was the sovereign's personal representative and this position was enhanced when the title of empress of India was added to the other titles of Queen Victoria in 1877.

India's direct rule from Westminster contrasted markedly with the forms of government that had developed in Britain and would develop shortly in the white settler colonies of Canada, Australia, New Zealand and South Africa. In these governments a clear separation of powers existed between the legislature, executive and judiciary but in India they remained merged and vested in a narrow-based government. This comprised the governor-general and his council. Made up of heads of the main government departments and some state princes, the council existed to assist the governor-general. Provincial governments existed in Bombay and Madras, each headed by a governor supported by a council that was similarly constituted.

The governor-general and the provincial governors and their councils combined legislative, executive and judicial functions and constituted Indian government. The decisions of this narrowly-based government were recorded as having been taken by the governor-general (or governors) in council and announced as such. All decisions had to be reported to the British Parliament through the secretary of state for India and ratified. We shall see shortly that the right of veto was exercised on occasion. In London there was a similar structure in that the secretary of state was supported by his own council which comprised fifteen members, eight of whom were elected by the directors of the East India Company. The powers of the Company had been seriously circumscribed by the 1858 India Act with its troops being absorbed into the British army and the Indian Civil Service (ICS) becoming answerable to the secretary of state for India. In fact, the ICS had been set up shortly before the Mutiny in an attempt to restrict the Company's power of patronage.[16]

After the Mutiny Indian government has been described in the following way. Under the viceroy or governor-general and his council came:

> the familiar, layered pyramid of Indian government with its hierarchy of presidency and provincial governors, collectors, commissioners, deputy commissioners, assistant commissioners, judges, magistrates, assistant magistrates, police superintendents and inspectors, and the legion of Indian clerks and tax gatherers . . . their every action was subject to [British] Parliamentary scrutiny, although Indian business was usually conducted before an-all-but-empty chamber.[17]

Compared with its counterparts in Britain or the white settler colonies the ICS was proportionately larger and more powerful. It was far less diffused than the Colonial Service which was responsible for the administration of all the other territories within the British Empire.

The vast ICS was significant in another respect. Because the upper échelons of the Indian government were narrow a far greater proportion of government originated in the middle and upper reaches of the ICS than in other British territories. Just as there was a plurality of political views at the highest levels of imperial administration, so the same existed in the higher levels of the ICS, some of those members were of a liberal persuasion. Thus, an important potential synergy existed in the Indian situation between the highest policy and decision makers and those senior members of the ICS who could promote ideas, some of which would later be co-operative.

One of the latter was Sir William Wedderburn who had followed his father into the ICS. While a district judge at Poona Wedderburn put forward his 'co-operative' proposals which will be discussed later. In the run-up to India's first co-operative legislation in 1904 the ICS proved valuable in practical ways. They gained awareness of co-operative developments in Europe through research and had the capacity to draw up legislative proposals on their findings. The point to underline is that the nature of the ICS owed much to India's form of government after the Mutiny of 1857.

Even after retirement members of the ICS could remain influential on Indian affairs. As we shall see later, the 'India of London'[18] as Henry Wolff termed them, would help to shape India's first co-operative legislation. Wedderburn remained active in Indian affairs after his retirement during which he helped to found the Indian National Congress, serving as its president in 1899 and again in 1910. He also regularly contributed to its journal, *India*. Between 1893 and 1900 Wedderburn was a British MP and took a leading role in the setting-up of the Indian Parliamentary Committee.

Another retired member of the ICS who remained active in Indian affairs was Hodgson Pratt (1824–1907). A founding member of the National Indian Association in 1872, he wrote frequently on Indian matters in the *Economist*. Besides maintaining his Indian interests, he also became heavily involved in the British Co-operative movement. Pratt was closely associated with the Christian Socialists and was prominent in many late-nineteenth-century co-operative initiatives in Britain as well as becoming a founding member of the International Co-operative Alliance in 1895.

Wedderburn and Pratt typify the liberal element within the ICS. We cannot know its extent but it does point to some degree of plurality there which also manifested itself at the top of the Indian administrative pyramid. Before exploring possible co-operative interests we should examine the aristocratic background of India's governor-generals and governors. As in other British territories they constituted the political and social apex. They were also the sovereign's personal representatives and a prerequisite of that was that they should have high social status. In 1900 they were still almost exclusively from the British aristocracy and had a number of shared characteristics.

These included a considerable knowledge of Britain's politics, national and imperial. Before inheriting their titles and therefore often the right to sit in the House of Lords, they had often sought election to Parliament's lower chamber, the House of Commons. In either chamber they shaped legislation and, if they gained ministerial or cabinet positions, they also exercised executive powers. Being well-versed in British politics meant that should they be given positions within the Empire they enjoyed influential connections with those in the imperial system back home. Politics, whether Conservative or Liberal, was therefore a cohesive factor.

Another cohesive factor was education. British aristocrats were traditionally educated at leading British public schools where patrician values, codes of honour and conduct were instilled. Marriage was yet another binding force. At that time aristocrats seldom married outside their class which made it even more likely that they moved within family and class circles strengthened further by their shared Anglican religion. The Test Act of 1673 had barred Catholics and non-conformist Protestants from holding public office. Under the Catholic Emancipation Act of 1829, Catholics were allowed to sit in Parliament but were required to take an oath denying the Pope's right to interfere in British affairs. Despite this provision, in 1900 British aristocrats, and particularly those with parliamentary influence, were still predominantly Anglican. It should also be remembered that Anglicanism was a communion with prelates stationed throughout the British Empire. It thus constituted another important imperial network which aided the transmission of ideas.

Aristocratic family connections can be seen at play in the spread of co-operative ideas within the British Empire. Neither Earl Grey nor Sir Horace Plunkett served in India but Earl Grey's brother-in-law, Earl Minto (1847–1914), was governor-general of India between 1905 and 1910, before which he had been governor-general of Canada.

Minto seems to have shared a number of his brother-in-law's characteristics. Like Grey, 'he was an open minded paternalist, a Whig grandee who, like so many of his kind, had fallen out of love with Liberalism when it embraced Irish Home Rule'[19] There is no evidence that Minto was directly involved in promoting co-operatives in India, but he did became governor-general a year after the passing of the 1904 Co-operative Credit Societies Act, and departed a year before the enactment of the larger and more comprehensive Act of 1912. He was therefore at the head of Indian government during the consolidation period of India's first co-operatives. His administration oversaw the implementation of the 1904 Act and moves to pass the second Act. Given the narrowly-based nature of Indian government it is likely that had he opposed these moves at any point his influence would have prevailed. Therefore, it seems reasonable to speculate that Grey's influence, possibly during family gatherings, helped to shape Minto's attitudes to co-operatives in India during their formative period.

Turning briefly away from India but illustrating the inter-connectedness between aristocratic imperial policy makers, we should note that Sir Horace Plunkett was not the only member of his family to become a co-operative enthusiast. William Lee, the Lord Plunkett was described by Henry Wolff as an 'ardent co-operator'. He actively supported Sir Horace's work in Ireland and between 1896 and 1903 was a leading member of the Irish Agricultural Organisation Society founded by Sir Horace to be the apex organisation of Irish agricultural co-operatives. In 1898 Lord Plunkett assisted Sir Horace in Parliament by supporting the passage of the Societies Borrowing Powers Act which was intended to assist the growing number of Irish village banks. Within the context of imperial administration the point is that in 1904 Lord Plunkett became governor-general of New Zealand.[20] His assistance to co-operatives there will be examined in greater detail in a later chapter. At this point we should merely note that members of aristocratic families could influence each other on co-operative matters and this assumes greater significance when those members were also leading imperial administrators.

Plunkett's period as governor-general of New Zealand roughly coincided with Earl Grey's in Canada. This opens up the possibility that both men spoke to others of similar rank on the potential of co-operatives when visiting London for state occasions or on other imperial business.

Two other imperial figures should be noted for their connection with India: the Lords Wenlock and Macdonnell. Although of lesser rank, both were co-operative enthusiasts and actively involved in moves towards India's first co-operative legislation. Lord Wenlock was the governor of Madras but had previously been involved in co-operatives in England, helping to set up a consumer co-operative on his family estate in Yorkshire and being a founding member and later president of the British Agricultural Organisation Society. This formed along similar lines to its Irish counterpart[21] which suggests that Lord Wenlock was well acquainted with the work of Sir Horace Plunkett and the Lord Plunkett.

Sir Anthony Macdonnell, later Lord Macdonnell, was lieutenant-governor of India's United Provinces, where he oversaw the setting up of co-operatives before any co-operative legislation had been passed. He has been described as a 'thorough believer in Co-operation' and in 1901 did 'pioneering work by establishing . . . two hundred co-operative credit societies in the United Provinces'.[22]

EVENTS LEADING UP TO INDIA'S FIRST CO-OPERATIVE ACT

From the foregoing it is reasonable to suggest that figures at the highest levels of Indian administration were familiar with co-operative ideas. By itself this would not have guaranteed their introduction. A number of other influences coalesced including a weakening of laissez-faire attitudes: government intervention to help ease economic and social problems was becoming more acceptable.

Development was taking new forms and was initially much concerned with building infrastructures. In India, as elsewhere, though, greater emphasis also came to be placed on planning and technology. Intervention increased but the policy of not interfering with the free market remained: 'humanitarianism was always balanced by pragmatism and the Raj never lost sight of the need to pay its way. Technical improvements which made Indians less vulnerable to the wayward forces of nature were also contrived to enrich them and, through taxation, the Government'.[23] Thus, when in 1882 Sir William Wedderburn made his legislative proposal to introduce a kind of pre-co-operative credit, it was turned down by the secretary of state for India in London because it meant intervention in the free market. Its failure illustrated the power of the London veto in Indian affairs because both the Bombay and Indian governments had already approved Sir William's proposal.

Progress towards India's first co-operative legislation was slow, taking over twenty years from this first attempt. Moreover, steps towards it were taken against a background of obvious need. Famines recurred for various reasons including the failure of monsoon rains. There were also persistently high levels of rural debt which were highlighted in a series of Famine Commission Reports. That of 1880 noted:

> We learn from evidence collected from all parts of India that about one third of the land-owning class are deeply and inextricably in debt and that about an equal portion are in debt, though not beyond the power of recovering themselves.[24]

That of 1901 also recorded that:

> In his evidence before us the chief secretary of the Bombay Government said that 28% of land in Broach had passed into the possession of the money-lending classes and from a report of the collector of Ahmedabad, it appears that in his district, expropriation of the land owners has also made considerable way. Taking all these statements into account and comparing them with the evidence we have received, we think it probable that at least one-fourth of the cultivators in the Bombay Presidency have lost possession of their lands, that less than one-fifth are free from debt and the remainder are in debt to a greater of less extent.[25]

These statements clearly illustrate the link between famine and rural indebtedness. Recognition grew slowly that co-operatives might offer solutions. Although Wedderburn's proposals were vetoed in London, a number of Indian histories credit him with being the first to propose co-operative credit in India.

> It was in 1882 on the initiation of Sir William Wedderburn, who was then District Judge of Poona, that the Government of India proposed to the Government of Bombay the experimental establishment of agricultural banks in the Puriandar Taluqa in that district, for providing capital to agricultural classes on reasonable terms. The principle of operation of the proposed bank was to borrow

> money at moderate interest from the big capitalists, whether Indian or European, and to hand it over to *ryots* at a higher rate, but at once considerably lower than the rates charged by the *sowcar*.[26]

Henry Wolff disputes how far Wedderburn's proposals were co-operative and, in any event, points out that, at that time, co-operative credit solutions were still largely unknown beyond a narrow circle of German and Italian pioneers.[27] Nevertheless, in the context of this study Wedderburn's proposals are significant because they mark a starting point and can be seen as stepping-stones to the 1904 Act inasmuch as they were partially incorporated in the Land Improvement Loans Act of 1883 and the Agriculturalists Loans Act of 1884.[28]

Other stepping-stones included initiatives taken by Lord Wenlock, governor of Madras, and Lord Macdonnell, lieutenant-governor of the United Provinces almost a decade later. By then thrift and credit societies were becoming more strongly based in Ireland, Germany and Italy. In 1892, Lord Wenlock sent Frederick Nicholson, later Sir Frederick, to study European credit co-operatives and to report back. His report appeared in 1895. In 1896, Lord Macdonnell sent Henry Dupernex on a similar mission. The reports of the two men undoubtedly contributed to a growing momentum which led in 1903 to the setting up of a committee to consider legislation to encourage and promote thrift and credit co-operatives in India.

Both Nicholson and Dupernex were members of this committee together with four senior members of the ICS and the British manager of the Commercial Bank of India.[29] The opening statement of the *Report of the Committee on the Establishment of Co-operative Credit Societies in India*, reflects how far it was based on European co-operative experiences. 'The "Agricultural banks" which have been so successful in improving the condition of the poorer classes in European countries rest upon cooperative credit, and we have confined our attention to banking on this basis.'[30] The committee noted how co-operative credit had assisted European agriculturalists and concluded that it could also benefit their Indian counterparts. It then proposed the lines along which credit societies should be established in India, the privileges that they should be given, and the extent to which they should be aided by, or subject to government control. The report also included a draft bill which then came under active consideration in India and in London.

Through the eye-witness accounts of Henry Wolff it is possible to glimpse some of the activities going on behind the scenes which accompanied these developments. He also recounts his own efforts to shape the Indian legislation:

> Retired members of the Indian Civil Service, to whom I had explained the Raiffeisen system, owned themselves greatly pleased with the idea and . . . declared . . . the system to be the one marked out for application in India. Prominent among these was . . . Sir Arthur Cotton, the constructor of the Kistna, Godavari and Cauvery Canals, and Mr. Gladstone's chosen confidential adviser on many Indian questions.[31]

Henry Wolff lobbied but he was also consulted on possible forms of the proposed Indian legislation. Both Nicholson and Dupernex visited him during their European fact-finding missions. Of Dupernex, Wolff wrote:

> Unfortunately [his] time seemed very narrowly measured. After he had read my book we had a long palaver in London, in the course of which I explained things as well as I could. But I wanted him to see for himself societies in Germany and Italy, which I still consider were the only ones to prove of real service to him. I offered to give him the necessary introductions. However, he had not time to do more than break his journey to Brindisi. And so I had to content myself with giving him an introduction to the People's Bank at Mentone, which never ranked in the opinion of co-operators as genuinely 'co-operative' and has long since renounced both the name and constitution of a co-operative society. That brief and exclusive visit has, I regret, left a mark upon the Co-operative Movement in India, which I cannot help looking upon as a *damnosa haereditas*.[32]

Wolff judged Nicholson more kindly and described him as a 'deserving officer'. Nicholson's report, including a draft Bill was 'privately communicated . . . along with the draft, for perusal and advice' by Sir Charles Bernard of the India Office. Wolff responded on 3 July 1900:

> Dear Sir,
>
> I have to thank you for your kind letter of 29th ultimo, and the two volumes of the Nicholson Report as well as a copy of the Madras Government Order.
>
> The last named I beg to return herewith.
>
> I have had to deal with the matter rather hurriedly, mainly on account of my imminent departure for Paris, and the organisation of one of the Congresses [Fourth ICA Congress held in Paris 18–21 July 1900][33] to be held there being thrown almost exclusively on me.
>
> I cannot too warmly recommend you to take the opinion of Mr. Brabrook, Chief Registrar of Friendly Societies. To deal with

the matter under an Amended Companies Act would, I am sure, be a tremendous mistake. We want a Co-operative Act.

I enclose a reference to Acts in force in this Kingdom.

Of course, if I can, be of any service in the matter, I shall be only too glad to be so.

Believe me, etc.,

Henry Wolff[34]

This seems to indicate that the Indian legislation was likely to take the form of an 'Amended Companies Act'. Wolff, however, pressed for a 'Co-operative Act' and refers specifically to 'Acts in force in this Kingdom'. This may seem strange. While Britain had legislation applying to co-operatives there was not one with 'Co-operative' in its title. In Chapter 2 we noted how the Industrial and Provident Societies Acts had been passed to apply to British co-operatives. Two points to emphasise here are that this legislation was incremental and that it had been almost fifty years before its codification provided a legislative framework acceptable to British co-operatives. A similar incremental pattern would be seen in imperial co-operative legislation but their starting points were to be greatly different.

In Britain co-operative development had preceded legislation which, to some extent, made it possible for legislation to reflect the needs that co-operators had themselves identified. Colonial co-operative legislation invariably preceded co-operative development and was therefore based on needs identified by colonial civil servants. Although undoubtedly well intentioned, civil servants' assessments of needs were likely to lead to prescriptive legislation. This would particularly be the case where it was judged that the lack of local development required safeguards to be incorporated. This proved to be the case in India. From the outset, then, there would be crucial differences between British and colonial co-operative legislation. Henry Wolff's comments, however, were firmly based on his British co-operative experiences.

Wolff's history of *Co-operation in India* deals at length with his response to Nicholson's report which he considered 'masterly'. However, he believed it contained contradictions on the question of 'State aid' which Wolff admitted 'is a very difficult subject'.[35] As president of the executive committee of the ICA, he would have been well aware of the debates then taking place within the ICA on this question.[36] While not rehearsing their arguments in his response to Nicholson's report he nevertheless highlights the existence of the debate although he comes down on neither side.

Wolff is less equivocal when he suggests that Nicholson is confusing two kinds of credit.

> The object of co-operative banking is *not at all* to foster what the Board [Madras Government] will call 'licentious' borrowing or 'facile' credit. It is, to create and make available a new security. So far from making credit to poor cultivators or labourers 'facile' or easy, as I have pointed out in my various writings, it makes it 'possible' only by making it 'difficult.' It does not ask the man to come and borrow. It distinctly tells him: You will have no money unless you can fully satisfy us as to having a good case. The presumption is *against* lending.
>
> Also, the object of co-operative banks is by no means merely to place fair credit in the place of unfair. It is to *create working capital*, without which the most fertile land, situated near the best markets, is worth very little.[37]

He illustrates this argument by quoting the thousands of German co-operative dairies set up without capital but with the help of co-operative banks whose 'claims have gradually been paid off at the rate of so much per gallon used'. In addition, Wolff cites steam thrashing machines 'which have never cost their owners, a society, anything, inasmuch as the bank has advanced the money and had been repaid out of the hire'.

Wolff also feared that Nicholson's draft Bill was far too large and complex; it 'altogether staggers a European by its ambition'.

> Here are a Companies Bill [for Joint Stock Banks] a Savings Banks Bill, a Land Improvement Bill, a Co-operative Bill, and one or two other things, all rolled into one. In this country we should want about five or six bills for all this, and five or six sessions [of Parliament] for their consideration.[38]

This seems to illustrate how a colonial civil servant's interpretation of needs and their required safeguards could lead to prescriptive legislation. Wolff is also aghast at Nicholson's suggestion of using some form of Companies Act.

> But what staggers a mere European quite as much as the comprehensiveness of Mr. Nicholson's proposal is his suggestion that the matter should be settled by an amendment of the *Companies Act*. In this country nobody would think such a thing. This Companies Act, quite apart from the intolerable expense which it involves, is very unsuitable, indeed directly adverse to co-operation. It means that a small number of persons should have as full as possible power of dealing with the money and interests of a much larger

> number; that things should be done oligarchically . . . and it emphasises 'profit'. Co-operation cannot succeed except the circumstances be exactly reversed.

Wolff also castigated Nicholson's proposal that 'profit should be divided according to the shares'. This idea was:

> an exceedingly bad one, which no co-operator in this country would dare so much as to name. That is the joint stock principle. The co-operative principle is that, since it is, not shares, but custom which makes the profit, it is the custom that the profit belongs in what the French call the *ristourne*, i.e., the return of what was paid in excess. We must not promise the ryots bread and give them a stone.[39]

He then reviews the legislation applying to co-operatives in Britain, Ireland and Germany, and finally commends Britain's industrial provident societies legislation, adding that he has asked the 'General Secretary of the Co-operative Union at Manchester to forward to Sir Charles Bernard a copy of their handbook on the Industrial and Provident Societies Act'. Wolff also commends the friendly societies law. He observes that there 'ought to be ample room in India for it', adding, that India needed 'an equivalent to our Registrar'.

Returning to the question of state financial aid, Wolff warns against loans being made into gifts and suggests that there were ways to prevent this.

> I do not see the harm of an advance. I have elsewhere compared this to the pail or two of water which we have used to pour into a new pump of the old type, *not to provide the water to be drawn up*, but only *to get the sucker to work*.
>
> We have had to accept some State aid in Ireland [£2,000] and, though it is too soon to speak positively, it does not appear to have worked any mischief. But it is true, the Irish village banks are exceedingly well officered.

In a footnote rather than in his response to Nicholson's report, Wolff states that this Irish state aid was 'subsequently arbitrarily withdrawn, to the no small embarrassment of the erst-assisted societies. That should serve as an *exemplum utile*'.[40]

Wolff's comments have been quoted at length because they illustrate contemporary co-operative ideas and legislation applying and facilitate comparisons with the Indian proposals. We gain a clearer insight to these from Sir Denzil Ibbetson's speech when introducing the Co-operative Credit Societies Bill to the Indian Legislative Council.[41] At that time Ibbetson was a senior member of the Indian civil service but was later to become lieutenant-governor of Bengal.[42]

His speech is reproduced in full in the book *100 Years Co-operative Credit Societies Act, India, 1904*. In it he clearly summarises the Indian background to the Bill and so provides interesting points of comparisons with Wolff's co-operative and British perspectives. Ibbetson emphasised that the Act had had to accommodate considerable Indian diversity which necessitated 'two cardinal objectives', namely, 'simplicity' and 'elasticity'.[43]

He dismisses a potential role for indigenous systems of credit, suggesting that they had been more appropriate at a time 'when the security which the agriculturalist had to offer was of far smaller value than at present'. Ibbetson also touches on the tensions in the legal system to which Sir William Wedderburn had previously referred. According to Ibbetson, difficulties had arisen due to 'the fact that into most Indian contracts there enters an element of oriental hyperbole, for which full allowance is made when the settlement is by mutual consent, but which our Courts of Justice are for the most part unable to recognise'.[44]

Criticisms of British imperial rule have included its failure to take into account Indian systems of credit. When introducing the Bill, Ibbetson held that they were not always relevant. In support of this argument he quoted the Nidhi which had emerged in Madras about the same time Schulze-Delitzsch and Raiffeisen had begun their experiments in Germany. Although relatively successful they had not been considered relevant in the present context because their clientele were the educated and advanced Indian classes. Moreover, they were organised along the lines of British building societies. By contrast, evidence collected in connection with the Bill now being introduced pointed to the need for legislation that was designed to raise the living standards of the poor, particularly the rural poor. Hence the Bill's focus on the promotion of thrift and credit co-operatives.

Ibbetson then turned to what form the legislation should take. He noted that the existing Companies Act of 1882 contained 256 sections, but felt that 'its elaborate provisions, however, necessary in the case of combinations of capital on a large scale, are wholly unsuited to societies of the kind which we wish to encourage'.

He continued:

> The first thing to be done, therefore, was to take such societies out of the operations of the general law on the subject, and to substitute

> provisions specially adapted to their constitution and objects. In the second place, it was desirable to confer upon them special privileges and facilities, in order to encourage their formation and assist their operations. And, thirdly, since they were to enjoy exemption from the general law and facilities of a very special nature, it was very necessary to take such precautions as might be needed in order to prevent speculators from availing themselves, under colourable pretext, of privileges which were not intended for them.[45]

Leading up to the legislation there had been an 'extraordinary diversity of opinion, which extended in many cases to matters of principle'. This was to have been expected but what was now necessary was that the legislation should be seen as an experiment: what succeeded in Europe would not necessarily succeed in India, 'nor indeed is it probable that what is suited to one part of this great country will always be suited to another'.

> Certain broad principles must be laid down, and certain precautions must be insisted upon; but within those principles and subject to those precautions, the people must in the main be left to work out their own salvation on their own lines, the function of government being confined to hearty sympathy, assistance and advice.[46]

The Bill aimed to foster:

> the encouragement of individual thrift and of mutual cooperation among the members, with a view to the utilisation of their combined credit, by the aid of intimate knowledge of one another's needs and capacities and of the pressure of local public opinion.

Thrift and credit co-operatives encouraged for this purpose were intended for 'small men' rather than the 'capitalist'. They should comprise members who lived in the same neighbourhood so that they would have knowledge of each other and new members should be admitted by election. Ibbetson continued:

> that a man must be a member before he can borrow from the society, and in that capacity have contributed to the funds of the society since our basis is mutual cooperation; that money shall not be lent on mortgage, so that the capital may be liquid and capable of ready realisation; that the interest in a society which may be

> held by a single member is to be limited, in order to prevent an individual from obtaining control, and that shares can be transferred subject only to certain restrictions which are intended to prevent speculation. We provide for a simple form of registration for compulsory dissolution, subject to appeal to the local government, in order to meet the case of fraud, or of bogus cooperative societies which may have obtained the benefits of the Act while not pursuing its objects; and for liquidation under a simple procedure and subject to appeal to the Civil Courts.[47]

The Bill offered considerable benefits to co-operatives including exemption from the payment of income tax, stamp duties and registration fees. Ibbetson reported that there would be compulsory inspections and audits by government officers in order to prevent people trying to form bogus societies or gaining control of bona fide co-operatives for personal gain, and also to foster public confidence.

In implementing the legislation local governments were to be given important powers. Ibbetson stated: 'we give them a wide rule-making power . . . while indicating certain heads under which it will probably be advisable to exercise it'. He continued that because of the experimental nature of the Bill's objects it was likely 'that we shall have to gain our experience as we go. Under these circumstances it is essential to proceed gradually and with the greatest caution'. Accordingly, local governments were asked to select a few places in each province in which they could undertake initial experiments.[48] Ibbetson's speech is significant because it set out the Bill's objectives. Let us now examine how these worked out in the final Act.

THE CO-OPERATIVE CREDIT SOCIETIES ACT, INDIA, 1904

The Act was to apply to two main groups: urban artisans and low-paid employees; and rural agriculturalists excluding 'wealthy rent-receivers'. It provided for residents of a specific area to be admitted as members by election; also for them to borrow from their society as long as they had previously saved with it. Registration of societies was to be simple but where there was fraud, or bogus co-operatives formed, they could be dissolved. There was, however, a right of appeal to the local government. Societies could also be liquidated by a simple procedure but again with a right of appeal, this time to the civil courts.

British industrial and provident societies legislation had conferred limited liability on all British co-operatives but in India this was to be available only to urban societies. Rural societies were denied it in the belief that unlimited liability would encourage loans to be made responsibly and strengthen societies' sense of mutuality.

Both types of co-operative were given corporate status. Each could place any surplus they made to reserves or use it to reduce their rate of interest. Urban societies were also allowed to distribute their profits in the form of a patronage dividend, so long as they had first created sufficient reserves. They could also lend to rural societies existing in the same district. Each kind of society was exempt from paying income tax, stamp duties and registration fees. To prevent the abuse of these privileges, the Act laid down that systems of audit and inspection by government officers should be put into place. Under these arrangements no co-operative could borrow money without prior approval. All these powers of supervision were intended to reassure society members, guard against mismanagement and fraud, and increase societies' credibility among the wider public.

One of the Act's more contentious features was the power it gave the registrar. This reminds us that Henry Wolff had called for an Indian registrar. He might not have anticipated the greater powers he would receive compared with his British counterpart. These included the ability to take the place of the courts on certain matters and to arbitrate on questions relating to co-operative principles. As far as the latter were concerned, registrars had to ensure that societies' by-laws remained in line with them. As a result it would now become necessary for Indian registrars and their staffs to be trained in what were co-operative principles and their operational ramifications.

This was a fundamental difference between British and Indian co-operative legislation. While it was true that legislation applying to British co-operatives also required that their rules should reflect co-operative principles, espousal of those principles had led to the formation of a voluntary and popular movement. Almost by a process of osmosis, those principles had become incorporated in the industrial and provident societies legislation,

In the process, they clearly distinguished it from British company law. A far more mechanical process would be required in India where registrars and their staff would first need to be trained in co-operative principles. After that, the members they wished to attract into thrift and credit societies would require to be trained. In this sense it is possible to view the 1904 Act as a continuation of attempts begun a century earlier to transfer Western enlightenment and British liberalism to India.

For those not of the legal profession it is difficult to characterise the Co-operative Credit Societies Act, India, 1904. While Wolff's fears that it would prove to be an omnibus piece of legislation did not materialise, doubts remain about how far it resembled Indian companies legislation. Ibbetson clearly said that that would not be appropriate. The judgement of history has been less sure. Thirty years later, H. Calvert in his *The Law and Principles of Co-operation*,[49] claims that the Act was indeed a 'modified code of company law'. Moreover, Calvert argued that this form of legislation was appropriate for India's stage of development in the early twentieth century and contrasts it with that in Britain and elsewhere in Europe. He suggests that even in Western Europe laws permitting voluntary association were of relatively modern origin. Calvert seems to take no account of indigenous traditional forms of association. Perhaps he was right as far as *democratic* voluntary association was concerned as the Indian caste system might not easily have accommodated it. However, Calvert's analysis might lead one to suspect that imperialism fostered over-simplification.

Nevertheless, his interpretation of the 1904 Act is important because he was writing with the benefit of hindsight and with considerable knowledge of how it had worked out in practice. It is therefore interesting to find him contrasting the Act favourably with Britain's industrial and provident societies' legislation.

> The rigid provisions of the various laws [I & P] . . . may seem to contrast strangely with the simplicity and elasticity of the Indian Act. They must be presumed to be based on the knowledge of the people with whom the legislatures were dealing and their absence from the latter Act must not be construed as reflecting the opinion that they were not necessary here. The Government of India has thrown upon Local Government and Registrars the responsibility for insisting on the necessary rigidity adapted to local conditions. It will not be seriously argued that a strictness which seventy or eighty years of experience has shown to be necessary in Europe can be lightly dispensed with in India . . . the simplicity and elasticity which characterise the Indian Act give Local Governments and the Registrars a free hand either in the determination or in the application of the principles of co-operation.[50]

This statement underlines the importance of local government and the registrars in attempts to accommodate India's geographical, social and cultural diversity. The enhanced role of the Indian registrar contrasts strongly with that of his counterpart in Britain, who was traditionally the vehicle through which societies could be registered or dissolved, and was the office through which annual reports and accounts were lodged in much the same way as the registrar of companies dealt with those of

British companies. The powers of the Indian co-operative registrar went much further. Both the British and Indian systems had a chief registrar under whom registrars and assistant registrars served and all were civil servants. In India, however, they headed much larger establishments of government officers whose remit was to encourage co-operatives into existence and then to supervise their management.

A second Act was introduced in 1912, which applied to the whole of India and to all kinds of co-operative rather than just to thrift and credit societies. It also provided for the establishment of co-operative banks and gave greater discretion to the registrar to determine the eligibility of different categories of people for co-operative membership. '. . . agriculturalists or non-agriculturalists, their caste, occupations etc. As regards admission of members, the right to determine whether the applicants have fulfilled all conditions and made all payments due to the society, was given to the Registrar'.[51]

This was an unwelcome development as far as supporters of voluntary co-operation were concerned because it breached the Rochdale principle of 'open membership'. Wolff criticised this in his *Co-operation in India*, arguing that it shifted the responsibility from a co-operative's members to the registrar as to who could join their society and in the process weakened their mutuality.[52] It reflected a tension between the traditional voluntary co-operation of the mother country and state-sponsored co-operative development in British colonies.

For the moment we should note that co-operative Acts followed in many Indian states, including the important Bombay Co-operative Societies Act of 1925; others followed in Madras, Bihar, Orissa, Bengal and Burma. At that time Burma came within Indian jurisdiction. 'These Acts retained the basic aspects of the 1912 Act, but introduced several provisions to deal with a variety of co-operatives and added many concessions as well as penalties and fixed responsibilities of various functionaries and members.'[53]

Within a few years there was wide legislative provision for the encouragement of all types of co-operatives in India. One can sympathise with Wolff for the departure such arrangements meant from the voluntary forms of co-operation he held dear, but there is no doubt that Indian co-operatives were an important imperial innovation which brought benefits to ordinary Indians. While it was true that the introduction of legislation brought with it a cadre of official leaders, it also prompted the emergence of unofficial leaders. Madhav Madane in his essay records:

> The beginning and the rapid spread of the cooperative movement in many parts of the Bombay State is mainly attributed to the

> efforts and devotion of non-official leaders. These leaders who were already active in the socio-economic field, seized upon the opportunity of starting credit co-operatives when the 1904 Act was enacted. Thereafter, there was no looking back for them and their zeal helped the registration and working of the credit co-operatives.[54]

Madane's perspective is interesting. Born in 1924 and dying in 2007, he was Indian and worked with Indian co-operatives for much of his working life, becoming steeped in their history. This runs counter to Calvert's belief that Indians had little experience of voluntary associations. Madane's reference to 'non-official' leaders 'who were already active in the socio-economic field' may well help to explain how Indian co-operatives were able to make such swift progress after the passing of the 1904 Act. In 1906–7 843 societies were formed with a combined membership of 90,844. By 1911–12 those numbers had risen to 8,177 and 403,328 respectively.[55]

CONCLUSIONS

This was a successful beginning but its significance extended far beyond India. The model it pioneered was replicated in Ceylon (Sri Lanka), Malaya (Malaysia), Cyprus and Africa. It had much to commend it but its speed of dissemination throughout the Empire was helped by the existence of networks created by the Indian and colonial civil services. These provided the means through which ideas and experiences could be exchanged. In addition, those involved in the Indian legislation and its implementation wrote much about it. Margaret Digby of the Plunkett Foundation, who did much to shape colonial co-operative legislation after 1945, once observed that the Indian legacy was 'carried by its own reputation and by the writings and travels of men like Mr. H. Calvert, Mr. C. F. Strickland and Sir Malcolm Darling who had first been connected with its administration in India'.[56]

The writings of Calvert, Strickland and Darling form an important part of this study, as do those of Margaret Digby herself. Each was heavily influenced by the Indian experience and this chapter has recorded it at length because many references will be made to it in future chapters. Above all, the 1904 and 1912 Acts point to lines of tension that emerged between imperialism and co-operation and were so clearly heralded in the writings of Henry Wolff.

7. Early Examples of British Imperial Co-operative Development: Southern Africa

INTRODUCTION

Co-operatives were a new form of business organisation that was to prove effective in a variety of settings in response to vastly differing needs. In India they had been introduced by government to help offset poverty, indebtedness and recurring famines among a vast and largely settled indigenous population. In Southern Africa they were seen mainly as a tool to help white settler farmers. Conditions in the region varied greatly as we shall see in our study of three territories: Rhodesia, Cape Colony and Bechuanaland (Botswana). Rhodesia wanted to increase its white population, particularly farmers. Cape Colony had a longer history but had still to achieve food sufficiency. Bechuanaland, secured for strategic reasons, remained largely undeveloped.

Throughout this chapter we speak of Southern Africa as a region. During the early years of the twentieth century it was still in a state of flux following the 'scramble for Africa'. Some territorial boundaries shifted again in the wake of the First World War. Not surprisingly the region was also constitutionally diverse. It contained a dominion under the British Crown, namely the Union of South Africa, formed in 1910. This comprised the British colonies of the Cape and Natal, and the former Boer republics of the Transvaal and the Orange Free State. It also contained colonies, of which Rhodesia was a prominent example. Still being settled, it was administered by the British Colonial Office on behalf of the Westminster Parliament. Lower down the constitutional order came Bechuanaland which was a protectorate administered by the British high-commissioner.

In India we had seen the introduction of co-operatives in a setting in which the British predominated. British rule in Southern Africa was more recent and less certain. Before examining the types of co-operative development that occurred there we should briefly note how the British operated in the region.

THE BRITISH IN SOUTHERN AFRICA

The second half of the nineteenth century saw vast virgin tracts of African land carved out and settled by Europeans with little or no regard for indigenous populations. It was a period of territorial competition between the British, French, Portuguese, Dutch and Germans and also one of adventure and pioneering. A motley assortment of people moved through this shifting landscape including missionaries, adventurers such as Edward Lugard,[1] romantics such as the author Rider Haggard[2] and earnest Salvation Army leaders who sought land on which to settle unemployed British workers.

British political and legal systems had become well-established in India but in Southern Africa they were more recent and far more fluid. As in India they emerged in response to economic advances spearheaded by trading companies. Prominent among these were Cecil Rhodes's British South Africa Company, the Royal Niger Company in West Africa and the Imperial British East Africa Company in the East. They 'succeeded in drawing huge tracts of Africa into British control. From the date of the BSAC'S charter – October 1889 – a new quasi-sovereign state began to emerge in Southern Africa'.[3]

Besides administering in London a growing number of African territories, the Colonial Office also needed to conduct relations with other European powers seeking to become imperial powers in Africa. For example, in 1890 Lord Salisbury, the British colonial secretary, successfully negotiated with the Germans and the Belgians that the British should control a route from the Cape to the headwaters of the Nile and onto the Mediterranean. Such a north–south route had immense strategic significance facilitating trade and strengthening security. A corresponding east–west route might have been established by the Portuguese had they been able to link their colonies of Mozambique in the East and Angola in the West.

Generally speaking the British proved more determined and adroit, helped by Colonial Office leadership and by growing public support for imperial adventures. Alongside such developments imperial theory also evolved. An example was the colonial conference held in 1884 that led to the founding of the Colonial League, whose aim was to form a confederation of self-governing British territories, an ideal that Earl Grey enthusiastically supported.

In Southern Africa the main vehicle for British economic development was Rhodes's British South Africa Company. Earl Grey joined its board as a relatively junior member when it received its royal charter in 1889. Higher up the aristocratic scale the Tory Duke of Abercorn and the

Liberal Duke of Fife were respectively appointed the Company's chairman and vice-chairman,[4] Despite Grey being junior Rhodes had been keen to recruit him because he saw him as 'the paladin of his generation' and a 'man of unquestioned rectitude'.[5]

Essentially, the 'Company' represented privatised imperial development in the region with the British state as yet little involved. Dealings were often adventurous and sometimes questionable, as in the abortive Jameson Raid. Grey appears to have been uneasy about events leading up to this and tried to alert Joseph Chamberlain, the colonial secretary:

> Lord Grey felt it incumbent on him to warn Chamberlain of Rhodes's intentions. In April 1895 Grey had forecast that 'rough times' lay ahead, and in August he had a private meeting with the Colonial Secretary in which the reason for the Bechuanaland base was made plain: it was to be the starting point for a company raid into the Transvaal with the aim of bringing down Kruger's government . . .
>
> Chamberlain, who might reasonably have been expected to express horror at Lord Grey's news, merely remarked that he took it for granted 'no movement will take place unless success is certain, a fiasco would be most disastrous'. He then went on a long holiday, leaving South Africa in the tremulous hands of a newly-arrived High Commissioner.[6]

Chamberlain later disclaimed any prior knowledge of the raid which, 'taking Lord Grey's testimony into account, can only be called a lie'.[7]

Colonial Office perceptions of Grey could have led Chamberlain to disregard his warnings. Some people considered him an ambiguous figure but one who could nevertheless be used. Sir Alfred Milner (1854–1925), who became the Cape's governor and high-commissioner in 1897, said that he considered Rhodes, 'thoroughly untrustworthy', but had found it necessary to work with him because 'Rhodes was one of the *arcana imperii* [imperial secrets] that could never be divulged except to the fully initiated augur'. Grey seems not to have been among that select group because Milner added:

> For goodness sake . . . do not let Grey . . . ever know what I think . . . Grey, excellent, simple-minded fellow, would not be one-tenth of the use he undoubtedly is, if he did not take Rhodes at his own valuation.[8]

Despite this, Grey remained an enthusiastic and whole-hearted supporter of British imperialism in Southern Africa. His links with Rhodesia grew and in 1896 he was appointed the colony's administrator. Although he held the position for only two years ever after he spoke enthusiastically of Rhodesia. At one point he declared that his 'heart was in Rhodesia'.[9]

Grey saw the development of Rhodesia entirely from the British point of view. He paid little regard to indigenous tribes, and continued to see the development and administration of Rhodesia purely in terms of settling white farmers.

CO-OPERATIVES IN RHODESIA

Because Rhodesia was less rich in mineral deposits than other parts of Southern Africa, agriculture assumed greater importance in its economy. There was, however, a shortage of farmers and the economics of settlement were not favourable. Grey believed that the formation of co-operatives could help reduce farmers' costs and thus increase their incomes to a point where farming became a viable occupation.

Working through the Company and after Rhodes's death the Rhodes Trust, Grey tried to encourage co-operatives and land settlement in a number of ways. He was a prominent figure and therefore a focal point for people to approach. One such approach came from Commander Booth-Tucker, son-in-law of General Booth, the founder of the Salvation Army, who impressed Grey with his successful organisation of settlements for unemployed British family men in Britain and America. Grey suggested that the Company should encourage similar experiments in Rhodesia and that it should 'select bits of land which shall be secured for him [Booth-Tucker] at the lowest possible prices'.[10]

After Rhodes's death in 1902 Grey became a trustee of the Rhodes Trust and we soon see him working behind the scenes to encourage co-operatives. Grey had been in correspondence with Mr Fischer in Mashonaland who, impressed by Plunkett's success in Ireland, wanted to try to set up a 'Farmers' Co-operative Association' at Rusapi. In supporting the idea Grey had suggested that the Association could purchase manures and farm seeds more economically and that farm implements and machinery might be as much as 25 per cent cheaper because farmer/members could deal collectively and directly with the manufacturer. He also believed that members should join together to obtain the use of thoroughbred bulls and boars and that collectively they could buy steam ploughs and other costly machinery to hire out to individual members.

Grey even suggested how the co-operative might be structured, illustrating his detailed local knowledge.

> I think Rusapi supplies opportunities for a successful Society. The farmers on Mr. Rhodes' estate at Inyanga would all become members, also the Laurecedale farmers and the farmers in your own District; further, the existence of such a Society might stimulate big land owners like the Zambesia Exploring Company, to place settlers on the large stretches of fertile and irrigable land in their possession . . .
>
> The establishment of a Society at Rusapi would, I hope, lead to the establishment of similar societies at Umtali, Mazoe, and Charter Districts. These Societies could then be federated to a Rhodesian Agricultural Wholesale Society which could be established at Salisbury.[11]

Grey then referred to German and Continental co-operative experiences which:

> recognised that men who, individually, have no credit on which they can borrow money, by joining together and entering into a joint unlimited engagement to be responsible for the liabilities of the Association, can provide the security on which Banks are glad to lend money at comparatively low rates of interest. It has generally been found possible to borrow money at 4% to 5% and lend it at 6% to 7%; the rates in Rhodesia would necessarily be higher.
>
> The difference between the interest paid and the interest received pays expenses and helps to form a reserve fund and in proportion as the reserve fund grows the credit of the Association improves, thus enabling it to borrow at cheaper rates.

Referring to correspondence he had had with 'Mr. Norris of Placefell, Inyonga', Grey continued:

> Mr. Norris points out that the worse difficulty in the way of the development of the country, is the enormous price everyone wants for a farm – 'This applies to this district, they are not worth it. Men with money won't pay it, men with small capital can't, which are the class to start in a new country and the country cannot go ahead otherwise – there are not big fortunes to be made farming and yet, decent livings for any amount of Englishmen with small capital who can obtain advances for productive purposes or to effect some economy at low rates of interest.'[12]

Grey copied his reply to Fischer to six other people, one of whom, Owen Thomas, had served 'on the Royal Commission on Agriculture

1893–1896'. He supported the idea of agricultural banks in Rhodesia, pointing out that Rhodesian farmers were charged interest rates three to four times higher than English farmers and that Rhodesian agricultural banks might ease that burden. His letter to Grey provides insights into this pioneering period in Rhodesia.

> I have during the three and a half years in South Africa travelled through almost every District. I did 2750 miles by road in the Transvaal after the war was over. I noticed in every District that the one man who undoubtedly flourished was the storekeeper, this parasite middleman had mortgages on most farms, the farmers were tied hand and foot, they could not buy or sell except to and from him, he is the one curse of the country, never satisfied with less than from 300 to 700% profit. I have had ample proof of this and from what I saw and the evidence I gathered I came to the conclusion that the middleman in South Africa more especially in the rural districts was after all the worst pest the farmers had, his aim has been to cripple and so secure the farmer's custom, Once a farmer gets into their clutches he seldom gets out until the farm and stock have gone.[13]

Others also referred to the stranglehold of the 'parasite middleman' and supported the idea that a co-operative store could help reduce members' living expenses. Some attributed the high cost of living to the charges of the Beira and Mashonaland Railways, compounded by the 'Merchants and Storekeepers . . . rigorously refusing to lower their prices of goods; as one man frankly stated to me "we must make provision for our bad debts"'.

He added that a short time earlier:

> the employees of the Railway Workshops in Umtali, at a meeting convened by themselves, decided that as the present cost of groceries etc., were so high, they should form a co-operative store and import all their goods direct for distribution amongst the members. This was decided upon, but before coming to a final decision, it was suggested that the storekeepers at Umtali be approached with a view to their making some reduction in their prices. This suggestion was carried out, with the result that a few days later, the Storekeepers presented a new price list, showing an all round reduction of 22%. This speaks for itself, therefore knowing of this, I am strongly in favour of embodying a Co-operative store if an Agricultural Society be formed.[14]

The nature of co-operative development changed over time. It would later become highly professionalised but in the early 1900s both in India and Southern Africa it was still experimental and largely unprofessional. An illustration of this is provided by the Rhodes Trust which, as part of its co-operative initiative, sent out a 'young man, lately assistant clerk of the Northumberland County Asylum, where he had an excellent character' to assess the feasibility of co-operatives in Rhodesia.[15] We do not know what, if any, co-operative experience Charles Bullock had. In 1903 he was given £50 'from the Rhodes Trust to enable him to proceed to . . . lay the foundation of a Farmers Co-operative Association'.

It seems reasonable to suppose that Grey was involved in this appointment. Bullock came from near Grey's family home at Howick and once in post he regularly reported to Grey as well as to the Rhodes Trust. For example, in December 1903 he wrote to Grey about the difficulties he had experienced in communicating with potential co-operative members over vast distances making it a problem to arrange meetings as first steps in forming co-operatives. He had been able to organise only two such meetings and both were 'small'. Consequently Bullock tried instead to visit farmers but sometimes they were 'absent from home'. Then he could only leave copies of his proposals and hope that the farmers would respond. Where Bullock did meet farmers, however, he felt that he had learnt 'a great deal as to the actual requirements of these people and [I] am now personally acquainted with them'.[16] Behind the scenes Grey was also active in seeking advice on possible legislative forms for Rhodesian co-operatives from J. C. Gray, general secretary of the Co-operative Union in Manchester.[17]

The quest for appropriate co-operative legislation reminds us that in overseas British territories it needed to come within their legal frameworks. This question was being discussed at the same time, 1903, in India. The issue recurs throughout the history of co-operative development within the British Empire. It also reflects the fact that the Empire never had a uniform system of law.

Besides the legal forms co-operatives might take, another issue concerning their development was how to communicate with potential co-operative members and to persuade them to consider co-operative action. An attempt was made to do this through the *Rhodesian Agricultural Journal*. Its edition of August 1903 carried an article headed 'Co-operation in Farming', and again it is possible to see the hand of Earl Grey in this. It began by briefly describing the experiences of agricultural credit societies in Germany and Ireland and argued that these showed that:

> neither member nor creditor has ever lost a penny by them. By thus 'capitalising the honesty' of poor men a security is obtained on which banks are glad to lend money at a comparatively low rate of interest. Members enter into a joint unlimited engagement to be responsible for the liabilities of the Association, and it has been generally possible to borrow money at from 4 to 5 per cent., the difference paying expenses and forming a reserve fund by means of which the credit of the Association is improved and still lower rates obtained.[18]

The article showed how Irish agricultural societies collectively purchased manures, seeds, livestock and machinery and jointly marketed their produce. By conducting their businesses co-operatively Irish farmers had shown that it was possible to operate at lower costs than they could have done individually. By contrast, 'In this country . . . we have hitherto been content with Farmers' Associations and their somewhat limited objectives'. The article continued that in Cape Colony such associations were already considering adopting 'co-operative lines'. It ended by summarising the arguments Earl Grey had used in his correspondence with Fischer to support the establishment of a Farmers' co-operative association at Rusapi.

CO-OPERATIVES IN CAPE COLONY

In Rhodesia the argument for promoting co-operatives had been that they could encourage white immigrant farmers to settle. In the Cape of Good Hope or Cape Colony the question was whether they could help boost home food production and thus lessen dependence on imports.

In 1905 a government report highlighted this issue. Its author was P. J. Hannon, later Sir Patrick Hannon. A close colleague of Plunkett, he was an IAOS organiser who had supervised a number of small co-operative experiments in the West of Ireland.[19] His report, addressed to 'The Secretary for Agriculture' within the Colony showed that he was well versed in co-operative theory and contemporary co-operative developments. Moreover, he had quickly grasped the essentials of Cape Colony's economy and the part co-operatives could play in helping it to fulfil its potential.

It remains one of the most impressive documents pertaining to early imperial co-operative development. Its fifty-six pages highlighted co-operative experiences in Denmark, Holland, Ireland and Germany. The Dutch references were both legitimate and politic in view of the part played by the Dutch in the history of Cape Colony. They were strengthened when Hannon quoted G. J. D. C. Goedhart, president of the Dutch Federation of Co-operative Societies:

> co-operation makes from a poor people a rich one; it makes the farmers hold together; it enables them to lower the cost of living; to gain property; to resist the trust of manure and seed merchants; to get together machinery, which one alone never could have; In short, it makes them better men.[20]

Goedhart became president of the International Co-operative Alliance (ICA) in 1921, until 1927.

On the question of the Cape's food self-sufficiency Hannon noted that:

> a point of time can always be marked out when the people were dependent, for some proportion at least, of their food, upon foreign sources, and in the attempt to make these Colonies self-supporting, we have the example of various other communities now phenomenally successful in agricultural export which were once themselves, importers.[21]

He quoted Canada's experience. In 1892 its agricultural exports had been just below £4,500,000 but by 1905 these exceeded £21,000,000, 'notwithstanding that the Canadian farmer is snowbound for at least three months of the year'.

> Self-help, on the part of the farmer, combined with well-devised practical schemes of education, experiment and subsidy, on the part of the Government, may at once be pointed to as the primary factors in this magnificent measure of success.

Hannon referred to the rapid growth of agricultural sectors in British imperial territories which were initially intended to feed their own populations and reduce dependence on imports but which were now becoming major agricultural exporters.

His tour of the Colony had revealed a willingness to 'undertake practical schemes in a truly self-help spirit'[22] and he identified areas of potential co-operative development including viticulture or wine-making, dairying and milk supplies, poultry production, bacon curing, supply of seeds and manures, co-operative granaries and marketing of grain, fruit production, water boring, mutual insurance of livestock, agricultural credit, abattoirs, tobacco growing and woollen manufacture including mohair. Hannon examined each possibility at length and his report provided a valuable benchmark from which subsequent developments could be measured. It illustrated the differences between the situations in Cape Colony and those in Rhodesia. They would also differ from those in Bechuanaland which we now consider.

CO-OPERATIVES IN BECHUANALAND

Rhodesia needed to attract white settler farmers; Cape Colony to achieve food sufficiency. Needs in Bechuanaland were far less clear. Dominated by the Kalahari Desert the territory was home to several impoverished tribes who subsisted with their cattle in vast areas of sandy wasteland. Yet it became strategically important because of what was happening around it. Lying north-west of Cape Colony, it found itself being trekked over by Boer freebooters from the Transvaal in the 1880s. They wanted to continue northwards and had little interest in Bechuanaland which contained no obvious wealth; their chief concern was to secure future lines of communication. However, the British saw such movements as a threat and in 1884, under the Convention of London, secured a border between the Transvaal and Bechuanaland.[23] This, however, did not guarantee the territory's status. Later the same year the British felt threatened again when Germany, under Bismarck, established a German colony on the Cape's north-west border. After the First World War this became a British mandated territory of South West Africa. In the 'scramble for Africa' in the 1880s, though, the British thought its establishment a possible limitation on their future expansion. If, for example, the Transvaal took Bechuanaland to secure its lines of communication but later formed an alliance with the German colony Britain might lose control of the corridor running between Cape Colony and Rhodesia. Cecil Rhodes had once described this as 'the Suez Canal of the trade' of the Cape.[24]

Britain saw two options. One was to absorb Bechuanaland within the Cape Colony; the other to declare it a British protectorate. In 1885 she decided on compromise when, with the agreement of native rulers, she agreed to Southern Bechuanaland being absorbed into the Cape while Northern Bechuanaland became a British protectorate.[25] In 1910 when the Union of South Africa was formed this protectorate did not join it and the British then rather neglected it until the 1930s. Little economic development occurred before the 1950s and the territory's economic mainstay was its provision of migrant labour to South Africa and limited cattle rearing.

Against such a background any co-operative development is somewhat surprising. Yet Bechuanaland's first co-operative proclamation was issued as early as 1910. Because it was a protectorate the territory's laws, including those applying to co-operatives, were issued as proclamations of the high-commissioner rather than as Acts passed by a legislative assembly. Thus it differed markedly from the Union of South Africa which achieved dominion status in 1910 and Rhodesia which remained a colony but with greater administrative powers than those in Bechuanaland.

Bechuanaland's first co-operative proclamation[26] is therefore a strange document in that it appears to anticipate agricultural development in an economy within which there was little overall development. Clearly, though, possibilities had been identified inasmuch as the proclamation paves the way for co-operative activities in marketing, manufacturing, irrigation, insurance and joint purchasing. All were within agriculture.

We have seen that there was little homogeneity in Southern Africa. Parts of the region were still being settled while competition for territory occurred in others and their status evolved or changed. There were also different government forms ranging from a self-governing dominion to a protectorate. Consequently, legislation applying to co-operatives was passed in various ways. That process was less important than the content of co-operative laws which we should now consider.

CO-OPERATIVE LEGISLATION IN SOUTHERN AFRICA

The region's constitutional diversity has been noted but needs to be emphasised because of its effect on co-operative legislation. In terms of status and development the most important was the Union of South Africa formed in 1910. It comprised the former self-governing colonies of Cape Colony and Natal and the Boer Republics of the Transvaal and the Orange Free State: the last two had achieved self-government in 1907 following the Boer War. As a dominion within the British Empire the Union of South Africa was self-governing and could pass its own legislation, including that applying to co-operatives. The British sovereign remained head of state and was represented in South Africa by a governor-general.

Rhodesia remained a colony with a colonial administration that was ultimately responsible to the Colonial Office in London and the Westminster Parliament. It later divided between Northern and Southern Rhodesia, the former becoming Zambia and the latter Zimbabwe. Neither achieved independence before the end of this study.

Mandated territories and protectorates comprised the lowest form of constitutional entity. Bechuanaland was a protectorate and its Acts were therefore issued by the high- commissioner as proclamations.

Before the Union of South Africa was formed some co-operative legislation had already been passed in its constituent territories. Examples include the Agricultural Co-operative Acts passed in the Transvaal and the Orange Free State in 1908 and 1910 respectively.[27] Specific Co-operative Acts had not been passed in Natal or Cape Colony but the Agricultural Development Acts which had been passed included provisions for co-operatives. For example that passed in Natal in 1904 had allowed government loans to be paid to farmers forming co-operatives. However, there was little take-up and co-operatives did not really begin until some years later, 'when a number of Joint Stock Companies with co-operative principles were formed under the Companies Act'.[28] These formed mainly in the dairy industry where the creation of a number of creamery companies subsequently spearheaded a strong dairy industry.

A similar process occurred in Cape Colony when an Act passed in 1905 allowed co-operatives to form as joint stock companies with co-operative features grafted on and registered under the Cape Companies Act.

These pseudo co-operatives ran into various difficulties. 'Little or no supervision was exercised by Government . . . and errors in management and organization after some years brought about virtual insolvency'.[29] At other times capital expenditure proved too high in relation to turnover, and shareholders sometimes paid themselves higher prices for their produce than trading returns justified. We can therefore conclude that the disciplines of Rochdale co-operation and the hard-headed business attitudes of British consumer co-operatives in the late 1800s were missing.

Although it takes us beyond the period of 1900 to 1918 which forms the first part of this study it is worth noting that in 1922 a comprehensive Co-operative Act was passed for the Union of South Africa. It subsumed earlier Acts and applied to other forms of co-operative as well as agricultural societies. The Act allowed for co-operatives' liability to be limited or unlimited.[30] It also contained elements of compulsion which ran counter to the voluntary tradition of Rochdale co-operation.

> Provision for the compulsory supply of produce is made in the model rules, also for pooling and pool payments. The Act also provides for fines to be imposed on members who fail to sell produce through the society.[31]

An Amending Act of 1925 reinforced these provisions:

> When the Minister is satisfied that in any district 75 per cent of the producers, producing 75 per cent of the local output of any kind of

> agricultural produce, are members of a co-operative society, he may give notice that in future all producers in the district shall market their goods through the society, whether they are members or not. Non-members coming under this regulation are then bound by the rules of the society, but may apply to have their produce inspected and graded by a Government officer at the expense of the society.[32]

Market disciplines were replacing personal disciplines that featured so prominently in co-operative traditions in the mother country where compulsory co-operation was not readily countenanced. The above provisions limited the freedom of potential co-operative members to decide in their best interests the activities they should undertake through collective and voluntary action, accepting in the process personal disciplines and democratic control. Already in the early years of the twentieth century Southern African co-operatives were departing from European co-operative traditions.

However, one lesson that the region took from the mother country was its effective use of secondary or federal societies. In Britain the two most notable examples were the English and Welsh Co-operative Wholesale Society and its Scottish counterpart. The 1922 Act in South Africa, and its Amending Act of 1925, went further by permitting the formation of co-operative federations extending beyond territorial boundaries. Thus, 'Co-operative companies in North and South Rhodesia, Bechuanaland and South West Africa may be members of the Union of South Africa Federal Co-operative bodies.'[33]

Today, in Europe, we still struggle with the legal problems thrown up by the formation of trans-national co-operative societies. Yet, against a background of constitutional and developmental flux, a cross-border co-operative body became possible in Southern Africa far earlier. The Union of South Africa Federal Co-operatives went on to include co-operatives in South West Africa after it became a British mandated territory following the First World War. Its co-operative legislation dated 'from the period of German possession'. In 1922, however, it 'was recast on the lines of the Union of South Africa'.[34]

Co-operatives in Bechuanaland were also able to join the Union of South Africa Federal Co-operatives. By 1922 its proclamation of 1910 remained its only piece of co-operative legislation probably because little economic development occurred in the territory. Limited to agriculture it did not extend to other types of co-operative but decreed that 'The word "co-operative" is compulsory but not protected. Liability is unlimited. Members must be farmers; each Member has one vote only.'[35]

In Rhodesia adherence to 'one member one vote' also weakened. Co-operatives were placed firmly under Companies Acts. In Southern Rhodesia a series of ordinances and an Agricultural Co-operative Act of 1925 applied only to agricultural co-operatives, whereas in Northern Rhodesia in the same year a General Co-operative Act was passed 'without special agricultural application'.[36]

Earlier we noted that Earl Grey had sought the advice of the Co-operative Union in Manchester on what type of co-operative legislation might be suitable in Rhodesia. He died in 1917. Had he lived he is likely to have been aghast at the type of legislation which was passed in Southern Rhodesia. We should recall that the territory's economy was heavily dependent on agriculture in which large-scale white settler farmers predominated. Their departure from the co-operative principles, which so strongly imbued legislation in the mother country and had been internationalised through the rules of the ICA, is perhaps therefore not surprising. Besides providing for the 'compulsory supply of produce' and 'for fines to be imposed on members who fail to sell produce through the society', subsequent Rhodesian legislation also allowed for members' share capital to be subscribed 'progressively in proportion to their business' with members' votes being linked to the number of shares held.[37] The co-operative principle of 'one member one vote' irrespective of share capital held was thus broken.

CONCLUSIONS

We have tried to trace the emergence of co-operatives in Southern Africa between 1900 and 1918 as a *regional* development. They were influenced by imperial relations in the region quite as much as they were by economic developments. The latter included the need to attract white settler farmers in Rhodesia and to reduce food and other imports in parts of what would become the Union of South Africa.

People joined co-operatives in Southern Africa for quite different reasons from those doing so in the UK. Such people were also vastly different from the working classes who formed the bed-rock of the British Consumer Co-operative movement. While economic imperatives shaped British co-operation, the ideological influences of Robert Owen, Dr William King and the Christian Socialists remained a powerful motivating force. These ideological influences were weaker in Southern Africa but economic imperatives far stronger. Nevertheless the seeds of collective economic action had been sown.

8. Early Co-operative Development in the Dominions

INTRODUCTION

Despite growing co-operative diversity British co-operatives and those elsewhere within the British Empire had a symbiotic relationship fostered by the imperial trading system. Governments were involved with co-operatives to varying degrees. Those in Australia, New Zealand and Canada wanted to improve and sustain their agricultural sectors because of their importance to their export markets. By the early 1900s these countries were virtually self-governing, their ties with the Crown and Westminster ensured under constitutional legislation and the Crown represented through their governor-generals. Consequently, the governments of these dominions were in pretty full control of their economies and the agricultural sectors within them. They were also free to take on the direction and guidance of their indigenous co-operatives.

An over-riding consideration, however, was ensuring the success of national export markets, particularly those operating within the imperial free trade system. Central to this was Britain's free trade system which had superseded its eighteenth-century mercantilism. It had been shaped by the theories of Adam Smith (1723–1790) who had argued that if restrictions such as protective tariffs were removed greater international trade would result and a more productive division of labour encouraged. A free trade system would also generate stronger incentives to exploit different geographical regions' natural advantages.

Such arguments propelled Britain towards the adoption of free trade policies. By the mid-1800s she had repealed most of her protective tariffs including, most significantly, her Corn Laws. The results included cheaper imports of wheat and other staples, which helped feed Britain's rapidly increasing population, particularly that in her industrial towns. The consequential decline of British agriculture was acceptable because

Britain was rapidly becoming 'the workshop of the world'. Her industrialisation before other nations and her rapid imperial expansion in the second half of the nineteenth century meant that she had a lead start in buying raw materials in the cheapest world markets and selling her manufactures in the most expensive. We have seen that this process had a disastrous effect on India's indigenous textile manufacturers.

British consumers, including the working classes who were the mainstay of the British Consumer Co-operative movement, benefited from such arrangements, particularly cheap food imports. Aided by the development of steam ships, refrigeration and bulk-buying techniques, quickly perishable goods could now be transported vast distances and were cheaper than those produced by British agriculture. Many of these goods came from the Empire, particularly from the dominions.

Both the British Consumer Co-operative movement and the International Co-operative Alliance (ICA) favoured free trade. They strongly opposed protectionism.[1] The ICA's concern with international trade can be judged from the fact that nineteen out of its first twenty-four congresses (1895–1969) debated aspects of it.[2] Such concern is likely to have been shaped by the fact that large-scale mass-membership consumer co-operative movements predominated in the Alliance at that time. Found mostly in Western and Northern Europe many of these had established co-operative wholesale societies which had entered into world trade markets.

Import issues were often raised in Britain at annual co-operative congresses. Duties on staple foodstuffs such as sugar[3] and wheat in particular were opposed.[4] Between congresses, the British movement's apex organisation, the Co-operative Union, appointed representatives to the Empire Marketing Boards set up by the British government's Imperial Economic Committee. The Co-operative Union reported to one congress on their work:

> We may say that in the main the evidence of the Imperial Economic Committee has been in harmony with the views expressed in our evidence to the committee on behalf of the Movement, viz., that any development of the market in this country for the products of our overseas Dominions can best be obtained by organising the voluntary preference of the consumer rather than by the means of food taxation for the purpose of giving Empire preference.[5]

Such statements indicate the British consumer co-operatives' ease within the imperial trading system; also the primacy they attached to the consumer. This recalls the movement's adoption of the consumer theory of co-operation rather than that of producer co-operation. Echoes of this debate surfaced elsewhere in the Empire but the issues raised were not as quite clear cut as they had been in Britain in the late nineteenth century. One reason was that primary production – agriculture, horticulture, fishing and their ancillary services – was more significant in the economies of British dominions and colonies than their industrial output.

As we have seen, the two British Co-operative Wholesale Societies (CWS) soon took advantage of the opportunities offered. As noted previously, they extended their vertical integration by establishing import depots at Britain's main ports and trading agencies overseas. Many of the latter were within the Empire.

Such developments undoubtedly assisted the overall expansion of the British Consumer Co-operative movement. They also helped solve an enviable problem. The movement constituted a tight self-supporting system. Its trading surpluses were re-employed within it and were not reinvested to any great extent in private capital markets. The expansion of the two Wholesale Societies into manufacturing had been made for a number of reasons including the need to ensure supplies. However, a consequence was the accumulation of 'too much capital'.[6] Investing in the Manchester Ship Canal and increasing their volume of imports therefore made good commercial sense. The question of whether such trade should be with colonial or dominion co-operative producers seems hardly to have been raised by British retail co-operators. Consequently, their Wholesales were free to trade with them or set up in competition as the CWS had done previously with the Irish co-operative creameries.[7] Both occurred.

The development of the Wholesales' foreign trade underlines how quickly they had advanced from their establishment in the 1860s. By the late nineteenth and early twentieth centuries their leaders were becoming a new élite that, unusual for Britain at that time was working-class. Its privileges included foreign travel. Records show that board members of the CWS and SCWS travelled not only in Britain but also overseas where they inspected foreign trading depots, made links with local producers and initiated deals. Examples can be seen as we consider co-operative developments within the dominions.

AUSTRALIA

Under the Australian Commonwealth Constitution Act of 1900 a federal form of government was adopted, which meant that the legislative and taxation frameworks of co-operatives would be determined by states rather than by the federal government. A consequence of this and also of Australia's geographical size and diversity was that a national co-operative identity would be slow to emerge. Australia's land mass was almost the same as that of the USA but its population was far smaller. In the early 1900s it was still less than 5 million. However, earlier settlements were now being boosted by voluntary British immigrants, some of whom had been co-operative members back home. As Gary Lewis, the Australian co-operative historian was to observe, however, the Rochdale model of co-operation proved difficult to establish and it would remain a 'weak co-operative transplant' in Australia.[8]

One reason for this was that Australia was regional, and crops could be grown in only a relatively small part: a long, narrow coastal belt which seldom stretched inland more than 300 or 400 miles. Moreover, it was divided between Western Australia and Southern Australia by semi-desert. The coastal area of tropical Queensland, New South Wales, Victoria and South Australia supported agriculture, fruit growing and dairying but further inland where the land was drier wheat was the staple crop. In the hinterland beyond only cattle and sheep farms were viable.

From this it can be seen that Australia's agricultural sector was very important within her overall economy. However, her small domestic market meant that she was heavily dependent on exports. To help boost these Australia established a number of marketing boards to ensure quantities, consistent quality and standardisation. This may have inhibited co-operative growth because to some extent they duplicated their functions. Some producers therefore questioned whether they needed to be in both types of organisation.

Australian co-operatives proved, however, to be independent, spontaneous and voluntary initiatives, forming in response to needs. The first known society was the Australian Mutual Provident Society of New South Wales which was set up by five men in 1849.[9] Another formed in Brisbane ten years later.[10] The collapse of the gold mining boom in the 1860s resulted in more co-operatives including the Adelaide Co-operative Society in South Australia, established in 1866.

Co-operative creameries were the first to form successfully in the agricultural sector. In New South Wales, Victoria and South Australia, however, they were initially registered under Companies' Acts. Co-operatives handling dried fruits were also established in these states and in Victoria co-operative bacon factories and meat freezing plants were set up along with societies handling eggs, onions, live pigs and other commodities. Co-operative insurance companies were also established in the three southern states and Queensland together with a few dairies and a poultry farmers' co-operative. As in Britain some of these societies advanced sufficiently to set up secondary co-operative bodies to perform specialist functions.[11]

Consumer societies were slower to emerge. As in New South Wales they were possibly hindered by inappropriate legislation and a lack of clear identity, particularly in relation to Australia's growing labour movement. Such difficulties were thought to have stemmed from 'ideological uncertainty' which:

> clouded the concept of co-operation: co-operators could not agree on its definition; unhelpful legislation tolerated 'bogus' co-operation; Christian Socialists, worker advocates and middle-class reformers evinced a confused and confusing array of co-operative visions, muddling co-operators and co-partnership . . . positing co-operation as an antidote to the strike weapon and mirroring the same free-trade protectionist dichotomy present in the broader community.
>
> What was the Labour Movement to make of this confused picture of a movement simultaneously affirming the transformation of society, the retention of existing class relations and the blunting of the strike weapon?[12]

Such a situation contrasted sharply with the British Consumer Co-operative movement whose mass membership and ideology justified its being termed a 'movement'. By contrast Australian co-operatives failed on both points: neither could they cohere around a clear ideology nor could they achieve a critical mass.

Links with British co-operation were maintained through immigrants with previous co-operative membership and relations with the English and Welsh CWS. The latter took a step forward in 1896 when, as part of its push for colonial trade, the Wholesale sent a three-man delegation to Australia. Its members were Ben Jones, Joseph Clay and William Stokes.[13] Ben Jones (1848–1947) was prominent in the British Co-operative movement and held various positions within it. As far as this trip was concerned the most significant of these was that he was manager of the CWS branch in London.[14] Joseph Clay (1827–1901) was a founding member and later president of the Gloucester retail society. He was elected to the board of the London branch of CWS and its chairman for nine years.[15] Details of a William Stokes have not been found but there may have been some misreporting. The third member may have been a William Stoker (1835–1902) elected to the CWS board in 1893.[16]

It is likely to have been significant that two members of the delegation were from the London branch of the CWS, which oversaw co-operative imports arriving at the port of London. The importance of the visit to the CWS is underlined by the fact that the only way to Australia in 1896 was by a lengthy steamship voyage. On arrival the delegation described their mission in rather flowery language. It was to further

> joyful marriage of Labour and Capital [through] the humane and god-like principles of co-operation . . . [to] spread the word [of] co-operation; a religious message to help put into practical operation through co-operation in every sphere of life the precepts of Christianity; a political message to develop ties to the colony and to foster exports to assist the working man of Britain.[17]

One significant point was that despite their according more importance to consumer rather than producer co-operation British co-operators still aspired to a close relationship between labour and capital; also that in line with co-operative thinking back home the delegation firmly linked co-operation with Christianity. However, there was little disguising the fact that the delegation's main aim was to develop ties with the 'colony' so as to 'assist the working man of Britain'!

By all accounts the three-man team were fêted in Australia. They were met by a 'cheering citizen's committee' and the New South Wales premier and they addressed town hall meetings. One report suggested that they were 'stirring colonial society to its foundations'.

The trip had resulted from an earlier approach by two Australian co-operators who sought closer links with the CWS. One was W. J. 'Billy' Nuttall (1835–1905) who had been a British co-operative leader before immigrating to Australia in 1883.[18] He had served as CWS 'cashier' and his assistant, Ben Jones, succeeded him.[19] Nuttall and Jones were therefore well-known to each other. Before agreeing to the visit the Wholesale had asked Nuttall and his Australian colleagues to tour New South Wales and Victoria to spread the message of 'co-operation with the old country'.[20] When doing so they told farmers that:

> they could benefit from a shortfall in CWS requirements for dairy products, then accounting for one-seventh of all British dairy consumption. They could do this by exploiting the 'co-operative barter system', a free-trade system of consignments direct to Manchester via the recently completed Manchester Canal, by-passing London markets where Australian produce generally presented poorly. By directly indenting CWS goods, farmers could

> avoid exchange-rate disadvantages affecting the Australian currency. Mississippi wheat growers had 'co-operated' in this way with British consumers . . . in exchange for CWS manufactures, including woollens, cotton goods, needles, nails, watches, jewellery, cutlery, locks, machinery, hardware, tinware, glassware, pianos, boots, shoes, leather goods, and other products.

The reference underlines the significance of the Manchester Canal to the CWS. Interesting also is the list of goods that the CWS could supply in a proposed 'co-operative barter system', which indicates the extent and nature of CWS production at that time. Nuttall's approach to the CWS was backed by the Victoria government who also sent a representative to Britain to investigate possibilities in greater depth. It has been speculated that he could have been 'the Australian delegate present at the formation of the International Co-operative Alliance in 1895'. Elsewhere he has been referred to as the 'Special Commission in the United Kingdom who kept colonial primary producers informed on market conditions and CWS requirements'.[21]

The ground had thus been well laid for the visit of the CWS's delegation which arrived in July 1896 to tour the 'eastern colonies'; it met both government and co-operative organisations. Amusingly, at a public meeting where one of the CWS representatives claimed that the CWS had 'too much capital' someone from the floor shouted back, 'Send it here!'.

On other occasions there were efforts to bridge the gap between the interests of producers and consumers. One of the CWS representatives stated:

> We started in England from the consumers' point of view, but from the producers' point of view in the colonies. The result will be the same, for all workers are ultimately consumers.[22]

In his historical study of consumer co-operation in New South Wales Gary Lewis suggests that:

> The terminology [of the CWS representatives] was deliberately vague: 'consumers', 'producers' and workers were employed as synonyms. Secondary workers in the audience might have reasonably concluded from this that they were 'producers' which indeed they were, but the CWS visitors meant 'primary' producers.[23]

During their visit the CWS representatives paid far more attention to Australia's primary producers than they did to her consumer co-operatives.

They spent much time investigating possible sources of various types of Australian produce[24] but far less on whether these might form the basis of independent agricultural co-operatives.

Lewis asserts:

> Apparently the visitors were wholly concerned with cementing links to Australian primary producers . . . Manchester's encouragement of rural co-operation and opposition to indigenous production co-operation which might compete against its own exports was an important reason for the retardation of co-operation in Australia.[25]

Elsewhere he concluded that they were:

> indifferent to colonial urban brethren [and] chary of indigenous production co-operation which might cut across its trading plans.[26]

This judgement appears harsh. If it is accepted, and with previous examples of the CWS's adverse influence on indigenous Irish creameries in mind it seems reasonable that it should be, then British co-operative influence on its Australian counterparts was not as benign as might have been wished or expected. It could then have been another sad example of the clash between two competing systems of co-operation, the consumer and the producer. It also represented a co-operative form of imperialism in which the more powerful consumer co-operators of Britain placed their trading concerns above those of colonial co-operative producers.

There were further visits by CWS representatives but outcomes changed little. A visit in 1926–7 illustrated this: 'Wherever the tourists went . . . the perennial question of local co-operative manufacture and the impact of this on CWS imports was raised: it was an issue that would never go away.'[27]

NEW ZEALAND

Co-operative development in New Zealand was less problematic than that in Australia perhaps because less was demanded of it ideologically. This was particularly so among agricultural co-operatives where pragmatism was a strong feature shaped by a number of factors, including the country's low population. By the early 1900s this was just over 1 million accommodated in an area slightly larger than Britain. Ten years or so later 54 per cent of that population lived in towns despite the fact that the country had little industry. It was sustained 'by means of extremely efficient agriculture, specializing in livestock and dairy products'.[28] That in turn depended for its success on the maintenance of export markets.

The first recorded co-operative in New Zealand was the New Zealand Farmers' Cooperative Association formed in 1881, followed in 1895 by the National Dairy Association New Zealand. These took their place in an agricultural sector heavily geared towards exports and one in which there were close relations with the New Zealand government. Crop marketing boards were a feature, and sat more comfortably alongside New Zealand co-operatives than those in Australia. A more distinctive New Zealand feature was the question of land rights,[29] over which there could be friction with the Maoris.

It has been suggested that New Zealand agricultural co-operatives' ease within the national set-up owed something to the Danish system which had incorporated co-operatives and adult education within its agricultural advances: 'As in the case of Denmark, there is abundant evidence that effective organisation, on the right principles and for proper objects, have been the key to the markets of the world for the New Zealand farmer.'[30]

New Zealand's co-operatives were possibly helped by their relative homogeneity of production within a compact land mass, assisting the formation in 1933 of a national federation, the New Zealand Co-operative Alliance. By forming their own Overseas Farmers' Cooperative Federation which was based in London, they also avoided the troubled relations their Australian counterparts experienced with the English and Welsh Co-operative Wholesale Society.[31]

New Zealand agricultural societies exhibited two important characteristics of other successful co-operative movements. One was the capacity successfully to establish secondary societies to perform specialist functions. The other was to merge to form larger co-operative units, for example the amalgamation of dairy factories into the New Zealand Co-operative Dairy Company which then controlled '59 factories and creameries scattered at intervals over a territory of 159 miles in length by 60 miles in width and catering for 8,000 suppliers'.[32]

The objectives of this amalgamation, which were likely to have applied to others in New Zealand's dairy industry were:

> to effect improvements in (1) manufacture; (2) quality; and (3) marketing power. Reductions in manufacturing costs were also secured by (1) cartage routes being properly organized and avoiding duplication; (2) each factory being organized to handle the supply

> most conveniently situated to it; (3) bulk buying of factory requisites being introduced.[33]

New Zealand's agricultural co-operatives seem to have been more concerned with practical issues than ideological ones. As a result they were not divided to the same extent as were their Australian counterparts by uncertainties of identity or relations with a wider labour movement. From a co-operative organisational point of view they were as much at home in company as in co-operative legislation, this despite ambiguities that might arise over voting rights and capitalisation.

In this connection Margaret Digby observed that:

> Various Acts exist relating to different types of associations – friendly societies, incorporated societies, agricultural and pastoral societies. Agricultural co-operative societies, however, are, it would appear invariably incorporated under Companies Acts of 1882 and 1908 (with amendments). Dairy Societies are frequently, but not always, also registered under the Dairy Industry Act, 1908, which consolidated the earlier Co-operative Dairy Companies Act. In the Act of 1908, a section is devoted to Co-operative Dairy Companies, but its provisions relate simply to the right of companies registered under it to require the surrender of shares, and to re-issue them, also to their exemption from certain sections of the Companies Act. The Articles of Association of New Zealand Co-operative Societies usually contain provisions as to the *maximum number of votes per member* [my italics] etc. which define their co-operative character, but these provisions do not appear to be statutory.[34]

This is a clear departure from the Rochdale co-operative principle of one member one vote irrespective of the number of shares held. New Zealand legislation also provided for the formation of rural credit associations with a minimum of ten members. Again they seem to point to some departure from co-operative orthodoxy as members, 'might also borrow from other sources', and accept 'joint and several liability with certain possibilities of exception'. Loans were at 'fixed rates of interest and for approved objects, usually on personal security but occasionally on mortgage or similar security'.[35]

Some of New Zealand's co-operatives were undoubtedly hybrid but they seemed to have worked and to have met the needs of their members.

CANADA

Between 1904 and 1911 the fourth Earl Grey was governor-general of Canada. He was therefore the personal representative of the king emperor and the link between Westminster and the virtually self-governing dominion of Canada. Within the imperial hierarchy, particularly between high-commissioners, governors and governor-generals, Grey ranked high. His Canadian position was far higher than that of administrator of Rhodesia, which he had held previously.

For all his high standing, and perhaps because of it, Grey could at times take an independent position. We saw this in Southern Africa where he warned Joseph Chamberlain, colonial secretary, of moves that would lead to the abortive and greatly damaging Jameson Raid in 1895.[36] He was also prepared to take an independent line in Canada in 1911 in connection with the Coronation Honours List of King George V. Grey wrote opposing an honour for Max Aitken (1879–1964) later Lord Beaverbrook, proprietor of the *Express* papers. Writing to Lewis Harcourt, secretary of state for the colonies, Grey said:

> As it is well known throughout Canada that the Crown in the exercise of its prerogative of Honour generally acts upon the recommendation of the Governor General, I venture to suggest that in justice to the Governor General, as well as in the interest of the Crown, he should be consulted before His Majesty's Government submits to the King a recommendation that Honour should be conferred upon a Canadian.
>
> Had His Majesty's Government done me the honour to consult me with regard to the suggestion that Mr. Max Aitken should be knighted, my advice would have been strongly opposed to its adoption. Sir Max Aitken may have rendered in the United Kingdom services to the Crown of a character which entitles him to be the recipient of special favours from the Crown. But I am not aware of any circumstances in the Canadian life of Sir Max Aitken which would justify the bestowal upon him of any honour. All that is known of Sir Max Aitken in Canada is that he is a young man of about 30 who has suddenly acquired enormous wealth by successful company promotions. The fact that he was recently well blackballed for St. James's Club of Montreal, and his candidature withdrawn from the Mount Royal Club, the two leading Clubs of Montreal, may be accepted as an indication of the opinion in which he is held by many of his fellow citizens.

> I have endeavoured, during seven years of hard work, to create an impression in Canada that disinterested devotion to the public service was more valued and appreciated by the Crown than the rapid acquisition of wealth; and I cannot refrain from giving expression to my regret that an Honour should have been conferred, the result of which must be to diminish that impression, and also to lessen greatly the value which has hitherto been attached to any mark of the Sovereign's approval.[37]

Such comments reflect Grey's personal values as well as his high imperial position. No doubt because of the former and despite the latter, Grey became very much involved in Canadian co-operative development while governor-general. At a personal level he became a member of the Caisse Populaire de Levis,[38] and maintained numerous co-operative contacts, while at a more official level he gave evidence to a federal special committee considering evidence in connection with the proposed Industrial and Co-operative Societies Act. Indeed, as we shall show shortly, Grey may well have been active in moves to initiate the Bill. While evidence is not conclusive, it could suggest that Grey was exceeding the constitutional powers of the sovereign he represented. In Walter Bagehot's famous words he had only the 'the right to be consulted, the right to encourage, the right to warn'.

Let us note Canada's position at the time Grey arrived. He was conscious of her swift overall development particularly that towards the Pacific. In 1910 he wrote to Sir Horace Plunkett: 'When I reflect that this rich West was, at the time I was at Cambridge, only known to the explorer and the fur-trader, the development is indeed astonishing.'[39]

By 1900 Canada was the world's third largest political entity, behind Russia and China,[40] but it lacked population. In 1861 this was just over 3 million. Later it was augmented by European immigrants, although in the late 1800s this was offset to some extent by migration to the adjacent and increasingly affluent America. Canada needed more immigrants to support her push into the prairies and on to the Pacific. As in Australia and New Zealand some of her new immigrants had been members of co-operatives back home: this was to become a favourable factor in subsequent co-operative development.

Like Australia, Canada had diverse geographical settings. In the West the fertile valleys of British Columbia supported the growing and marketing of fruit and dairying and lumbering. The prairies became vast wheat-growing areas while the eastern Maritime Provinces proved suitable for small-scale farming, fishing and lumbering. Provinces were sometimes divided by physical barriers such as the Rocky Mountains and a stretch of some 800 miles in Northern Ontario comprising rock and moraine: both discouraged settlement. Other less tangible barriers existed, such as those of language and religion between Southern Ontario and Quebec.

However, Canadian co-operatives took root more easily than perhaps their Australian counterparts had done. Margaret Digby even suggested some competition when she wrote of 'one province after another . . . taking up the leadership, devising its own form of co-operative enterprise and ultimately influencing and enriching the achievement of others'.[41]

Canada's first recorded co-operative formed in 1852 in Nova Scotia as an insurance society against fire.[42] In the 1860s a number of co-operative stores were set up by miners who had possibly brought this idea from the 'mining villages of Britain, probably of Scotland'. Co-operatives also emerged in agriculture and sprang from earlier collective activities that had grown naturally 'in a hard country and an exacting climate, far from sources of supply and reserves of labour'.[43] Such community activities included 'barn raisings' and 'threshing bees'. There were also 'beef rings' in the prairies, through which fresh meat was supplied to a circle of farmers before they had refrigeration or cold storage facilities. Co-operatives seemed a natural stepping stone from such collective activities.

Another important factor assisting their development was that of helpful legislation. W. B. Francis in his book *Canadian Co-operative Law* noted that while informal co-operatives had existed since 'the earliest stages of agricultural development' in Canada, they had been 'unincorporated' which meant that there had been 'little organized co-operation in Canada for purchasing or marketing . . . before 1860'. Legislation in 1865, influenced by Britain's Friendly Societies Act of 1846 and her first Industrial and Provident Societies Act of 1852, led to an increasing number of formal societies becoming 'incorporated'.[44]

The purpose of the proposed Act was to:

> authorize the formation of companies of co-operative associations for the purpose of carrying on, in common, any trade or business . . . [by] raising voluntary subscriptions of the members thereof, a fund to enable them, as such societies, to carry on or exercise in common any labour, trade or business, or several labours, trades or businesses, except the working of mines, minerals or quarries, and except also the business of banking and insurance.[45]

In the grand Rochdale tradition the 1865 Act also prohibited credit trading. It is suggested that it prompted subsequent legislation favourable to co-operatives at provincial levels and helped to swell growing support for co-operatives in 'Legislatures, Departments of Agriculture and Universities'.[46] Co-operatives began to appear in growing numbers and in Western Canada included the Grain Growers Grain Company, established in 1906. It was followed four years later by the Saskatchewan Co-operative Elevator Company which encouraged the setting-up of similar organisations in Alberta. In 1906 a retail society, the British Canadian Co-operative Society was registered and about the same time fruit marketing societies were formed in British Columbia and Nova Scotia. Among such developments there were also secondary societies. Notable among these were the United Farmers Co-operative Company of Ontario in 1914 and the Cooperative Federee de Quebec in 1921.[47] In Quebec the Desjardins credit union movement began in 1900 with the formation of Le Caisse Populaire de Levis. It gave rise to a major co-operative movement which will be described in greater detail later.

Help from federal and provincial governments went to co-operatives in the agricultural and horticultural sectors. Examples included the Federal Government's subsidy through its Dominion Seed Branch to the Seed Growers' Association of up to $Canadian 10,000, and its channelling of up to $Canadian 300,000 through the provinces for 'buying suitable seed cleaning machinery for co-operative cleaning'.[48] The Federal Live Stock Branch also assisted 'co-operative shipments of live stock, particularly lambs and hogs, from the Maritime Provinces to the Boston and Montreal markets'. Through provincial governments the federal government also provided:

> market intelligence to the various local associations, advising them as to the quality and finish of stock and assisting in local arrangements for locating and shipping . . . It has been their policy to stimulate local buying as much as possible, at the same time facilitating outside competition to the greatest possible degree and in this way they have been able to net co-operative shippers full market value for the stock which has been offered for sale through this channel.[49]

Provincial governments worked with agricultural and horticultural co-operatives through their agricultural departments. The Saskatchewan government was particularly strong in its support and formed a co-operative branch in the 1920s. In the 1940s it set up Canada's first specialist Department of Co-operatives.[50]

Such help was designed to assist primary producers to supply national and international markets. Co-operatives in the service sector were not similarly helped and they remained dependent on self-help. An attempt to redress this imbalance was made with the proposal in 1907 for 'Bill No. 2, An Act Respecting Industrial and Co-operative Societies' which came before the Federal House of Commons. Its title reflects its main thrust towards co-operatives in industrial rather than rural settings.

Although it was not passed its failure is worth noting for two reasons. First of all it reflected a degree of opposition to service sector co-operatives that could be mobilised by private traders, showing the degree of political influence they could wield. Secondly, the Bill's failure meant that co-operatives in Canada's cities and urban areas would have to rely on their own resources. In sectors like thrift and credit where a simple business form easily took root, or in situations where strikes provided motivation for the setting-up of retail societies, initiatives could be sustained particularly where other favourable factors also existed. These might include their being linked to adult education programmes or propagating agents such as the Catholic clergy operating alongside them. In such circumstances viable co-operative developments could occur without the kinds of government support available to agricultural or horticultural co-operatives.

Although the Bill failed evidence submitted to its Special Committee is of considerable interest. Eleven witnesses gave evidence between December 1906 and April 1907, including: 'His Excellency the Governor General', 'A. Desjardins', 'King, W. L. Mackenzie, C. M. G.' and 'Trowern, E. M'. The governor-general was, of course, Earl Grey. Desjardins was Alphonse Desjardins (1854–1920) who founded the Caisse Populaire de Levis in 1900. King, W. L. Mackenzie, CMG, was better known as W. L. Mackenzie King (1874–1950). At the time of the Special Committee he was a career civil servant and Ontario's deputy minister of labour. He later became Liberal leader and three times Canada's prime minister. These three spoke in favour of the proposed Bill and presented considerable evidence in support of it. E. M. Trowern was the dominion secretary of the Retail Merchants' Association of Canada. His Association strongly opposed the Bill.

It is possible that the idea of the Bill arose from exchanges between Desjardins and Grey shortly after Grey arrived in Canada in 1904. Grey sought Henry Wolff's views on Desjardins and later his support for the proposed Bill. At that time Wolff was still chairman of the Executive Committee of the ICA and Earl Grey the Alliance's president. Through these positions both had ready access to information about co-operative developments elsewhere.

In early 1905 Grey wrote to Wolff from Ottawa:

> I have had an interesting talk with Mr. Alphonse Desjardins. He impressed me favourably. They tell me he is a man of one idea; an enthusiast who bores people by endeavouring to enthuse them with his convictions on a subject to which they are profoundly indifferent.
>
> I am in hopes that we may be able to do something here. I have given your letter to Mr. Lemieux, the Solicitor General, and he has had a three hours talk with Desjardins and one or two talks with me. I have asked Mr. Mackenzie King in the Labour Department, to go down to Quebec to inspect Desjardins bank at Levis and write a report upon it in his Labour Gazette. He will probably make use of his opportunity to write a full description of the workings of the Raiffeisen and Schultz de litz Banks.
>
> When the House of Commons here, which is very ignorant upon the subject of Co-operative Banks, has been partially educated by this article in the Labour Gazette, I hope Mr. Bourassa, a French member, will bring the subject before the House.[51]

A little over a month later Mackenzie King had completed the proposed article and Grey sent 'an advance proof' to Wolff.[52] A 'R. Lemieux' chaired the Special Committee and it is perhaps too easy to suppose that he could have been the 'Mr. Lemieux, the Solicitor General' to whom Grey referred in his letter to Wolff. Such developments point to Grey orchestrating behind-the-scenes moves, a view that is buttressed to some extent by the complementary evidence given by Grey, Desjardins and Mackenzie King to the Special Committee. This was appointed by the federal parliament prior to its formal consideration of the Bill.

In his evidence Grey stressed that he was not speaking as the governor-general but as the president of the ICA. He briefly described its aims and objectives, and continued:

> I do not propose to refer to the provisions of the Bill which is the subject of your consideration. The possibility that they contain matters which may prove to be of a controversial character, make it undesirable that I should do so, but having been informed that under the existing law in Canada co-operative associations of workingmen have no legal status, I have come here in order to state that I am heartily in sympathy with the object of the Bill now before parliament, which I understand is to give co-operative associations of workingmen that legal status which is now wanting, and which it is most desirable should be secured in order to help workingmen in their endeavours to help themselves.[53]

A considerable part of Grey's evidence focused on the work of the Caisse Populaire. Grey said:

> I have no hesitation in saying that if a new Act is required to facilitate the multiplication of banks like that which Monsieur Desjardins to his great credit, has established, the sooner the Act is passed the better.[54]

Grey cited ways he felt that the Caisse Populaire and institutions like it could help many Canadians, including farmers. He went on to compare it with similar bodies in Europe, Ireland and India adding:

> A joint stock bank as a rule will not lend to an individual who has no security but his character to offer, but when a group of men known to be honest and thrifty and of good character, give their collective guarantee for the repayment of an advance, then experience has proved conclusively that a security is provided on which a bank can safely lend. The character of this security is shown by the fact that on the advances made to 2,169 Raiffeisen banks not a single cent has been lost.[55]

Grey submitted[56] a long contribution from Henry Wolff, whom he introduced as the 'author of "Peoples Banks", "Co-operative Banking" etc. and chairman of the International Co-operative Alliance'. Wolff had already copied this submission to the Canadian press. Continuing his evidence Grey quoted at length Danish co-operative experiences. After Denmark's war with Germany in 1864 'her people had rallied their broken strength, calling to their aid the principles of association and education ...' Grey believed that Danish experience, along with that in Ireland, France and the United Kingdom, offered 'many lessons for Canada'.[57]

Alphonse Desjardins's evidence had two parts: the first comprised a question and answer session with members of the Special Committee on how the Caisse Populaire differed from conventional banks;[58] the second was a general statement that later appeared as an addendum to the report,[59] which outlined how the Caisse worked.

Desjardins's inspiration came from European thrift and credit movements, particularly Raiffeisen in Germany of which he had gained knowledge through his work as a verbatim reporter in Canada's federal parliament. His motivation, though, derived from his Catholic faith and a wish to ease poverty in his native Quebec. He set up the Caisse with his wife, Dorimène, and initially they had operated from their home, though quickly becoming able to operate on a more formal basis. Soon their model was being copied throughout Quebec and other parts of Canada. From its outset the Desjardins movement, as it became known, had close association with the Catholic Church and its clergy assisted its propagation.

Grey's and Desjardins's evidence was complementary as was that of William L. Mackenzie King. He was a civil servant but his evidence to the Special Committee reflects considerable co-operative enthusiasm and experience in Canada and elsewhere. For example he described how as an undergraduate of the University of Toronto he had studied political economy and co-operative movements in different countries. Later he had undertaken post-graduate study at the University of Chicago and at Harvard where he had given 'additional study to the subject of co-operation'.[60]

After Harvard he had spent a year in Britain and Europe 'studying industrial conditions' and co-operative movements. As a result he endorsed John Stuart Mill's view that it was better to look more 'to the co-operative movement for the great betterment of the working classes than any other single movement'.[61] In Britain Mackenzie King had visited the St Rollox Co-operative Society Ltd in Glasgow and he tabled as evidence some of its literature.[62]

He added that at Harvard he had belonged to two co-operatives: the Harvard Co-operative Association; and the Dining Association. Students formed these to eke out their scarce resources because while they were anxious to obtain a 'college education' they did not enjoy 'considerable means'. Formed in the 1880s, the Harvard Co-operative Association retailed furniture, blankets, fuel and books to its members who paid a joining fee of US$2.50. Officers were elected to manage the society and at the end of the year its profits were divided between members according to the value of their purchases.

The Dining Association operated on similar lines and paid elected members to manage their society. The payment

> helps them to go on with their college work. Then some of the students act as waiters and they are also paid for their services . . . At the end of the year the profits of the concern are divided among the men who have been members . . . A record is kept of every purchase . . . at the end of the year the total amount of purchases are added up and the profits instead of going to some landlady . . . are returned in part to himself.[63]

Mackenzie King believed that similar university co-operatives existed at Yale, the University of Michigan and at the Massachusetts Institute of Technology.

The most important part of his evidence to the Special Committee, however, detailed Canadian co-operative developments to date. These were based on reports from local co-operators, observers and published sources.[64] The last relied heavily on articles that had appeared in the *Labour Gazette* previously mentioned by Grey in connection with a report on the Caisse Populaire. Referring to a retail society that had emerged from workers' strike action Mackenzie King observed that it was,

> helping the workingmen to appreciate the difficulties of the capitalist, as well as enabling them to meet some of the difficulties with which they had to contend themselves . . . co-operation . . . teaches the working classes something of the . . . risks that capital has to take, it familiarizes them with matters of trade, the kind of management that is required, the kind of skill . . . necessary to enable a business to be carried on profitably . . .[65]

The Special Committee also received evidence opposing the Bill. It was led by the Retail Merchants' Association of Canada. Its dominion secretary, E. M. Trowern,[66] spoke at length and included in his evidence views of a member of St Rollox Co-operative Society in Glasgow, suggesting that it was not as good as Mackenzie King had argued. However, the Retail Merchants' Association's opposition to the Bill rested largely on two main points. The first was that the Bill was hardly likely to help farmers as they were already largely covered by suitably amended companies legislation; consequently an Industrial and Co-operative Societies Act would not be appropriate for them. Their second objection was that there was no need for a Federal Bill. It is likely, however, that the real objections of the Retail Merchants' Association arose from fears that an increased number of successful retail co-operative societies would heighten competition.

Possible reasons for the Bill's failure were the success of the Retail Merchants' Association in opposing it and the argument that existing provincial legislation was sufficient for co-operatives.[67] Whatever the reasons Canada's co-operatives found, like their Australian counterparts, that it was difficult to establish national cohesiveness and identity. In Canada, however, the failure led to positive action. Co-operators now recognised that like the Retail Merchants' Association of Canada they needed a dominion-wide voice capable of representing co-operatives and speaking on their behalf to politicians and civil servants.

In 1909 the Co-operative Union of Canada (CUC) was formed. Although not an immediate success it was nonetheless a positive response to the failed Bill; it also highlighted the importance of leadership in successful co-operative development. Canada already had one notable leader in Alphonse Desjardins. The founding of CUC brought to the fore another, George Keen (1869–1953) who had moved to Canada from England in 1904. He became president of the Brantford, Ontario Co-operative Association and later the CUC's secretary-treasurer.

Like Desjardins Keen was Catholic, which shaped his co-operative views. To a greater extent, though, these were influenced by his experiences in the British Co-operative movement. He had seen what the British Co-operative Union had achieved as a national co-operative organisation in its organisational support for primary society members, educational and propaganda facilities, and the representations it could make to Parliament. Keen also had a good understanding of British co-operative theorists such as George Jacob Holyoake, Henry Wolff and Edward Vansittart Neale. Although a consumer co-operative enthusiast Keen readily recognised that the CUC needed to include different types of co-operative; that it could not be predominantly consumer-led like its British counterpart.

Despite Keen's pragmatism the CUC was slow to develop. One reason was its need to focus on provincial issues. Consequently Keen,

> had to work for an organisation that had a limited liability to create national momentum. Almost all the organization's resources would be concentrated on assisting small bands of co-operative enthusiasts and in advising on co-operative legislation . . . The focus on provincial movements imposed special pressures on the national co-operative leadership.[68]

While national co-operative leadership was emerging Keen became a notable propagandist. In the early decades of the twentieth century he edited the *Canadian Co-operator* and wrote co-operative study materials for the Workers' Education Association of Ontario and the Antigonish movement in Nova Scotia. He also broadcast a weekly programme on co-operatives on radio station WCLF in Chicago.[69] The CUC did not really become an effective national organisation until the mid-twentieth century.

Grey continued to support co-operatives in his later years as Canadian governor. He remained in regular contact with Horace Plunkett on a number of co-operative issues. Two days after Christmas in 1910 he wrote:

My dear Plunkett,

I hear you are on this side of the Atlantic and hope before you return you may be able to spare time to come up and see me at Ottawa. I want much to have a talk with you on many matters, affecting both Ireland and the United Kingdom, as well as the Dominion.

A blizzard of western farmers blew down over Ottawa the other day: over 500 strong: backed by all the force of $300,000,000 behind them. It was stated that the poorest member of the deputation was worth $10,000.

When I reflect that this rich West was, at the time I was at Cambridge, only known to the explorer and the fur-trader, the development is indeed astonishing.

I telegraphed to your publisher for 400 copies of your book on the 'Rural Life Problems in the United States': my wish being to send back every western farmer with a copy. Your publisher however, was not able to send me more than 100 copies. These were given to members of the deputation coming from Alberta, Saskatchewan and Manitoba.

Although Nature has done so much for the west, I cannot help feeling alarmed as to the future. These farmers are not farming the land: they are mining it. They are skimming the cream which Nature has accumulated there for centuries, and they are putting nothing back! You probably know the story of the farmer who when the pile of manure outside his stable door reached so high a level that it was impossible for his horse to enter without scraping the skin off his back, resolved, not to remove the pile of manure, but to build a new stable! The spreading out of manure being a practice regarded as at once expensive and unnecessary.

My object in dealing out your volume to these farmers was to bait the ground for you to fish in at a later date. I do not think you could be rendering a greater service to Canada and to the Empire than by giving up six weeks or a couple of months to a tour of lectures in our Prairie Provinces. I know you are so busy that it is perhaps unkind of me to make you this request; but I recognise that the present is the moment to strike and that no one can strike the malleable iron more effectively than you.

I shall be very glad to hear from you what your plans are on this side and whether there is a chance of seeing you at Ottawa.

Yours [and added in Grey's own hand] very sincerely. Grey[70]

It seems likely that Grey bore personally the cost of the one hundred copies of Plunkett's book. Notes in his archive at the University of Durham suggest that he was prone to such gestures and was the poorer for them. They underline, however, the genuine nature of his co-operative enthusiasms.

His letter to Plunkett has been recorded in full because it reflects the ease of relations between Grey and Plunkett. It was born out of long co-operative association although they still addressed each other formally as 'Plunkett' and 'Grey'. Use of family names even when signing 'Yours very sincerely' was still a British upper-class practice. The letter also demonstrates Grey's unease over Canadian farming practices although he was impressed with the speed at which Canadian agriculture was advancing. Above all the letter shows his eagerness to propagate Plunkett's co-operative ideas by gifting copies of his recent book to Canadian farmers in preparation for a possible Plunkett lecture tour.

Plunkett replied to Grey on 6 January 1911 and did so with similar warmth. He wrote:

> If there is anything that would add to the pleasure [of the proposed] visit, it would be the prospect of doing useful work in the Western provinces where you have given me a magnificent send-off by your extraordinarily generous assistance to my rural reform propaganda.[71]

However, Plunkett's health was poor. That and his concerns with the current Irish political situation led him to decline Grey's invitation.

Grey left Canada in 1911. Back home in England he retained his interest in Canadian co-operatives. For example in February 1912 his secretary wrote to Alphonse Desjardins on Grey's behalf. He congratulated him on the advance his banks were making in the province of Quebec and asked a number of questions. The letter continued:

> Lord Grey has still his card recording the fact that he has invested $5 in the Caisse Populaire de Levis, and will be obliged if you will until further notice credit his account with the bank with the dividends and interest as they become due.[72]

CONCLUSIONS

The dominions give many examples of spontaneous co-operative growth. These occurred in response to a variety of needs and in diverse geographical regions. An important difference between the dominions and India, where the government had taken the initiative in introducing co-operatives, was that they attracted white settlers many of whom came from Britain. In 1900 South Africa was still in turmoil but quietened sufficiently for the Union of South Africa to form ten years later and become a dominion. During the same period Australia, New Zealand and Canada had become virtually self-governing. Their legislation was still approved by the Westminster Parliament and their governor-generals represented the British sovereign. However, as we have seen in the case of Earl Grey and attempts to pass the Industrial and Co-operative Societies Bill in the Canadian parliament, a governor-general could still be involved in the pre-legislative process. The failure of that Bill and the appointment of a Special Committee to consider evidence for and against it illustrate a growing parliamentary maturity.

Within dominion economies we noted the importance of export crops particularly those going to British markets. Producer co-operatives became part of the export system helping to ensure deliveries, quantities and quality. Government created marketing boards that had much the same functions and sometimes lessened the reason for co-operatives. However, some governments supported co-operatives through subsidies, information on market conditions and technical advice. Such facilities were usually channelled through the agricultural departments of provincial or state governments. The close links between the Danish parliament and co-operatives in that country became the model for such developments.

Whereas some co-operatives in the dominions found it relatively easy to establish their credibility and identity, others did not. Those with limited functions, for example in agricultural supply or marketing, rather than co-operatives operating in urban or city locations, found it easier. An exception was the Desjardins credit movement whose function was simple and therefore easy to understand and support. Moreover, its cohesion was reinforced by its Catholic and French environment. Like the British Consumer Co-operative it benefited from subliminal propinquity. Its strong visible presence, arising from its many credit unions, helped create cohesion and identity.

Co-operative identity in the dominions was also sometimes blurred by inappropriate legislation. In Australia, New Zealand and Canada, agricultural co-operatives often came under amended Company Acts. In New Zealand this led to capitalisation and voting rights at variance with the Rochdale model. One reason for this was that the British Industrial and Provident Societies Acts applied only in Britain; they were not readily replicated or appropriate to rural settings. Moreover, dominion political systems lagged behind those in Britain where ideologically motivated interest groups such as the Christian Socialists could lobby for innovative legislation. In the dominions it was often easier to amend well-established company legislation which had the merit of already being well understood. Within such legislation, however, the concept of limited liability was enshrined as it was also in the British industrial and provident societies legislation. Familiarity with this and reasons for it meant that the concept of unlimited liability was less easy to grasp. Yet it had become a central feature of the German Raiffeisen system. Grey, Wolff and Plunkett understood its importance particularly as a bulwark of mutuality but largely failed to persuade budding dominion co-operative movements of its merits.

Ideology played a lesser role in dominion co-operatives than among British consumer co-operatives. It was not entirely lacking for in Canada many rural co-operatives grew out of earlier collective or community activities necessary for survival in pioneering conditions. In Canada also the Desjardins movement and co-operatives for 'workingmen' displayed a limited ideology. Elsewhere in the dominions, though, co-operatives were functional organisations with specific and sometimes limited purposes. Australia illustrated the difficulties that could arise from trying to graft on a metropolitan ideology. In New South Wales, Rochdale co-operation would prove a weak transplant.

Leadership was to become important in dominion co-operatives but was only beginning to appear during this period. Leaders emerged in Australian and New Zealand co-operatives but hardly registered in co-operative histories in the way that Desjardins and Keen did in Canada. Consequently external leaders such as Grey, Wolff and Plunkett became significant. They had no fixed roots in any one area but were effective propagators of co-operative ideas. Local leaders would, however, build institutions that would assist future co-operative development.

PART TWO: Institution Building and Professionalisation

9. The Plunkett Foundation and its Conference at the Empire Exhibition, Wembley, 1925

INTRODUCTION

This chapter begins Part Two of our study and covers the period between the two World Wars. It focuses on the building of institutions involved in co-operative development within the British Empire and examines how their support services became more professional. Such features distinguish it from our first period between 1900 and 1918 when it was first realised that the creation of co-operatives could assist the Empire's development agency functions. That first period had essentially been one of experimentation. It had produced lessons that aided successful developments during the inter-war years.

Assisting this was an increasing exchange of experiences and information between co-operatives through an expanding International Co-operative Alliance (ICA) and the Plunkett Foundation set up in 1919. This chapter focuses on the latter, noting how and why it was established and its early functions. A point to note, however, is that the Empire was changing; also that early enthusiasts within it were ageing or dying. Earl Grey had died in 1917. Sir Horace Plunkett and Henry Wolff remained active through the 1920s despite advanced years. Wolff died in 1930 at the age of 90 and Plunkett in 1932 at 78.

Grey had held high imperial positions but apart from occasional speeches and pamphlets wrote little on co-operative matters. We can only learn therefore of his co-operative ideas through his personal archive and that of the ICA. Although lower in the imperial hierarchy Wolff and Plunkett remained energetic activists and writers even in old age. Wolff's last book, *Co-operation in India*,[1] appeared only three years before his death. Plunkett's books gathered influential support. Earl Grey, as we saw, distributed copies of one to Canadian farmers. Theodore Roosevelt (1858–1919) US president between 1901 and 1909 and a personal friend of Plunkett, adopted his slogan 'Better Farming, Better Business, Better Living' to spearhead American agricultural policy.[2] The writings of Wolff and Plunkett allow later generations to trace their co-operative ideas.

Both men were also institution builders. Wolff is primarily associated with the ICA as chair of the steering committee that led to its foundation in 1895 and thereafter as chair of its executive committee until 1907. Plunkett helped set up individual co-operatives in Ireland but more importantly support organisations such as the Irish Agricultural Organisation Society and the Irish Agricultural Wholesale Society.

In terms of co-operative development within the British Empire, however, his most important creation was the Plunkett Foundation which he set up and endowed in 1919.

THE PLUNKETT FOUNDATION

It had antecedents. Plunkett was a man of politics and co-operatives. He also divided his time between Ireland, England and the US, and earned himself the label of an 'Anglo-Irish American'.[3] His later Irish years were troubled as nationalists pressed for Home Rule and Unionists opposed it. In 1919 Plunkett led the formation of the Irish Dominion Party. It sought to attract moderates from both the North and South and to press for Home Rule as a united country with dominion status in the British Empire. During its short life the new party aroused strong hostility and Plunkett was denounced by both Nationalist Republicans and Unionist politicians.

An Act of 1920 granted Home Rule under which the South became self-governing while Northern Ireland remained in the United Kingdom. It led to a bitter civil war during which, in 1922, Plunkett was nominated to the Irish Senate. Only months later, while he was in America, his house on the outskirts of Dublin was burnt down possibly as part of a campaign against senators. After his return from America Plunkett set up home in England, at Weybridge, although he continued his work in Ireland and retained strong connections there.

Plunkett set up what was originally known as the Horace Plunkett Foundation in 1919, the same year as he formed the Irish Dominion Party. While the latter was short-lived the former continues to the present day. It grew from the Co-operative Reference Library, Dublin that Plunkett founded with Father Tom Finlay in 1914. This was initially based in Plunkett House, Merrion Square, which had been given in tribute to Plunkett by Irish co-operative organisations. Plunkett and Fr Finlay donated its first books but later acquisitions came through a grant of £2,000 from the Carnegie United Kingdom Trustees. One of the Co-operative Reference Library's two librarians was Francis Cruise

O'Brien, father of Conor Cruise O'Brien, who became well-known in the later twentieth century as an author, politician and UN figure.

The Library's aim was: 'to supply accurate information as to the progress and distinctive features of co-operative organisation in *all countries* [my italics] to genuine inquirers and more especially to the field workers of the three Agricultural Organisation Societies of the British Isles'.[4] It became: '. . . world famous in a short time, its services being extensively used by co-operative organisations in every continent despite the difficulties caused by the Great War; a great deal of business was done with India and the USA'.[5]

Part of its success derived from the quarterly publication *Better Business* which the Co-operative Reference Library published from October 1915. It attracted subscriptions and contributors 'from all over the world' reflecting increasing interest in co-operatives and presaging the future Horace Plunkett Foundation.

On 21 December 1918 Plunkett wrote in his diary: 'Most of the day with Adams. Agreed to make him and A. D. Hall trustees of my new rural reconstruction bequest and donation. I meditate starting this thing during my life, centring it at Oxford and the Plunkett House, Dublin.'

Less than a month later, on 13 January, he wrote again in his diary: 'Founded the Horace Plunkett Foundation with a first endowment of £5,000 and made it the recipient of a provision in my will.'[6]

Plunkett invited three trustees to oversee the Foundation. One was Sir Daniel Hall, chief scientific adviser to the Ministry of Agriculture, another Professor W. G. S. Adams, warden of All Souls, Oxford, both of whom he had mentioned in his diary. The third was Dermod O'Brien, president of the Royal Hibernian Academy and treasurer of the Irish Agricultural Organisation Society (IAOS).[7] Besides holding important public positions these men were also friends and associates of Sir Horace.

Although Plunkett had originally thought of basing the Foundation in Oxford and Dublin the troubles in Ireland and the destruction of his Dublin house possibly led him to choose London. It was initially set up at 10 Doughty Street, which lay between Grays Inn Road and Russell Square. Another possible reason for locating in London was that although the quarterly *Better Business* had a wide circulation elsewhere it was small in Ireland. The Co-operative Reference Library was moved to the new Foundation where it boosted its research capabilities. Plunkett set about shoring up the Foundation's finances by seeking support from wealthy benefactors in the UK and overseas and by increasing his own contribution to £20,000.[8]

The Foundation initially aimed to 'promote courses and studies on co-operative subjects and to support good causes in allied fields'.

London proved a good location for the new Foundation but it was additionally fortuitous when the Empire Exhibition was held at Wembley between 1924 and 1926. Sir Horace seized the opportunity to organise a conference bringing together the many leaders of co-operative movements in the Empire who would be attending the Exhibition. His initiative gained the support of the Agricultural Organisation Societies of England, Ireland, Scotland and Wales as well as the approval of the Departments or Ministries of Agriculture for England, Ireland and Scotland.

THE EMPIRE EXHIBITION AT WEMBLEY AND THE PLUNKETT CONFERENCE

While the Plunkett conference was concerned only with agricultural co-operation and in particular its 'application to the industry, the business, and the life of the farmer in the British Empire', it nevertheless concerned an important part of the Empire's trade. Moreover, as we have seen in previous chapters, agriculture included a wide range of activities such as horticulture, viticulture and fishing as well as involving support services such as marketing, supplies, insurance, credit and banking. We are able to follow the conference's debates through the report the Foundation produced the following year, which includes a preliminary survey of agricultural co-operative movements in the British Empire in the early 1920s.[9] Altogether the conference report provides a valuable historical document.

Its preliminary survey was undertaken by Karl Walter. By all accounts, even his own, Plunkett was not reckoned to be a good public speaker. Yet he was very good at persuading others to support his causes and choosing people for particular roles. This is seen to good effect in the early years of the Plunkett Foundation and the person he invited to head its small staff, Karl Walter. Walter has been described as someone who had

> been trained in banking and had gone over to journalism. He had known Plunkett for a number of years and had helped him, notably in his campaign to explain Allied war aims to the Americans. He had considerable personal charm, could play brilliantly with ideas, including the idea of co-operation . . .[10]

The survey Walter undertook was presented to the Wembley conference. It runs to some 123 pages, and covers Australia, New Zealand, Canada, South Africa, India, Lesser Antilles (Caribbean), Barbados,

Jamaica, Antigua, British Guiana, Mauritius, Ceylon and Malaya. Besides its considerable statistical detail it describes the evolution of different agricultural co-operative movements and the issues they faced.

When addressing the conference Walter noted that it was the first to be held on agricultural co-operatives in the Empire. Previously they had enjoyed only limited exchanges of information. He believed that the conference could remedy this and underline the fact that agricultural co-operative movements had 'many interests in common'. For example, they helped farmers achieve better returns through:

> effecting the economies of large scale purchases and sales, and by substituting as far as possible agricultural control for that of the independent middlemen during the passage of produce from the farmer to the consumer. As essential supplements to such organisation, the co-operative purchase of farm requirements has generally been developed, as in many cases the co-operative supply of facilities for credit and insurance. The broader justification of the co-operative movements has been to render more efficient, economically and socially, national agriculture, as a fundamental factor of national welfare.[11]

The Empire Exhibition provided the opportunity for the Plunkett conference and we should briefly note how and why that came about. Its idea was not new, having first been suggested by the British Empire League in 1902. Mounting tensions leading to the First World War and the war itself had delayed its organisation and changed its rationale. By the end of the war Britain and the world had changed. Some kind of reassessment of the Empire and reinterpretation of the imperial ideal were now required, quite apart from any celebration of Empire.

Ironically, at the time of the Exhibition the British Empire had reached its zenith. Post-war settlements had brought it a number of previous German colonies such as South West Africa and Tanganyika (Tanzania), which would now be administered as British mandated territories. Yet, for all its global spread, British power was about to wane. There were a number of coalescing reasons. During the First World War Britain's armed forces had been swelled by combatants from her colonies and dominions but some had returned home questioning British hegemony. Calls for national independence grew within British colonies and particularly in India. Another reason was that the war had economically weakened Britain, depleting her exchequer and causing a loss of markets: America and Japan now challenged her earlier trading dominance.

Her political landscape was also changing. It could not yet be known that traditional swings between Liberal and Conservative governments had ended and that there would not be another Liberal government: moreover that the Labour Party would become an increasing political force. In 1924 it was elected to form a minority government under Ramsay MacDonald and although it survived only ten months it was a portent of things to come. Consequently, the Labour Party's views on Empire assumed greater importance but at the time of the Empire Exhibition they were still somewhat equivocal. The Labour Party was part of a wider labour movement which encompassed the trades unions and the Consumer Co-operative movement. Both had muted vested interests in Empire. Trades unions recognised that the Empire helped shore up employment at home while the Consumer Co-operative movement was happy with imperial imports as long as they were distributed in the best interests of the consumer. Despite such interests calls for colonial freedom began to be heard within constituency Labour Parties whose members invariably included active trades unionists and co-operators. Moreover, some leading Labour figures were already involved in campaigns for Indian independence.[12]

The Empire Exhibition was held at a time of imperial uncertainty but set out to celebrate Britain's imperial might. It rivalled the Great Exhibition of 1851 which had been held to celebrate Britain's growing industrial might. That had been held at the Crystal Palace originally erected in Hyde Park whereas the Empire Exhibition was held in a newly constructed exhibition complex in the north London suburb of Wembley: Wembley Stadium had held its first football cup final the previous year. The Exhibition site covered some 220 acres and included pavilions housing displays from the dominions, India and the colonies as well as an amusement park, and palaces of art, engineering, industry and government. Some 27 million people visited the Exhibition during the two years it was open.[13]

Quite where the Plunkett conference was held is not clear: the industry or government buildings seem likely candidates. It convened, however, between 28 and 31 July 1925. Attendees numbered 168 with the largest group coming from the UK. Others came from Newfoundland, which did not become a province of Canada until 1949, Canada, Australia, New Zealand, South Africa, India and Malaya. Interest groups represented included agricultural co-operative leaders, prime ministers, ministers, civil servants and academics. Agricultural co-operation was less well developed in Britain than elsewhere in the Empire which may account for the fact that its Consumer Co-operative movement was well represented with delegates from the Co-operative Wholesale Society

(CWS), the Co-operative Union, individual retail societies and the Co-operative College.

Although Sir Horace Plunkett was now living in England he opted to be placed with the Irish delegation which also included the Irish high-commissioner, the Hon. James MacNeill. Earlier in his career MacNeill had been the first registrar of co-operatives in India's Bombay province.[14] Other notables included the high-commissioners of Australia and New Zealand and the secretary of state for India, The Rt Hon.the Lord Olivier.

Two unusual groups comprised representatives from dominion marketing boards and co-operative registrars in India. The latter were members of the Indian Civil Service. All were Indian except C. F. Strickland who was British-born. During the inter-war years he became a leading colonial co-operative registrar and an authority on co-operative development.

While these roll calls are interesting in themselves the importance of the Plunkett conference lies in what it reveals about agricultural co-operatives and in particular how quickly they had developed since the turn of the century. The conference discussed other issues but its four main debates were on 'State Policy in respect of the Organisations of Agricultural Co-operation', 'The Co-operative Organisation of Rural Credit', 'The Co-operative Marketing of Agricultural Produce' and 'The Relationship between Co-operative Movements of Agricultural Producers and Urban Consumers'.

A major theme of this study is the relationship between co-operatives and the state and for this reason we will focus particularly on that debate; also where other debates touched upon it. A fact that emerged quickly was that agricultural co-operatives were less developed in Britain than in other parts of the Empire. Early British speakers including the Rt Hon. Noel Buxton, MP, the British minister of agriculture, and chairmen of Agricultural Organisation Societies in England, Ireland and Wales tried to explain this. Before that, in opening the conference, Sir Noel quoted remarks by Sir Horace Plunkett that '. . . co-operation is of value not only because it improves the economic position of farmers, but also for its moral and social influence'.[15]

Buxton then described contemporary British agriculture and the part that co-operatives played within it. As far as their relations with the British government were concerned, Buxton believed that British farmers first needed to show that they could emulate what 'agriculturalists abroad have done to help themselves before they are entitled to the assistance which economically and justifiably the State can give'.

He was followed by Sir Daniel Hall, from the Ministry of Agriculture, who was also chairman of the Plunkett Foundation. He advanced three reasons why British agricultural co-operatives were less well advanced than those in other parts of the Empire; all derived from British agriculture being older and more developed. Firstly, that 'the typical British farmer is a capitalist upon a comparatively large scale'. Secondly, that unlike other farmers in the British Empire he was not a 'single-man or family-unit farmer' for whom 'co-operation can do more, and can do that much more quickly'. Britain's agriculture comprised comparatively large-scale farmers who formed a 'fairly efficient economic unit'. The third reason why British farmers were not enthusiastic about co-operatives was that 'we are not doing an export trade'. British farmers were less dependent on export markets because the home market provided a ready alternative which is 'an old, organised and efficient trade service for both sale and purchase'. Because Sir Daniel believed that the conference was 'all agreed about the principle' of co-operation, he went on to focus on the 'techniques' by which co-operatives met their goals. Those concerning their relations with the state were essentially those between governments and voluntary organisations. By way of example, he quoted those fostered by Sir Horace Plunkett between the Department of Agriculture and the voluntary co-operative movement in Ireland which sadly had recently been disrupted by 'political divisions . . .'

Education and training was a prime area for collaboration between the state and co-operatives. Sir Daniel noted the current debate about whether education and training should be undertaken by agricultural colleges and farm institutions or by co-operatives themselves with technical advisers attached. He did not believe that co-operatives should seek subsidies to organise such facilities themselves but should rather use the services that were already provided by the state. Hall disapproved of co-operatives claiming 'to run the educational movement' and believed that they should 'content themselves with using it'.

His speech revealed paternalistic attitudes that were perhaps understandable in a senior civil servant but less so in the chair of the Plunkett Foundation, an organisation which saw co-operatives as 'voluntary' organisations. His comments also reflect a tension that would colour co-operatives' relations with the state. It had existed from the time of Rochdale and supposed that co-operatives might assume certain state functions appropriate to their credo of democratic self-management and self-government. Such ideas had permeated general co-operative attitudes but were probably stronger in consumer rather than agricultural co-operative movements.

Fourth Earl Grey (1851–1917), President of the International Co-operative Alliance 1895–1907, Administrator of Rhodesia 1896–8. Governor-General of Canada 1904–11

Henry Wolff (1840–1930), Chair of ICA Executive Committee 1895–1907, Co-operative author and authority on thrift and credit unions

Sir Horace Plunkett (1854–1932), Pioneer of Irish co-operatives and founder of the Plunkett Foundation

Margaret Digby (1900–1985), Secretary of the Plunkett Foundation and authority on co-operative legislation

Will Watkins (1893–1995), Director of the International Co-operative Alliance 1951–1963

Dr Robert Marshall (1913–2008), Principal UK Co-operative College 1946–76

Bert Youngjohns, Post-war Colonial Co-operative Registrar

Archie Macintosh, Post-war Colonial Co-operative Registrar

Trevor Bottomley, Post-war Colonial Co-operative Registrar

Sir Daniel was on firmer ground when he asserted that governments should become responsible for audits where they granted co-operatives credits: '. . . the Government which lends the money must see that the money is being properly applied, and that assets are being preserved. The introduction of Government audit in itself involves giving the society technical advice'.[16]

As we shall see later responsibility for audit became a central part of government involvement in co-operatives in India and British colonies.

Sir Daniel recognised, however, that there were areas where governments had little part to play as, for example, when co-operatives sought to improve 'the life and the social betterment of the community'. The reason was that such work depended on the enthusiasm of individuals and the spirit they engendered.

> I do not believe that the machinery of a great Government Department is precisely the best machinery for developing that spirit. I think in that respect we must trust to voluntary action outside the State, and it is in this direction the Horace Plunkett Foundation hopes to make for progress.[17]

Sir Daniel said that Sir Horace had endowed his Foundation with 'extraordinary liberality'. It now sought to foster the aims of rural communities, 'not merely from the business side, but especially from the vital social side of the betterment of the human being'. Hall added that Sir Horace wished the Foundation to use its funds for the 'promotion of the spirit of fellowship'. Sir Daniel said, 'Here I believe we have an example of the voluntary action which can put a soul into the co-operative movement.'

Generally speaking British agricultural co-operatives added little to the debate on co-operatives' relations with the state: the main contributions came from elsewhere in the Empire. Important among these were two speeches by the Hon. C. A. Dunning, prime minister of Saskatchewan who had earlier been the first general manager of the Saskatchewan Co-operative Elevator Company.[18] His transition illustrated how co-operative leadership could prove to be a stepping stone to a political career. This had already been seen in Europe and would be seen again in newly independent states in the post-imperial period.

Dunning spoke on co-operatives' relations to the state and again on 'The Co-operative Marketing of Agricultural Produce'. In both debates he illustrated ways in which the Saskatchewan government had assisted co-operatives. His starting point was that progressive agriculture was essential to 'Empire well-being'. Agricultural success depended on a number of factors which included state guidance; the application of scientific knowledge to the farming industry; the existence of voluntary organisations of farmers for business purposes on co-operative lines; and a reconstruction of rural social life to reduce disparities between town and country.[19]

Canadian government assistance to agricultural co-operatives on marketing varied from province to province but was primarily provided 'along legislative lines'. Each province had 'legislation facilitating co-operative organisation for marketing purposes among farmers'. Such legislation had three main characteristics: it facilitated cheap and easy incorporation; it provided a fair degree of standardisation; and it encouraged the organisations created to remain

> co-operative in spirit, and not become an ordinary capitalistic corporation dominated by a majority financial interest. In these organisations the man, the producer counts rather than the investment of the producer in the capital of the organisation.[20]

Dunning did not mention any safeguards to prevent such degeneration. He went on to describe another form of state assistance in Canada, namely the state management of co-operative marketing. This was particularly strong in Saskatchewan where it had been 'markedly successful in placing co-operatives on their feet which had they been left to tread the thorny road of experience . . . would never have lived through it'.

Elsewhere, particularly among consumer and thrift and credit societies, appreciation had grown of the educative aspects of co-operation through which ordinary people learned to manage their businesses. Speaking about Saskatchewan agricultural co-operatives Dunning offered plausible arguments why such a process should be replaced by state help.

> It is characteristic of the co-operative movement wherever we find it that the first class individual in connection with it is what I might term the co-operative evangelist, the enthusiast who is imbued with the ideal, who sees fully the possibilities and who can arouse his fellows to organise. Usually, however, the evangelist is not the type of a man to look after the practical business of co-operation once the organisation is established . . . we do not throw up enough men who have [the] capability of evolving from the evangelist, from the enthusiast into the practical man of everyday business which is absolutely necessary for the successful management of any business whether co-operative or otherwise.[21]

To offset such shortcomings the Saskatchewan Department of Agriculture had set up a Co-operation and Markets' Branch whose purpose was to assist the co-operative marketing of 'any product of the farm'. Dunning stressed that the state was not trying to force co-operation on the farmer or to become a means of co-operative propaganda. Rather it sought to assist the co-operative marketing of any product including 'subsidiary' products which were not the farmers' main 'money crop'. Such crops were usually insufficiently important to warrant setting up an organisation to handle them. In such circumstances the Co-operation and Marketing Branch of the Department of Agriculture undertook to market these subsidiary products,

> but on the distinct understanding that just as soon as the product assumed a sufficient importance in the eyes of those producing it and was produced in sufficient volume to allow it to be done, a co-operative organisation entirely composed of farmer- producers should undertake the work of marketing.[22]

Dunning acknowledged that the scheme had not always proved easy. It was natural for civil servants to want to improve the reputation of their department and this sometimes made it difficult for them to cast loose their creation. Another problem was 'that it is human nature apparently to lean upon the Government as long as the Government will let you lean on them'. For these reasons it was important to start with clear understandings. Dunning went on to describe how the co-operation and Marketing Branch had worked to market two 'subsidiary' products, namely wool and dairy products. Successful transitions had been made and co-operative marketing organisations established. A similar process was under way with potatoes. In engaging in such undertakings the state was not 'pap-feeding' the industry: the cost of initial state-marketing was charged against the commodity and was passed to the producer who 'must stand on his own feet'.

The Saskatchewan government was also involved in the early capitalisation of the Saskatchewan Co-operative Elevator Company of which Dunning had been the first general manager. He described how Western Canada had suffered from a 'grain monopoly', a situation that had given rise to public indignation and had prompted scores of 'Utopian' remedies. After thorough investigation, however, it had been decided to try to deal with the problem 'co-operatively'. The view was that if farmers owned the handling facilities that they would be able to control how their produce was handled and so counter 'monopolistic tendencies'.

As a result a centrally managed organisation was created with separate 'local' organisations that were represented at the Company's annual meeting:

> Each shareholder had one vote and no shareholder could hold more than 20 shares of a par value of 50 dollars, that is 1,000 dollars or £200 in English money, of the stock of the Company. Each local co-operative elected one of their number to represent them at an annual meeting.[23]

The question had arisen as to how such an enterprise should be funded. Dunning had earlier spoken of the problems of capitalisation and had noted the inimical effects of dependency on external funding. In this case it was resolved through an agreement between the Saskatchewan government and the Saskatchewan Co-operative Elevator Company that if the latter's 'locals' subscribed 15 per cent the government would fund the remaining

> 85 per cent of the cost of erecting ... facilities, taking as security a mortgage on the uncalled capital liability of the individual shareholder. The relationship of the State to the institution therefore was that of first mortgagee on the facilities and the first mortgagee on the uncalled capital liability of the individual shareholder. The repayment to the State was arranged on an amortised basis over 20 years with the understanding that the State would loan money to the institution at a rate of interest not to exceed the cost of the money itself to the State, the idea being that there should be no contribution from the general taxpayer for the scheme, but rather that the credit of the Province should be placed behind it, because of its vital importance to welfare of all the people.[24]

This is an important statement because it shows government preparedness to combat monopoly power. Schemes to do so, however, were not only for the immediate benefit of individual producers but also for the welfare of 'all the people'.

Dunning reported to the Plunkett conference that the Saskatchewan Co-operative Elevator Company then had 25,000 shareholders in some 425 local organisations of farmers, each with its own elevator: '... the Company ... met religiously on the dot every dollar of its obligation to the Province' and was now operating 'without one dollar of Government guarantee'.[25]

His contributions to the conference showed how a government sympathetic to co-operatives, perhaps out of government self-interest, could facilitate and animate co-operative development. It also illustrated government withdrawal after success. The following speech from C. F. Strickland of the Indian Civil Service (ICS) provided sharp contrasts. Thrift and credit societies had been introduced in India with the short-term aim of preventing famines by reducing rural indebtedness and poverty but with the long-term aim of staving off social unrest with its threat to law and order. This represented another kind of governmental self-interest and had led to a top-down approach to co-operative development. It contrasted with the mixed kind that had evolved in Saskatchewan. Strickland's opening remarks made this clear when he said that India more than any other country had 'placed co-operation under the guidance of the State'. It was a Civil Service driven form of co-operative development that had originated the Co-operative Credit Societies Act of 1904.

Since then experience had produced results that might not have been expected. For example, Strickland disagreed with the view expressed elsewhere in the conference that a 'State servant cannot be a fervent co-operator'. He asked, 'Why not?'

> It is easy to take into your co-operative work those of your State servants who are keen co-operators. Place them in such conditions as co-operative work in India does place them, and they will not stay unless they are co-operative enthusiasts; you will find only those men will stay who are really heart and soul in the work; the other people will go back to their more pleasant duties.[26]

Strickland believed that if a state worker were a keen co-operator he could be 'as successful a propagandist or supervisor as any voluntary organiser'. He acknowledged, however, that Indian conditions were different from elsewhere. Consequently, Indian methods of co-operative development might not be appropriate in England, Ireland or other countries where 'the smaller farmer is more educated, where you can reach him by means of literature etc.' thus making it possible to work through voluntary organisations.

His experience in India also led him to dispute another view expressed in the conference which had been that 'co-operation must be originated by the farmers and carried on by the farmers'. Strickland focused on the role of the co-operative leader and where he might be found. He said in India,

You must call upon the farmer, point out to him what he wants, ask him whether he wants it; if he rejects it very well, but you must go on trying to evoke a response from him. Farmers are very scattered and very busy, they cannot throw up from themselves their own leaders unless those leaders are able to devote themselves to this work only.

He agreed with other conference speakers who suggested such work should be maintained by 'whole time workers'. A problem, however, was whether these should come from voluntary organisations such as the Agricultural Organisation Societies, presumably like those existing in England, Ireland, Scotland and Wales which were funded by private subscriptions with a certain amount of government help.

Strickland asked:

Is it fair to ask any voluntary body supported by its existing societies to provide funds for protecting persons who are not at present in any co-operative society? I think not. Therefore, for propaganda at least, if you are not going to employ a State service, it is reasonable that every State should finance to some extent the chief co-operative body.[27]

Such bodies were required not only for 'propaganda' but also for audit. All too often co-operatives suffered 'inefficient auditing' for a number of years and when they eventually called for help it sometimes it came too late.

What is required is a regular audit . . . by a man who knows what co-operation means, an expert with regard to the difficulties of co-operative societies, and trusted by and personally known to the people whose organisation he is visiting. If you do not have a co-operative audit, you are going to have a very cold-hearted audit, indeed. Somehow or the other you want a co-operative audit and I do not think you are going to get that except out of a voluntary body, and I do not think it fair to call upon a co-operative body to finance itself if it is carrying on propaganda as well as maintenance.

Points emerging from Strickland's speech relevant to subsequent co-operative deveopment were: that it was possible for a state official to be a 'fervent co-operator'; that audits should be conducted keeping in mind co-operatives' distinctive nature; the issue of whether it was right for embryonic co-operatives bodies to be funded by members of existing co-operatives.

It is important to place this last point in context. The question was raised when there was still a close correlation between co-operative membership, capitalisation and risk. That link would eventually weaken, particularly among consumer co-operatives. Examples of established co-operatives helping new ones emerged during the post-imperial years of the later 1900s when movement to movement schemes evolved. These well-established co-operative movements in Northern and Western Europe and later Japan encouraged co-operative development in Africa, Asia and South America, usually with government agreement and sometimes support.

Strickland's experiences in India undoubtedly shaped his belief that civil servants could be co-operative enthusiasts.

A number of issues were thrown up by the debate on co-operatives and the state, including a number of dualities. Dunning had spoken of co-operatives conferring benefit first to their members and secondly to the wider society and economy. Several speakers acknowledged that co-operatives were both businesses and social entities. A third duality arose in conference recognition that both state and voluntary organisations had roles to play in co-operative development. Such dualities had the potential to make co-operative development more complex than some other forms of development.

A fact barely alluded to in conference debates but which could be inferred was that co-operative development would also be influenced by the nature of the state in which they emerged. It was, however, touched upon by a question from T. W. Mercer of the UK Co-operative Union who asked:

> Inasmuch as the development Mr. Dunning speaks of depends upon the assistance of a sympathetic Government, does he not think it necessary for co-operative societies to take political action in order to make their needs known?[28]

Dunning's reply clearly distinguished between 'political action' and 'Party political action':

> I believe that Party political action is fatal to Co-operation . . . I believe that, if the spirit of Co-operation is strong in a country, if the people are imbued with it, it will find its reflection in the minds of men that are sent to Parliament whatever their Party. You will have no trouble with an unsympathetic Parliament provided the

> groundwork of co-operation is well laid among the people. God help a Government in Saskatchewan that was not sympathetic to co-operative enterprise![29]

This was a sweeping assumption. True, the Saskatchewan government had been sympathetic to co-operatives but the British government had proved less so during the First World War despite the fact that co-operative membership was almost 4 million and societies had considerable reach into British life. During the war government schemes involving the commandeering of co-operative property, the mobilisation of co-operative workers and the unfair distribution of scarce commodities adversely affected co-operatives: they believed that they were more harshly treated than their private trade competitors who achieved higher rates of exemption. Failing to achieve redress the movement, which over the three previous decades had inconclusively debated its political stance, decided on direct political action. In 1917 it formed its own Co-operative Party and sponsored its first parliamentary candidates in the 1918 general election.

The examples of Saskatchewan and Britain demonstrate that they were different kinds of state and that the nature of a state depended on which interest groups had political power.

Where co-operatives reach a certain size and influence they can threaten existing interest groups. If these are sufficiently powerful within a state they can prejudice co-operative advancement. That in turn can prompt co-operative political action. At this stage, however, we should note that the co-operatives we have studied so far, in Britain, Ireland, India, Australia, New Zealand, Canada and Southern Africa, all developed in vastly different states; moreover, that states can change through time. An obvious example was the granting of Home Rule to southern Ireland which then prompted a civil war that in turn damaged co-operatives. It also led to the Plunkett Foundation being set up in London rather than Dublin.

In the short term, however, Mercer's question and Dunning's response to it prompt questions about the political awareness and skills that co-operatives need. At the time of the Plunkett conference, however, such needs were only beginning to be recognised.

For the future work of the Plunkett Foundation the conference's recognition that both the state and voluntary organisations such as Plunkett had a role to play in co-operative development was crucial. How did the Plunkett Foundation respond? It was helped by the fact that the conference endorsed Karl Walter's view that agricultural co-operative movements throughout the Empire faced many common problems but had little means of exchanging information. It therefore passed the following resolution:

> That in view of the importance and urgency of reliable information as to the position and progress of the agricultural co-operative movement in all its branches, there should be established in London a clearing house of such information for the service of the movement primarily throughout the English- speaking world.
>
> That the Trustees of the Horace Plunkett Foundation be hereby asked to consider steps to give effect to the above Resolution.[30]

Comments from A. V. Alexander and others suggest that there were fears that this proposal could lead to an international organisation that would rival the ICA. Alexander easily commanded attention because he was a notable British co-operative leader and parliamentarian. He had been elected to Parliament as a Co-operative MP in 1922 and at the time of the Plunkett conference was parliamentary secretary to the Board of Trade in Labour's first minority government. Subsequently he served in three governments as first lord of the admiralty including that under Winston Churchill during the 1939–45 war.[31] Alexander also acted as parliamentary secretary to the UK Co-operative Union. Speaking at the Plunkett conference he observed that agricultural co-operatives had not formed federal organisations to the same extent that consumer co-operatives had and that these were necessary to form the base of an international body.[32]

Fears that the Plunkett Foundation might become an agricultural counterpart to the ICA were countered by Harold Barbour of the Irish Agricultural Organisation Society (IAOS) who paid tribute to the 'great value and work of the Co-operative Alliance'. Barbour added, however, that its great accomplishments had been achieved by something that agricultural co-operatives lacked, 'namely a very accurate knowledge of our own position'.

He continued:

> Now while it may be that in time our interests will be well and safely confided to the International Co-operative Alliance, I feel strongly that there is an intermediate step to be taken. We have to put our own house in order to learn our own weaknesses and our strengths . . . I think we will have accomplished a great deal, if we establish a clearing house for the benefit of the English-Speaking co-operative agricultural co-operative movements of the world.[33]

Other comments, and particularly those by Dunning, point to a divide between agricultural and consumer co-operatives. When it was suggested that the ICA 'might fill the bill' as a clearing house Dunning said that:

> it raised that old question as to the diversity of motive existing between producers and consumers' co-operative effort, a diversity of motive which must exist until agricultural producers are well enough organised to meet industrial consumers on equal terms. There can be no agreement except between equals. We are not content to wag the tail of the industrial co-operative dog.

He continued that he did not think that the ICA could provide agricultural co-operatives with the services they needed: 'It is specialised services we need,' adding 'I think the Horace Plunkett Foundation will do this work admirably.'[34] Such comments reveal that tensions survived from the late-nineteenth-century debate between producer and consumer co-operation. Co-operative records were also showing that it was not easy to marry the supply of producer co-operatives with the demands of consumer societies; indeed that any kind of symbiotic relationship was difficult to establish.

On the question of relations between the ICA and the Horace Plunkett Foundation it was unlikely that they would ever become competitive. They were two quite different organisations. The ICA, based on national co-operative apex organisations was representative, democratic and under its rules open to all kinds of co-operative, although consumer societies predominated at the time of the Plunkett conference. The Plunkett Foundation focused on agricultural societies at least in its early years but did not seek to represent them. Moreover, it was never likely to be particularly democratic. Only its trustees, nominated by the great and the good, were elected by its annual conference, suggesting that it would be a rather paternalistic organisation. That was not out of keeping with its limited functions of research and propagation.

The conference had brought together agricultural co-operators from throughout the British Empire. It had provided their first international forum and initial exchanges of information as well as the discussion of mutual problems. It had also laid the foundations of the future work of the Plunkett Foundation. The conference resolution specified that London was where its clearing house should be based, possibly because the Plunkett Foundation was already there but also because it would be near Westminster and the political and administrative heart of the British Empire.

THE PLUNKETT FOUNDATION AFTER THE WEMBLEY CONFERENCE

The conference report was entitled *Agricultural Co-operation in its Applications to the Industry, the Business, and the Life of the Farmer in the British Empire in 1925* and included Karl Walter's preliminary survey. Two years later the Foundation began publishing its *Year Book of Agricultural Co-operation in the British Empire*. Its title was changed in 1930 to *Year Book of Agricultural Co-operation* reflecting, perhaps, growing unease about Empire but more likely a broadening geographical coverage in content and readership.

This work and the additional staff recruited to do it were funded by Sir Horace who 'more than doubled his original gift'.[35] One of the new recruits was Margaret Digby (1900–1985), who became a leader of the Foundation and an important figure in co-operative development in the British Empire and later the Commonwealth. Initially employed in 1927 as a part-time research assistant she became secretary of the Foundation in 1932 and headed it until her retirement in 1967.

Margaret Digby was an obvious 'blue stocking' who never married. Despite an undoubted intellect she had little formal education. She had been raised by two spinster aunts of radical persuasions. Her friends were left-wing and she became a socialist. Early co-operative jobs included one in the office of the Co-operative Women's Guild led by Margaret Llewellyn Davies (1862–1944). Llewellyn Davies helped form the International Conference of Women Co-operators which in 1924 became the International Co-operative Women's Guild. An Irish friend was Florence Marks, who had moved to London from Dublin with the Co-operative Reference Library and had told Margaret Digby about the research position with the Foundation.

Despite differences in attitude and background she and Sir Horace developed a close working relationship which is well-reflected in her biography of him, *An Anglo-American Irishman* (1949).

In her memoirs Digby wrote excellent pen portraits of her fellow workers as well as descriptions of Plunkett's final years:

> His slight, bent figure was familiar to all who worked there. He had a thatch of grey hair and a short, neat beard, a good forehead, a very alert, rather cold, eye and long, firm mouth. He had fine hands, both sensitive and capable; he had been a horseman before he was a motorist. He had most beautiful manners . . . His courtesy was reassuring to the young and diffident, but there was a steely quality underneath. Shoddy thinking or laziness . . . would be met, not so much with blame as with contempt. He had a sharp,

> wry sense of humour and could sum up those of whom he did not approve in a few tart words – 'If that man is not a rogue he ought to take an action against his face.' He liked to talk (though he never rambled) about his early life, his 'cowboy days' when 'you should always sell cattle in the dusk. They look larger'.[36]

Plunkett liked to gather the entire Foundation staff around him to discuss his current work including his writings. On occasion he would ask 'What did you think of that paragraph, Miss D? Could you suggest a different form of words?' He noted the drift of staff comments and once wrote in his diary 'Relevancies from Miss Digby'. Their mutual regard led to closer working relations.

Digby also wrote engaging descriptions of those who visited the Foundation. They included Leonard Wolff, husband of Virginia Wolff, whom she described as,

> Seeming younger than he probably was, but haggard and bony and wild, with pale blue eyes, long hair and a humane expression. He always spoke in a low voice but was pleasant and natural. 'I am writing a silly sort of pamphlet,' he would say, before coming to the Library for material.[37]

A less publicly well-known figure was Patrick Hannon who had produced the report on co-operative potential in Cape Colony which we noted in Chapter 7. According to Digby, Plunkett had picked him up as 'a shoeless and penniless country boy in Ireland, and had trained him as a co-operative organiser'. He was later believed to 'have married money and had become a rich man and a Member of Parliament'.

Digby gives us insights into the Plunkett Foundation's early work. Besides its research and a growing list of publications, there were talks at the highest levels on agriculture and on agricultural co-operatives. She was asked to handle an early enquiry that had been started by the Ministry of Agriculture but had not progressed very far, since it was an immense job to look 'into the legal position of co-operatives throughout the world'. It was perhaps an indication of the growing interest of officialdom in co-operatives. It gave Digby important groundwork for her career. It 'introduced me to the logical fascinations of the law, which can only be deduced step by step, from its written base, however ill-conceived that base may sometimes be'.[38] She found that much of the research material she required was already housed in the Foundation's library, but it required summarising or translating. Despite having little formal education Digby had mastered five languages which obviously stood her in good stead. This new work also brought her into the official world and included trips to the Colonial Office library. Significantly she concluded:

> I was little impressed with the mind that governed the empire, at least in the lower reaches of Whitehall. At this time, however, I was fairly certain, like many of my contemporaries, that the empire had better not be there.[39]

She learned to be discreet about her views, particularly when 'Plunkett himself brought me into the penumbra of official life at a higher level'. On one occasion she found herself in the presence of Prime Minister Stanley Baldwin. She gives a delightful vignette of herself and Sir Horace on the doorstep of 10 Downing Street with Sir Horace pausing to ask 'with apparent earnestness, "Now is there anything you specially want the P.M. to say?" ' Sir Horace had been asked to brief Baldwin on a coming debate on agriculture.

Despite such high-level work Digby observed that 'I never took my role as professional statute drafter or cabinet adviser seriously, but I do not think I realised what an excellent training it was.'[40] This training stood her and the Plunkett Foundation in good stead during the inter-war years. The Foundation was weakened by Plunkett's death in 1932, and complications with his will; also growing financial problems and worsening international relations as the world headed towards the 1939–45 war.[41] Nevertheless its research and advisory work grew. It became even more significant in post-war years as the Empire that Digby thought 'had better not be there' evolved into the Commonwealth and its colonies gained independence.

CONCLUSIONS

This chapter has traced the setting-up of the Plunkett Foundation. Horace Plunkett was already a renowned builder of institutions, including various co-operative support organisations in Ireland such as the IAOS that was later copied in England, Wales and Scotland. His Plunkett Foundation, which he generously endowed, should be viewed in this light. The Foundation built on the library he had begun with Fr Tom Finlay. Known as the Co-operative Reference Library it moved from Dublin to London after the Wembley conference of 1925 which had called for a 'clearing house' of information for agricultural co-operatives throughout the British Empire. It was not intended to become a competitor of the ICA but rather a complementary and mutually beneficial body.

The 1925 conference was significant because it attracted considerable co-operative interest and was attended by co-operative leaders from Britain and the Empire. The latter were largely from agricultural co-operative movements while those from Britain included many from the Consumer Co-operative Movement. We have focused primarily on the discussions relating to co-operatives and the state. These revealed how the state could assist co-operative development, with examples quoted from Canada and India. However, state officials needed to be imbued with co-operative spirit and to be aware that their roles should be temporary until co-operatives could become self-funding and self-managing. Various dualities were highlighted. For instance co-operatives were both economic and social institutions; and voluntary organisations, rather than government departments, were better placed to encourage the latter. Another duality was that governments could benefit society in general by promoting co-operatives. An example quoted was the improvement to Canadian exports by the development of co-operative wheat pools.

Plunkett had been a vital force in co-operative development in Ireland and elsewhere; in his later years he advised about agricultural co-operatives in India. Earlier his ideas had been taken up enthusiastically in America and to a lesser extent in Canada. His Plunkett Foundation provided a means for his work to continue after his death. Margaret Digby, who had proved such an admirable helper during Plunkett's final years, was to lead the Foundation for the next thirty-six years during which time the British Empire, the framework in which the Foundation had been formed, came to an end. Sir Horace was an imperialist by birth. Margaret Digby was not and was well-placed to take the Plunkett Foundation through these final years of the Empire.

10. Civil Servants in Colonial Co-operative Development

INTRODUCTION

This chapter traces the emergence of other support systems in British colonial co-operative development, and focuses largely on the role of the Colonial Service. Doubt was expressed at the Plunkett Foundation's conference at Wembley in 1925 whether civil servants could work effectively in co-operative development. Some believed that voluntary workers, non-government organisations and co-operators were better suited. C. F. Strickland had argued, however, that colonial civil servants could also be co-operators. Nevertheless, the background of British colonial administrators was so different from potential colonial co-operative members that we need to examine how they overcame such differences and become an important part in British colonial co-operative development.

In addition, this chapter explores ways in which colonial civil servants learned about co-operatives, such knowledge forming no part of their formal education and training. Before that, however, we need to look at the nature and role of the Colonial or Indian Civil Services and the backgrounds of their recruits.

THE COLONIAL AND INDIAN CIVIL SERVICES

Recruits to the Colonial and Indian Civil Services (CCS and ICS)were likely to be high flyers from the professional upper and middle classes. Both services demanded high entrance qualifications. The ICS was the more specialised in that its appointees were expected to operate only within the Indian Empire including Burma. Potential candidates were identified at school or university and sat two entrance examinations (the second was not taken unless the first was passed). Successful candidates in the first exam followed this with a year's probation at an English or Scottish university, where they prepared for the second exam, which included compulsory papers in the Indian penal code and procedures, the principal language of an Indian area and the Indian Evidence and Contracts Acts. There were additional papers from which candidates could choose, including other aspects of Indian law and languages. Before motor cars successful candidates also had to show that they could journey on horseback.[1]

The CCS was the more general of the two, covering wider and more disparate areas. Applicants heading for work in Malaya, Ceylon and Hong Kong had to take the ICS exams while those seeking positions in Africa and the lesser tropical colonies were often appointed by private interview after prior assessment had been made at their schools or universities. Once appointed they could sometimes stay in the same position for long periods. They learned on the job which possibly led to the view that many colonial officials were 'recruited more for character than brain power'.[2] In either the Indian or Colonial Service appointees were expected to work hard. The ICS conduct rules stated that they could be asked to work twenty-four hours a day.

Appointments to both services were made in London. This enabled a centralised recruitment process, avoiding the risks of local patronage. Nevertheless it led to the recruitment of similar types: upper-middle-class males educated in British public schools and universities who could be easily viewed as an 'old-boy network'. Their shared backgrounds may have fostered cohesiveness and an esprit de corps, helpful once out in the field and facilitated communications possibly including knowledge of co-operatives.

In the 1920s recruitment to the CCS was widened to include candidates from the dominions. The end of the First World War brought a dramatic expansion. One reason was 'the expanded establishment of the territorial government'. Another was a 'need to fill the backlog of vacancies brought about by four years of non-recruitment, natural wastage and the heavy casualties among Colonial Service officers killed or wounded in action or drowned at sea'. Preference was given to applicants with wartime service, many of whom retained their armed forces rank after joining the CCS. A further reason for recruitment being spread to the dominions was the division of the Colonial Office into two in 1925. One office dealt with the colonies and the other the dominions but they shared a technically interchangeable staff.[3]

Members of the ICS and CCS could have learned about co-operatives in a number of ways. Officers journeying to the far corners of the Empire needed to be kitted out and this could have brought them into touch with a group of civil service 'co-operatives'. Prominent among these was the Army and Navy Stores which had developed the specialist trade of clothing and equipping colonial officers for the field.

Extensive advice was given on shipping orders. For example, officers going out to West Africa were warned 'never be parted from your mosquito net' or 'never eat tinned food if you can get fresh'. As far as local food was concerned they were urged to avoid all over-ripe fruit, meat or fish which was the least bit tainted:

> When a tin of provisions – animal or vegetable – has been opened, its contents must at once be emptied into a glass or earthenware vessel. Neglect to do this is a frequent source of ptomaine poisoning, and one's servants have to be constantly kept up to the mark in this respect, as they cannot see the necessity for the precaution.[4]

Recruits were advised that working hours varied in different colonies and protectorates. A general recommendation was that they should get up early and do as much work as possible before 11 a.m. thus leaving the more mundane and routine matters until the hotter part of the day. An early breakfast of bacon and egg by 6.15 a.m. was also suggested as it was important to eat before going out. Other meals during the day could be taken at times appropriate to a location and work routine. Officers were told that working hours in West Africa were similar to those in England but they were advised that all work should be done 'regularly and with method'. Those who needed to travel were also advised to arrange their journeys to ensure that 'the in-coming and out-going official mails are not neglected'.[5] Keeping a work diary was also recommended as it helped remind officers of things to be done.

Extensive advice was also given on how officers should be equipped. Recommendations included:

> Mosquito net
> White pith sun hat, with puggaree [thin scarf of muslin worn around hat sometimes falling to shield back of neck from sun]
> White umbrella, lined
> Large kettle or camp saucepan, to hold at least five pints of boiling water
> Lantern, to burn candles or vegetable oil
> Medicines [long list provided]
> Two cases of provisions
> The most recent map or maps of Colony or Protectorate[6]

Dress should include 'several flannel tennis or khaki suits, an old serge or tweed suit and a light waterproof . . . also an overcoat . . . chiefly on the voyages'. Officers of higher grade were advised to pack a dress suit with dinner jacket which would also be needed on the voyage out and home, along with heavy underclothing. Summer woollen underclothing was suggested once in post. It was recommended that a woollen undervest should be worn beneath a flannel, linen or cotton shirt. Shirts, vests and 'drawers' should be changed 'when possible' once every day; so at least eight sets of each were needed plus 'Needles, thread. Buttons &c'. Two pairs of brown leather boots were required 'and dubbin should not be forgotten'. Bush boots should be 'well nailed' and mosquito boots also taken. 'Shoes should only be worn when playing tennis, cricket or other games.'

Advice was also given on how to store clothes so as to guard against moth and mould. Besides household items officers who travelled should also take camping equipment. Tents would be supplied by the government but officers should take items such as pump, camp bed, bedding and mosquito net, waterproof sheet approximately 8ft by 6ft, bath and washstand combined, canvas bucket, camp table and chair, large water bottle, cooking and eating utensils. Twenty yards of muslin was recommended to make houses mosquito proof, along with two air-tight uniform cases, revolver with ammunition, small compass, hammer, nails and case opener.

At base officers were advised to eat fresh rather than tinned foods but items of a 'less perishable kind' could be bought more cheaply in England and transported. These included tea, coffee, cocoa, tinned milk, rolled oats, tinned sardines and assorted meats, tins of marmalade, jam, butter and plain biscuits, salt, pepper and mustard, soda siphon with sparklets, tinned soups, soup squares, tinned curry power, rice, beef dripping and tins of assorted vegetables, fruit, bottled pickles, Worcestershire sauce and lime juice. In some postings the government provided home furnishings; in others officers had to ship out what they needed, including a latrine pan with rim, cover, sand box and sand scoop; pantry equipment should always include a meat safe and in kitchen equipment there should be a water drum and water bucket.[7]

Such requirements created a considerable specialised market. One famous stockist was the Army and Navy Stores in London which claimed to be a co-operative. It was one of a number of civil service 'co-operatives' set up in the late 1800s. The first had been the Civil Service Supply Association founded in 1867 by a group of civil servants. Its success encouraged other 'co-operatives' including the Army and Navy Stores in 1871 which registered under the Companies Acts of

1862 and 1867 rather than the Industrial and Provident Societies Acts. Its membership was drawn from the:

> Army and Navy: Militia or Yeomanry; Peers, Privy Councillors, Lords Lieutenant and Deputy Lieutenants; foreign and English ambassadors and senior officials of the Foreign Office; Secretaries of State; Cabinet Ministers or Heads of Department of Cabinet offices; members of the Royal Company of Scottish Archers; officers of the Royal Irish, Indian and Colonial Constabulary; Civil officers of Government of India, and last but not least, the secretaries or other recognised officers of the Naval and Military messes and canteens. In addition those entitled to be shareholders could introduce life or annual Members, who paid for the privilege. This list in effect includes the whole of the Establishment.[8]

The membership and registration under company legislation did not prevent the Army and Navy Stores being a co-operative nor hamper its aim 'to supply Members with goods of the first quality at the lowest possible price'. Where the rules of the Stores took it away from the co-operative form was when they breached the principle of open membership by specifying 'the class of persons entitled to apply for shares'. Likewise, when it provided for its members' shares to appreciate in value rather than remain fixed. To the undiscerning the Army and Navy Stores could seem to be a co-operative and thus provided some kind of introduction to members of the Indian and Colonial Services.

Civil Service co-operatives also formed in other parts of the Empire and usually registered under company law. The New South Wales Civil Service Co-operative, formed in Sydney in 1871, was said to have confused co-operative identity because:

> It was quoted on the Stock Exchange, paid fixed and higher than bank Rate levels of interest on capital and was effectively controlled by a small coterie of investors and managers. Long held in contempt by [trades] Unionists as an expression of co-operation's dubious democracy, it sullied co-operation's reputation in worker circles, stole potential patronage from genuine Rochdale stores.[9]

Whether the Civil Service Association formed real 'co-operatives' or not is perhaps a less significant point than the fact that they played a major part in equipping officers of the Indian Civil and Colonial Services for their overseas service.

THE FLAG FOLLOWS TRADE

An early maxim of the Empire had been that 'the flag follows trade'. In other words trade came first and the British flag followed to protect and advance it. Throughout this study we have noted the pioneering role of various British trading companies such as the British South Africa Company spearheaded by Cecil Rhodes. Their employees operated alongside officers of the Indian Civil and Colonial Services who had to take account of these British interests. Often they included representatives of the British Co-operative Wholesale Societies. Insight into their operations and the ex-patriate lives of their representatives can be gathered from a number of articles in the British co-operative press, for instance in *The People's Year Book* (1921) dealing with the operations of the CWS in West Africa. The article immediately claims that the CWS was trading in the area for quite different reasons from those of its capitalistic competitors:

> Today is the day of 'Big Business'. Gigantic aggregations, amalgamations, and combinations of capital exist whose policy is to monopolise, to 'corner' the natural resources and wealth of the world, in the interest, and for the benefit of the few, at the expense of the many. The Co-operative Movement, the trade union of the consumer, is the only substantial bulwark against the complete exploitation of the workers, and the development of these huge trusts and combines has compelled the C.W.S. in self-defence, to go direct to the sources of supply for the requisite quantities of raw materials necessary to meet Co-operative requirements.[10]

An important part of the CWS's business in West Africa was the purchase and shipment of large volumes of palm kernel and palm oil to CWS factories in Britain which manufactured soap, paints, lubricants and, increasingly, margarine. The CWS had developed a strong presence in Sierra Leone and Nigeria – the Palm Belt.

Apparently 'Big Business' was also well established in the region with branches in even 'the most remote places where the solitary white manager leads a most monotonous and lonely life'. There were many work problems including poor transport systems that were 'totally inadequate to deal with the volume of trade'. Often goods had to be stockpiled until transport became available.

The prime reason for the presence of the two British CWSs in the colonies was to serve the British co-operative consumer. Their representatives may have given the colonial officer only a limited insight into co-operatives. However, wider perspectives could have been obtained from international co-operative bodies such as the Plunkett Foundation and particularly from the ICA which undertook a review of co-operative principles in the 1930s and clarified the definition of co-operatives.

1930S ICA REVIEW OF CO-OPERATIVE PRINCIPLES

By the 1930s formal co-operatives had existed for almost one hundred years and had appeared in the four corners of the globe. However, they still lacked a clear and universally accepted definition, Co-operatives interpreted or expressed co-operative principles in different ways. For example, consumer co-operatives and thrift and credit societies could begin operating on members' share capital whereas this was usually insufficient in agricultural co-operatives, various productive societies and housing co-operatives. Sometimes additional capital came from the state which created new dynamics and relationships. Consumer and thrift and credit societies could also observe the principle of open membership. This became difficult, however, in worker and housing co-operatives where the sales of goods produced influenced the number of worker/members who could be employed or where housing stock restricted the number of member/inhabitants.

The ICA was the natural candidate to conduct such a review being the senior international co-operative organisation in terms of age, geographical spread and democratic structure. By the 1930s it also recognised that it needed a clear definition. From its inception the Alliance's constitution was closely based on the Rochdale principles and national co-operative movements were admitted according to how closely their rules observed those principles.

Moreover, the ICA faced difficulties from the rise of Communist and Nazi and fascist regimes which imposed changes on national co-operative movements causing doubt as to how far they remained voluntary and independent co-operative movements and therefore eligible for ICA membership. For these reasons, the ICA needed a modern restatement of co-operative principles.

A review was agreed at its congress in Vienna in 1930.[11] This proved inconclusive and the first report of the Special Committee appointed to conduct the review was not accepted. The ICA's London congress of 1934 called for a further review. Its report was accepted by the Alliance's congress in Paris in 1937 but with reservations.

This was a rather unsatisfactory outcome but hindsight suggests reasons. One was that consumer co-operative movements comprised the predominant group in the Alliance at that time and were strongly represented in the Special Committee appointed to conduct the review. It was not surprising, therefore, that they should adopt the yardstick of the Rochdale principles by which to conduct the review.

Their influence was bolstered by that of the ICA's general secretary, Henry May, who administered the review. A Briton, he had served in the British Consumer Co-operative movement before becoming secretary, and made the Rochdale principles the basis of his questionnaires to ICA member movements in order to assess how far they were still being observed.[12]

Another reason why the principles of consumer co-operation featured so heavily in the 1930s review was that the theory of consumer co-operation had triumphed over that of producer co-operation in the late nineteenth century and consumer co-operatives were still expanding and achieving considerable commercial success.

Consequently, Rochdale's influence can be seen in the Special Committee's first report. This declared that fundamental co-operative principles were:

Open Membership
Democratic Control
Dividend on Purchases
Limited Interest on Capital
Political and Religious Neutrality
Cash Trading
Promotion of Education[13]

It also identified 'Other Basic Principles of Co-operation', which although not expressly included in the Rochdale formula were considered central to the 'Co-operative System'. These were mutuality with trade between members only; voluntary membership; and sale at current or market prices. It was recognised that it was not always possible to apply these. For example, changed circumstances might make it no longer feasible to restrict trade to members only although it should remain the ideal because it was basic to mutuality. Where an 'arbitrary interpretation' could not be sustained a 'limit as narrow as possible' should be imposed to meet the 'casual or accidental demands' of non-members.[14]

The Special Committee also acknowledged that open membership had not been specifically stated within the Rochdale principles but believed it to be inherent in the Society's rules and operations. New dictatorships created conditions quite different from those experienced by the Rochdale Pioneers who lacked economic resources but were free voluntarily to risk their savings in a Utopian enterprise. The demands of modern authoritarian regimes sometimes led to people compulsorily joining co-operatives which meant that the voluntary principle could not apply. Yet the freedom the voluntary principle represented was fundamental to a true co-operative and should therefore remain an ideal.[15]

The principle of sale at current or market prices was acknowledged by members of the Special Committee as a device by the Pioneers to blunt the opposition of private traders, but they believed that it should be retained because its absence could prove 'inimical to the interests of the community in general'.[16]

The Special Committee's proposal that 'inalienable assets' should be considered another 'Basic Co-operative Principle' ran into strong opposition which revealed a fundamental divide between Rochdale and co-operative movements in other countries and traditions. Rochdale and British societies following its model provided in their rules that should they be dissolved the balance of their assets over liabilities should be divided among their members. Some co-operative movements elsewhere laid down that if societies were liquidated their collective assets should be passed to other co-operatives, disinterested organisations or to public utilities. Their reasoning was that a rule that allowed division among members could become a motive to wind up a society. The strong and opposing evidence received by the Special Committee led it to take no definitive position. Instead it recommended that co-operatives should make regular allocations to inalienable reserves and that national legislation should clearly lay down what should happen to collective assets if liquidation did occur.[17]

The question of inalienable assets aroused heated discussion at the ICA congress in London in 1934 when the Special Committee's first report was submitted, as did the issues of cash trading and co-operatives' observance of religious and political neutrality. In the heat of these debates a French delegate appealed for latitude and suggested that co-operative principles should not be applied in ways that restricted co-operatives as 'living organisms'. It was far more important that they should retain the 'co-operative spirit'.[18] This phrase 'the co-operative spirit' found its way into British colonial co-operative development as we shall see. The congress concluded that the Special Committee's report had been too consumer oriented. It referred it back and asked the Special Committee to enquire into other co-operatives' application of co-operative principles. Consequently, the Special Committee extended its enquiries to CWSs, workers' productive societies, agricultural productive societies, credit societies and co-operative banks but reported to the ICA's next congress in Paris in 1937 that responses had been so inadequate that it had found it 'difficult to draw firm conclusions'.[19] The inadequate responses may, however, have been a measure of the difficulty of accommodating co-operative principles under one formula such as Rochdale and then using it to define co-operatives.

The 1930s review of co-operative principles therefore proved somewhat unsatisfactory and inconclusive, yet the principles were clearly adopted by colonial officers involved in co-operative development. Officers' writings reveal that they had read widely about co-operatives, were aware of various definitions and that they had recognised that co-operatives represented a form of business distinct from the investor-led. The fact that many headed their departmental reports 'Co-operation' rather than 'Co-operatives' also suggests that they recognised co-operatives as an ideological as well as an economic system.

THE WRITINGS OF COLONIAL CO-OPERATIVE REGISTRARS

Co-operative literature had grown massively from the mid-nineteenth century. Its extent is illustrated in various co-operative bibliographies. These became so large that by the 1950s some were compressed into 'select' versions containing the most important references. Such an example was published with the Plunkett *Year Book of Agricultural Co-operation, 1954* and some idea of its scope can be gathered from its subject headings which were:

> Co-operation General – by continental regions and countries; Bibliographies and libraries; Biographies; Book-keeping and audit; Congresses; Consumers' co-operation; Co-operative and collective farming; Credit and banking; Directories; Education and Training; Electrification; Films; Fisheries; Forestry; Grass-drying; Health; History; Housing; Insurance; Irrigation; Legislation; Marketing; Novels; Organisation, administration and finance; Petroleum; Politics and relations with the state; Post-war relief and construction; Press; Producer–consumer relations; Purchasing and machinery; Refrigeration; Religion and co-operation; Statistics; Taxation; Transport; Women and co-operation; Workers' productive societies and labour contracting; Year books and annual reports; Youth and school co-operatives.

These were then divided geographically into over eighty countries.[20]

During the inter-war years British colonial co-operative registrars began to contribute to co-operative literature and so assisted colonial co-operative development.

Both company and co-operative registrars existed under colonial legislation but because co-operatives had become part of the Empire's development agency functions their registrar had additional responsibilities including promoting, nurturing, supervising and auditing societies. He headed a specially created Department of Co-operation or a co-operative branch within a Department of Agriculture which operated within a specific area of British imperial administration, usually a province or 'state'. Within this he and his department also liaised with non-governmental organisations such as co-operative unions or institutes and provincial 'apex' banks.[21].

The co-operative registrar's promotional work assumed increased importance but took time. Co-operatives did not necessarily form spontaneously in under-developed areas. Often future members needed to be persuaded to form one and further persuaded that they could safely invest their limited savings in it. They often also required training in appropriate organisational and business skills and such training became a further responsibility of the co-operative registrar and his department.

It is not always easy to establish statistically the rate of colonial co-operative growth. Different territories tended to compile statistics differently or they varied between different types of co-operative or were complicated by shifting monetary values. Growth, however, is suggested by the increasing number of co-operative registrars among whom a sense of identity began to emerge. Some in India started to hold periodic conferences to discuss policy and administration and exchange experiences.[22] It is from among these registrars that early authors on colonial co-operative development appeared.

Prominent among them were H. Calvert, C. F. Strickland and M. Darling whose writings have been said to have done much to lay the foundations of British colonial co-operative development.[23] Their books suggest an almost encyclopaedic knowledge of co-operatives from which they appear to derive an enthusiasm for the role they could play in development. Few personal descriptions of them survive. Sir Malcolm Darling seems to have been 'a man of wide experience, mainly in India, commanding character and distinguished mind; also with a sense of humour',[24] while Strickland whom we first met at the Plunkett conference at Wembley in 1925 was 'one of the three great co-operative registrars of the Punjab' and was 'quietly amusing'.[25] Later Darling became chairman of the Plunkett Foundation and Strickland one of its trustees, thus creating symbiotic links between colonial co-operative development and the Foundation.

At this stage we are mainly concerned with the writings of Calvert and Strickland. Darling wrote less and his main contribution during the period was his book, *Some Aspects of Co-operation in Germany, Italy and Ireland*, published by the Lahore government in 1922. It suggests that colonial co-operative registrars in the 1920s were still focusing on European co-operative experiences and that insufficient of their own had emerged to write about. That changed in the 1930s particularly with two books published in 1933.

Calvert's *The Law and Principles of Co-operation* has been termed a 'co-operative classic',[26] and went into five editions. Its importance can be gauged from the dedication B. J. Surridge and Margaret Digby made when their *Manual of Co-operative Law and Practice* was published in 1948. They dedicated it to:

> H. Calvert, Esquire, C.S.I., C.I.E., I.C.S. (retired) whose *Law and Principles of Co-operation* has been taken, with his permission, as a basis for this book and to whom one of the authors, an ex-Registrar of Co-operative Societies [Surridge], remains always indebted for his counsel.[27]

Friendship and a sense of identity can also be detected from the fact that Calvert dedicated his seminal work, 'To my Colleagues M. L. Darling and C. F. Strickland'. His book is important for the way it links co-operative law and co-operative principles which are illustrated by references to the Indian Co-operative Societies' Act of 1912. Unlike the preceding Act of 1904 this applied to the whole of India and to all kinds of co-operative and influenced subsequent Indian co-operative legislation.

In Chapter 6 we traced how Henry Wolff had campaigned for a 'co-operative' Act in India rather than one that comprised an addition to company law. Calvert explains why company legislation proved appropriate. He noted that in Britain Industrial and Provident Societies Acts had evolved from friendly society legislation and that this had recognised a right of voluntary association. No similar tradition existed in India. Even in Britain the right of association was relatively new because it had not been possible before the repeal of the Combination Acts in 1824. Calvert argued that because no similar transition had yet occurred in India, it made sense to adapt Indian company legislation. Moreover, that offered greater 'simplicity and elasticity' than the Industrial and Provident Societies Acts in Britain.[28]

Under the Indian Co-operative Societies Act of 1912 ultimate responsibility for the observance of co-operative principles was passed to the co-operative registrar. Framing co-operatives' rules and by-laws was the responsibility of local government in order to take account of regional conditions. However, the registrar was ultimately responsible for approving these before the registration of a co-operative.[29]

> The Indian Act suggests (section 4) that a Co-operative Society is a society which has as its object the promotion of the economic interests of its members in accordance with co-operative principles. But it leaves to the Registrar the decision as to what co-operative principles are.[30]

Calvert interprets these in his opening chapter entitled 'What is Co-operation?'. He examines various definitions and links them with examples from Austria, Japan, British Columbia, Romania, Belgium, America, Tunisia, French West Africa, South Africa and Germany, with frequent references to the legislation applying to them.

His premise is that poverty leads people to form co-operatives and that this becomes their common bond. From this he advances four co-operative principles:

> As all [members] lacked a sufficiency of capital, capital could not be the basis of association. The only other basis was the human individual, and accordingly the first principle of co-operation is that the members join as human persons and not as capitalists. The second principle follows from the first: for if all persons meet to satisfy the common need, there should be no distinction between them in the satisfaction of this need. They must meet on a basis of equality. The third principle is not peculiar to co-operation, but its importance in the life of a society is so very great that it deserves a special place. The act of association must be voluntary. The fourth principle is that the members join to promote the economic interests of themselves, and not of anybody else.[31]

This analysis emerges from extensive study of co-operatives as had the conclusions of the ICA's 1930s review into co-operative principles. Yet they are somewhat different inasmuch as Calvert opts for more general rather than specific operations. Those responsible for the ICA analysis might not have disagreed with Calvert's but would, no doubt, have wanted to put more flesh on the bone. The important thing for Calvert and his registrar-friends is that he gives a working definition that is appropriate for colonial co-operative development.

He can be somewhat contradictory. At one point he states that co-operation is 'not primarily an ethical movement but a strictly business one and many failures in India would have been avoided if this had been more stressed'.[32] Yet elsewhere he says:

> Human beings, and not capitalists, bind themselves together to 'work each for all and all for each' . . . Co-operation stands out for moral uplift, for honesty and for the homely virtues that count so much in the daily lives of the people. It possesses the peculiar faculty of making virtue pay . . . Moreover, the morals of an individual cease to be a purely private matter for his own conscience, they become of importance to the whole community to which he belongs.[33]

Calvert also clearly recognises that 'Co-operation differs from its rival, capitalism, in that it promotes peace and not strife, unselfishness and not self-seeking.' He acknowledges that European co-operative leaders saw it being more than just a means that enabled 'a farmer to save or make more money':

> Many of its most ardent apostles look upon it as a sort of social reform, indeed in some cases, as religion. They consider it not only as an economic, but also as a moral movement. And there is little doubt that many helpers are attracted by the evidence they see on every hand of social improvement wherever co-operation has obtained a firm foothold. It seems impossible to study the progress of the movement in any country in the world without being impressed by the great moral gain accompanying the spread of these societies for self-help through mutual help.[34]

Calvert turns later in his book to practicalities and deals with topics such as the objects of co-operative societies, liability, interest, conditions necessary to create a credit society and the provisions of the 1912 Indian Act. He says less than Strickland did in *Co-operation for Africa*[35] about the role of the co-operative registrar as someone who animates and motivates potential co-operative members. Strickland illustrates the central importance of this but also shows, like Calvert, that co-operative development is shaped by its location and target population.

His book was published in the same year as Calvert's and deals with African co-operative experiences. Strickland emphasises how African history and tribal conditions impacted on co-operative development. The text also reflects a shift in imperial thinking in its introduction written by the Rt Hon. the Lord Lugard.

Son of a British chaplain in Madras Lugard failed the ICS entrance examination and joined the army instead. After serving in campaigns in Afghanistan, the Sudan and Burma he joined a force raised by the African Lakes Company and became involved in East African developments. Later recruited into the Imperial British East Africa Company he virtually became known as 'the father of British Uganda'. His subsequent fame rested on the way he secured Britain's position in Nigeria where he later became governor-general.[36] There Lugard developed new ideas about imperial government central to which was the concept of indirect rule. It postulated that indigenous populations could maintain their own social and political forms.

> Under his inspiration indirect rule was carried in Nigeria to a pitch and subtlety and complexity never equalled elsewhere. Lugard began as a mercenary of Empire: but he was already acquiring the habits of an apostle, a dedicated champion of imperial trusteeship, of a paternal imperialism which would allow native peoples to develop, not in their own time, but at least according to their own cultures – while ensuring that the resources of their territories were developed for the benefit of the world as a whole . . . He was one of the very few British theorists of Empire to apply his ideas in the field – the very antithesis of the proper, unobtrusive bureaucrat the Indian Civil Service might have made of him.[37]

Lugard was therefore an important colonial administrator and theorist. The fact that he was prepared to write the introduction to Strickland's book suggests that he believed co-operation was relevant to his ideas. He noted that co-operation was practised from 'Iceland to South America, from Belgium to Japan, but so far has been little understood or practised by the European nations who control the continent of Africa south of the Mediterranean sea-board'. Lugard continued:

> The fundamental principle of the [co-operative] system is identical with that of 'Indirect Rule' – which could better be named 'Co-operative Rule' – the essential aim of both being to teach personal responsibility and initiative. Nowhere more than in Africa among a people too prone to act on the instinct of the mob without individual thought, and too prone to indiscriminate imitation, can the principle of deliberate and organised co-operation towards a

> definite and recognised objective be of greater value. The immemorial social systems of Africa are, as we all know, in danger of complete disintegration today as a result of the contact with 'Western civilization': systems which amid the tribal conflicts of the past succeeded in maintaining unity, provision for the old and disabled, and obedience to the tribal law – whether based on religion and superstition or on tradition and custom – which have now lost their compelling force.
>
> Chaos cannot be averted by imposing the European institutions of the 20th century. Obedience may be enforced without understanding, but the innovations will neither produce contentment nor will they be permanent. So the task of the administrator is summed up in one word – 'Adaptation'.[38]

Lugard obviously believes co-operatives could be part of the adaptation process but was on more dubious ground when claiming that 'Indirect Rule' and 'Co-operative Rule' were synonymous.

Throughout the book that follows Strickland emphasises the influence of location on co-operative development. After his opening chapters explaining 'What is Co-operation?' and 'What Co-operation has Done' he deals with 'African Society'. In this he notes that the stages of development of African societies were 'extremely diverse' and that 'all degrees of sophistication and civilization are coexistent in African society'. He felt that co-operation was suitable only for 'detribalized' Africans whose

> mentality and . . . economic position are similar in many respects to those of European and the more educated Asiatic races, and since the restoration of tribal rule among them is no longer practicable, the co-operative types of Europe and Asia will for the most part be suitable to them. They will need credit, housing, consumers' societies, &c.[39]

Strickland acknowledged that some Africans still lived 'wholly or partly' under tribal rule. He believed co-operation could help these but that it would need to be suitably adapted by colonial administrators who had a strong knowledge of both 'Co-operation' and 'Africa'.

Like Lugard Strickland recognised that Africa was in a state of flux. He believed that 'a synthesis of western and native cultures has to be achieved', by retaining past heritage but absorbing 'the wealth, material and ideal . . . from the modern world'. It was necessary to give place to the 'educated and critical man' but to hold him in 'the midst of his community to contribute towards and interpret its new morality and understanding'.

Strickland saw some affinity with Lugard's ideas on indirect rule when he says:

> The intention of indirect rule is not to immobilize the native race at the stage of civilization which it has already reached, but to ensure to it the protection of the surroundings and the institutions which it knows and loves, while these are, gradually and with the consent and collaboration of the people themselves, reshaped and (where necessary) purified to admit fresh economic ideas and to reconcile them with higher social and moral requirements.[40]

Advancing African society, Strickland believed, would prompt 'a growing number of associations for specific purposes, operating in connection with the local authority, but not directly operated by it'. He makes an important point when he suggests that such associations should be 'relieved of all functions which are outside their competence and which therefore hamper their growth and that of the differentiation of interests'.

> People who have no cattle will not be particularly interested in co-operative dairying. That is why it would be a mistake to entrust co-operative dairying to the village autonomy, which must devote its fullest capacity to really common interests, and should not be used for private or sectional purposes.[41]

This is an important point because it touches on the concept of mutuality and the fact that at some point there is likely to be a natural boundary in terms of the members who can meaningfully contribute to and benefit from a co-operative's operations. Widening membership, perhaps through compulsion as in the Soviet Union during the 1930s, often weakened the 'common bond' by slackening members' links with the contribution they made and the benefits they received. In economic terms Soviet 'co-operatives' might also have exceeded their optimum size. Again in Tanzania in the post-colonial period compulsory multi-purpose village co-operatives were introduced. While a 'common bond' existed in the sense that members were villagers it was weaker than the more specific common bond that would have existed, say, in Strickland's example of a dairy co-operative.

Strickland emphasised the importance of a specific 'common bond'. He believed that co-operatives were an important example of the autonomous associations he wished to see in African development encouraging the growth of welfare and the development of 'social fibre'.[42] Additionally he believed they helped advance Lugard's ideas of indirect rule.

After his chapter on African society Strickland followed a similar pattern to that in Calvert's book. He noted what co-operatives have achieved elsewhere, described different types of co-operative, and dealt with co-operative law, finance, audit and supervision. Whereas Calvert's book dealt at great length with the 1912 Indian Act, Strickland highlights the Co-operative Ordinance No. 7, 1932 of Tanganyika.[43]

The writings of colonial co-operative registrars suggest that during the inter-war years colonial co-operative development became specialised and professional. Their experiences also shaped their view that the appropriate people to carry out such work were the officials of the ICS or CCS. Strickland had suggested at the Plunkett conference, however, that such a person could also be a co-operator and that it was indeed desirable that he should be. Colonial co-operative registrars clearly preferred a symbiotic relationship between co-operatives and government officials. Calvert in particular saw little place for the external well-wisher.:

> The society exists for the members, and not for anyone else. Special significance, therefore, attaches to the words 'of their members' which are found in most Acts dealing with Co-operative Societies. In some provinces the management is apt to fall into the hands of honorary workers who act more from feelings of charity towards their neighbours than from any desire to train them to dispense with their guidance and help. If a business is such that it cannot be limited to its members, it cannot truly be a co-operative . . .[44]

His statement touches upon a complex issue that might be termed 'paternalism'. That is defined as well-wishers performing functions for co-operatives which they are not yet strong enough to carry out for themselves. In his reference to 'Non-official Leadership' and 'Designated Honorary Organisers' Calvert no doubt meant those identified by Madhav Madane in his essay[45] whom he argued played a beneficial and significant role in the development of Indian co-operation. Calvert was closely involved in that and therefore had the right to disagree. His comments, however, overlook the role that 'paternalism' played in fledgling co-operative movements in non-colonial settings.

It was discernible in Horace Plunkett's assemblage of different interests, aristocratic and Church, in support of his work with Irish co-operatives. Another example was the support the Catholic hierarchy gave for the Desjardins Thrift and Credit Societies in Canada. Even the sturdy and self-reliant British Consumer Co-operative movement[46] owed much to the Christian Socialists not only for their ideas but for their campaign for the first Industrial and Provident Societies Acts at a time the movement carried no political weight.

These examples suggest that young co-operative movements attract well-wishers who are ready, willing and able to help. History shows that that help is eventually withdrawn as movements become self-sufficient. We should note, however, that it seemed to last longest in movements promoted by colonial administrations, thus prompting fears recognised by C. A. Dunning at the Plunkett conference that feelings of dependency had been created.[47]

CONCLUSIONS

British colonial co-operative development in the early 1920s was still being guided by what co-operatives had achieved in Europe and North America. Ten years later that was changing. Accrued colonial experience was being distilled in reports and books written by leading co-operative registrars. Prominent among these were Calvert and Strickland who approached co-operation from different perspectives from those of the early pioneers, Wolff, Plunkett and Grey.

One reason was that they were taking co-operatives into new geographical areas as part of a hierarchical imperial administration. They also came from different élites, being highly educated, but essentially from Britain's professional upper and middle classes. This meant that there was a huge divide between them and the peasants they wanted to organise into co-operatives although this was in part overcome by good intentions and good will.

Calvert and Strickland wrote at a time of a shift in imperial ideas. Some fifty years earlier Sir William Wedderburn, a judge at Poona, had illustrated plurality of thought in the ICS through his ability to propose pre-co-operative ideas. During the inter-war years Lugard advanced ideas of indirect rule in which both he and Strickland saw a role for co-operatives. In between Wedderburn and Lugard the British Empire had accepted ideas that economic and social development was necessary if the Empire was to make its resources fully productive but also as a means of preventing political unrest. Co-operatives had become part of the Empire's wider development agency functions.

Strickland in particular suggested that co-operatives could be part of the 'adaptation' that the British Empire needed to make particularly in a changing Africa.

We have also noted a growing co-operative literature which revealed co-operatives to be world-wide and not only a phenomenon of the British Empire.

11. Co-operative Development in the Middle East between the Two World Wars

INTRODUCTION

This chapter completes Part Two which has explored aspects of co-operative development in the British Empire during the inter-war years. Earlier we noted how such development was prompted for a number of economic and social reasons. We also saw that it occurred within a variety of governmental systems ranging from a total British imperial regime in India to emerging self-governments in the dominions. In the Middle East, however, co-operatives would emerge in far more uncertain and shifting political conditions.

The British Empire grew through the need to secure routes for trade and strategic purposes, and pre-empt other empires expanding into British controlled territories. An example of this was Russia's attempts to expand south-eastwards into Asia and threaten British India. A new dimension occurred in the late nineteenth century in the 'scramble for Africa' in which European powers competed for the continent's newly discovered natural resources. In the Middle East another new dimension opened up with the decline of the Turkish Ottoman Empire. Its imminent demise sparked new competition between Britain and France as to how they might benefit from this.

THE MIDDLE EAST AND THE BRITISH EMPIRE

Britain extended its influence in the region in the late nineteenth and early twentieth centuries when parts of the Middle East became known as Britain's 'informal Empire'.[1] They came under British influence not so much for purposes of trade but rather for diplomatic and strategic reasons. Oil had not yet been discovered and the region, splintered by feudal sheikdoms and emirates offered little in the way of intrinsic value. During the decline of the Ottoman Empire Britain gained virtual control of Egypt without giving her the formal status of a colony and was granted mandated powers over Palestine by the League of Nations in 1920.

When the Suez Canal opened in 1869 Britain needed to re-evaluate her Middle East policies. Up until that point her main interests in the region had been to ensure access to India and to contain French and Russian ambitions in the Levant and beyond. Such foreign policy objectives Britain had largely been able to achieve through a softly, softly approach under which she made generous offers to fragmented feudal Arab emirates and sheikdoms if they placed themselves under British protection. This was relatively easy to provide from the nearby British navy and Indian army. It was about this time that the term 'British gunboat diplomacy' was coined.

Although subject to the Turkish sultan, the ruler of Egypt, the khedive, had the power to grant the concession to the Suez Canal Company to build the canal. Britain had initially opposed it, believing it to be a French plot to facilitate her expansion into the Levant and beyond. The canal was opened by the French empress, Eugenie, in 1869 and linked the Mediterranean and the Red Sea thus shortening the sea route to India.

In 1875 the British government under Disraeli changed tack, seeking to control the canal by buying from the khedive 40 per cent of the Suez Canal Company's shares. This made it the largest shareholder although its power was somewhat tempered by the Suez Canal Convention of 1888. Signed in Constantinople, this guaranteed free and open navigation to all vessels during war and peace although Britain and France, now allies, effectively denied their enemies access to it in both World Wars!

The importance of the canal to Britain and her changed policy meant that she now sought greater power over Egypt. Although the khedive remained nominal ruler Britain increased her influence by appointing in 1883 the Earl of Cromer (1841–1917) as British agent and consul-general, a position he held for the next twenty-four years, ensuring continuity of policy. Under Cromer's influence Egyptian administration was brought more and more into British hands.

Cromer was effectively governor of Egypt, reforming its government, economy, military and agriculture. Born Evelyn Baring into the prestigious banking family, his early career had been as an artillery officer in India but later as a financial adviser to the viceroy's council. He was also a skilled diplomat. French and British rivalry in the region could have meant that he would take strong positions with the French. Instead he sought good relations and was probably instrumental in helping to overcome Britain's reservations to the proposed Entente Cordiale between the two countries agreed in 1904.[2]

During the First World War Turkey entered hostilities on the side of Germany. This meant she and her empire became the enemy of Britain and France and that the Middle East became a war zone. Several important diplomatic initiatives within these new parameters reshaped the region after the war and thus the context in which Middle East co-operative development would occur.

One of the most significant of these diplomatic initiatives was the Sykes–Picot Note agreed between Britain and France in 1916. Initially secret it was revealed by the Bolsheviks in 1918. In it Britain and France agreed to divide the Ottoman Empire at the end of the war. Directly or indirectly France would take the whole of Syria, the Lebanon, Cilicia and Mosul. Britain would take what subsequently became known as Transjordan, Iraq and northern Palestine. Britain and France also agreed that other parts of Palestine should come under international control as was later agreed with the League of Nations. The Note also provided for the establishment of an as yet undefined Arab State.[3]

The perhaps better-known commitment that Britain entered into during the war was the Balfour Declaration of 1917. Under this Britain supported the creation of a Jewish homeland in Palestine after the war.

The Balfour Declaration has been ranked alongside the Bolshevik Revolution as one of the two most 'momentous developments' in 1917.[4] It should be seen, however, as part of Britain's overall strategy in the Middle East, which was now a war zone. She had made military advances within an area broadly known as Palestine and had sent General Allenby (1861–1936), previously commander of the British Third Army in France, to take charge of the British army in Palestine. He captured Jerusalem in December 1917 and pushed the Turks back through Syria in early 1918. In October that year he signed the Armistice of Murdros on behalf of Britain and helped ensure British control. In the circumstances it is perhaps not surprising that the League of Nations agreed to Palestine becoming a British mandated territory. This, together with her de facto control of Egypt formed a large part of what became known as Britain's 'Informal Empire in the Middle East'.[5] Allenby was raised to the peerage in 1919 and the same year was appointed British high-commissioner in Egypt, a post he held until 1925.

British and French control in the Middle East, however, was hardly secure. The Arabs were disillusioned with the post-war settlements, but it is difficult to asses how realistic was the prospect an Arab state. There were:

> conflicting 'angles of vision'. The French, the Syrians, the Hashemites, the Zionists, the Palestinians and the Government of India all pulled in different directions while President Wilson insisted on his 'Fourteen Points' on the universal right to self-determination. To add to the confusion, Britain and France issued within hours of the Ottoman surrender a joint declaration in which their war-aim in the area was defined as 'the establishment of national governments and administrations deriving their authority from the initiative and free choice of the indigenous populations' . . . In making this joint governmental declaration now and giving it maximum publicity, France and Britain doubtless had one eye on President Wilson, the other on the kind of control they planned to exert over 'national governments' in their respective zones.'[6]

Post-war co-operative development would take place within a considerably fractured region.

CO-OPERATIVE BEGINNINGS IN EGYPT

Egypt's initial co-operative development might have occurred earlier for at one point it seemed likely that it would become part of the development and reform programmes of the Cromer administration. Indeed, Henry Wolff, that authority on thrift and credit societies whose advice had been sought on Indian co-operative legislation, was told that he was about to be consulted, but an alternative policy was adopted. Clearly co-operatives were not an automatic element within development programmes.

Lord Cromer's wide-ranging reforms included the establishment of the National Bank of Egypt within which was an agricultural section charged with improving Egyptian agriculture and the position of Egypt's fellaheen or peasants. In 1902 the agricultural section was made autonomous and named the Agricultural Bank of Egypt. It then considered how best to channel loans to the fellaheen. At this point a possible role for thrift and credit societies was explored.

Henry Wolff noted that:

> the Egyptian Government had been considering how Co-operative Credit might be made available for the native cultivating population, who certainly seem to have stood in urgent need of judicious financial assistance. Lord Cromer at the time had spoken of likewise thought and in the first instance of Co-operative Credit. I was informed by the late Lord Ilkeston that I was about to be consulted on the matter.[7]

When he was not consulted and co-operatives were not encouraged pique may well have coloured Wolff's assessment of the results. He described in pejorative terms how the Agricultural Bank's 'emissaries literally had . . . to stalk about the country with bags of gold coin on their backs, with the clink and glitter of which to allure reluctant fellaheen to accept advances' and had 'its reward in a huge number of seemingly irrecoverable loans'.[8]

Sir Frederick Nicholson, who was to play a major part in India's first Co-operative Credit Societies Act of 1904, was also dismissive. After visiting Egypt on a fact-finding tour prior to the passing of the Indian legislation he declared that 'the Egyptian system would not at all do for India'.[9] This raises the interesting prospect that it might have been Egypt rather than India that had passed the first notable co-operative legislation within the British Empire.

It later transpired that the sticking point had been the nature of the Egyptian peasant. When the House of Lords appointed a select committee to consider Wolff's Thrift and Credit Societies Bill in 1910 Cromer was a member. Wolff then had an opportunity to speak to him on the matter and Cromer told Wolff that he had been:

> altogether, and enthusiastically in favour of co-operative credit, in opposition to paternal action – more particularly of Co-operative Credit as a help for cultivators. His explanation was that, at the time he carried through the formation of the National Bank of Egypt he did not consider the Egyptian fellaheen quite 'ripe' for Co-operation.[10]

This raises a point of pivotal importance in co-operative development: the nature of a client population. Strickland in his *Co-operation in Africa* refers to ways in which Egyptian peasants differed from their counterparts in other areas of Africa:

> The Egyptian mentality and the economic and social state of the Egyptian peasant are semi-Asiatic, and dissimilar from those of eastern, western and central Africa. Money-lenders abound, and the peasant is habituated to debt. His agriculture is, in Lower Egypt at least, comparatively intensive, and fertilizers bulk large in his requirements. The commercial world is familiar to him, and he regards himself, however, inaccurately, as a man of understanding and ability, qualified to deal in an international market. The consequence in Egypt, as in Asia, has been the

> increasing substitution of commercial for subsistence crops, and a growing subjection of the peasant farmer to the financing individual or institution.[11]

Strickland emphasises that not all peasants are the same and that their economic circumstances can alter as market conditions change. Co-operative developers would need to take account of such nuances.

Tracing the difficulties of the Agricultural Bank of Egypt Strickland noted how the small peasantry were 'unwilling to pay with punctuality'. As a result the Bank was 'compelled to seize many of their holdings' on which it had granted loans on a mortgage basis. In 1912 the Egyptian administration passed the Homestead or Five Feddan Law which exempted such small properties from attachment. This led the Bank to realise that it could no longer lend to 'individual peasants whom it could not supervise' and prompted a reconsideration of the co-operative option. The outbreak of the First World War delayed action and Egypt's first co-operative legislation was not passed until 1923. Apart from a few 'scattered societies', Strickland believes this marks the start of the Egyptian co-operation movement.[12]

Inasmuch as those few 'scattered societies' were spontaneous non-governmental initiatives they should be noted. They owed much to the pioneering work and vision of individuals including Omar Lutfi (1867–1911) who helped found Egypt's first agricultural co-operative in 1908. He had studied European co-operatives and believed that they offered lessons relevant to Egyptian conditions. Lufti was head of the State School of Law at Cairo and a founder of the New University of Cairo.[13] As commendable as his efforts and those of a few others were, they were not widely copied: the real take-off period for Egyptian co-operatives therefore did not come until after the passing of the 1923 Act and its replacement in 1927 by an improved Act.

By 1930 there were over '500 co-operatives with 50,000 members and an owned capital of £176,000'. They were largely rural and agricultural and were helped by more favourable lending arrangements. In 1930 a new Agricultural Bank was established by leading European and Egyptian banks. It, and Bank Misr, Egypt's State Bank, became the main means of channelling government funds to co-operatives. Money was lent to co-operative members for productive purposes such as the purchase of agricultural equipment and supplies, and for some marketing.

Such developments required the appointment of specialist co-operative staff and an autonomous unit was set up in the Department of Agriculture. Writing in 1933 Strickland observed that:

> The Egyptian movement . . . has attained valuable results in establishing a system of credit and of purchase among the villagers. Co-operative education is given to the staff and members, and the importance of an efficient supervision and audit is realized. The breadth of Co-operation as a social agency is acknowledged, though little has yet been done in practice to fulfil its potentialities. The defects appear to be in an excessive closeness of control in certain ways, an unfortunate dependence on State finance, and an omission to form local or central unions for mutual supervision or audit of societies.[14]

Strickland went on to suggest that co-operatives that did not 'provide the bulk of their own finance will not generate a real co-operative spirit'. He therefore hoped that state control would lessen as local co-operative unions developed and was heartened by a statement in a pamphlet produced by the co-operative section of the Department of Agriculture which said:

> We believe that unless a co-operative society has something to its credit more than the improvement of the material condition of its members, and unless it develops their capacities and helps to form character and to elevate social life, it is of little real significance.[15]

It is debatable how far Egyptian co-operatives advanced towards this ideal by the end of the inter-war period. But the nub of the problem had been identified of how to ease dependency on government funding and supervision and encourage self-reliance and control.

We should now turn to consider how during the same period co-operatives emerged in neighbouring Palestine but, sadly, here we need to divide them between Arab and Jewish societies.

ARAB CO-OPERATIVES IN PALESTINE

Zionism during the First World War pressed for a Jewish homeland in Palestine. Such aspirations were endorsed by the British government in its Balfour Declaration of 1917. General Allenby's military successes in the region helped Britain take practical control of Palestine after the war with powers mandated by the League of Nations. This arrangement would continue until 1948 when the United Nations took over responsibility for Palestine: a year later the State of Israel was created.

During the inter-war years Palestine was administered by Britain and by 1940 457,000 Jews, 941,000 Moslems and 119,000 Christians were estimated to live there.[16] These figures are interesting for two reasons. One is to note a population classified by religion rather than ethnicity. The other is that these figures come from a document prepared by the London-based Secretariat of the International Co-operative Alliance (ICA) in 1942. Entitled *Co-operation in the Colonies* it gave an in-depth account of co-operatives in British colonies.

The report reveals that in Palestine by the end of 1939 there were 1,081 Jewish co-operatives, twenty-four Arab societies and six others with a combined membership of around 150,000: 'Own funds (share capital, reserves, etc) amounted to £3,750,000, and deposits to £1,500,000.' However, there were big differences between Arab and Jewish societies. Whereas Jewish ones were spontaneous and diverse, their Arab counterparts were largely agricultural and were far more reliant on government.

Under Ottoman law Jewish co-operatives had no legal status but in 1920 the British administration introduced the Co-operative Societies Ordinance: the ICA report describes this as closely following the 'Bombay Law'. Palestinian co-operative legislation took a step forward in 1933 following a review carried out by Strickland in 1930. Sent to study the co-operative position in Palestine he was asked particularly to look into the possibility of encouraging agricultural co-operatives among the Arabs. So far there had been little Arab co-operative development and his visit and subsequent report[17] paved the way for the legislation of 1933 which applied to all co-operatives whether Arab or Jewish, improved auditing arrangements and also provided for the appointment of a registrar.

A little subsequent progress among Arab co-operatives is reported in an article by Harry Viteles, general manager of the Central Bank of Co-operative Institutes in Palestine in the *Year Book of Agricultural Co-operation 1936* published by the Horace Plunkett Foundation.[18] Even so they remained less spontaneous and self-perpetuating than their Jewish counterparts and more dependent on government encouragement and assistance. Strickland had already recognised in his report that while Jewish co-operatives had arisen in diverse economic and social activities, Arab societies were most likely to form in rural areas and be linked to agriculture. By the end of 1935 forty-four Arab credit and thrift societies had been established along with eleven 'Transportation societies'. The registrar was reported as being 'awake to the dangers of a too rapid expansion unaccompanied by patient education and constant supervision', and for this reason had 'proceeded cautiously in the formation of new societies among Arab cultivators'.[19]

There were hopes that Arab and Jewish co-operatives would eventually come together in one movement:

> Co-operators in Palestine and abroad would like to see the Palestine Government make some efforts to merge the two movements – Arab and Jewish – particularly in those districts having a mixed population and in those fields, such as marketing of citrus and other agricultural products where the interests of both sections are identical. The co-operators would also welcome a more active Government policy in carrying out the hope expressed 'that advantage will be taken of Jewish experience and the goodwill expressed by Jewish central co-operative organisations'. In view of the wide gap which still exists between the two movements, there is some doubt as to the practicality of setting up immediately one central official co-operative council for both movements. There is a feeling that until the Arab co-operative movement is more extensive and varied and has its own representative organs [auditing unions] such a combined council would reduce the usefulness to the Jewish co-operative movement of this forum for discussion of general co-operative questions without contributing much to the development of the Arab co-operative movement.[20]

Thus the politics and dynamics of the situation are summed up.

JEWISH CO-OPERATIVES IN PALESTINE

An important dynamic in the growth of Jewish co-operatives was the need to settle land. Co-operatives became part of a land settlement strategy to help Jewish immigrants. They arrived with skills and talents developed in their countries of origin but often applied them quite differently in Palestine. For example Viteles notes that only 16 per cent of Palestinian Jewish co-operatives were credit societies 'whereas the Jewish co-operative movement in Europe is almost wholly credit'.[21] Both the ICA report and Viteles's article emphasise the diversity of the co-operatives they now established in Palestine. The report, quoting figures for 1940, shows that there were 115 thrift and credit societies in both urban and rural areas, 109 agricultural societies involved in general activities, marketing and supply, 109 housing societies, 106 workers' productive societies and 109 consumer co-operatives. Societies had also formed in less traditional co-operative areas such as water supply, smallholders' settlements, suburban development, communitarian settlements and transportation. Palestinian Jewish co-operatives had also formed six audit unions.[22]

Viteles explains how and why these developments were diverse and large:

> The underlying motive is still that of colonisation – the co-operatives being the instrument for facilitating and expediting the settlement of Jews on the land. The special characteristics which have been developed are attributable for the most part to the mixed character, individualism, and social-political structure of the 250,000 Jews who have come to Palestine since 1919 (the present estimate of Jewish population is 360,000) and to the fact that Palestine is still a country in the making.[23]

It seems that the demands of settlement encouraged changes in behaviour. Speaking of Jewish Palestinian marketing societies Viteles noted that: 'in no other country have Jewish farmers, considered as extremely individualist, shown such an aptitude for this type of co-operation which requires discipline, mutual trust and confidence, a long range point of view and business acumen'.[24]

There was co-operation between organisations as well as individuals, for instance that between Jewish co-operatives and the Jewish labour movement. The latter had 'specially adapted its structures to the requirements of its co-operative work. Parallel with the Histadruth [General Federation of Jewish Labour in Palestine] is the Hevrat Ovdim [Brotherhood of Workers] to which are affiliated all the Labour co-operatives'.[25]

Perhaps the most striking innovation of Jewish co-operatives, but one appropriate for land colonisation, was their development of agricultural land settlements. These were known as kvutzoth and kibbutzim and combined co-operative production, marketing and living. Their aim was to settle the maximum number of members on the minimum area possible at minimum cost. No private property was held within them and everything the members produced went to the co-operative. On entering voluntarily members had to be prepared to work for and with the group to which all assets and liabilities belonged. Important decisions were made by the general meeting and implemented by committee. Robert Owen's nineteenth-century schemes for co-operative communities come to mind although the Jews seemed to look more to the kolhoz or collective farms in the Soviet Union. A fundamental distinction between them was that in Palestine co-operative communities membership was voluntary whereas it was compulsory in the Soviet kolhoz. In

Palestine Jewish co-operatives recognised four basic principles, namely: 'variable capital, unlimited membership, joint liability and equal rights'.

CO-OPERATIVES IN CYPRUS

Co-operative development in Cyprus is interesting not only for the actual societies that were established but also for the role played by B. J. Surridge, co-operative registrar between 1934 and 1943. Although the movement had begun two decades earlier it had advanced little before his arrival. Within a short while he had influenced its legislation and helped improve its economic infrastructure and trading arrangements. He was appointed adviser on co-operatives in the Colonial Office in 1947 and for many years he was also a trustee and vice-chairman of the Plunkett Foundation thus assisting a non-governmental organisation involved in colonial co-operative development.

We should first trace how Cyprus had become part of the British Empire. She was located in the eastern Mediterranean rather than the Middle East but was nevertheless part of the Ottoman Turkish Empire. For administrative purposes she was ceded to Britain in 1878 under a convention agreed with the sultan of Constantinople. This brought her into what has been called Britain's 'informal Empire'. When Germany entered the First World War, as an ally of Germany Britain annexed Cyprus in November 1914 and in May 1925 raised her to full colonial status. Her status within the British Empire was thus more definite than that of Egypt or Palestine. Like the latter, though, her population was divided, this time between Cypriots of Greek or Turkish origin. However, unlike those in Palestine, Cypriot co-operatives combined in a single movement.

Essentially it was a government prompted movement. Its growth began with the passing of the Co-operative Credit Societies Law in 1914. This was only ten years after India's first Co-operative Credit Societies Act and it is temping to speculate how far that legislation inspired the Cypriot version. Credit societies were considered the most appropriate form of co-operative for the island's 'peasant proprietors'[76] operating within its large agricultural sector.

The first co-operative was registered in 1916 but progress was slow. Indeed, it was suspected that some 'co-operatives' were co-operative in name only. Until the 1930s their main function had been to channel long-term loans from the Agricultural Bank and this led to their being perceived as little more than the Bank's lending and collecting agents. A weakness of the system was that deposits were small and could fail to match the long-term loans made. Often short, rather than long-term credit was what was required and generally the link between thrift and credit was weak.

When Surridge arrived in Cyprus in 1934 the situation began to improve. First the 1916 Act was revised in 1935.[27] A specialist Department of Co-operation was created and began to undertake 'the reorganisation of societies on sounder lines'.[28] These included the introduction in 1936 of new arrangements under which the repayment of long-term loans were to be made by individuals directly to the bank rather than through their co-operative societies. This allowed co-operatives more time to 'devote their energies to their proper purposes, namely the encouragement of thrift, the provision of short-term credit and collective supply and marketing'. In addition societies believed to be co-operative in name only were reduced from 324 in 1934 to 262 in 1937.[29]

One of Surridge's reforms that assisted co-operatives' financial infrastructure was the creation in 1937 of a Co-operative Central Bank, with an initial membership of seventy-one co-operatives, but 'with funds provided by Barclays Bank (D.C. and O) [Dominion, Colonial and Overseas]'[30] when it began operations in 1938. This was a novel departure in co-operative development. Until then co-operative banks in Britain and her Empire had traditionally been established and capitalised by their member societies, although there had been examples of government funding being channelled through a state bank such as Egypt's Misr Bank. The Cypriot Co-operative Central Bank was the first to be funded initially by a major capitalist private enterprise bank.

It was presumably a short-term measure until co-operative funds could replace the initial capital. A question raised, however, was how far it ran counter to Strickland's maxim and the widely-held co-operative view that 'co-operatives that did not provide the bulk of their own finance will not generate a real co-operative spirit'. Another was whether this initial funding was repaid from the Bank's operations and if so, at what rate and how soon. And what were Barclays' motives? Why should such an arch-competitor to the co-operative system wish to assist a form of business that was so much at variance to its own both in structure and ethos.

However questionable from a co-operative point of view Barclays' participation in Cypriot co-operative development might be it nevertheless illustrated that the co-operative form was considered sound enough to attract private investment and assure a profit.

Whatever the role of Barclays within the Cypriot Co-operative Central Bank, it became an important adjunct to future Cypriot co-operative development. Its focus shifted to providing short- and medium-term credit and accepting deposits from societies. In addition it began to arrange the importation and distribution of commodities such as fertilisers, sulphur and seed potatoes to its member societies.[31] The importance of thrift was emphasised among co-operative members as a corollary to the Bank granting them short- and medium-term credit.

Thrift and credit became the backbone of the Cypriot co-operative movement and gave it considerable strength. Although this chapter is primarily concerned with colonial co-operative development during the inter-war years we can perhaps jump forward a few years to note that in Cyprus 'During the war-time period of comparative prosperity deposits with societies increased enormously'.[32] By 1945, in a total population of approximately 430,000, Cypriot co-operatives had a membership of 56,881. Of these 44,242 belonged to credit societies linked to the Co-operative Central Bank.

The role of Surridge and ipso facto that of the co-operative registrar in helping the Cypriot movement achieve a firm foundation should be noted.

CONCLUSIONS

One important factor in the background to this chapter was British and French rivalry in areas previously governed by the Turkish Ottoman Empire but which was now collapsing. The First World War hastened its disintegration. It also encouraged Allied bargaining with Jews and Arabs for support during the war with post-war promises of land. The Jews were promised a homeland in Palestine under the Balfour Declaration of 1917 while less formal undertakings were made to Arabs. The peace settlements failed to deliver to the Arabs and they felt betrayed. However, it was possible to implement the Balfour Declaration inasmuch as the League of Nations granted Britain mandated powers to administer Palestine after the war. It was always likely that the promises made to the Arabs would be negated by implementation of the secret Sykes-Picot plan of 1916. To a large degree its provisions were carried out resulting in the Middle East being mostly divided into areas of British or French control.

It has been said that 'The concept of Co-operation is . . . versatile and universal.'[33] The truth of this statement is amply borne out by examples we find of co-operatives taking root in a troubled Middle East during the inter-war years. In Palestine two separate movements grew, one Arab the other Jewish; but in Cyprus, divided between Turkish and Greek Cypriots, a combined movement developed.

Motivation in Egypt and Cyprus was negligible and needed to be encouraged by government initiatives and guidance before firm roots took hold. Jewish co-operatives in Palestine were quite a different story. Motivation among these was strong and was usually linked to the need to colonise the land and secure incomes in hostile environments. Outside Palestine Jews had been noted for individual entrepreneurship but once in the Jewish Homeland they exhibited strong communal and collective traits: their need to establish themselves proved a strong motivating force.

In Cyprus we noted the important influence of the co-operative registrar from 1934 until 1943, B. J. Surridge.

PART THREE: Co-operative Development in the Dying Days of Empire

12. Colonial Co-operatives in the Twilight of Empire

INTRODUCTION

The First World War put in train events that redrew the Middle East, and hastened the end of the Turkish Ottoman Empire. The Second World War hastened the end of the French, Dutch and British Empires.

The First World War was seen as an imperialists' war. From its outset the Second World War claimed to be a moral war. This time Britain had no expansionist war aims and the Allies fought to free countries from the aggression of dictatorships so that they could once more become sovereign and self-determining. It was only a short step to ask whether calls for self-determination were not equally applicable to colonial territories. Ideas of empire were fading and an important factor in this was heavy dependence on American might during hostilities. Her initial reluctance to join the war had been fuelled by her wish not to be seen helping prop up a British Empire she had fought her way out of almost 200 years earlier. American support for calls for self-determination brought them high in the Allies' war agenda.

Whether or not the British Empire would survive the war, its territories quickly mobilised. Canada's prime minister, Mackenzie King, warned Hitler that if Germany attacked Britain 'there would be great numbers of Canadians ready to swim the Atlantic'.[1] Britain's war-time leader, Winston Churchill, returned the compliment when he declared that if Britain fell, he and 'the fleets and armies of the Crown would sail with him to Canada' to continue the war.[2] Along with Canada, Australia and New Zealand quickly joined the fray, perhaps out of fear of Japanese aggression as much as loyalty to Britain. South Africa was more equivocal and entered on Britain's side only after a long and bitter parliamentary debate. British colonies and other territories were brought into the war by decision of their administrations or, in the case of India, by the decision of her viceroy 'in council'.

At the end of hostilities Britain was still ostensibly a great power. Churchill had sat with Roosevelt and Stalin at major war-time conferences determining war aims and settlements. Moreover, during the war Britain lost no parts of her empire and after it, along with the USA, France and the Soviet Union, she became responsible for the governance of a divided Germany, Austria and Italy. Her influence also extended to such an extent elsewhere that it was observed:

> To an unprecedented degree the Mediterranean was a British lake . . . The whole of the North Africa littoral, the whole of the Levant was held by British arms, southern Persia was occupied and even Greece was more or less a British sphere of influence. With imperial armies deployed across the world, with a Royal Navy of 3,500 fighting ships and a Royal Air Force of unparalleled prestige, in theory the British Empire was a Power as never before . . .[3]

It was not going to last. The war proved a major catalyst for change, both of Britain's empire and at home. The changes at home and particularly the election of a Labour government in 1945 heralded changes in the Empire. The war also encouraged economic and social changes in many colonies. Increased economic activity derived from growing demand for their products or from the stationing of large numbers of service personnel had brought greater prosperity and a possible opening up to new outside influences. These could be unsettling where they interacted with movements pushing for colonial independence.

Attitudes had also shifted in British dominions. Canada, Australia, New Zealand and South Africa had not been invaded or economically weakened to the extent that Britain had. They had begun to see themselves as partners of Britain in a commonwealth. Moreover, they were influenced by the USA's call for self-determination which prompted questions of what Britain should do with the remainder of her empire. The war cost her so dear that maintaining her hold over them by force would be economically unsustainable.

At home, gratitude and admiration for Churchill led to expectations that he and his Conservative Party would win the first post-war general election. Had Churchill remained Britain's prime minister, the British Empire might have staggered on longer than it did. An 'incorrigible imperialist romantic' Churchill declared that he had 'not become the First Minister of the Crown in order to preside over the liquidation of the British Empire'.[4]

He and the Conservatives were not elected and a Labour government under Clement Attlee was. It seems even to have been a surprise to

Labour. At the founding conference of the United Nations (UN) in San Francisco in 1945 Attlee spoke to Wallace J. Campbell, assistant secretary of the Co-operative League of the USA, who was representing the International Co-operative Alliance (ICA). Attlee admitted privately that he was not expecting a Labour victory.[5] Yet the Labour Party with its Co-operative Party allies won handsomely and formed the government between 1945 and 1950. A reforming government, it introduced the welfare state and bought the 'commanding heights' of the economy into state ownership against a background of a weakened economy. War-time austerity, including the rationing of some basic foods, continued into the early 1950s. Labour lost popularity but won the 1950 election with a slender majority of ten. Attlee went to the country again in 1951 and this time the Conservatives won. The Labour Government of 1945–50 had, however, set a clear colonial policy that continued under the Conservatives. It set the pace for the dissolution of the British Empire and found a clear place for co-operative development in colonies moving towards independence.

BRITISH COLONIAL POLICY IN 1945

A number of factors influenced the 1945 Labour government's colonial policy. One was the moral arguments the war had introduced. Another was the growth of national independence movements in some colonies; while at home there was uncertainty about the costs and benefits to the national exchequer of maintaining the Empire. The exchequer bore the costs of manning and defending imperial territories but commercial undertakings took the resulting profits, although some of these no doubt found their way back to the exchequer in tax receipts.

Overall it was difficult to sustain arguments in favour of retaining the Empire. Britain began the fastest retreat from empire the world has ever seen. In the meantime, though, colonial policy needed to take account of development needs and how co-operatives might help meet them. A number of factors contributed to a clearer co-operative policy, including the wartime coalition government's Colonial Development and Welfare Act of 1940, and also moves in the embryonic UN in support of co-operatives. At home the Fabian Society set up a special committee in 1945 whose *Co-operation in the Colonies* report helped shape British colonial policy.

The Colonial Development and Welfare Act 1940 extended the provisions of the 1929 Colonial Development Act passed by Britain's second Labour government by adding welfare objectives. Moves towards the new Act were made in 1938 when Parliament set up a royal commission under the chairmanship of Lord Moyne to investigate and make recommendations on the social and economic conditions in the British West Indies. It reported in December 1939 and the secretary of state for the colonies, Malcolm MacDonald, realised that its recommendations could have wider application. A year earlier he had set up a Colonial Office departmental committee to consider how a broader legislative programme of colonial development and welfare could be introduced. The result was the 1940 Act.

Shaped by the threat of war, the Act reflected changing ideas about the kind of role Britain could play. 'Before the outbreak of war MacDonald had recognised the propaganda value which such a programme of colonial development could have during wartime. He regarded an untarnished colonial reputation as an essential part of Britain's defence policy.' The 1940 Act provided unprecedented levels of funding from the British government: £5m yearly for a ten-year period and an annual £500,000 to be spent indefinitely on research.[6] Although the war prevented full implementation of the Act it gave a promise of things to come whichever party was elected to government.

Inherent in the Act was a change in how development should be funded in British colonies. Previously the Colonial Office earmarked little for development, believing that once a territory had been opened up and its infrastructure of roads, railways and harbours created, little further needed to be spent. Trading companies and businesses operating within a territory were expected to be self-supporting and raise the finance they required in London. The Colonial Office required 'that each Colony should be self-supporting and that its budget should be balanced annually'.[7] This created a 'Catch 22' situation. Backward colonies had the greatest need of development but because they had the lowest tax returns they were the ones least able to fund their own. By setting up the Colonial Development Fund the 1929 Development Act went some way to remedying this situation but limited its impact by stipulating that grants from it could only be made to colonies providing 'commerce with or industry in the United Kingdom'.

The genesis of the 1940 Act lay in the 1938 royal commission chaired by Lord Moyne, whose focus had been on the economic, industrial and social unrest in the British West Indies. Britain's need to resolve these problems stemmed from her unease about America's growing influence in the region:

> Colonial Office officials regarded the US government not only as unrelentingly critical of the Empire but also as a threat to British dominion in the Caribbean. By the 1920s US economic penetration

> of the region was considered so far advanced that the Colonial Office envisaged Canada as a countervailing influence in the western hemisphere through strengthened economic ties with the colonies.[8]

America's economic might was growing but in foreign policy she had shown strong isolationist tendencies. She had not joined the League of Nations despite the role President Woodrow Wilson had played in shaping the peace settlements after the First World War. The role she eventually played in the Second World War brought her back to centre stage. Her political influence was such that after the war she became the home of the UN that replaced the earlier League of Nations.

Although ultimately fully engaged in the war America was not war-torn like Europe and the Far East. One consequence was that many wartime conferences organised by the embryonic UN were held in America. The American Co-operative movement played an important part in these, often representing the ICA. The British and American movements both helped influence early UN thinking on co-operatives, including those in colonies. At national and international levels co-operatives were increasingly entering the corridors of power. War provided the catalyst for this increase in influence.

BRITISH CO-OPERATION IN 1945

To a considerable extent the British Co-operative movement sustained the ICA during the Second World War. The war disrupted the workings of the Alliance but unlike similar international organisations, including the Socialist International and the International Federation of Trade Unions, it survived. During the 1930s the ICA had lost its member organisations in Italy, Germany, Austria, Spain and Japan, and this helped its remaining members to unite behind the Allies. Although it remained ideologically united the war badly affected its organisation. Improvisation became the order of the day. Since its formation in 1895 the Alliance had based its head office in London, which meant that it was in a country at war but not in one that was invaded. It was further helped by being in the country of the ICA's strongest affiliate, the British Co-operative movement.

In May 1940 a meeting of a reduced ICA executive convened in Paris and appointed R. A. Palmer, general secretary of the British Co-operative Union and already an Alliance vice-president, as acting president for the duration of the war. It also appointed for the same period Gertrude Polley, previously its administrative secretary, as the ICA's acting general secretary.

Palmer and Polley worked well together and took a number of important policy initiatives during the war. One was the ICA's survey of British colonial co-operative movements which, as we will see, helped form the basis of the 1945 Labour government's policy on post-war colonial development. Another initiative, through its American affiliate, the Co-operative League of the USA was to contribute to UN war-time conferences and other activities. One was the United Nations Relief and Rehabilitation Administration[9] and the other the Food and Agricultural Conference at Hot Springs in 1943, which led to the founding of the UN Food and Agricultural Organization (FAO). Such participation in early UN activities undoubtedly helped the ICA gain consultative status with the UN in 1946.[10]

The war provided the catalyst for many changes. In Britain and Europe co-operatives had established their credibility. Their mass memberships and trading success showed that bottom-up, democratic businesses could be a viable alternative form of business and helped establish co-operatives' credibility at international levels. Co-operatives, through the ICA, contributed to debates and initiatives in the embryonic UN particularly in post-war relief and rehabilitation and in colonial co-operative development.

POINTERS TO POST-WAR COLONIAL CO-OPERATIVE DEVELOPMENT

Calls for democracy, self-determination and freedom from want heightened interest in colonial co-operative development. They were boosted by the Atlantic Charter of 1942 setting out the Allies' war and peace aims and speaking of 'United Nations', a term President Roosevelt had first used in 1941 to describe nations fighting the Axis powers. It led on 1 January 1942 to twenty-six states signing up to the United Nations' Declaration in which they pledged to continue their joint war effort, not to make peace separately,[11] and supported the call for 'Freedom from Want'. This had ramifications for colonial development. The UN conference on food and agriculture held in Hot Springs, Virginia in May and June 1943 helped push Freedom from Want higher up the agenda. It also led to the founding of the UN's Food and Agricultural Organisation (FAO) which would come to have a special interest in less developed regions of the world.

North America's influence in international affairs increased during the Second World War. The Japanese attack on Pearl Harbor in December 1941 led her to abandon her earlier isolationist policies. Because Germany was allied to Japan, America also found herself at war with Germany. Another factor that helped to increase her international influence was that many war-time conferences had to be held in America because war made difficult venues in Europe, the Middle and Far East.

Consequently, the ICA based in London had to channel its views through its American affiliate, the Co-operative League of the USA (CLUSA) which often represented it at these conferences. We have already noted the interview that one of its representatives, Wally Campbell, had with Clement Attlee during the founding conference of the UN in San Francisco in 1945. Another representative for the ICA was Dr Peter Warbasse, president of CLUSA. Additional but indirect representation was occasionally achieved when co-operators also happened to be part of government delegations to UN conferences, as happened in the case of neutral Sweden.

In December 1943 the International Co-operative Alliance (ICA) formally requested representation on the United Nations Relief and Rehabilitation Administration (UNRRA); its council of administration as well as on its European regional committee. Although the former was not possible because only governments were allowed to appoint representatives, the ICA was informed that its request that co-operative movements in occupied countries, neutral and free countries should be mobilised to help post-war relief and reconstruction would be looked upon favourably.

The ICA also developed long-term relations with the International Labour Organization (ILO). The ILO had been one of the more important League of Nations agencies and was carried over into the UN system after the war. From its inception in 1919 it had had close links with the ICA. Its first director, Albert Thomas (1878–1932) had been a French co-operative leader, a delegate to ICA congresses and a member of its central committee between 1910 and 1930. A French socialist politician he had also served as Minister of Munitions during the First World War. One of his first acts on becoming the ILO's director was to set up within it a co-operative branch, later termed Co-operative Services. Thomas argued that co-operatives and trades unions should work closely together because they were complementary: co-operatives enabled workers to improve their conditions through maximising what their wages would purchase.[12]

A consequence of the ILO's move to Canada for the duration was that its war-time conferences were also held in North America. One in 1944 paved the way for collaboration between the ILO and international co-operative organisations in the post-war world, with the ILO's Co-operative Service publishing two important guides: Co-operative Organisations and Post-war Relief' and the 'Co-operative Movement and Present-day Problems'.[13]

These raised the co-operative profile in the ILO but a similar process also occurred in its sister organisation the UN's FAO. Earlier we noted its genesis in the UN's food and agriculture conference at Hot Springs in 1943; its aim had been to give practical expression to the principle of 'Freedom from Want' expressed in the Atlantic Charter. The conference was primarily concerned about how agricultural productivity and food standards could be improved, and envisaged a role for co-operatives in two resolutions; one directly encouraged co-operatives, while the other acknowledged the importance of agricultural credit and within that recognised the role that credit co-operatives could play in helping reduce peasant indebtedness.

The first resolution read:

> Whereas:
>
> 1. The cooperative has been of very great importance in many countries, both to urban and rural populations, especially in agricultural districts, where farming is based on small units and in urban areas of low-income families;
> 2. The proper functioning of cooperative societies may facilitate adjustments of agricultural production and distribution, as members have confidence in the recommendations and guidance of their own cooperative organizations, which they know operate in the interests of their members and of society in general;
> 3. The democratic control and educational programs, which are features of the cooperative movement, can play a vital part in the training of good democratic citizens, and assist in including a sound conception of economic matters;
>
> *The United Nations Conference on Food and Agriculture Recommends*
>
> 1. That, in order to make it possible for people to help themselves in lowering costs of production and costs of distribution and marketing:
>   (a) countries study the possibilities of the further establishment of producer and consumer cooperative societies in order to render necessary production, marketing and purchasing, finance and other services;
>   (b) Each nation examine its laws, regulations and institutions to determine if legal or institutional obstacles to cooperative development exist, in order to make desirable adjustments;

(c) Full information as to the present developments of cooperatives in different countries be made available through the permanent organization recommended in Resolution 11 [This refers to the establishment of the UN's FAO].[14]

The second resolution on agricultural credit stressed the need for credit facilities if agriculture was to be 'restored, increased and intensified'. It also observed that in some countries it was available only at rates the farmer could not afford to pay and noted that agricultural communities in many countries were unable to obtain information on agricultural credit systems in other countries.

It went on to urge that 'full use be made to ensure an adequate supply of credit to agriculture' by 'all types of suitable private, cooperative and public credit institutions', that 'the rate of interest be as low as possible and the conditions regarding initial cost, redemption etc. be as favourable as possible for the borrowers, particularly . . . the small farmer'.[15] This resolution gave co-operatives only a partial role in the provision of agricultural credit but when linked to the previous resolution it strengthened the focus on co-operatives. The role they could play in the post-war world was becoming clearer. Moves nearer home were no doubt encouraged by international developments. An important one was headed by the British Fabian Society but also involved the British Consumer Co-operative movement and the Plunkett Foundation.

The Fabian Society was founded in 1884 mainly among middle-class intellectuals who opposed revolutionary Marxism but aimed to spread more evolutionary socialist ideas. Well-known members included the writer George Bernard Shaw (1856–1950) and Sidney (1859–1947) and Beatrice (1858–1943) Webb. The Fabian Colonial Bureau was founded in 1940 and along with the 1940 Colonial Development and Welfare Act, indicated that British policy and decision-makers were looking towards a more enlightened future for British colonies.

In 1945 a report from a special committee to the Fabian Colonial Bureau entitled *Co-operation in the Colonies*[16] was published. Amongst the people it brought together on the committee was Arthur Creech Jones, MP, who was to become secretary of state for the colonies in Attlee's 1945 Labour government. Others we have already met such as Sir Malcolm Darling the noted co-operative registrar and Margaret Digby from the Plunkett Foundation. Other members were Dr N. Barou, the famous economist who had written on co-operative insurance and banking, and Leonard Wolff, who had written 'Socialism and Co-operation' and 'Co-operation and the Future of Industry'.[17]

The committee also had senior representatives of British consumer co-operation: Neil Beaton, chairman of the Scottish Co-operative Wholesale Society (SCWS); R. G. Gosling, a director of the CWS; and the Rev. G. S. Woods MP, who sat on the executive committee of the Co-operative Union. There was also Percy Redfern, author of *The New History of the C.W.S.* and formerly managing editor of CWS Publications, and other members included C. W. Greenidge, secretary of the Anti-Slavery and Aborigines Protection Society and Lord Winster who chaired the special committee.

The foreword to the report was written by C. F. Strickland who quoted Lord Passfield, previously Mr Sidney Webb, who said as secretary of state for the colonies in the short-lived Labour government of 1929, 'The Colonies shall have more Co-operation.' Webb was in office briefly but out of it he retained close links with the Fabian Society and its Colonial Bureau, which now took the lead in proposing post-war colonial co-operative development policies.

The report helped the 1945 Labour government's colonial policy in respect of co-operatives. It also provided an objective review of what co-operatives had and could achieve in British colonies and suggested that co-operatives were not always successful. They were at times not even an appropriate option. In his foreword Strickland stated:

> I do not associate myself with all the hard things that have been said about the Colonial Office and colonial administration. Civil Servants are busy people, with little knowledge of technical matters. Many of them were under a delusion that Co-operation in the Colonies is concerned only with agriculture; Some not realising the technical nature of Co-operation, tried to found co-operative societies, which sooner or later came to grief. They had attempted a task for which only a trained co-operator is qualified.[18]

Strickland expressed his support for what would be the committee's three main findings: the need for 'suitable co-operative law' that was simpler than the Friendly Societies or the Industrial and Provident Societies Acts; provision for a registrar who was 'fully trained for his duty, and independent of other departments'; and recognition that 'Co-operation is adult education in the business of life'.[19]

To reach these conclusions the special committee carried out a survey of 'co-operation in the British dependencies' which can be found in part two of the report. The survey covered the British West Indies, British West Africa, British East and Central Africa, Malaya (Malaysia) and Ceylon (Sri Lanka), Palestine, Mauritius, Cyprus and other dependencies.

Part one provided an overview of 'Co-operation and the Colonies' while part three looked to future 'Lines of Progress'. Part four comprised Conclusions and Recommendations, the latter being divided between what governments could do and the help that the British Co-operative movement and international co-operative organisations could give.

The work of the committee was based on a series of papers prepared by C. F. Strickland, H. Calvert and Margaret Digby, A. Cavendish, formerly director of co-operation in Malaya, Dr Arthur Lewis, reader in economics, London School of Economics, C. W. Greenidge and the secretariat of the ICA. It is likely that much of the survey in Part Two of the report was based on the 1942 survey conducted by the ICA to which we referred in the last chapter.

A point to note is the standardised reference throughout the report to 'Co-operation' rather than co-operatives. We had seen this in the inter-war writings of leading colonial registrars. Its continuing use suggests that the special committee also recognised that co-operatives expressed an ideology, theory and comprised a distinct system.

What also emerges strongly in part one is the committee's anger at 'Colonial Poverty'. This had not been so clearly expressed before. Shame at continuing poverty had obviously entered British imperial consciousness in a way hardly seen previously. This perhaps owed much to war-time rhetoric. The committee's analysis, though, blamed colonies' poverty on their dependence on cash crops and noted that in the twentieth century the terms of trade had moved against 'producers of primary products'. Moreover,

> the colonial peoples have been unable to develop any defensive organisation against such modern business methods, or against the fluctuation of markets. They lack any sort of economic independence, and one of the main reasons for this is indebtedness.[20]

Rural indebtedness had been made worse by inappropriate systems of land tenure and by the fundamental fact that many colonies were in the tropics where nature was harsh and hostile and 'where man has not yet succeeded in controlling his environment'.

Having posed the question 'Why has this degrading colonial poverty been allowed to continue?' the committee proceeded to blame it on British governments earlier laissez-faire policies:

> Colonial policy was less directed to promotion of colonial welfare and prosperity than to the maintenance of law and order so that trading companies might pursue, without interruption, their

> business of securing a steady flow of raw materials to the wealthier industrialised countries.[21]

The report suggested that the 1940 Colonial Development and Welfare Act represented a step in the right direction that was reinforced by the Hot Springs resolutions referred to previously.

Recognising that co-operatives were not the only means of reducing colonial poverty the committee did, however, emphasise the part that thrift and credit co-operatives could play in overcoming the 'inveterate ... habit of borrowing, of instilling through education the need for individual responsibility' and recognition 'that in most instances there is only one practical alternative to co-operative credit for the small producer – and that is usury'.[22]

The committee believed that the reorganisation of agriculture should be 'one of the first aims of colonial economics' but acknowledged that this required much 'scientific and technical research'. It further recognised that the findings of such research would have to be implemented by colonial populations that had 'very limited education'. The question therefore arose as to how essential improvements could be brought 'within the capacity of colonial peoples' The committee's answer was:

> The co-operative organisation offers the most acceptable means. It provides a platform for the instructors, pools the use of apparatus, makes the adoption and enforcement of new methods a communal responsibility, and is able to link improved production with a better return for the product and hence to a direct and readily understood economic advantage.[23]

They then emphasised that 'The principle of sound business is a fundamental principle of all co-operative activity.'[24] The nine recommendations made for government action included the proposal that the Colonial Office should appoint a co-operative advisory committee to make recommendations on co-operatives to the secretary of state for the colonies. Linked to this was the proposal that independent co-operative departments should be set up in all colonies, and that these should be headed by co-operative registrars responsible only to the governor or equivalent colonial authority. While not subordinate to any other department, co-operative departments should consult and collaborate with them and the Colonial Office's advisory committee on co-operatives. In order to strengthen the work of colonial co-operative departments it was proposed that a model co-operative ordinance should be drafted. These were organisational proposals. Included among the aims of co-operative departments were: attempting to eradicate indebtedness; expanding and making more efficient co-operative marketing; encouraging the development of consumer co-operatives; and reviewing colonial land tenure so as to avoid fragmentation, uneconomic mortgaging and the accumulation of land by mercantile interests[25]

Moving onto 'How the British and International Movements Can Help' the committee's proposals illustrate the economic and trading tensions between the mother country and her colonies. Part of the success of the British Consumer movement rested on the trading ties its Wholesales had developed with colonial primary producers which proved to be little more enlightened than those of traditional private traders. We have seen, based on annual co-operative congress reports, only occasional colonial co-operative concerns among British co-operators; even fewer were of an organisational or systematic nature.

Co-operatives had been emerging in British colonies over the past forty years but only now were British co-operative leaders becoming involved through their membership of the special committee. Reasons for their earlier hesitation are likely to include trading interests and scepticism as to whether government-encouraged co-operatives could ever be true co-operatives; also their belief in the primacy of consumer co-operatives. The British movement's strong international impulses had traditionally been directed towards the ICA rather than to co-operatives in the British Empire. The war and changes in attitude in government and international systems were prompting a major re-evaluation by British co-operatives.

For example, the special committee believed that help from the British Co-operative movement:

> might take the form of help in the primary stages of developing societies in areas which have hitherto been co-operative deserts – laying the necessary foundation of education in co-operative principles and of training in organisation of co-operative societies. Or it might take the form of developing the many potential opportunities which exist for mutual help in the sphere of trading relationships, once sound co-operative associations have been established in the colonies.[26]

It believed the ICA might also help through its International Committee for Inter-Co-operative Relations. This was established in 1931 to promote close relations between consumer and agricultural societies, but the Special Committee now suggested that it could act as a liaison between the world-wide co-operative movement and international institutions. Up until that time the International Committee's secretarial work had been undertaken by the co-operative section of the ILO in Geneva.[27]

Returning to the question of the help that could be given by the British Co-operative movement, it was suggested that this should include market research, advice from the CWS bank, the popularisation of colonial producers among British co-operative consumers, the forging of links between colonial producer co-operatives and the encouragement of colonial consumer co-operatives. More specific proposals included giving advice on co-operatives to the Colonial Office and colonial co-operative departments, producing training materials for use in colonial co-operatives, awarding scholarships to colonial students to study co-operation at the British Co-operative College, sending educational and technical experts to work with colonial co-operatives and raising a fund to encourage 'Co-operation in the Colonies'.[28]

References were also made to the British Agricultural Co-operative movement but the special committee's report made clear that 'This is not part of the consumers' movement although the two are associated through the Co-operative Union and the International Co-operative Alliance'. Instead it emphasised the role that the Horace Plunkett Foundation had already played and could still play rather than on any possible contribution of British agricultural co-operatives:

> This Foundation with its excellent Co-operative Reference Library, is available as a centre of information on the Co-operative Movement, particularly as regards agriculture, all over the world. A large number of colonial officers and administrators have already received training in Agricultural Co-operation at this institution, and it is hoped that its unique facilities, together with those of the Co-operative College, will be of increasing value in the important work of training co-operative personnel for the Colonies.[29]

We should briefly examine the responses of the British government to the special committee's recommendations. They were likely to be favourable given that Arthur Creech Jones had sat on the special committee and was now secretary of state for the colonies. Under him the Colonial Office established a co-operative advisory committee, and in 1947 appointed a co-operative adviser in the person of B. J. Surridge. A year earlier dispatches from the Colonial Office reported 'a proper legal framework in the form of a Co-operative Ordinance and Rules for the appointment of a Registrar of Co-operative Societies assisted by a staff of the necessary quality and strength' which had generally been accepted.[30] Colonial governments were urged to set up co-operative departments headed by co-operative registrars. The Colonial Office also appeared to move closer to the British Co-operative movement with the appointment to its economic advisory committee in 1947 of J. MacFadyen, director of the CWS.[31]

Recommendations to the British Consumer and International Co-operative movements were only partially implemented. Traditionally the CWS and to a lesser extent its Scottish counterpart, had been generous in the help they gave to co-operative causes but more through the ICA than the British Empire. However, the special committee's recommendations would now prompt the British movement to take initiatives in co-operative education and training, which we now consider in some detail.

LINKS BETWEEN BRITISH AND COLONIAL CO-OPERATIVES

In Part Two of this study we saw how co-operative registrars and their assistants became an important element in colonial co-operative development. The 1904 Co-operative Credit Societies Act, India, and subsequent Indian legislation widely copied throughout the British Empire, provided for the position of co-operative registrar. In doing so it copied British legislation in respect of co-operative and private enterprise businesses. The position of co-operative registrar became enshrined in colonial co-operative legislation but early holders of these positions often lacked knowledge of co-operatives. In time some became noted co-operative registrars and we have mentioned H. Calvert, C. F. Strickland and Sir Malcolm Darling. The distillation of their experiences in conferences, research and writings helped co-operative registrars or assistant registrars to become more specialised and professional.

The rhetoric of the Second World War, the landslide election of a British Labour government in 1945 and the recommendations of the special committee in its report to the Fabian Society helped advance colonial co-operative development. Such advances, however, took place against a changing background where calls for colonial independence and the end of empire became ever stronger. The founding of the Movement for Colonial Freedom in London in 1954 added weight to these calls.[32]

During the late 1940s and early 1950s a growing number of colonial co-operatives were formed. Illustrating this growth statistically is difficult because of the problems of comparing like with like and changes in currency values over time. However, two sets of figures quoted by Surridge in his essay on co-operative advances give us some idea:

> In 1945 there were 1,885 societies in ten territories with 266,000 members, paid up share capital of just under £1,000,000 and reserves of £410,000. In 1954 in 26 territories there were 8,626 societies with just over 1,000,000 members, out of an estimated total population of 82,000,000 and it may be assumed that in one out of every 16 households there is one member of a co-operative society. Six thousand seven hundred of these societies are mainly concerned with thrift and credit, and marketing and processing. Few societies have a large membership, the average being 105 members, and they operate mainly at the village level . . .
>
> The total paid up share capital of all societies amounted in 1954 to £5,000,000, or around £5 for each member, deposits to £5,000,000 and reserves to £3,800,000.[33]

Even Surridge fails to compare like with like because first he refers to ten territories and later to twenty-six. India had become independent in 1947 and so we can deduce that her statistics are not included in the 1954 figures. Nevertheless, the two sets of figures point to growth. How was that growth being managed? Surridge suggests with difficulty:

> In numbers the staffs of Co-operative Departments have grown considerably. To some extent a modification of Parkinson's Law . . . has tended to operate in that as societies increase in number more staff is required to supervise them and with more staff more societies come up for registration. A recent examination of estimates of revenue and expenditure in the territories shows that in all the territories there are 32 Registrars, 162 Deputy and Assistant Registrars and 809 other Co-operative Officers.[34]

This statement touches on several themes of this study, such as whether governments can be appropriate developers of co-operatives. A tendency for co-operatives to become over-dependent on government officials was recognised as early as the 1925 Wembley conference organised by the Plunkett Foundation. Strickland had then advanced the view that government officials could assist co-operative development because they, too, could become co-operators. Experience was not necessarily showing this to be the case. Surridge's reference to increasing numbers of government co-operative officials also prompts the question as to how much they knew about co-operatives and how enthusiastic they were about them.

The answer was not likely to be encouraging. Surridge went on to quote Strickland who had said in 1938 that the training of co-operative staffs had often been neglected. As a result, 'The ignorant have been sent to lead the ignorant, the blind to guide the blind and the result has naturally been disastrous.'[35] Strickland's hopes in 1925 must necessarily have therefore been moderated and comments in his foreword to the report of the special committee to the Fabian Society confirm this. We may recall he said that some government officers 'not realising the technical nature of Co-operation, tried to found co-operative societies, which sooner or later came to grief. They had attempted a task for which only a trained co-operator is qualified'.

From where, then, would these trained co-operators come? A two-part answer emerged: colonial co-operative officials would be trained in house or in other relevant institutions such as co-operative colleges; or the Colonial Office would recruit trained British co-operators to serve in colonial co-operative movements. Let us examine the first of these two options.

By the mid-1950s special co-operative training institutions had been set up in a number of territories. They included the East African School of Co-operation near Nairobi which ran two five-month courses for junior co-operative officers and employees of co-operative societies. There was also the recently established Co-operative College in the Federation of Malaya which was about to start offering courses. Funds provided under the Colonial Development and Welfare Acts had also been used to provide two-month courses for senior co-operative staff in Tanganyika and Kenya and there were plans for similar courses in West Africa. Less formal provisions were provided annually in Oxford at the Overseas Services Club where British registrars and assistant registrars on leave in the UK could gather to discuss matters of general co-operative interest.[36]

The premier co-operative education and training facility among these establishments was the British Co-operative College which after the war began courses for senior colonial co-operative officers. It was established in Manchester in 1919, evolving from the strong educational tradition of British co-operatives. Education had featured strongly in the teachings of Robert Owen and the tenets of the Rochdale Pioneers. Following these leads mid-nineteenth-century retail societies set up reading rooms which pre-dated compulsory formal education and public libraries. Societies expressed their dedication to education in their rules which invariably provided for the election of education committees that ranked only slightly behind the board or committee of management in seniority. Each level of the movement, district, section and national, had education functions. These culminated in the Co-operative Union's Education Department.

A decision to set up a Co-operative College had been taken by the 1914 Co-operative congress. From its beginning the British Co-operative College attracted occasional overseas students, so when courses for colonial co-operative officers were introduced in 1946 they represented a continuation of an existing tradition. By then the College was better able to accommodate them. A year earlier it had moved from Manchester to Stanford Hall near Loughborough. The movement's purchase of this eighteenth-century manorial hall standing in 300 acres of park and farm land was intended to celebrate the end of the Second World War and the centenary of the Rochdale Pioneers in 1944.[37]

At the same time the College needed a new principal and adviser of studies and Dr Robert Leckie Marshall (1913–2008) was appointed in 1946. This brought into British co-operation one of its most influential and respected figures. Marshall came from a Scottish mining family and on gaining a miners' welfare scholarship had studied at St Andrews University where he gained a first class honours MA. In 1935 on a Commonwealth scholarship he went to America where he was a junior lecturer at Yale University in government and politics.

On the outbreak of war he enlisted in the army and rose to the rank of lieutenant-colonel. He was also awarded the OBE. Shortly after his return to Britain after Dunkirk he had joined the Army Education Corps and pioneered informal methods of education, editing *The British Way of Life and Purpose*, a series of booklets issued throughout the army as the basis of weekly instruction. In 1942 he became commandant of one of the army schools of education.[38]

At 33 Marshall was principal of the College and he was later head of the education department of the Co-operative Union. In the latter role he oversaw the Co-operative Union's continuing correspondence courses which often acted as feeder courses for British students aiming to study at the College. In post-war years the College offered managerial, secretarial and social science diploma courses. Secretarial qualifications may sound inappropriate but they were designed to prepare students to become secretaries of co-operative societies, a position equivalent to that of company secretary. Whereas under company legislation the company secretary was required to protect shareholders' interests, under the Industrial and Provident Societies' Acts it was the members' interests rather than those of shareholders that predominated. A society secretary was the guardian of these which meant that he or she needed to be fully trained in co-operatives' legal and financial requirements.

In 1946 the college had well-established teaching programmes and after its move to Stanford Hall facilities to accommodate an intake of colonial co-operative officers. In the context of this study the Co-operative College under Robert Marshall should be seen as being central to melding Britain's two co-operative traditions, Rochdale and the colonial.

Despite these developments the British Consumer Co-operative movement still believed that consumer co-operatives were the best form of co-operative. When a deputation from it met the Secretary of State for the Colonies in February 1946 it urged him to give greater priority to them in subsequent colonial co-operative development.[39]

However, the education executive's report to the same congress revealed a wider emphasis:

> *Special Course for Colonial Students.* – The first special six months' course for students sent by the Colonial Office from the Colonies is being instituted in the session 1947–48. This course, for which 10 students are expected, will deal particularly with Co-operative agriculture, marketing and credit.[40]

Elsewhere there may have been doubt whether the College with its emphasis on British consumer co-operation was an appropriate venue for training of colonial co-operative officers; also about the level of its courses. While the Colonial Office would have been well aware of the College's status and the facilities it could offer from reports of the Education Department to annual co-operative congresses, it would also have known of a more critical and independent assessment. This came in a book by A. M. Carr-Saunders, P. Sargant Florence and Robert Peers entitled *Consumers' Co-operation in Great Britain* first published in 1938. In it the authors made an in-depth study of the history and organisation of education within the British Consumer Co-operative movement.[41]

They noted that the College's courses were not of university standing and called for the movement to have closer links with universities. Parallels were drawn with religious organisations The movement:

> has a belief in Co-operation and a special point of view about social problems; it may be said to have certain tenets. Its position is not unlike that of the religious organizations. The latter often maintain colleges in university cities; the students avail themselves of the facilities offered by the universities for non-sectarian instruction. This should be the relation of the Co-operative College to the University of Manchester.[42]

When this book was published the Co-operative College was based in Manchester and calls for it to have closer links with Manchester University were not inappropriate. Some individual co-operative societies such as the Royal Arsenal in south-east London had forged links with their local universities and in post-war years the Co-operative College, now based on the borders of Leicestershire and Nottinghamshire, developed close links with Nottingham and Loughborough Universities.

However, at the time of the negotiations between the Colonial Office and the Co-operative College there was a possibility of mismatch inasmuch as the Colonial Office wished entry requirements for colonial co-operative offices to the College to be of university level. The way that this and other problems were successfully overcome owe much to the synergy that developed between Marshall and B. J. Surridge who was appointed the Colonial Office's adviser on co-operatives in 1947.

We already know the kind of man Surridge was and are familiar with the Colonial Office characteristics he exhibited. In Marshall he met a man equally able but from quite different background and employment. Marshall was well-read. A polished and witty speaker his aphorisms and ready quotations reflected eclectic literary tastes. Perhaps more to the point he also proved to be a good manager of staff and students, although a noted disciplinarian.

In his negotiations with the Colonial Office, Marshall was able to build on friendships made at St Andrews University; one with Eugene Melville who after the war worked in the Colonial Office. Their personal friendship gave Marshall informal links with the Colonial Office that added weight to the more formal negotiations.

He later recorded that although the Colonial Office believed that the Co-operative College could mount the courses they wanted they nevertheless found the British Co-operative 'mysterious'. However, visits to the College reassured. Now based at Stanford Hall outside Loughborough it offered many facilities. Its previous owner, the furniture magnate Sir Julian Cahn, had built a bijou theatre in the 1930s about the same time he had a superior cricket pitch laid out. During his time visiting professional cricket teams played on it and their members were accommodated in bedrooms located above the theatre. When the College moved to Stanford Hall it continued to maintain both the theatre and cricket pitch along with a swimming pool, football pitch, tennis, badminton and squash courts, putting green and Italian Gardens and the 300 acres of park and farm land surrounding the College.

When later asked about the Colonial Office's motivation in sponsoring the courses for colonial co-operative officials Marshall said he believed that it was to 'help discharge British responsibilities'.

The Colonial Office recognised that a transition from Empire to Commonwealth was inevitable and was chiefly concerned about managing the pace of that transition. He had readily agreed with the Colonial Office that the Plunkett Foundation should have been the natural home for the proposed courses. It had developed a considerable reputation through its Co-operative Reference Library, advice to colonial administrations of co-operative legislation, and personal study visits that it had organised for individual officers. Nevertheless it lacked 'the fabric' which the Co-operative College could provide. It would always be possible for the College to invite visiting specialist tutors and these would include Margaret Digby, secretary of the Plunkett Foundation, and Surridge. Together they produced *A Manual of Co-operative Law and Practice*[43] for the Co-operative College courses.

To qualify for entrance students had to be serving colonial co-operative officers, have good English and be able to study in that language and meet university entrance requirements. It was not unnatural, therefore, for the Colonial Office to wish university qualified staff to teach and for certificate and diploma courses to be validated by a university as later happened through the University of Loughborough.

A great strength the College could offer was its teaching of co-operation. It had featured in Co-operative Union correspondence course curricula and had become a feature of the College's social faculty. By the 1940s the College offered a social science diploma and a co-operative honours diploma. In the first and in the extra-mural diploma in politics, economics and social studies which was later offered by the University of Nottingham for students at the Co-operative College, distinct areas were maintained for co-operative history, theory, organisation and economics. Given that Britain was an important cradle of co-operation it was not surprising that the British Co-operative College became pre-eminent in its teaching of co-operative studies.

In the academic year 1946–7 ninety-eight students studied at the College: ninety-one were men. Twenty came from overseas countries. Those outside the British Empire were China, Denmark and Poland. Colonial and mandated territories within the British Empire included Assam, Pakistan, Nigeria, Gold Coast [Ghana], Barbados, British Guiana, Malaya, Cyprus, Mauritius, St Lucia, Palestine and Iraq. The College came to use the term 'overseas students' rather than colonial which was quite in keeping with its long tradition of enrolling students from countries outside the British Empire. That term also served to lessen the colonial and imperial distinction.

Apart from separate courses no distinction was made between British and overseas students. All became full members of the student body and of the student union, participating in the same activities as other College students from the UK. In a taped interview Marshall spoke of how the College, while recognising the importance to it of government-sponsored colonial co-operative students also pushed for voluntary or non-government officials such as those of larger colonial societies or co-operative unions to also be offered places. While no progress was made on this point the College arranged for its overseas students to visit voluntary British co-operatives. Study visits were arranged to both consumer and agricultural societies, to the Plunkett Foundation and the Welsh Agricultural Organisation Society. During the Christmas and Easter holidays overseas students were hosted by large retail societies.[44]

CONCLUSIONS

The British Co-operative College brought two British co-operative traditions closer together, one voluntary the other imperial. Its work contributed significantly to the impetus for colonial co-operative development that occurred between 1945 and 1960. The Colonial Development and Welfare Act of 1940 was passed in partial expectation of war and the need Britain would have for its colonies' support but it also reflected shifting and more positive attitudes to colonial development within which co-operatives could play a part.

War emphasised issues of democracy and self-determination. They were central to the Allies' war aims and stated clearly in the Atlantic and UN Charters. Imperial ideas became more difficult to justify or sustain particularly given America's central role in the war and her opposition to empire.

The role that co-operatives could play in the post-war world began to be seen more clearly in the early workings of the UN. Examples could be found in the UN Relief and Rehabilitation Administration but more clearly in its Hot Springs conference of 1943 which led to the setting-up of the UN's Food and Agricultural Organisation in 1945. FAO like the International Labour Organization set up in 1919 began to support co-operatives in undeveloped countries.

At home the advent of a Labour government in 1945 hastened the end of the Empire and increased focus on the role co-operatives could play in colonial development. The work of the special committee and its report and recommendations to the Fabian Society helped shape the Labour government's attitude to co-operatives as a means of development, aided by the fact that a member of that special committee was Arthur Creech Jones who became secretary of state for the colonies. Not only was he well acquainted with the findings of the special committee but also with leading figures in the British Co-operative movement. The Colonial Office privately recognised that the Empire would be replaced by the Commonwealth and considered that its role should be how best to pace and manage that transition. The Colonial Office appointed a co-operative advisory committee, a co-operative adviser in the person of B. J. Surridge and issued a dispatch to colonial governments urging the creation of specialist co-operative departments headed by co-operative registrars.

Echoes of the earlier divide in British co-operation between the merits of consumer over producer co-operation resurfaced in the movement's call to the Colonial Office to encourage consumer co-operatives in colonial territories. However, the Co-operative College set about organising courses for colonial co-operative officers in agricultural, market and credit societies. A productive synergy developed between the College principal, Dr Marshall, and the Colonial Office's co-operative adviser, B. J. Surridge.

Colonial co-operative students at the Co-operative College helped increase the interest of the British Consumer Co-operative movement in colonial co-operatives.[45]

13. British Co-operative Colonial Officers

INTRODUCTION

In the last chapter we noted how co-operative development rose up the agenda of the 1945 Labour government's colonial policy, influenced by the recommendations of the special committee that had reported to the Fabian Society's Colonial Bureau in the same year. The focus was now exclusively on colonial co-operative movements, their dominion counterparts being well able to look after themselves. Moreover the colonial remnants of the British Empire were quickly diminishing. India became independent in 1947 and divided between India and Pakistan. A year later Britain withdrew from Palestine, Burma and Ceylon. In 1956 the Sudan became independent as did the Gold Coast renamed Ghana the following year. Cyprus and Nigeria became independent in 1960 and were followed in the next two decades by Sierra Leone, Tanganyika (Tanzania), Uganda, Nyasaland (Malawi), Northern Rhodesia (Zambia), Malta, Malaya, Gambia, Basutoland (Lesotho), Bechuanaland (Botswana), Mauritius, Swaziland, Fiji, Guiana and Barbados. Some newly independent territories remained within the Commonwealth even when they became republics but others, like the Union of South Africa in 1961, left the Commonwealth.

The retreat from Empire meant that the India Office and the Indian Civil Service were abolished while the Colonial Office became smaller despite sometimes having to administer massive changes. These included the regrouping of colonies such as the formation of the Central African Federation which in 1953 combined Northern and Southern Rhodesia and Nyasaland. Elsewhere the Colonial Office became part of the response to violent threats to British rule with states of emergency being declared in Malaya in 1948 to counter a communist insurgency and in Kenya in 1952 to put down the Mau Mau rebellion.[1] As a result colonial co-operative development sometimes occurred within shifting and troubled frameworks or among populations that were ethnically or religiously divided.

Among its recommendations to the Fabian Colonial Bureau the special committee proposed that personnel from the British Co-operative movement should be recruited to serve in colonial co-operative movements and courses for officials from those movements should be organised by the British Co-operative College. In the academic year 1959–60 colonial officials numbered twenty-five; a further nine enrolled from newly independent territories[2]

BRITISH CO-OPERATIVE COLONIAL OFFICERS

The British Co-operative movement in terms of membership, turnover and capital was the largest in the British Empire. The bulk of the movement comprised consumer co-operatives. Consequently recruits drawn from these were well-versed in co-operative theory, history and organisation but might not necessarily have the skills appropriate for colonial co-operatives. By reasons of climate, geography and requirements of imperial trade, the agricultural sector predominated in most colonies. Were the skills of those recruited from the British Co-operative movement, therefore, transferable or appropriate?

British co-operative recruits were exclusively from working-class backgrounds and few had been to university. Most were unlikely to meet the traditionally high entry requirements of the Colonial Office. Another potential problem was how well British co-operative recruits would fit into colonial administrations once in post.

Close working relations evolved between the Co-operative College's principal, Robert Marshall, and B. J. Surridge, the Colonial Office's adviser on co-operatives. Surridge made frequent visits to the College and became well-acquainted with its staff, particularly those involved in courses for colonial students. Over a number of years he recruited figures such as Bert Youngjohns, Bill Craw, Stan Maudsley, Archie Macintosh and Trevor Bottomley.

In the early 1950s the Colonial Office was not alone in promoting colonial co-operative development. UN agencies such as the International Labour Organization and the Food and Agricultural Organisation were also turning their attention to co-operative development in undeveloped countries and among their recruits was Basil Loveridge, also a past student of the British Co-operative College with a long career in British co-operative education. His post was on a contract basis and he was employed in an advisory capacity with the title of consultant or expert; he never held the position of co-operative registrar.

Although the wives of recruits followed their husbands to colonial postings no woman was appointed in her own right. Given the harsh living conditions this is perhaps not surprising. However, Margaret Digby, secretary of the Plunkett Foundation, undertook short-term assignments such as training programmes or advising colonial administrations on aspects of co-operative law. She was already involved in courses for colonial students at the Co-operative College. In 1948 her *Manual of Co-operative Law and Practice*, written with B. J. Surridge, was published and became widely used in British colonies.

Digby was an experienced traveller. Sartorial anecdotes of her abound. Asked by a woman what to pack for the tropics she suggested that if she flew from London in January she should wear three pairs of knickers. When the plane touched down in Rome she could remove one pair and a second pair on reaching Cairo and thus be comfortably dressed when arriving at her destination. Basil Loveridge contributed to a number of African co-operative seminars with Margaret Digby and he recalled that she only ever packed two dresses. These were changed daily and one would be worn while the other was washed and dried.

Despite the fact that British co-operative recruits differed in many ways from traditional Colonial Service recruits they nevertheless proved able and made meaningful contributions to colonial co-operative development.

They appeared readily to accept the new emphasis on promotion in colonial co-operative development. It had traditionally been part of a co-operative registrar's function from the time of India's early co-operative legislation but its significance increased under the 1946 Model Co-operative Ordinance.

The Colonial Service, later HM Overseas Civil Service, had two main branches, the administrative and the technical. The former was the more important and from it permanent secretaries, district officers and magistrates were drawn. The technical branch covered specific functions such as those of agriculturalists and road engineers. However, the branches could overlap where a technician rose to become head of his particular function. Then, perhaps as director of agriculture or director of works he could join the administrative branch. Surridge argued that while a co-operative department was a technical department, its head, the co-operative registrar, should join the administrative grade. The Colonial Office accepted this view although no co-operative registrars appear to have risen up the colonial administrative hierarchy. The designation of co-operative departments as technical departments is important in two respects. One will be seen more clearly in our final chapter when we consider the 1964 publication by the Department of Technical Co-operation entitled *Co-operatives Overseas Policy on the Recommendations of the Advisory Committee*. The other was that it helped ease the entry of British co-operative recruits particularly where their experience in co-operative education and training experience could assist increased promotion in co-operative development.

We should now consider the experiences of British co-operative recruits. Two recruited in the 1950s were Archie Macintosh and Bert Youngjohns. Macintosh became assistant co-operative registrar in the Owerri and Rivers Provinces of Nigeria and later head of the Department of Co-operatives and co-operative registrar in the Gambia, while Bert Youngjohns became assistant and later co-operative registrar in Basutoland. In the 1970s Youngjohns became the co-operative adviser in the Foreign and Commonwealth Office and thus a successor to Surridge although there had been considerable institutional changes in the meantime. Remnants of the Colonial Office had merged in 1966 with the Commonwealth Relations Office to become the Commonwealth Office and two years later this became the Foreign and Commonwealth Office. The age of empire was then almost over.

It has been possible to trace the experiences of British co-operatives recruits through their written accounts and taped interviews. All came from similar working-class backgrounds with strong family co-operative connections. Most had mothers active in the Co-operative Women's Guild and they themselves had invariably studied at the Co-operative College. They had gone on to hold a variety of positions in the British Co-operative movement, many in its educational and training wing.

How were these recruits, well-versed in British co-operation but in the main without degrees, viewed by the colonial officers with whom they would now work? The rationale of their deployment lay in the recommendations of the special committee to the Fabian Colonial Bureau and the recognition by the 1945 Labour government of co-operatives as a tool for development in British territories. Co-operatives had already developed a track record of success and even affection among those involved in earlier schemes of co-operative development. Archie Macintosh recalled that:

> I never met Captain Cheeseman, W. H. K. Campbell or 'Captain' Strickland but their ethos pervaded the Movement in Nigeria and they were held with awe and affection there . . . I still have the 78 record of one of my Co-op. Choirs singing 'Captain Strickland, O Ye Co-operative'. Bert Youngjohns told me that on one of his Solomon visits he found the two launches he had procured for them on an aid project for inland hopping were respectively named 'Surridge' and 'Digby' at the members' request.[3]

A few existing colonial officers had already become interested in co-operatives as Macintosh also recalled:

> One man who had an enormous effect on my Co-operative approach was Ronnie Leslie my first Registrar. A truly fine man he had sacrificed a promising career as Senior D. O. on the way to a probable Residency or Governorship to join the Co-op. Department . . .[4]

Examples of such support for co-operatives and the Labour government's acceptance of the recommendations of the special committee might almost confirm a suspicion that the Colonial Office proved less stringent in processing applications from British co-operators. It seems that once Surridge had identified possible recruits their applications were handled sympathetically, as two accounts suggest. Archie Macintosh recorded:

> I knew B. J. Surridge quite well. He was on the panel which interviewed me for the Col. Service in 1953. He asked me most of the really relevant questions but I could see his quiet amusement which I found out later was occasioned by my rather simplistic not to say naïve attitudes to colonialism and the job.[5]

Trevor Bottomley described his interview at greater length:

> . . . when I studied the job description provided by the Colonial Office I got cold feet. It seemed to me to call for more accountancy knowledge than I had which was virtually none. I consulted an accountant friend of mine . . . and was advised by him to be sure I knew the difference between 'income and expenditure' and 'receipts and payments'. So long as I knew this, he suggested, I would be alright . . .
>
> On the due day I was interviewed by four people, one of whom was introduced by the Chairman as our 'technical member'. After a few friendly, preliminary remarks the Chairman handed the questioning over to this gentleman. His contribution went like this: 'Well, Mr. Bottomley, normally I should have to ask you several questions about accountancy and auditing but, with your experience, we need not take up time with that. And of course, some legal knowledge is necessary and I see you have studied company and Co-operative law so that's alright. The post definitely requires a sound background in education and training and you have

> excellent qualifications in this field. Can I ask you why do you want to work overseas and why this post? On receiving some bumbling answer to that he then said to the Chairman, 'Well, that's it Mr. Chairman, all very satisfactory I think.[6]

Bottomley's appointment as assistant co-operative registrar in Basutoland was confirmed within a week. The question then arises as to how he and other British co-operators were received once in post. Bottomley found little distinction between himself and existing colonial officers.

Almost a decade earlier when class attitudes might have been stronger, Archie Macintosh trod a more difficult path to acceptance. He wrote:

> Many people who joined the Colonial Service were related to people in it and were, therefore, already paid up members of an old Boy network so our arrival as working class practitioners of slightly odd doctrines was not too auspicious in terms of social or job acceptance but two incidents . . . seem to me to have importance way above their triviality and probably says something about the 'snobbery' of the C.S. . . .'

The co-operative registrar knew his wife's aunt and uncle:

> albeit more as 'servants' than equals . . . the relationship was quite irrelevant – the Mackintoshes knew people Ronnie knew so they must be O.K. so doors opened at HQ Enugu and at Provincial HQ in Calabar Province.
>
> The next incident was that two weeks after my arrival I was taken to be introduced to the Resident of the Province at Port Harcourt – a very important geezer and greatly respected. As I sat a bit nervously before him his face seemed very familiar so after he had asked me all the usual questions in gubernatorial manner I very tentatively enquired – did you used to be called Jumbo, Sir? Sharp intake of breath from the Assistant Registrar of Co-operative Societies I was relieving who was quite frankly a bit of a prat though efficient at the job. He'd been a wartime Naval Commander and was considered to be a damn fine fellow – which he was, prat or no. Jumbo started laughing and said 'you're Archie Mackintosh, aren't you?'

The background to this exchange was that when Macintosh left school in Form 3 to join the SCWS, 'Jumbo – or David Smith' had been in the sixth form and the school captain. He was also assistant scoutmaster of the troop that Macintosh had joined some years earlier.

After the courtesy visit to the resident of the province in Port Harcourt Macintosh returned to his post, with a journey that involved a 'three hour ferry crossing and four hour very slow car journey'. He recalled that within a week 'every DO, Agric. Officer, Education Officer, et. etc., knew that I had been at school with David' so that I must be 'the right kind of material . . . it could have taken us up to a year to be easily accepted. It actually took about a month and personally and workwise saved us from quite a bit of misery and loneliness though it could still be pretty lonely'. Even so he found it was about six months 'before we had any social life – occasional drinks or dinner parties and there was a club of sorts'.

British co-operative recruits experienced loneliness in a variety of ways. They usually travelled in advance of their wives who would join them when they had settled and found reasonable accommodation. Their wives also needed to be stout-hearted. Poor travelling conditions and far-flung co-operatives meant that their husbands could be away for long periods. Their living accommodation could be quite Spartan. The Macintoshes found theirs 'pretty ropey' but considered themselves lucky to have running water and electricity although the water was not safe to drink from the tap and the electricity available only 'when it didn't break down'.

The new recruits soon found that their promotion of co-operatives was determined to a considerable extent by their location. It was not only a question of climate and topography but also of class, race and government. Basutoland and Bechuanaland, later Lesotho and Botswana, were British protectorates but enclaves within the borders of the white racialist Republic of South Africa. That had repercussions on marketing and transport. Loveridge recalled an example of the latter when working in Botswana. He and a colleague, Derek Heffer, also a past student at the Co-operative College, were travelling by car but had to transfer to a train when it broke down:

> We had Pitso, the driver, with us, and Derek was worried about how he would be received on what was, although it was passing through Botswana, a South African train. He bought three first-class tickets, and when we presented ourselves on board told the conductor that Pitso was the Minister's driver. We all got on and settled into a carriage and stayed there. We could not take Pitso into the dining room, so we all ate in our compartment.[7]

Bottomley quickly found how topography and class affected what could be developed. Basutoland occupied the foothills and high ranges of the

Maluti Mountains and the southern ridges of the Drakensberg Mountains. Its people were the Basotho, a Bantu tribe that had a strong tribal identity. Apart from some land in its capital and some small areas used for district administration the land belonged to the tribe, and 'its use, occupation, and distribution was entirely under the control of the Paramount Chief through a structure of chiefs and sub-chiefs. There was no white settlement or farming'. Moreover, Basutoland had a low level of commercial activity with an economy 'based on sheep, some arable farming in the western foothills, employment in Government service, and the repatriated wages of men working in South African mines'. Raising cattle was an important part of Basutoland's economy but the mountainous terrain restricted the supply of grazing land. As a result only the chiefs had cattle herds while the majority of tribesmen had to content themselves with raising sheep and goats. Bottomley found the Basotho 'argumentative, and highly articulate; but generous and friendly people who, in the main, cheerfully accepted the status quo of rule by Britain'.[8]

Archie Macintosh found the situation in West Africa quite different. He observed:

> that West African British colonies had no settler problems. There were no settlers and there was none or very little of the apartheid or near-apartheid attitudes of East, Central and Southern Africa. The divisions were class based rather than colour based though even between 'classes' relations were pretty relaxed and informal. All Govt. Depts. and commercial firms had pretty well-informed indigenous senior and junior officers.

When moving on to the Gambia as co-operative registrar he found that his development efforts were helped by the governor who was 'dead keen to get Co-ops. of some kind started. He was Sir Percy Wyn-Harris who found Mallory's axe on Mount Everest in the 1930s'.

Returning to the question of what new British co-operative recruits brought to colonial co-operative development, this now had a distinct niche within overall British colonial policy. Shaped by India's early co-operative legislation, the influence of leading inter-war co-operative registrars and the recommendations of the 1945 Fabian report co-operative development became an important element in the colonial policy of the post-war Labour government. The Colonial Office's 1946 model co-operative ordinance formed the ground rules under which British co-operative recruits operated. It contained two essential features. One was that the administration of a colony should include a government officer, usually the co-operative registrar, who supported by staff of suitable quality, strength and sympathy would head the development of co-operatives with a strong emphasis on promotion. The other was that co-operatives should have a proper legal framework which would often become known as a co-operative societies ordinance.

B. J. Surridge has described this as usually having 11 parts:

1. Preliminary
2. Registration, including the appointment of the Registrar and his staff
3. Duties and privileges of registered societies
4. Rights and liabilities of members
5. Property and funds of registered societies
6. Audit, inspection and enquiry
7. Dissolution
8. Surcharge and attachments
9. Disputes
10. Power of the Government to make Rules having the force of law on certain matters
11. Miscellaneous[9]

Rules 'having the force of Law on certain matters' gave the registrar powers to ensure that a society's rules were in line with co-operative principles'. This had been a feature of colonial co-operative legislation since India's initial Acts of 1904 and 1912 and it gave the registrar legislative and arbitration functions over and above those exercised by other colonial officers.

The 1946 model co-operative ordinance and the rules made under its authority became the foundation of British colonial co-operative development. It emphasised the importance of promotion and made the co-operative registrar directly responsible for it. Experience had already shown that few co-operatives formed spontaneously in communities where there was little knowledge of them or of their potential.

The promotion of co-operatives began with field officers identifying possible opportunities and then introducing education and training programmes to prepare future members. When a viable trading stage was reached it was necessary to register embryonic co-operatives to gain corporate status within legal and taxation frameworks. Only the co-operative registrar could register. In law his decision to register permitted a society to engage in any commercial activities stated in its registered by-laws and to do so without reference or obligation to any other authority except those relating to taxation and criminal law.

Consequently, the co-operative registrar and his staff had to be fully conversant with a territory's co-operative law.

Co-operative promotion had been emphasised in the model co-operative ordinance and Surridge made it a central element in his development strategy. He also stressed how the ordinance reflected co-operative principles by recalling that the Fabian report had stressed their relevance in diverse circumstances. The example the report had given was of co-operative legislation in Saskatchewan, Canada. There an Act in 1944 had created a Department of Co-operation and Co-operative Development under a minister. A deputy minister, a civil servant, was the registrar and he exercised powers similar to those under the British 1946 ordinance. A further Act in 1950 spelled out more clearly what a co-operative enterprise needed to show to prove that it was observing co-operative principles in order to gain registration. These were:

1. Each member or delegate one vote
2. No voting by proxy
3. Race, creed or political beliefs no bar to membership
4. Services primarily for members
5. Interest on share capital not to exceed 5% per annum
6. Services to members and patrons as nearly as possible at cost in that savings and surpluses arising from operations are paid to members or members and patrons in proportion to patronage, use or contribution after provision for operating expenses and valuation reserves subject to the bylaws.[10]

Surridge held that the above 'enshrined the Rochdale principles'. He also argued that to maximise effectiveness a co-operative registrar had to have well-trained local staff. Consequently:

> It thus becomes *his first duty to train them* [Surridge's italics], i.e. those who will train the members of committees and employees of the societies and in due course the whole body of members.[11]

A discernible push to train colonial co-operative staff followed in the 1950s. Courses for senior colonial staff at the UK Co-operative College were the precursor but attention was also focused on junior indigenous staff through the establishment of a number of Co-operative Colleges in British colonies. Those in Ceylon and Malaya will be discussed in greater detail in the next chapter.

For the moment, though, we should note that the 1946 British model co-operative ordinance set out the parameters within which British co-operative recruits would work. Coming from the movement that had propagated Rochdale co-operation they were well-versed in co-operative principles. Did this, however, give them an edge over traditional colonial officers? Bottomley tended to think not, nor that a comparison would be particularly 'useful':

> In the former group (traditional colonial officers) there were several hard-working, brilliant and committed (and underpaid) men, and no doubt many time-servers . . . It comes down . . . to individuals. In that sense the 'colonial' group had the advantage of (generally) being well educated and well-trained in colonial administration . . . Their training included local languages and law and promotion prospects depended on this. Graduates of the (Co-op) College knew and were committed to Co-op. principles and organisation but for the most part had little experience of management except in theoretical terms . . . They also rarely had any language ability.

Once more emphasising the importance of the individual officer Bottomley suggested that it could reasonably be assumed that colonial officers took a job in co-operative development and stayed with it,

> because they believed this was a very worthwhile occupation. In that context, it should be remembered that every 'Colonial' officer worked within a hierarchical system in which he hoped, eventually, to become a Governor and a Knight. Calvert and Campbell et al presumably believed that their proclaimed interest in Co-ops. would not be a barrier to that career ambition.[12]

Neither Calvert nor Campbell became a governor or a knight. A rare example of a colonial co-operative registrar becoming a knight was Sir Malcolm Darling.[13] We have already met H. Calvert but have spoken less about W. H. K. Campbell who, as a co-operative registrar, came to prominence somewhat later The work for which he is best known, *Practical Co-operation in Asia and Africa*[14] was published in 1951 and reprinted in 1955. Both he and Calvert were held in high esteem by British co-operative recruits who were grateful for their major written works and sometimes for their ephemera. Trevor Bottomley recalled that:

> When I was in Basutoland with Bert Youngjohns I found in the files in the Co-op. Office a very thick, yellow binder marked *Ceylon*

> *Co-operative Manual.* It was a collection of official forms, specimen by-laws, commentaries, reports, and other papers and documents issued, often written by Calvert. It was an amazing source of information – for instance, several of the documents were lecture notes (eg. On economics) written by Calvert and used for staff training. I asked Bert [Youngjohns] where it had come from but he had no idea. Presumably the previous, or even previous, Registrar had known Calvert and had obtained it from his friend. (Bert was the first Co-op. trained Registrar, as distinct from civil servants given the job, in Basutoland.) Once discovered we used it often – a proposal to register a 'house construction society'? No problem, what did the draft of Calvert's By-laws for such say? A gold mine![15]

Basil Loveridge also admired the work of Calvert and Campbell. He wrote that he had:

> been fortunate to arrive in Ceylon just four years after independence and while the influence of the old colonial Registrars was still there. In those days the post of Registrar was reserved for elite members of the Ceylon Civil Service (CCS): ICS in India. They all had good degrees from British universities, many Oxford and Cambridge. Originally they were British. . . . They were followed by two or three Singhalese, also appointed under British mandate.[16]

Campbell had written *Practical Co-operation in Asia and Africa*[17] to help incoming co-operative registrars who might be precipitated into co-operative service, as he had been, without previous experience. He described how after '15 years of the ordinary revenue and judicial duties of an Administrative officer in Ceylon' he had been suddenly been appointed the country's registrar of co-operatives. His lack of experience was compensated for by the opportunity of undertaking extensive co-operative study tours which helped make him enthusiastic about co-operative development.

He and Calvert also endeared themselves to British co-operative recruits by the importance they attached to co-operative education and training. Loveridge wrote:

> Both men saw the importance of education in co-operative work. Of the two I got the impression that Calvert had the bigger influence although he was only there [Ceylon] one year. He was remembered by many of the older staff I worked with as a tower of strength.

> I retain vivid memories of Campbell's contribution and he had a lasting impact on my work. The bye-laws of Credit Societies provide much of the good principles and practice of co-operatives and Campbell insisted that officers taught them seriously. Campbell would visit any group applying for registration and conduct an examination. Did they know their bye-laws? If they failed the test he refused to register.[18]

Returning to the question of what other British co-operative recruits brought to colonial co-operative development, their writings suggest that they perhaps had a more democratic and egalitarian attitude towards local populations than traditional colonial officers. Loveridge believed that he and his colleagues came as 'helpers'.

> We were called many things – Expats, Advisors, Consultants – but I would much have preferred to have been called 'Helper'. We did not sit in an office in the capital and say what should be done. We drove out to the site and helped. It meant driving on some of the world's worst dirt roads.[19]

He was employed under contract within the UN system, which differed from employment within the British Colonial Service. Under that officers became part of the government structure and were required to execute policy and be held responsible for doing so. This did not necessarily preclude a hands-on approach and there is much evidence to suggest that other British co-operative recruits also got out of the office and listened.

For example Archie Macintosh recalled how he applied the management and organisational skills gained during the year he had spent as the SCWS's canteen supervisor in Benbecula in the Scottish Hebrides. There he had learned that people were concerned with only two times of day. These were the ferry time and the milking time. The West African equivalent appeared to be 'cool skin small'. Locals like their Hebridean counterparts felt little concern about the rest of time. Such relaxed attitudes prompted Macintosh to spend his first three months becoming part of the scene rather than attempting to organise co-operatives.

> During these three months I mainly sat on the Bantaba – (an open air platform where the old, the sick or lazy farmers foregathered daily) until I was part of the furniture exchanging the odd comment either in pidgin or through my interpreter about village

> happenings. The breakthrough came when the three village headmen started asking my interpreter/Inspector in training why I kept coming. I had a similar if slightly easier experience in the Hebrides when trying to buy local produce for the canteen direct from local crofters.

In Basutoland part of Bottomley's role was to reorganise and renew a co-operative credit system damaged by earlier failures. The process involved:

> Argument, cajoling, persuasion using both carrot and bludgeon . . . intimidation . . . bribery, as well as an immense amount of litigation, explanation, friendly discussion and genuine effort to find sensible answers to difficult problems.
>
> The Basutho have a long established oral tradition and make fine barrack-room lawyers. These two qualities made for many long, long sessions in village meetings (*pitsos*) often in the most remote areas, and continuing well after sundown, when no light except that of a communal fire was available, trying to establish fact and to decide what best to do.[20]

British co-operative recruits proved sensitive to indigenous populations in a variety of ways. One was a willingness to take advice from locals. Loveridge recorded:

> . . . an old man with very few teeth said to me, 'You know, Mr. Loveridge, we have boys out at our cattle posts near the borehole, and if we don't go to check on them we lose cattle, and if you don't check on your co-operatives, you will lose them.' How true: regular visits to co-operatives became an essential part of our work.[21]

Another way they were sensitive to their client groups was in ensuring that they took their own decisions. This was illustrated when Loveridge and a colleague visited a co-operative and found that its committee was meeting. The subject under discussion was whether the society's treasurer was dishonest. Loveridge insisted that he and his colleague would only observe and advise and that any eventual decision had to be made by the committee itself. The meeting broke up without any decision and a further meeting was arranged for the next day. Loveridge and his colleague then returned to their 'camp'. Early next morning the treasurer's father rode in to report that his son had admitted his guilt. At the committee meeting which followed he offered to repay his son's debt in instalments, which the co-operative's committee accepted. Loveridge then expected them to dismiss the young man. Instead:

> They told him he was no longer Treasurer but could stay on the committee. When I asked the reason for their decision they replied, 'If we send him away he will not learn to mend his ways. We are going to keep him with us and maybe we can give him some help.' Solomon would have been proud of them.[22]

Apart from the adjustments that British recruits needed to make to sometimes difficult housing and social circumstances they also experienced rough travelling conditions. Often they had to travel over vast distances to remote areas. Loveridge estimated that in five years he travelled around 100,000 miles in the Kalahari desert. Unmade roads were exhausting and damaging to vehicles. An ability to make repairs and to improvise was paramount. Sometimes there could be danger from wild animals. Often they drove with 'six five-gallon plastic bottles in the back' of their vehicles filled with petrol which made them feel like a 'mobile Molotov cocktail'.[23]

On a number of occasions they needed to camp out and that required the packing of appropriate equipment and foodstuffs. Loveridge described how on one occasion they decided to make camp beside a road. 'We got out the pot and made a stew with some vegetables in it, and turned in for the night. No camping gear had been brought, so we slept in the sand in our sleeping bags.' He found onions a good source of food; they also 'kept' better than potatoes.

Earlier we noted that the Indian Civil Service required that officers should be capable of riding on horseback for long periods and distances. In Basutoland Bottomley found that under 'ancient Government regulations' officers were still required to make at least one trek by horse each year, 'presumably to get lazy HQ types off their bottoms occasionally'. In any event, visits to some co-operatives in mountainous areas could only be made on horse. Having decided to make such a visit he called for the necessary arrangements to be made.

The trek started from a government supply shed in the mountains and on arrival Bottomley recalled:

> To my total astonishment I found assembled 18 horses, 8 pack mules, six grooms and a mountain of equipment. It seemed a bit excessive for five people on a five day trek . . .

> I accepted this logistical deployment while shuddering at the charge which might be laid against my travel budget. It was explained that, because of the nature of the country we would be travelling in, it was customary to take several spare animals . . .
>
> From the first day I found it very difficult to keep up. My horse quickly realised it had a complete novice on its back and would not do more than amble along at its own pace. So, as we progressed, I tended to fall further and further behind . . . By the second day I knew there would have to be a substantial amendment to the programme . . .
>
> The few tribesmen we met on the trail usually exploded with laughter at the obvious discomfort . . . One insisted that since I rode so badly I must be a priest; and that he had been waiting for such a fellow to turn up as he wanted his daughter married. He accepted reluctantly, and it seemed disbelievingly, that I had no such qualification.[24]

Air travel also threw up problems. Most of it was by Cessna and Bottomley needed to hire one to visit a South African farmers' co-operative in East London in an attempt to circumvent the hold that Afrikaner speculators had on the sale of the Basutoland wool crop. Each year they crossed the Caledon river to 'buy wool, cash on the nail at the cheapest price they could get away with. They had divided the country up between them to avoid competition and so cheated the Basotho farmer of a fair market price'. To break this hold the Basutoland government's co-operative department negotiated an annual deal with a South African farmers' co-operative under which a price was agreed and advertised; 'the South African Co-op's agents would then be given every facility to enter the country and buy wool at that price from our local Co-ops. If speculators from the Orange Free State wanted to buy our wool they would have to offer at least the same price . . .'[25] To negotiate a deal Bottomley and a colleague flew to East London in a chartered Cessna. It developed navigational difficulties soon after take-off and gave rise to a hair-raising adventure. Although a return flight had been booked they decided they could not face it and instead drove all the way back by car.[26]

After serving as assistant co-operative registrar in Basutoland, Trevor Bottomley became co-operative registrar in Bechuanaland. By then the Colonial Office no longer existed and its co-operative functions had been transferred to the Commonwealth Relations Office. Moreover, other agencies, particularly those in the UN, were entering developing world co-operative development. This shift allowed British co-operators to be recruited through new channels and is well-illustrated by the deployment of Edgar Parnell and Bernard le Bargy.

Both were employed in a joint project set up in Bechuanaland where Trevor Bottomley was the co-operative registrar. The project stemmed from a visit made earlier by OXFAM's Southern Africa regional director, James (Jimmy) Betts. He was the brother of Barbara Castle, a minister who had served in several of Harold Wilson's Labour governments. Betts had previously worked in the Fabian Society's Colonial Bureau. He was impressed by Bechuanaland's co-operative ventures and proposed, following his visit, a project that would be funded by the Commonwealth Development and Welfare Scheme, OXFAM and the British Co-operative movement.

The direct involvement of the British Co-operative movement is interesting and brings to mind its call twenty years earlier to the Colonial Office to support the development of consumer societies in British colonies. Little had occurred but an opportunity arose now after it had successfully launched several cattle marketing schemes. There then was an opportunity to include a consumer co-operative element in the project although difficulties were anticipated as summed up by Bottomley:

> They (consumer societies) were notoriously difficult to organise and run successfully for two particular reasons. First, poor communities which have to cope with adverse conditions of marginal agriculture to make a living (most of rural Africa) have virtually no regular cash income.
>
> What income they did have depended on the harvest-time sale of surplus crops (if any), the sale of cattle, and help from family members employed as migrant labour elsewhere . . . this was the situation in Bechuanaland. Diamonds and other mineral wealth, and the employment it brought was in the future.
>
> Traditionally, as much of their income was seasonally-based, many people relied heavily on credit, usually at an extortionate rate of interest to cover the high risk of default, for much of their regular necessities; which only made them poorer. As a matter of both commercial and ethical principle, Co-ops could not give credit: if they did so it inevitably led to rapid business failure, and failed business could help no one.
>
> Successful, and that meant profitable enterprise was basic to our development strategy. While seeking to improve the conditions of the poor we could not be concerned with charitable objectives. So Co-op business policy was to make a profit while trading at the

> lowest practicable prices, but not to give credit. Profitable enterprise based on self-help, not charity, and with an in-built capacity for growth, was the objective.
>
> Secondly, there were always serious problems of inefficient and dishonest management, and the consequent cash and stock loss and theft. The temptations of available cash and merchandise in conditions of great poverty are almost too great to be resisted. The private traders had no such handicap: they obviously didn't steal from themselves or treat their own merchandise carelessly.[27]

The aim of the project set up by OXFAM and the British Co-operative movement was to organise and manage five consumer co-operatives, one in each of the largest tribal towns. Edgar Parnell was recruited. Like Bottomley he had studied at the UK Co-operative College but as a managerial student. He then worked in several British consumer co-operatives and was recommended to the project by the College principal, Robert Marshall. Bottomley was pleased to accept him because he believed that:

> His personal and technical qualifications admirably suited the requirements of the job. He was a natural manager and organiser; a quiet, undemonstrative fellow who could make things happen – and did. A man of few words, he inspired and impressed others by his ability to get things done, his coat-off, hands-on approach to work (not a common trait among Europeans in Africa) and his calm demeanour.

Part of Parnell's strategy was to base a consumer society in the rapidly growing new town of Gaborone. Parnell recognised, as Barclays Bank had already done, the potential significance of Gaborone which was to become the capital of Botswana when, after independence it was no longer known as Bechuanaland. Gaborone's population was increasing quickly although when Parnell arrived it was only around 1,500. Barclays had already opened premises but initially could only use half the building. The joint project conducted 'Some rapid and astute negotiations [and] procured a two-year lease on the other half of the premises for a co-op. shop.'

Parnell managed to find shop fittings on a trip he and his wife made to Johannesburg in a second-hand truck. Parnell explained to Bottomley that on their way to Johannesburg they had passed a small supermarket that was closing down and selling its fixtures and fittings. He bought them all: baskets, shelving, gondolas, check-out counters and cash registers. The truck returned piled high and wide. While in South Africa he had also placed an initial stock order with a grocery wholesaler.

Safely back Parnell announced he would open a co-operative supermarket in Gaborone within two weeks. Bottomley observed:

> And so he did, with outstanding success. A rail-truck load of sugar to be offered for sale as a loss-leader, was brought in from Rhodesia – another breach of the international embargo. Orders were placed with wholesale agencies throughout the Eastern Transvaal and the new store stocked with merchandise. Staff were recruited and trained. A giant Afro-American who, being enamoured of a local girl, had stayed on after completing a stint as a Peace Corp volunteer was appointed store manager.
>
> Two weeks later, to the astonishment of the local populace, not to mention the Government hierarchy, there it was – a shop, the Gaborone Co-op Supermarket open for business. The very first shop in the new town, the first supermarket in Botswana, and the first store in our consumer development project.

Bottomley recorded that its success 'demonstrated to public and politicians alike that, given good management, there were good prospects and considerable potential for co-op. retail trading'.[28]

The other significant arrival in the joint project was Bernard le Bargy. Like Bottomley and Parnell he had also studied at the UK Co-operative College but his recruitment was as an overseas volunteer, the first in the joint project. Bottomley sent him, together with a Tswana school teacher, a refugee from South Africa who could speak very good English and who was now recruited as a co-operative development officer, to organise and run a cattle marketing co-operative. It would cover the whole of the Bamangwato region, an area larger than Wales.

Le Bargy's appointment illustrated another aspect of co-operative development strategy as embodied in the 1946 model co-operative ordinance. When carried into Bechuanaland law it allowed the co-operative registrar to delegate to staff functions prescribed in the co-operative law. The exception was that of registration. The mechanism was that they could be deputed 'for the time being' and this was done by a simple announcement in the *Government Gazette*. Le Bargy and his partner were thus 'gazetted' and this meant that they could act with the full authority prescribed by law. It is worth mentioning, however, that the conditions in which they lived and worked showed that a pioneering spirit was still required: Bottomley wrote:

> Within a month of arriving in Botswana, Bernard was living in a mud hut in the bush; miles from anywhere, and in very rudimentary domestic conditions with no running water, primitive cooking facilities, no electricity or sanitation. With his Tswana colleague, he stayed there as an unpaid volunteer Manager for fifteen months and built up an immensely successful marketing operation. They also trained local people to take over the control and management of the co-op. individually, and as a team, they did a magnificent job.[29]

CONCLUSIONS

This chapter has followed the experiences of a new kind of person recruited to assist in co-operative development in British overseas territories. They came from the British Co-operative movement and were frequently closely associated with its Co-operative College. Their recruitment had been recommended in the report of the special committee to the Colonial Bureau of the Fabian Society and implemented in the colonial policy of the 1945 British Labour government. Two figures central to their recruitment were B. J. Surridge, co-operative adviser to the Colonial Office and Robert Marshall, principal of the Co-operative College. Few British co-operative recruits had been to university. Nevertheless they exhibited innate abilities that allowed them to function well in colonial settings. They showed a sense of identity with the co-operatives with which they worked; a pioneering spirit in adapting to difficult living and travelling conditions; and, on many occasions, considerable initiative.

14. Co-operative Developments in Malaya and Ceylon

INTRODUCTION

In each part of this study we have examined examples of co-operative development that occurred in different parts of the British Empire. Within Part Three we trace those in Malaya (Malaysia) and Ceylon (Sri Lanka) and do so for three main reasons. One is that both became independent during the period and so allow us insights into how co-operative systems could change after British rule. The second is that both movements came within Indian co-operative influence: they were physically near; their co-operative legislation was based on India's; and some of their notable co-operative registrars were closely associated with the Indian co-operative model. The third reason is that both movements were dramatically affected by the Second World War. Malaya was occupied by the Japanese. Ceylon was not but her national life was drastically affected. Yet the co-operative movements in both territories expanded remarkably after the war.

This was at least partly due to the emphasis placed by the Colonial Office's 1946 dispatches and co-operative model ordinance on the training of government and co-operative officials in co-operative organisation, administration and management. We will note the impact of this policy particularly in the way it facilitated the increased recruitment of indigenous personnel into senior positions in government co-operative departments.

CO-OPERATIVE DEVELOPMENTS IN MALAYA

Co-operative development in Malaya proved robust despite its fractured setting. The Malay Peninsula comprised a number of states, including Singapore. Some were federated, others were not. It covered an area of some 50,000 square miles and a population of almost 6 million. These came from a number of races and religions: Chinese and Indian labourers had been brought in to work in the tin and rubber industries. Later some moved successfully into shop-keeping and commerce and helped form socio-economic groups different from the original native Malays who tended to remain in traditional farming and over time became the poorer section in the Malay economy.

British rule was overthrown by the Japanese invasion of 1941 but restored when Japan was defeated in 1945. Besides increasing antagonism to British rule there were tensions between the Malay, Indian and Chinese populations. On top of this a communist insurgency occurred between 1948 and 1960. A state of emergency was declared and British troops brought in to help restore law and order.

Despite such tensions Malaya became independent in 1957. Britain's hand-over was helped by a long-term imperial objective aimed at preparing colonies for independence. It was well summed-up by Sir Hugh Foot, later Lord Caradon:

> We of the Colonial Service ... were engaged in creating and working in many institutions – parliaments, municipalities, rural councils, courts, schools and universities, hospitals, agricultural stations and the whole range of departmental services – but none of our tasks was more important than that of building up civil services capable of of taking the strain when independence came and making the institutions of government work.[1]

The policy to which Sir Hugh Foot referred was implemented at different speeds in different colonies but in Malaya it began as early as 1910 with the creation of the Malayan Administrative Service (MAS).[2] It concerned more the administrative side of the Colonial Service rather than the technical side which included co-operative departments. As we noted in the last chapter, though, heads of co-operative departments became part of the administrative element. Implementation of the policy helped increase the recruitment of indigenous populations: in co-operative departments they began reaching senior levels.

The policy was well under way when five Indian co-operative registrars attended the 1925 Wembley conference of the Plunkett Foundation. Throughout this chapter we will note co-operative registrars who were born in Malaya and Ceylon moving into senior co-operative positions. An important shift was occurring and one appropriate to approaching independence. It was another policy that illustrated a plurality of thought and governance within the British Empire.

Malaya's first co-operative legislation was not passed until 1922. It sought to help her subsistence farmers who had become the poorer section of its economy. Malay farmers had little incentive to change. They worked in a hot and moist climate which discouraged hard physical labour that was hardly necessary in any event because the rich soil easily produced sufficient foodstuffs. There was also a good supply of land which meant that if a peasant needed to sell to pay a debt, he could easily move to new land and begin all over again. While the younger and more ambitious gave up and moved to a town the majority remained in the countryside and became even poorer.[3]

Co-operative development was initially hindered by the more conservative Muslim Malay peasants who argued that the payment of co-operative interest on loans was contrary to Islamic teaching. They resisted joining thrift and credit societies. However, the Malay Department of Co-operation set up under the 1922 legislation was able to show that Indian Muslims had felt no similar reservations and had joined credit co-operatives to their considerable benefit. Malay peasants remained unconvinced. The Department then approached senior Muslim clerics in Arabia and Egypt who declared that co-operative credit was within Islamic law. This enabled the Department to approach Malay sultans and to persuade them to issue rulings to this effect and in this way religious objections were overcome.

Even then co-operatives were slow to form and only some 800 existed by 1941 when the Japanese invaded. Although the Malay peasants had been the initial target group societies had also formed among Indian labourers working on rubber plantations. Their benefits were immediate. Because they were migrants rather than permanent settlers they lacked access to suitable banking and secure means of saving or transmitting money back to their families. Thrift and credit co-operatives were the answer and by 1941 there were over 400.

Thrift and credit societies were also established among urban salary-earners particularly in the public services like the Malayan state railways. Salaries were usually paid monthly and workers could experience cash-flow problems which they could ease if they opened an account in a thrift and credit co-operative. Large surpluses resulted from their successful running and were then invested in municipal and government loans. Eventually secondary banking unions were formed to handle these investments along with a number of other functions.

When the Japanese invaded there were also around 150 rural Raiffeisen-type credit societies formed to finance farmers dependent on a single crop. Once that was sold the loan had to be repaid immediately. Several small rubber factories and egg marketing societies had limited success. More successful were general purpose or village welfare co-operatives, organised to clean up villages; repair bridges; make paths; arrange rat hunts, sports days, social gatherings and so on.[4]

Malayan co-operatives were hit hard by the Japanese invasion and the centre of their movement was devastated. The British director of the co-operative department, R. Boyd, was interned along with many of his staff.

> Half the trained audit staff died during the occupation or had to be invalided out of the service. Many of the members and office-bearers of local societies, especially among the estate labourers, were carried off in Japanese labour gangs, and died on the Siam railway. The books of many societies were lost or destroyed so that no record of their affairs remained.[5]

Boyd recalled that the Japanese permitted some societies to continue and allowed them to withdraw one-quarter of the sum at their credit 'to refund savings to members'. Little new saving followed because employment was uncertain and prices fluctuated. Matters worsened when the Japanese made it an offence to hold Malayan currency and issued instead the Japanese dollar. Difficulties arose from the fact that its value could not be determined as its notes were not numbered. Its value continued to fall until 1945 when it ceased to be legal tender. Surviving co-operatives then suffered further losses when they had to write off those assets held in Japanese dollars: many had to close.[6]

In addition:

> The head office of the department [of co-operation[in Kuala Lumpur was used by the Japanese as a military Headquarters. As a result all the departmental records were lost and the excellent co-operative library built up over many years was apparently burnt. The Japanese discouraged the reading and speaking of English. The loss of all records was a very severe blow. The prevailing shortage of paper rendered any rapid replacement impossible.[7]

Most societies lost records while some 'had no books left at all'. There were also severe transport shortages. 'Up until August 1946, only one car had been allocated to the Co-operative Societies Department which now covered the whole of Malaya.'

Happily the pre-war momentum of co-operative development quickly resumed despite immense difficulties. There was an enthusiasm to rebuild as a further article in the Plunkett *Year Book of Agricultural Co-operation 1948*, reveals:

> By the end of year [1947] all but 46 of the 891 Co-operative Societies which were in existence prior to the war in the Malayan Union had re-written, where necessary, their lost books and accounts and had them audited. Nearly all the pre-war societies were therefore in a position to resume normal working provided that they so desired . . .[8]

The article points to positive growth in a number of different kinds of co-operative including rural co-operative credit societies, fishermen's co-operative credit societies, credit societies linked to seasonal crops, labourers' co-operative credit societies, salary earners' thrift and loan societies and general purpose co-operative societies. Moreover, thirty-eight thrift and loan societies had established four unions which engaged in conventional union activity and in education.[9]

In 1945 the special committee report to the Fabian Colonial Bureau had noted:

> The outstanding feature of the Malayan Co-operative Credit Movement is that it has been built up without any direct financial assistance from the Government or the use of outside funds. It was the policy of the Co-operative Department to make societies independent of outside finance and *to deny them the use of other people's money until they had learned to use their own wisely* [my italics].[10]

This tradition continued as the 1948 article quotes:

> At no time has Government ever advanced money to a co-operative society in Malaya and no inducement is held out that if a society is formed the members will be able to get working capital from outside.[11]

A co-operative superstructure was emerging. It included a national co-operative union. In 1958 a co-operative central bank was established. By 1967 there were 2,967 co-operatives with a combined membership of 477,358. They existed mainly in agriculture, consumer supply, credit, banking, fisheries and housing and were supported by fifty-two secondary level federations or unions. Despite financial independence government influence was not totally lacking and could been seen in the decision taken in the 1970s to hive off agricultural and fisheries societies from the Department of Co-operatives and to place them under the newly created Farmers' Organizations Authority and Fisheries

Department Authority. It was later held that this hampered 'the overall integration' of the movement.[12] This may well be true and illustrates that the role of governments could be benign in their promotion and encouragement of co-operatives but also shape them in ways that co-operatives themselves might not have adopted had they been totally autonomous and independent.

This power becomes even more evident in Ceylon.

CO-OPERATIVE DEVELOPMENTS IN CEYLON

Ceylon was not invaded by the Japanese. Her existing government remained in power and, as part of the national war effort, became far more involved in co-operatives.

Unlike Malaya Ceylon comprised a uniform system of government and geographical entity. Its population, however, was divided between the Sinhalese and the Tamils. The 1945 special committee report to the Fabian Colonial Bureau noted some similarities with Malaya:

> Export production is largely in the hands of European plantations owned by London companies and supervised by managing agents. Ceylon's small holders are primarily growers of rice for domestic use, but also grow a small proportion of economic crops. The burden of debt is almost as heavy as in Malaya, due to the same fundamental cause – a bad credit system whereby the small farmer has recourse to the moneylender, to whom he is already heavily in debt . . . As in Malaya, the paralysing effects of this indebtedness are only too obvious – miserable standards of living, apathy to progressive ideas, inability to take advantage of the economies of co-operative marketing and preparation of crops.[13]

Solutions to these problems had been sought as early as 1909 when a committee was set up: its proposals led to the Co-operative Credit Societies Act of 1911. Similar to India's 1904 Act its aim was to encourage the formation of thrift and credit co-operatives so as to help reduce rural indebtedness and the pernicious hold of money-lenders, and enhance the economic position of small farmers. A broader Co-operative Act followed in 1921.

Until the war thrift and credit societies predominated. Initially the director of agriculture acted as co-operative registrar, but in 1926 a joint registrar was appointed under the designation of 'co-operative colleague'. He became the co-operative registrar and in 1930 a separate co-operative department was set up. The 1945 Fabian report noted:

'Whilst the first Registrar and Assistant Registrars were Europeans, the present Registrar and his staff are Sinhalese or Tamils.'[14] As in Malaya, indigenous populations were moving into senior co-operative development positions.

By the time war broke out little progress had been made in co-operative marketing and processing One reason was members' indebtedness and another was the difficulty of gaining entry to markets that were unregulated and often glutted. Several handicraft co-operative societies did exist, mainly in the weaving industry, as well as a growing number of better-living societies along the lines of those in Malaya. They encouraged their members to save, keep cleaner homes and develop kitchen gardens. A novel co-operative ran a daily motor-launch service between islands off the north coast and the mainland. All point to a diversification and growing awareness of co-operatives.

The war boosted both. The strongest growth, though, occurred when the government actively intervened to encourage the formation of consumer co-operatives. At the outbreak of war thirty-eight had existed, with a total membership of 17,675, and were found mainly on estates where they had been encouraged by the estate-owners. It is not clear how far they were self-managing, independent and democratic. Inasmuch as the costs of their members' purchases were deducted from their wages there was a hint of the truck system that had been banned in Britain a century earlier. Few independent retail societies existed. They were difficult to establish because '. . . cash purchases are foreign to local habits. Either people did not buy at all, or they bought on credit which was not repaid'.[15]

During the war government-sponsored consumer co-operatives were encouraged as reports of the co-operative department reveal:

> The remarkable events during 1942–45 were the result of war conditions. The economic background of the period was one of severe scarcity and rigid controls, and although this background was full of what normally would have constituted retarding factors to the highest degree, it actually fostered Co-operative development to a most surprising extent. Despite the introduction of controls, profiteering in consumer goods had by the beginning of 1942 grown so rampant throughout the country (the situation became very acute after the Japanese air raid of April 1942) that the people themselves were led to ask for co-operative distribution as the only remedy to their pressing ills. The result was a very rigorous 'Stores Drive', yielding a crop of 4,000 new co-operative stores.[16]

War conditions also led to an increase in the number of marketing and production co-operatives, from seventy-one in 1942 to 160 in 1945.[17] However, consumer co-operatives or 'stores' showed the most spectacular growth: 'Within two years more than half the population were being fed and clothed through Co-operative Stores.' A later estimate put this nearer two-thirds.[18]

The Administration Report of the Working of Co-operative Societies 1942–1945 stressed:

> that the Drive was the result of a great and insistent popular demand and that the part played by Government was merely to collaborate with the people in giving effect to their wishes.[19]

In the drive the co-operative department was assisted by the civil defence commissioner, the food controller and revenue officers. Food supplies were drastically reduced when Malaya, Burma and other nearby territories were overrun. Japanese air raids in 1942 threatened supplies further, particularly those from India. A food control scheme was introduced which created a network of private authorised distribution and guaranteed a basic ration of rice and flour. Other commodities were not guaranteed and a black market and profiteering resulted. Store co-operatives were encouraged so as to be a countervailing force.

These wartime initiatives proved a springboard for post-war co-operative development in Ceylon. They helped co-operatives establish their credibility and to make them a household name. Post-war development was also helped by two other elements: the war helping to modernise Ceylon's economy; and the continuing influence of earlier co-operative registrars such as Calvert and Campbell.[20] Sinhalese and Tamils who had worked with them now moved into leading positions. One was G. De Soyza, who had first been co-operative registrar and was later commissioner. In 1948 he became permanent secretary to the Ministry of Food and Co-operative Undertakings.[21] Another was T. D. L. Peiris who had been an assistant commissioner of the co-operative department and was later principal of the School of Co-operation at Polgolla.[22] There were also others in a greatly enlarging Department of Co-operatives that had resulted from the war-time stores drive. We can trace its growth by comparing its establishment figures in 1942 with those for 1945.

In 1942 the Ceylon co-operative department comprised:

1 Registrar
1 Deputy Registrar

5 Assistant Registrars
33 Inspectors
55 Sub-Inspectors
18 Clerks
1 Bookbinder
7 Others (peons)

The stores drive led to the appointment of 'a large army of Sub-Inspectors'; '. . . considerable additions also had to be made to the Inspectors' cadre'. A new deputy registrar was appointed.[23] By March 1945 when the co-operative department became the Department of Co-operative Development its staff comprised the following:

1 Registrar
1 Deputy Registrar
1 Senior Assistant Registrar
7 Assistant Registrars
1 Probationary Assistant Registrars
3 Temporary Assistant Registrars
1 Lecturer in Economics
88 Inspectors
5 Temporary Inspectors
709 Sub-Inspectors
34 Clerks
2 Translators
1 Bookbinder
12 Others (peons)
8 Labourers[24]

In relation to its commitments the Department was still considered to be under-staffed. The war had hindered recruitment and a number of designated posts remained unfilled. In addition to a greater emphasis on education and training reflected in the appointment of a lecturer in economics the Department was now also placing greater emphasis on field work: 'A new system of administration has now been devised for field work, the object being to speed up development.' Provincial structures within the Department were introduced to help in this and co-operative organisations were encouraged to form provincial unions or even a co-operative federation of Ceylon.[25]

As part of its drive for increased education and training, the Department established the School of Co-operation in 1943 which then became an important part of its education and propaganda branch.

Its functions included the 'systematic training' of inspectors and sub-inspectors already in service and of new recruits. It was also required to make provision for the 'training of office-bearers of societies' and to create a system of syllabuses and examinations.[26] Together the Department and the School of Co-operation encouraged co-operatives to organise propaganda meetings and arranged for a touring mobile propaganda van to be available.

Both the School of Co-operation and the Department became actively involved in other war-time initiatives. One was the 1942 All-Ceylon Food and Foodstuffs Exhibition in Colombo where they erected a co-operative pavilion. Such efforts along with the stores drive helped make co-operatives better known than they had been before. They became a 'household word in Ceylon' with the result that the need for co-operative propaganda was reduced.[27]

In 1947 the School of Co-operation found a permanent home at Polgolla near Kandy in premises that had previously belonged to the British Royal Air Force. A year later, when Ceylon became independent, it had become a considerable establishment with a large teaching programme: 'The officer in charge of the School is the Assistant Registrar (Education) who is assisted by a Lecturer in Economics, 3 Inspector-Lecturers, and two Visiting Lecturers.' Co-operative inspectors and sub-inspectors were sent to the School 'for training in batches of about 100 at a time'. Their training programme lasted six months and included classes in 'Co-operation, Accounts and Audit, Elements of Banking, Economics and Law, Economic History, Economic Geography, the last mentioned subject being given by the officers of the Department of Agriculture'. These classes led to examinations. 'Last year 812 candidates sat for these examinations and 549 passed the test, while 10 were "referred" in various subjects.' The School also held short courses 'in Co-operation for the Food Production Officers, who were to be attached to new Agricultural Production Societies'.[28] The Central Co-operative Library was now housed at the School with around 1,500 volumes and a reading room that offered a number of journals and periodicals in 'Co-operation, Economics and other allied subjects'.[29]

The size of staff of the Department of Co-operative Development, its provincial organisation closely linked to co-operatives' provincial unions and federations and the extent and nature of the School of Co-operation at Kandy suggest that a substantial co-operative movement had formed by the time Ceylon became independent in 1948.

Nine years later the *Report on the Ceylon Co-operative Movement for 1957*[30] shows that this expansion and diversification continued after independence. It reported that in 1956 there had been '10,812 societies

. . . 9,368 registered societies and another 1,444 (comprising Co-operative School Societies, Youth Clubs and Women's Guilds) which were recognised by the Co-operative Department'.[31] The total membership of the 'registered' primaries was 1,228,971, and of 'recognised' primaries 124,055. We assume that 'recognised' primaries were those awaiting registration. In a population of 8.9 million this represents a high degree of co-operative penetration. In addition 'the number of persons served by consumer societies was 5.2 million'.[32] Because a distinction is drawn between them and the membership of primary societies it is deduced that they were consumers rather than actual co-operative members.

By 1956 the School of Co-operation at Polgolla had accommodation for 150 students and ran courses for three or six months for 'officers of the Department as well as foreign students and three months' courses for prospective employees of co-operative Societies'. The principal of the School was now T. D. L. Peiris. A qualified librarian was about to be appointed to the School's library whose volumes had now risen to around 4,000.[33]

In addition, the Department of Co-operative Development now ran six education centres 'under the immediate supervision of the Provincial Co-operative Extension Officers'. Three more were planned and 'The funds required for acquiring these Centres has been made available by Canada under a Colombo Plan grant . . .'[34]

This and the recent completion of an education project funded by the International Labour Organization remind us that the framework of co-operative development was changing. Earlier patterns set by the Colonial Office were being replaced with specific and more limited aims funded by international organisations. The importance of education remained but its remit was changing.

For example the 1957 report of the Department of Co-operative Development underlined the importance the government attached to educating people in 'the principles and methods of Co-operation'. It was felt that this should be possible in a country that already had a literacy rate of 65 per cent. Such education would become even more important as the business and size of co-operatives grew. The report stressed that co-operation's 'fundamental principles need to be worked out in the light of practice in relation to changing conditions'.[35]

Education and training were features of most co-operative movements. Their relevance had been recognised from the time of the Rochdale Pioneers. Now we see a government department recognising their importance because its co-operatives had been encouraged from the 'top down' and because the war had produced the most compelling of circumstances. Newly independent governments similar to that in Ceylon were also attaching similar importance to their co-operative education and training provisions and for the same reasons. Many set up co-operative colleges similar to that at Polgolla. Their role was not only to train co-operative department staff but also co-operatives' senior officials.

During the 1950s we see an increase in study tours arranged between co-operative movements. In 1957 Polgolla attracted a number of foreign students while senior Ceylonese co-operative officers studied abroad, mainly in India. The Ceylon Co-operative movement attracted fifteen foreign visitors[36] from Iran, Manila, Japan, USA, Indonesia, Italy, Singapore and Malaya. Some were co-operative leaders while others were academics or civic dignitaries. A notable figure was M. Marcel Brot, president of the ICA, who on visiting the Polgolla School declared: 'the College will make a sure and effective contribution to the Co-operation in this country'.[37]

In 1957, nine years after independence, we find a large and diverse co-operative movement in Ceylon. It was consolidating and becoming part of a wider international co-operative movement reflected in its visits to and from other co-operative movements. The *Report on the Ceylon Co-operative Movement for 1957* also reveals its growing diversity. Besides the large consumer co-operative sector there were also credit societies with both limited and unlimited liability, production and sales societies, agricultural co-operatives, co-operative dairies, fishermen's societies, coconut production and sales societies, cottage industry co-operatives, textile societies, co-operative rubber production and sale societies, tea production and sale co-operatives, tobacco production and sale co-operatives, transport societies and a number of co-operative hospitals and dispensaries.

Such a list shows the large Department of Co-operative Development as successful in bringing co-operatives into many areas of national economic and social life. The Second World War, the needs it created and the stores drive response had exponentially raised co-operatives' profile and increased their numbers. Yet doubts would later be expressed about whether true co-operatives always resulted. De Soyza was reported to have asked 'to be forgiven for his errors',[38] thus pointing to internal doubts. Stronger external reservations were also expressed:

> The government mechanisms designed to assist and supervise cooperatives had similarly grown, and the earlier well-articulated plans to de-officialize the cooperative structure and make it dependent on its own resources rather than those of government

> fell by the wayside. First reduced during World War II when co-operative structures were created to handle distribution of food and other consumer goods, cooperative independence gave way to a Sri Lankan government decision to use cooperatives to achieve a variety of development tasks, whether or not the cooperatives agreed, and whether or not they had the needed capacity. Each cooperative shortfall brought further governmental planning and involvement and strengthened a government cooperative relationship that is still a brake on independent cooperative development.[39]

It has to be remembered, though, that this was the era of big government during which it was believed that the state should play a large part in a nation's economic life. National plans, often for five or ten years, became a feature along with an increased number of national authorities to oversee national production levels, prices and perhaps regulation of consumption. While such arrangements were the norm in communist regimes they were also evident in Britain and other parts of Western Europe in the late 1940s, 1950s and 1960s. It would be surprising if newly independent colonies did not follow suit. Thus in newly independent Malaya we see the government hive off agricultural and fishery co-operatives from the Department of Co-operatives to a newly created Farmers' Organisations Authority and Fisheries Authority without regard as to whether the integration of Malayan co-operatives could be hampered. Now in Ceylon we see it being argued that co-operative ideology could change because the nature of the state had changed.

The Ceylon government now wanted to promote multi-purpose village co-operatives. Precedent lay in the wartime decision to mount the stores drive. It ran counter, though, to earlier co-operative orthodoxy that co-operative membership should be based on interest or a shared or common bond: a grain farmer would have little interest in joining a dairy farmers' co-operative. The new proposals were outlined in the *Report on the Ceylon Co-operative Movement for 1957* which noted that a committee of the Ministry of Agriculture and Food had argued that changes were necessary in agricultural co-operation. It quoted a directive issued by the 'Hon'ble Minister' dated 1 July 1957 which said:

> Multi-purpose Village Co-operatives
>
> The Co-operative Movement in Ceylon is 45 years old, but unfortunately does not possess the stability and maturity normally associated with such long years of experience. I attribute this to two fundamental defects which have prevented the growth of a virile and healthy movement.

The minister attributed the first defect to a 'faulty ideology'. This resulted from co-operatives first appearing in a period when the dominant political philosophy argued that the state should not interfere in economic and social life. Co-operatives became an attempt 'to mitigate the severity of unregulated economic forces'. He stressed, however, that they now operated 'in an age in which the State is actively regulating economic and social affairs' and they should now see themselves as 'being an active partner of the State in the task of National Development . . .'[40]

The statement analysed further examples of how 'an allegiance to an obsolete ideology . . . imprisoned the Co-operative Movement of our country in narrow confines' and later considered the 'second defect', that of organisation:

> The Co-operative Movement of Ceylon, I believe, is unique in its apparent variety of forms. The 10,500 odd Co-operative Societies that exist today are of about 70 different types. This cumbersome organisational structure has resulted in an enormous dissipation of time and energy. An individual's interests as a consumer, a borrower of money, a seller of paddy, a seller of milk, a seller of coir products etc. would necessitate his being a member of a number of societies some located outside his village, with a result that he becomes no more than a 'sleeping partner', so to speak, of each of them. His interest in the societies gradually declines, his vigilance slackens and corruption among office-bearers and employees goes unchecked. The supervisory and audit roles of the staff of the Co-operative Department are made more difficult by the existence of numerous petty societies. Above all the dearth of managerial ability is made all the more pronounced by these numerous societies with very little business activity each having to employ its own manager on a paltry salary.[41]

These statements reflect an important change in co-operatives' environment. What was happening in Ceylon, soon to be known as Sri Lanka, was also happening in other post-colonial territories. Their ideas of the big state as a prime organ of development were widely held. Likewise ideas of merging and rationalising co-operative structures also gained ground in them as well as in market economies. For example, in Britain in 1955 the Consumer Co-operative movement set up an independent commission to consider how the movement might respond to a quickly shifting economic environment in which the nature and function of retailing was changing. The commission proposed the rationalisation of co-operative structures in line with enlarging markets, as well as changes in co-operative production and management.[42]

The idea of multi-purpose village co-operatives hardly took off in the West, although community co-operatives developed in the 1970s in the Highlands and Islands of Scotland and Ireland had some similarities. Generally speaking, Western economies had advanced to an extent that village-based multi-purpose co-operatives had little relevance. Nevertheless they were relevant in many developing countries where urbanisation was only just gathering pace.

Ideas of the big state, even in mixed economies like Britain's, lasted for fifty years or more in many countries throughout the world. They forced co-operatives to reorient themselves. By the 1960s the ICA felt the need to review co-operative principles once more, in the light of these changes.

With a growing number of post-colonial territories joining it the ICA also needed to take account of changes in third-world co-operative development. Earlier imperial frameworks were fast disappearing. Their place was being taken by UN agencies such as the International Labour Organization and the Food and Agricultural Organisation. Our final chapter will trace that handover and the developments surrounding it.

CONCLUSIONS

This chapter has allowed us to trace the co-operative movements in Malaya and Ceylon as these became independent. The war prompted enlarged co-operative departments particularly in respect of education and training where officials and members recruited under special conditions such as the stores drive in war-time Ceylon needed to understand what co-operatives were. The need for education and training continued as government direction and control of co-operatives grew. It was recognised that without members understanding their roles a co-operative was in danger of becoming a 'leaning tower'.

Greater government involvement in their co-operative movements sometimes led to their realignment with departments or ministries. Attempts were also made to streamline their structures and rationalise and improve their management. Such government involvement inhibited co-operatives' independence and autonomy. They were now seen as adjuncts of government rather than as non-governmental organisations. Governments' response to such accusations was that traditional co-operative ideology was no longer relevant once the state for the good of all became actively engaged in welfare and the economy.

We also noted in this chapter how the co-operative movements in Malaya and Ceylon began to stretch out to the wider co-operative world. They attracted co-operative visitors from abroad. Increasing foreign co-operative contacts were made. Important among these were links with the ICA and with the co-operative branches of the International Labour Organization and the UN's Food and Agricultural Organization. Post-colonial co-operative movements would increasingly become part of an international co-operative movement. They made it more diverse. The ICA was now not only bringing together co-operatives from communist and market economies but also those from earlier colonies. It found it more difficult to sustain its unity and in the 1960s once again felt the need to review co-operative principles.

15. Sunset to Sunrise: The Journey from Empire and Commonwealth to World-wide Co-operative Development

INTRODUCTION

In this final chapter we trace the shift of developing-world co-operative development from the British Empire to post-war international organisations often under the umbrella of the United Nations (UN). Other agencies such as OXFAM also became involved. Some national co-operative movements channelled assistance to fledgling counterparts in developing countries. An old order was passing and along with it earlier means of delivering major co-operative development. The British Empire was not the only one on the way out. Other European empires were also disappearing, some of which had also encouraged co-operatives in their colonies. Reasons for their decline were complex and varied but a major catalyst had been the Second World War.

A PERIOD OF TRANSITION – NEW AGENCIES INVOLVED IN CO-OPERATIVE DEVELOPMENT

Earlier we noted how the Allies' war aims had been summed up in the Atlantic Charter. This had initially been agreed between Britain and America in 1941 but was later endorsed by the Allies, including the Soviet Union. It not only spelt out the Allies' war aims against Germany, Italy and Japan but also the principles on which a post-war world should be built. These included the renouncing of territorial aggrandizement, that territorial changes should be made only with the consent of their peoples, and that all peoples had the right to choose their own form of government. The Charter also urged an easing of trade restrictions, an equal right of access to raw materials, increased international economic collaboration and a guarantee of the freedom of the seas.

Radically it also signposted a more democratic international order in which empires would be anachronistic. The new order was to be headed by the UN which was to be more firmly based than its predecessor, the League of Nations, set up at the end of the First World War. Although not formally established until 1945 the UN developed some momentum during the war when some of its embryonic agencies became engaged in relief, rehabilitation and food supplies. Moreover, the International Labour Organization (ILO), part of the old League of Nations system, continued to operate throughout the war and would become part of the new UN system. It had already had a strong co-operative record.

Just as the British Empire had realised that economic stagnation or decline could lead to social unrest and that to mitigate this there needed to be development, so too did the new UN now acknowledge that economic progress was needed to help preserve peace. Consequently, the UN Charter pledged UN members to 'employ international machinery for the promotion of the economic and social advancement of *all* peoples [my italics].'

Article 1 of the Charter asked for 'international co-operation in solving international problems of an economic, social, cultural or humanitarian character'. This was reinforced in Article 55:

> With a view to the creation of conditions of stability and well-being which are necessary for the peaceful and friendly relations among nations based on respect for the principle of equal rights and self-determination of peoples, the United Nations shall promote:
>
> (a) higher standards of living, full employment, and conditions of economic and social progress and development;
> (b) solutions of international economic, social, health and related problems, and international and cultural and educational co-operation;
> (c) universal respect for, and observance of human rights and fundamental freedoms for all without distinction as to race, sex, language or religion.[1]

All this was in accord with the aims of the International Co-operative Alliance (ICA) which gained Category A consultative status with the UN. It was one of the first three non-governmental organisations to do so.[2] Part of this success was due to its close work during the inter-war years with the co-operative branch of the ILO. In the late 1940s it also became associated with organs within the UN, in particular its Economic and Social Council, its Food and Agricultural Organization and its Educational, Scientific and Cultural Organization (UNESCO).

All this made it even more important that the Alliance should take account of the widening framework in which co-operative development was occurring. Besides the UN system co-operatives were becoming part of the policies and strategies of inter-governmental bodies. These included the Organization of American States (the Pan-American Union) which created a special division for co-operatives within its Division of Labour and Social Affairs. A development vehicle of the Commonwealth now replacing the British Empire was the Colombo Plan which promoted mutual aid schemes between Commonwealth members and arranged for an interchange of information and advice on co-operatives. The Caribbean Commission and the Commission for Technical Co-operation South of the Sahara also recognised the contribution co-operatives could make to economic and social development while the South Pacific Commission had appointed a co-operative officer and was energetically propagating co-operative ideas in Oceania. In addition to all this inter-governmental activity NGOs were also showing interest in co-operatives.[3]

The ICA, as the global organisation of co-operatives, needed to take account of such developments.

THE RESPONSE OF THE INTERNATIONAL CO-OPERATIVE ALLIANCE

The ICA became actively involved in co-operative development in under-developed countries from the 1950s onwards. At its Paris congress of 1954 its director, W. P. Watkins, presented a paper entitled 'Co-operative Development in Under-developed Countries, with Special Reference to the Activities of Inter-governmental Organisations'.[4] Interestingly it made no reference to co-operative developments within British colonies perhaps out of sensitivity to the Alliance's wider audience reflected in the debate which followed which drew speakers from Israel, Japan, Belgium, USA, Britain, Holland, Soviet Union, France, Italy, Czechoslovakia, Yugoslavia, Denmark and Canada.[5] It responded to a paper that had welcomed UN and other initiatives, noted the new parameters of co-operative development and stressed the co-operative movement's own responsibility in advancing co-operatives in under-developed countries.

It shied away from too precise a definition of 'under-developed' countries, opting instead for a more general one:

> Under-developed countries are commonly understood to be those whose natural resources are neglected, unexplored or not yet

> harnessed to production, whose agricultural and industrial techniques are out-moded, sometimes primitive, and whose populations are unenlightened and dominated by their physical environment. Labouring under these disabilities their inhabitants are under-nourished, under-housed, and under-educated, not merely in comparison with more advanced nations, but relatively to the minima science has shown to be necessary to be necessary to maintain health and working efficiency.[6]

Regions considered under-developed were the 'Middle East and North Africa; South-Eastern Asia and the East Indies; Africa south of the Sahara; the Caribbean and parts of Latin America; Oceania'.[7] One problem was their diversity which made it difficult to generalise about their problems and possible solutions.

Moving on to UN and other provisions the paper noted:

> Most of the action undertaken by Inter-Governmental Organisations to foster co-operation takes the form of technical assistance, which is the term adopted by the U.N. to cover all the knowledge, training, advice and experience provided for the under-developed countries in order to enable them to employ modern methods and techniques. Technical assistance in the most general sense is one of the obvious means which the U.N. Organisations would employ to further the economic and social advancement of all peoples.[8]

The paper also noted some earlier 'technical assistance' initiatives had proved inadequate because of massive post-war needs. When dealing with technical assistance methods the paper described how countries applied for help after which a preliminary survey of their needs was undertaken. Technical experts were then employed to work with appropriate government departments to meet those needs. In the case of co-operatives they worked with co-operative departments or with those responsible for co-operatives in other government departments. To date the majority of experts appointed came from Europe and North America and their experience was building up to the point where specialised agencies such as the ILO and the Food and Agricultural Organization could bring their co-operative experts together in periodic regional conferences to exchange experiences. Representatives of NGOs also working with co-operatives were invited to join such gatherings.

Watkins saw limitations in these new provisions, adding 'that Co-operators are not entitled anywhere to relax any of their own efforts to propagate their system'[9] He continued:

> Experience in colonial territories with government-sponsored Co-operation indicates that the best and most enduring results are achieved where the Registrar or other Officers are able to pursue their work consistently over several years, a decade or even longer.
>
> Inability to offer anything but a short-term engagement handicaps the Agencies in their search for experts of the right type and limits their choice.[10]

In any event Watkins considered that the new agencies involved in co-operative development were tending to rely overmuch on their own resources and expertise. Consequently they ignored those in the established co-operative movements. Perhaps this could be overcome if the ICA set out to foster closer collaboration between them and the new agencies.

He reported widening ICA membership in Israel, Egypt, India, Japan, Pakistan, Eastern Nigeria, the Cameroons, Gold Coast, South Africa, Argentina, Brazil, Columbia and Jamaica. Co-operative movements in these countries were 'not strong, either numerically or in any other sense'[11] and he wondered if it might be possible for them to be 'brought into official relations with the Alliance even before they become eligible for membership under the Rules' thus giving them access to ICA services and strengthening their international co-operative links. Above all, Watkins felt that the ICA needed 'a programme, funds and the missionary spirit'[12] to become actively engaged in co-operative development in under-developed countries.

The resolution of the ICA's 19th congress stressed the need for co-operative development in under-developed countries currently undergoing far-reaching economic, technical, social and political changes. It welcomed UN initiatives but urged that these should be carried out in close co-operation with the ICA so as to achieve the ultimate aim of self-help and mutual aid. The resolution also called on ICA members to give 'every kind of aid and encouragement to co-operative pioneers . . . in the under-developed countries'.[13]

Following its approval two important addenda were proposed. Each had significant policy implications. The first, proposed by Israel, urged that 'an International Fund under the auspices of the International Co-operative Alliance' be set up to 'foster, encourage, and develop co-operative activities and enterprises in under-developed countries'.[14] This was passed unanimously.

A second resolution, from Japan, called for the establishment of an Asian regional sub-committee of the ICA to foster friendly relations between Asian co-operative movements. The sub-committee should also promote trade between Asian co-operatives, facilitate exchanges of techniques, experience and information and organise study of the problems of legislation and government administration experienced by co-operatives in the region. Finally the resolution called for an annual or biennial Asian co-operative conference to be held. It was remitted to the Alliance's executive and central committees for them to take action.

These two proposals resulted in the establishment of an ICA development fund, which by 1957 stood at £45,896; and of a technical assistance sub-committee, which had responsibility for the administration of the fund and exploring the feasibility of an ICA regional presence in Asia.[15]

In 1956 a delegation of ICA officials and executive committee members visited the Far East. They held meetings with government officials in Lahore, New Delhi, Kuala Lumpur, Bangkok, Rangoon and Bombay and in India with the prime minister, Pandit Nehru. These discussions and those with co-operative movements in the region encouraged belief that an ICA regional office would be welcomed and was feasible. It was agreed to hold a conference in Kuala Lumpur in 1958, whose significance was underlined by the fact that it was opened by the Malayan prime minister, Tungku Andul Rahman Putra and attended by delegates from co-operative movements in Australia, Ceylon, India, Japan, Malaya, Pakistan, Burma, Indonesia, Singapore, Thailand and Sarawak as well as a number of government representatives and UN specialised agencies.

When the ICA held its next congress in Stockholm in 1957, there was increasing awareness that it was heavily Euro-centric. Its delegation to the Far East, except for B. J. Patel, the honorary general secretary of the All-India Co-operative Union had been 'wholly European'.[16] Consideration of how the ICA could become more involved in third-world co-operative development was forcing it to redress this imbalance. One way was to change the format of debate on the question. Thus instead of the one paper that was presented at its Paris congress three would be given at its Stockholm congress, from different perspectives: the UN, existing practitioner, and co-operatives in developing countries. They were presented under the title 'The Promotion of Co-operation in Lesser Developed Countries'.

The first was given by David Owen, executive chairman of the UN Technical Assistance Board,[17] the second by W. J. W. Cheeseman, who had been co-operative registrar in Nigeria and British Guiana[18] and the third by B. J. Patel.[19] Owen referred to the political difficulties the UN had experienced in its early years and were now being offset by the work of its specialised agencies in the economic and social fields to which he believed co-operatives could make important contributions.

However, they needed to take account of governments' procedures particularly where national development plans were involved. On the question of how the UN funded its development programmes Owen reported that some eighty-three countries had made voluntary contributions amounting to US$31.5 million to its special account for technical assistance.

Coming from a client group Patel's paper was somewhat different. Despite his co-operative movement having a longer history than most Patel said little about Indian co-operative experience. Having recalled Watkins's paper to the ICA's Paris congress in 1954 and describing the developments that followed, he went on to assure congress that India was attempting to stimulate co-operative activity in accordance with basic co-operative principles: much importance was attached to research and education. He ended his paper by stressing that co-operation had to be a people's movement but, 'first and foremost we ought to obtain the goodwill and approval of the country . . .'[20]. This statement reminds us of the delicate relationship between co-operatives and states particularly when the nature of the latter changes.

Cheeseman's paper represented a closing statement of the kind of co-operative development that had occurred under the British Empire. His paper elaborated on the ideas underlying the earlier model, his opening paragraph succinctly describing the benefits co-operatives could bring:

> In the first place, a Co-operative Society can provide its members with economic advantages with which they would be unable to provide themselves individually; in the second place, and in the long run possibly even more significant, Co-operative Societies have a most important educative value. Thrift, self-help, fair dealing and, above all, practical training in the operation of democratic control are all fostered by the association of the people in Co-operative Societies.[21]

In 'Asia, Africa and Europe' co-operatives had shown how they could meet the needs of 'economically backward people'. Consequently they had been able to:

> combat indebtedness, increase the production of peasant farmers, give the producers a fair return for their labours, reduce exploitation by middle-men and grasping landlords, provide farming and household necessities of good quality and at reasonable prices, and even improve health and living conditions. Also by teaching thrift

> and encouraging saving, they have improved individual and national economies. Obviously Governments should be interested in the establishment of flourishing Co-operative Movements particularly in the economically under-developed countries.[22]

Nevertheless, Cheeseman warned: 'There is danger in too much Government finance and attempting a rapid build-up from the top.'[23] He argued that it was necessary for Co-operators' to provide sufficient of their own capital so as to be able to look on 'their Societies as their very own, to give them a sense of responsibility and to make sure the Societies are credit-worthy'.[24]

The role of the co-operative registrar was important:

> In British under-developed territories most laws give the Registrar very considerable powers. Experience in many countries has shown that at times these powers are necessary to ensure the development of a healthy movement, but they are generally used with discretion, many of them I have never used myself.[25]

There was, however, a danger that young co-operatives might rely overmuch on their registrars and their services. He cautioned that such a 'state of affairs must not be allowed to continue indefinitely'. Cheeseman praised the 1946 dispatch and model ordinance issued by the British colonial secretary and said that he believed it to be 'the "Magna Carta" of Co-operation in the British colonial dependencies'. Two other important features of the British system were the 'provision of suitable co-operative legislation and the establishment of a Department for Co-operative Development'.[26]

At the end of a lively debate a resolution was passed unanimously and reasserted co-operatives' role in 'achieving social and economic benefits . . . for millions of people' and for the advancement of developing countries. It called for co-operative movements in these countries to become closely associated with the Alliance and for their national governments to provide developing co-operative movements with appropriate 'legislation, administrative supervision and adult education'. Having praised UN initiatives the resolution believed that still more 'effective co-ordination' was necessary between 'the work of Inter-Governmental Organisations . . . and the ICA . . . in the field of co-operative promotion'. It endorsed the work of the ICA's technical assistance subcommittee and called on ICA member organisations to increase their contributions to the Alliance's development fund. Finally, the resolution urged 'established Co-operative Trading, Agricultural, Banking and

Insurance Organisations' to forge closer relations with 'Co-operative Organisations in the lesser developed countries'.[27]

At this stage no representatives from co-operative organisations in developing countries were members of the Alliance's technical assistance sub-committee. This could point to a somewhat paternalistic attitude.

Its 1957 Stockholm congress heralded growing Swedish influence within the ICA and the leading role it would play in co-operative development in the developing world. One of its leaders, Dr Mauritz Bonow, was elected president of the ICA in 1960, a position he held for the next fifteen years when he led moves to set up the ICA regional office in New Delhi. During that time the ICA's policy on co-operative development in under-developed countries continued to evolve. Its Lausanne congress in 1960 helped clarify objectives and policy and its debate again had three papers, with different perspectives, this time under the heading of 'The Promotion of Co-operation in Developing Countries'.

The first, 'How the Work of the ICA might be Co-ordinated with that of the United Nations and International Bodies', was presented by R. N. Henry of the UN's Food and Agricultural Organization.[28] Henry's paper outlined UN provisions and those of its specialised agencies. On the question of how this work and that of the ICA might be better co-ordinated, Henry was not very clear. A general distinction was that he believed that the ICA should concentrate on improving co-operatives' organisation, management and the training of members and office bearers, while the UN and its specialised agencies should advise and assist governments and their co-operative services.

The second speaker was B. J. Surridge, co-operative adviser, British Colonial Office. His paper was entitled 'The Role of Governments in Developing Countries in Promoting Co-operation'.[29] In it he explored ways of reconciling Western ideas about the independence and autonomy of co-operatives with the needs of co-operatives in developing countries for early state support. Surridge recalled Georges Fauquet, the renowned French co-operator and first chief of the co-operative section of the ILO between 1921 and 1932 whose classic book, *The Co-operative Sector*, had identified four economic sectors: the public or state; the capitalist; the private or family economy; and the co-operative. Fauquet outlined how each of these sectors related to the state. Moving to the present Surridge noted that even where co-operatives were independent of the state as in Denmark, they could still play a prominent economic role. He also cited the Federal Credit Union Act in America which assisted credit unions by providing means of registration as well as supervision and guidance. In developing countries, however, the role of the state was more critical in meeting basic needs for co-operatives to take root. UN specialised agencies had helped identify some of these. For example, a recent ILO report had revealed a lack of educated men in Turkey which the government needed to remedy to give co-operatives a better chance of succeeding. In Cyprus, where Surridge had been co-operative registrar for nine years, the government had had to improve transport, and provide education and credit to protect small peasant farmers from private money-lenders in order to help co-operatives.

The third speaker was Dr Mohammed Hatta and his paper was entitled 'The Needs of Co-operative Organisation in Developing Regions and the Contribution of the ICA'.[30] Hatta has been described as an 'Indonesian statesman and father of the Co-operative Movement in his native country'.[31] He outlined co-operative experiences in Indonesia, illustrated the role played by government, but stressed the importance of the ICA's role in promoting the spirit of self-help. It could also provide education for members, training for co-operative managers and give support through its information and documentation services.

The debate which followed revealed that a number of ICA member organisations were becoming directly involved in third-world co-operative development. For example, the Swedish organisation Kooperativa Forbundet, which had organised an exhibition entitled *Utan Gransar* ('Without Boundaries') at the Stockholm congress designed to stimulate ideas about the potential of world-wide co-operation, now announced its readiness to finance the proposed ICA New Delhi office, initially as a co-operative education centre. It would do so as an international project and U Nyi Nyi, a former co-operative registrar in Burma was being appointed to head it. The French Co-operative movement also informed the congress that it was raising funds to provide technical assistance under the Dahomey project (a general development programme in French West Africa) and that part would be allocated to the ICA development fund. Delegates from Eastern European co-operative movements also reported that they were arranging seminars for participants from developing countries while attempting to develop trading links with their co-operatives.

At the end of the debate at the ICA's Lausanne congress no resolution was tabled but the technical assistance sub-committee had proposed instead a long-term programme of technical assistance which was unanimously approved. It argued that what had gone before had been too small-scale. More was needed, and better co-ordination. Proposals within the programme came under five headings:

1. The continuation and completion of the exploration of the developing regions, especially Africa and Latin America.
2. Intensive research into problems of the various types of co-operative in the regions.
3. Promotion of education at all levels through permanent educational institutes, regional seminars and the financing of books and teaching materials.
4. Collaboration with the UN and other agencies.
5. Promotion and expansion of trade between co-operative organisations in developing countries and the highly-developed movements as well as the promotion of co-operative insurance societies, banks and credit institutions.

This programme required adequate funding from the ICA and to help ensure this, additional appeals would be made for contributions to its development fund.[32]

Implementation of the long-term programme of technical assistance helped the Alliance to become less Euro-centric. It also brought it into areas that had previously been part of European empires. By helping younger co-operative movements it was also growing its future membership.

This slow process was assisted by its embryonic regional offices. The 1958 Kuala Lumpur conference had been followed by exchanges between ICA representatives and co-operative and government representatives in regional centres. These led to the opening of the education centre, funded by Swedish co-operatives in 1960. Government support was indicated by its inauguration by the Indian prime minister, Pandit Nehru, whose address was reckoned to have shown 'his grasp of the nature of Co-operation and its problems'.[33]

Delicate constitutional balancing arrangements then had to be made. What eventually became the regional office was made part of the ICA's administration, its costs being met from the Alliance's budget and its regional officer responsible to the ICA's executive through the ICA's director, general secretary and technical assistance sub-committee. The original education centre remained funded by Kooperativa Forbundet and was headed by a Swede, Bertil Mathsson. However, an Indian deputy was appointed, Dr S. K. Saxena who became ICA director in 1968 and moved to London. He held this overall position until 1981, emphasising once more the Alliance's declining Euro-centric nature. Initiatives to establish an ICA presence in the regions continued from its leading European affiliates although with strong local support.

Co-operative movements in the region appointed representatives to the advisory council of the Alliance's regional office and education centre in New Delhi. The council's honorary president was Mrs Indira Gandhi, Nehru's daughter. She later became prime minister and was assassinated in 1984. In 1964 the regional office and education centre were combined and Saxena became the regional officer.[34]

The ICA's regional office for East and Central Africa began operations in 1968, again with considerable Swedish co-operative finance.[35] Another for West Africa was opened in 1981 but in this case was heavily financially supported by Norwegian and French co-operative organisations.[36]

Although we are now beyond the 1960s when the British Empire largely ceased to exist in any meaningful form we should briefly note that these moves were accompanied by the ICA declaring a co-operative development decade. This was to celebrate its 75th anniversary in 1970 but was also in response to the UN's Economic and Social Council decision to assess the contribution co-operations could make to its second development decade. The Alliance's co-operative development decade ran between 1971 and 1981 and a preliminary report of its outcomes was made to its Moscow congress in 1980. Among the decade's aims was increased flow of knowledge and experiences between ICA regional offices. Conferences and seminars, education and training programmes, research and planning also took place with particular focus on how women, young people and the poor could become more involved in co-operatives. Attention was directed towards development strategies in the rural sector, along with employment in rural communities and the development of human resources. Various problems were identified including landholding systems, lack of capital, poor industrial and commercial infrastructures, and an absence of technology alongside an abundance of manpower.[37]

As part also of its development decade the Alliance established in 1973 an advisory group for international training of co-operators (AGITCOOP) to advise it on the education and training for co-operators in developing countries. AGITCOOP worked closely with the Co-operative Education Materials Advisory Service (CEMAS) established a year later: although funded by Swedish co-operative organisations it was based in the ICA. Both organisations worked closely with a similar body set up by the ILO in 1978, the Material and Techniques for Co-operative Management Training (MATCOM).[38]

This last mentioned was just one example of the close relationships that the ICA had developed with UN agencies; also with NGOs involved in third-world co-operative development. A number came together in

1971 to form the Committee for the Promotion and Advancement of Co-operatives. Its initial sponsors were the UN's Food and Agricultural Organisation, the ILO, the ICA, the International Federation of Agricultural Producers and the International Federation of Plantation, Agricultural and Allied Workers.[39]

Therefore from the 1950s onwards international co-operative development formed a large part of the ICA's agenda. It became involved with others in territories that had previously been part of the British Empire. That empire was withering fast but it still needed to manage its withdrawal from responsibility for co-operative development.

THE BRITISH RESPONSE

As the Empire withdrew, its principal offices needed to be reorganised. An obvious example was the Colonial Office. One of its major functions had been recruitment but in 1961 responsibility for this was transferred to the newly created Department of Technical Co-operation. Account needed to be taken that patterns of recruitment were changing. The large administrative element that had been required to run the Empire was declining, but the demand for technical personnel was increasing. In 1957 the Colonial Office recruited only 109 administrative officers, fewer than half the number ten years earlier while its technical appointments rose to approximately 1,350. These included 'engineering inspectors of works, radio and telecommunications technicians, agricultural superintendents and livestock officers, railway and marine technicians, accountants, health inspectors, assistant meteorologists, and hydrological inspectors'. Increasing numbers of women were also being recruited, 'all graduates'. Earlier they had been called 'Assistants', but now they became 'Women Administrative Secretaries'.

Another shift had also occurred. Appointments were now made to 'Overseas Governments' rather than to colonies or dependent territories. By 1960 they numbered around 20,500.

Later the Department of Technical Co-operation (DTC) became known as the Ministry of Overseas Development (MOD), then the Overseas Development Administration (ODA) and most recently the Department of International Development (DIFID).[40] While still the DTC it retained responsibility for co-operative development with Surridge as adviser on co-operatives. He was supported by an advisory committee on co-operatives whose chairman was Lord Peddie. He was a leading British co-operator, who was a director of the CWS and chairman of the Co-operative Party. His appointment reflects the shift towards increased collaboration with NGOs, in this case the British Co-operative movement.

In 1964 the secretary for technical co-operation, Robert Carr MP, presented to Parliament a statement on the 'Policy on the Recommendations of the Advisory Committee on Co-operatives'.[41] It is significant inasmuch as it represents the views of a Conservative British government on co-operatives in the twilight of the British Empire. The statement stresses all-party support: 'It has long been the policy of successive British Governments to encourage the growth in co-operatives overseas'. Note the emphasis on 'overseas' territories whether or not they had been part of the British Empire.

It indicated that the UK government welcomed the committee's report and proposed to implement its recommendations through the DTC as quickly as possible. It would do so 'in consultation with other interested bodies, notably British co-operative organisations' who had already indicated their willingness to 'assist by providing most of the experts and facilities that are likely to be needed'. These would be co-ordinated by the DTC under its function of 'co-ordinating, promoting and carrying out arrangements for furnishing countries outside the United Kingdom with technical assistance'.[42]

The statement then deals with the mechanics of delivering co-operative technical advice, education and training. A register had been proposed of British co-operative organisations prepared to release specialist staff for overseas work. They had already shown that they 'are nearly always ready to release individual members of their staffs . . . when asked to do so.' The committee recommended that they should be guaranteed re-employment and that British co-operatives should view overseas assignments as a qualification rather than a hindrance to normal promotion. Lists of retired senior co-operative staff would also be compiled. It was not thought necessary, though, to mount a training scheme for such recruits although a 'few short vacation or week-end courses on co-operatives overseas might be a useful way of stimulating the interest of British co-operative employees in work in the developing countries'.[43]

The statement then moved to the question of training overseas co-operative personnel in Britain. There would be funding to continue the Co-operative College courses and also 'to arrange study tours overseas by members of its staff and to establish a special overseas section of its library'. The DTC would also continue under its 'regional programmes of technical assistance, to meet all the expenses of students from overseas . . . when requested to do so by their governments'. The committee considered it desirable that the Co-operative College should gain 'university recognition' for its overseas diploma course and the Department was ready to help with negotiations because 'such a diploma would be a useful contribution to British technical assistance.[44]

A role was also seen for the Plunkett Foundation: 'The Committee recommended that the annual two-month residential school in Africa and the correspondence course organised by the Plunkett Foundation for Co-operative Studies should be continued' even when a grant from the Nuffield Foundation ended. It was hoped that the correspondence course could become 'self-supporting' but an alternative sponsor would need to be found should demand for its African residential courses continue. If there were difficulties, the Department would be ready to explore 'jointly' with the Foundation 'what further steps might be taken'.

In addition to provisions by the Co-operative College and the Plunkett Foundation the statement envisaged scope for a short course for overseas students 'in agricultural marketing with special reference to co-operatives, and that similar courses for other specialist co-operative subjects should be considered in the light of experience'. The DTC and committee were therefore exploring whether there was a British university 'willing and suitably equipped' to provide such a course. It was also proposed to prepare a 'memorandum' 'indicating the facilities available in Britain for the reception of overseas visitors and students who wish to see co-operative organisations in this country'. It would be sent to 'organisations, government departments and overseas governments introducing visitors to Britain'.[45]

Regarding overseas co-operative training facilities the DTC accepted the committee's view that in addition to its support for the Plunkett Foundation, it should also assist 'international organisations such as the Food and Agricultural Organisation (FAO) and the International Labour Organisation (ILO)'. This statement reflects interplay between two systems, one presiding over the run-down of empire, the other a new international relations order led by the UN and its agencies.

There was also acknowledgement that co-operatives in developing countries were attracting other kinds of support including that from individual countries. Note was taken of the links established 'by the Chairman of the Committee, the Lord Peddie, with members of the International Co-operative Development Staff of the United States Agency for International Development and others concerned with co-operatives in Washington'.[46] Other kinds of involvement included that of commercial banks. For this reason 'Mr. E. V. Whitcombe, CBE, a director of Barclays Bank, DC & O' was to become a member of the advisory committee on co-operatives.[47]

The main impression given by the 1964 statement is that the DTC would retain a co-ordinating and information role but that much of the work previously undertaken by the Colonial Office was being transferred to NGOs such as the British Co-operative movement, its Co-operative College and the Plunkett Foundation. These now also worked alongside other diverse international organisations. Earlier we described how the British Co-operative movement in conjunction with OXFAM had assisted co-operatives in Botswana. Later the British Co-operative movement encouraged well-qualified co-operative store managers experienced in staff training to join a scheme to help consumer co-operatives in Jamaica.[48] Co-operatives had become fashionable. But could their new standing be sustained?

Although there were increasing ad hoc provisions two main organisational systems existed in the 1960s in previous British territories. One was the remnants of the earlier colonial system; the other was led by UN agencies. Although their aims were similar their methods of delivery were different. The Colonial Office system was more long-term and offered permanent employment while the UN system was based on fixed-term projects that offered short-term contracts of employment.

Co-operatives were not necessarily amenable to short-term arrangements. We have seen that viable co-operatives took time to establish. Potential members often had to be persuaded and reassured. Sir Horace Plunkett was reckoned to have held forty meetings before succeeding in organising a single co-operative.[49] In developing countries they also often formed among the poor and dispossessed. In the 1950s W. H. K. Campbell had written:

> I am as brave as anyone when it is a question of losing a certain amount of government money in a good cause. The trouble with Co-operation in new countries is that the stakes with which the game has to be played are the savings for the most part of very poor people. These have not easily been acquired, nor has it been easy to persuade their owners to risk them in a co-operative society . . . If the stakes are lost, the effect on the owners and the resulting set back to the prospect of the movement are serious beyond all proportion to the amount of money involved.[50]

Whatever system was in place governments, as papers to ICA congresses had suggested, needed to provide suitable environments. These included not only appropriate legislative and taxation regimes but also educational and infrastructural supports. While governments could be helpful they could also damage co-operatives' credibility. This had been shown in communist and fascist regimes but examples also occurred in newly independent states where five- or ten-year national plans were adopted and co-operatives subsumed into wider goals.

As we saw in Ceylon such moves might not seem unreasonable in a war-time situation, although there was a later admission that they had hampered the development of an independent and autonomous co-operative movement. In post-colonial times other criteria became fashionable. For example, in Tanzania it was felt that socialism was the best means of development and that this could be achieved through establishing *ujaama* villages organised as multi-purpose co-operatives. Although these represented a bottom-up approach their overall direction came from central government. In the 1980s the experiment was acknowledged to have failed.[51] It had damaged the reputation and credibility of co-operatives. Various reasons for failure were adduced but little note was taken of the experiment's weakening of an important dynamic within co-operatives, namely that of their members' self-interest. It was not allowed to become selfishness because it operated in a self-help and mutual aid framework but nevertheless constituted an important motivation. In effect, the *ujaama* experiment had overlooked Strickland's maxim that a peasant rearing cows and primarily interested in dairy co-operatives would be less concerned with other co-operative activity impinging less directly on his main activity.

Remnants of the old system did not always approve of the new. When Archie Macintosh told Surridge that he had received 'a good offer to join the ILO' Surridge warned that if he accepted he would most likely become 'frustrated': there was not 'anything wrong with the UN people, just that it was all too bureaucratic'. Macintosh later observed:

> I noticed in various countries in other specialities that the short term 2 to 3 year contracts in UN prevented any build up of esprit de corps and tended to result in the people concerned spending a lot of time making their name at cocktail parties and other shindigs getting known so that contracts might be renewed. There was a myth among UK Overseas Officers that UN personnel spent the first six months of a tour making their name on the social ladder and the last six months organising their renewal of contract. Like most myths there was a bit of truth in it.[52]

It was a moot question whether one system was better than the other for co-operative development keeping in mind that that could often be slow. The British system was on its way out and the new UN one was gathering momentum. Some British co-operative registrars appointed by the Colonial Office were invited to remain by newly independent states and thus witnessed the transfer of power.

CONCLUSIONS

Conclusions can be drawn from two perspectives; the imperial and the co-operative. Because they had different histories, ideologies and traditions it might have been expected that any collaboration would be unproductive yet the opposite proved to be the case.

From India's first co-operative legislation in 1904 there was close interaction between the Empire and co-operation. Co-operatives became a tool for development and welfare. Their versatility and universality made them as relevant in Asia, Africa, the Antipodes and the Americas as in Britain and Europe and their usefulness to the Empire meant that it helped spread them to the four corners of the earth.

This symbiotic relationship stemmed in part from the pluralistic nature of the British Empire. It was not driven by a single ideology but rather by a mixture of ideas as exemplified in the divergent views of Disraeli and Gladstone. Essentially these had been shaped by two major political traditions that had evolved from the seventeenth century and divided on issues of sovereignty, by whom its prerogatives might be exercised and whether their acceptance involved some kind of social contract. The more traditional of the two schools of thought came to be labelled Tory or Conservative, while the other and the more radical was called Whig or Liberal. It was this latter tradition that would prove more receptive to the ideas of the European Enlightenment and ultimately to those of co-operation.

Co-operative ideas had an even longer history dating back to feudal times when peasant lands were held in common. They were based on the idea of resources being held in common or on the notion of the collective good which we saw come to the fore during Cromwell's Commonwealth under the concept of the 'commonweal'. Ideas of association grew stronger in the late eighteenth century when they became the rationale for collective action by those who owned nothing but their labour. Out of such ideas emerged the trades union and co-operative movements. Robert Owen brought moral and community dimensions to the latter while Dr William King and the Rochdale Pioneers added ideas of democracy, self-help, self-management and mutuality. Thus by the second half of the nineteenth century a complete and distinct co-operative philosophy existed with the underlying concepts of equitability, democracy, fraternity or mutuality, and solidarity and economy.

Throughout this study frequent references have been made to 'co-operation' rather than 'co-operatives'. The reason for this is that co-operative registrars so often headed their departmental reports in this way. It suggested that they saw first the ideology and then co-operatives as its outward expression. The co-operative ideology was more acceptable to Britain's Liberals than to her Conservatives and it would be British Liberalism that played the greater role in advancing co-operation throughout the British Empire.

The existence of pluralism had other ramifications including an ability to prompt divergent developments. For example at the height of 'new imperialism' when Cecil Rhodes and his British South Africa Company were carving out large parts of Africa Sir William Wedderburn in Poona could still advance ideas that eventually led to India's first co-operative legislation in 1904. Pluralism also allowed different ideas to lead to similar conclusions as when development became an imperial objective and 'development agency' functions part of the imperial remit.[53] On the one hand Joseph Chamberlain, the colonial secretary, argued that colonies should become more productive so as to defray their costs and lessen their burden on the Westminster Parliament. On the other hand some argued that poor colonial economies prompted social unrest which could possibly threaten British rule. With memories of the Indian Mutiny still potent it seemed prudent to counter economic decline with policies of development; and it would be within these that co-operatives found a role.

Although British pluralism proved enabling, effective methods of delivery were also crucial. Here co-operatives were helped by the enthusiasm of co-operative registrars. Co-operatives proved less easy to establish where registrars were ambivalent, as in New South Wales in Australia. However, a sufficient number of co-operative registrars were enthusiastic and able to provide a critical mass to propagate co-operatives in literature and through personal contacts. Co-operatives may have appealed to them because they offered a clear identity. They had a formula first set down in Rochdale and later reaffirmed by the ICA in its reviews in the 1930s and 1960s. By their very nature civil servants liked clear points of reference.

At the end of this study less definite conclusions may also be drawn and perhaps merit further research. For example it seems reasonable to suppose that co-operatives became building blocks in post-colonial territories through the development they assisted and in the way that they inculcated self-management and methods of democratic control and accountability. They obviously contributed to the building of a civil society in advance of independence. A question also arises as to how far their leaders and members became involved in national independence movements and, thereafter, what part they played in newly independent states. Undoubtedly members of co-operatives constituted clearly identifiable groups which became a source of votes and through which politicians could be identified and become known.

This brings us onto the convoluted and complex question of co-operatives' relationship with the state and with political parties. A wide range of relationships has been revealed in this study, from the distant to the very close. At one extreme co-operatives relied on the state for reasonable legislative and taxation frameworks and little more. Quite early on, though, co-operatives in Ireland and Denmark benefited from technical assistance provided by the state and as we later saw effective co-operative development in poorer sections of the world often depended on the state creating a favourable and supportive infrastructure.

A history of co-operatives also has to be placed against a background of shifting popular attitudes to the state. During the laissez-faire period the state was little involved in anything. A small state was prized. That changed during the late nineteenth century when it became more concerned with creating educated workforces and preventative medicine and when the bases of modern educational and health systems were formed. During the two World Wars the state became more interventionist and even more so in authoritarian communist and Nazi regimes. Flirtation with socialist ideas in the mid-twentieth century encouraged continuation of ideas of the big state but that period has passed. In the early twenty-first century the role of the state is once more a live issue and in some countries is likely to become smaller again.

In their early history co-operatives may not have been classed as NGOs although this is what they were. Since the Second World War and the growth of new systems of international relations headed by the UN they have been designated NGOs with their international representatives such as the ICA known as international NGOs. Consequently they have a clear and acknowledged status independent of states, yet demarcation between them is always shifting and sometimes creates tensions.

On the one hand, particularly where the intervention of the state in co-operatives has proved inimical it is tempting to subscribe to the view of Dr King that co-operation must be voluntary and 'that all the power in the world cannot make it compulsory, nor is it desirable that it should depend on any power but its own – the interference of Governments would only cramp its energies and misdirect them'. On the other, this study shows that a supra-state in the form of the British Empire helped develop co-operatives throughout the world though their ideology was markedly different from that of imperialism.

Notes

CHAPTER 1

1. Jan Morris, *Pax Britannica*, Faber and Faber Ltd, London, 1998, p. 42.
2. Ibid., p. 51.
3. Sir John Seeley, *The Expansion of England*, a series of lectures delivered by Seeley (1834–1895), as Professor of Modern History at Cambridge, publication details unknown.
4. Willie Thompson, *Global Expansion – Britain and its Empire 1870–1914*, Pluto Press, London, 1999, p. 16.
5. Ibid.
6. Huw Bowen, '400 Years of the East India Company', *History Today*, Vol. 50, 2000.
7. Sources on the East India Company can be found in John Keay, *The Honourable Company: The History of the English East India Company*, Harper Collins, London, 1991.
8. Morris, *Pax Brittanica*, p. 185.
9. Henry W. Wolff, *Co-operation in India*, W. Thacker & Co., London, 1927, p. 45.
10. Anthony Kirke-Greene, *On Crown Service – A History of HM Colonial and Overseas Civil Services 1837–1997*, L. B. Tauris, London, 1999, pp. 7–11.
11. Morris, *Pax Brittanica*, p. 183.
12. Ibid., p. 192.
13. *Whitakers Concise Almanack 2000*, The Stationery Office, London, 2000, p. 112.
14. Morris, *Pax Brittanica*, pp. 67–9.
15. R. Hyam, *Britain's Imperial Century, 1815–1914: A Study of Empire and Expansion*, 2nd edn, Macmillan, London, 1993, p. 104.
16. J. A. Hobson, *Imperialism: A Study*, cited in D. Graham, *Goodlad's British Foreign Policy 1865–1919*, Routledge, London, 2000. pp. 29 and 39.
17. Lady G. Cecil, *The Life of Robert, Marquis of Salisbury*, Vol. 4, Hodder & Stoughton, London, 1932, p. 310.
18. *Chambers Biographical Dictionary*, revised edn, Chambers, Edinburgh, 1984, p. 404.
19. Graham Goodlad, *British Foreign and Imperial Policy 1865–1919*, Routledge, London, 2000, pp.14–19.
20. Andrew Roberts, 'Salisbury – The Empire Builder who Never Was', *History Today*, October 1999, pp. 45–51.
21. *Chambers Biographical Dictionary*, p. 264.
22. Morris, *Pax Brittanica*, pp. 249–50.
23. Ibid., p. 109.

24. Ibid., pp. 109–10.
25. Goodlad, *British Foreign and Imperial Policy*, pp. 14–15.

CHAPTER 2

1. Report of the Thirty-Second Annual Co-operative Congress, Cardiff, June, 1900, Co-operative Union Limited, Manchester, 1900, p. 267.
2. Prof. A. Briggs, *Robert Owen in Retrospect*, Co-operative College Paper No. 6, April 1959, p. 6.
3. Ibid.
4. Arnold Bonner, *British Co-operation*, Co-operative Union Ltd, Manchester, 1961, pp. 494–5.
5. Briggs, *Robert Owen in Retrospect*, p. 9.
6. The 'Early English Socialists' include John Gray (1799–1850), *Lecture on Human Happiness*; T. R. Edmunds (1803–1889), *Practical Moral and Political Economy most Conducive to Happiness and National Power*; John MinterMorgan (1782–1854), *Revolt of the Bees*; Thomas Hodgkin (1783–1869), *Labour Defended against the Claims of Capital, Popular Political Economy*; WilliamThompson (d. 1833), *Inquiry into the Principles of the Distribution of Wealth most Conducive to Human Happiness, Labour Rewarded or How to Secure theWhole Product of His Exertions, Practical Directions for the Speedy and Economical Establishment of Communities.*
7. Bonner, *British Co-operation*, p. 24.
8. Dr S. Pollard, *Dr. William King: A Co-operative Pioneer*, Co-operative College Paper No. 6, April 1959.
9. Ibid., p. 19.
10. T. W. Mercer, *Co-operation's Prophet. The Life and Letters of Dr. William King of Brighton with a Reprint of the Co-operator 1828–1930*, Co-operative Union Ltd, Manchester, 1947, p, 54.
11. Ibid., p. 84.
12. A. F. Laidlaw, *Co-operatives in the Year 2000*, Studies and Reports No. 15, International Co-operative Alliance, London, 1980, pp. 8–9.
13. Brett Fairburn, *Social Movements and Co-operatives: Implications for History and Development, Review of International Co-operation*, Vol. 94, No.1, 2001, p. 28.
14. Bonner, *British Co-operation*, p. 42.
15. Ibid., p. 50.
16. G. D. H. Cole, *A Century of Co-operation*, Co-operative Union Ltd, Manchester, 1944, pp. 402–9.
17. Bonner, *British Co-operation*, p. 50.
18. Ibid., p. 46.
19. Ibid., p. 57.
20. Ibid., p. 61.
21. Ibid., pp. 488–94.
22. Cole, *A Century of Co–operation*, p. 200.
23. J. J. Dent, 'Hodgson Pratt and his Memorial', *Better Business, A Quarterly Journal of Agricultural and Industrial Co-operation*, Vol. 111, No. 2, February 1918, p. 141.
24. Bonner, *British Co–operation*, p. 63.
25. Ibid., p. 115.
26. C. R. Fay, *Co-operation at Home and Abroad*, Vol. 11, P. S. King, London, 1939, p. 244.
27. W. J. Chappenden, *Handbook to the Industrial and Provident Societies Act 1965*, Co-operative Union Ltd, Manchester, 1966, p. 1.

28. Ibid.
29. Ibid., pp. 2–5.
30. Prof. Charles Gide, *The International Co-operative Alliance*, The International Co-operative Alliance, London, presumed date of publication 1920.

CHAPTER 3

1. Philip N. Backstrom, *Christian Socialism and Co-operation in Victorian England*, Croom Helm, London, 1974, pp. 29–30.
2. Arnold Bonner, *British Co-Operation – The History, Principles and Organisation of the British Co-operative Movement*, Co-operative Union Ltd, Manchester, 1961, p. 65.
3. Ibid., p. 134.
4. Backstrom, *Christian Socialism*, p. 99.
5. Bonner, *British Co-operation*, p. 81.
6. Backstrom, *Christian Socialism*, p. 9.
7. Ibid., pp. 11–28.
8. Bonner, *British Co-operation*, pp. 491–2.
9. *CWS Annual 1896*, Co-operative Wholesale Society Ltd.
10. Percy Redfern, *John T. W. Mitchell: Pioneer of Consumers' Co-operation*, Co-operative Wholesale Society Ltd, Manchester, 1923, p. 39.
11. Durham University Library: Letter to Earl Grey from Edward Owen Greening, 1 September, 1898, *Archive Papers of 4th Earl Grey*.
12. Rita Rhodes, *The International Co-operative Alliance during War and Peace 1910–1950*, The International Co-operative Alliance, Geneva, 1995, pp. 19–20.
13. William Maxwell, *Lecture on Wholesale Co-operation – A Necessity*, delivered by William Maxwell, president of the Scottish Co-operative Wholesale Society Ltd at Leeds on 4 February 1888.
14. *CWS Annual 1900*, Co-operative Wholesale Society Ltd, Leeds, 1900.
15. Rhodes, *International Co-operative Alliance*, pp. 55–64.
16. *Co-operative Union Congress Report, Bristol*, Co-operative Union Ltd, Manchester, 1920, p. 121.
17. Bonner, *British Co-operation*, p. 192.
18. *Chambers Biographical Dictionary*, p. 699.
19. Rita Rhodes, *An Arsenal for Labour*, Co-operative Union Ltd, Manchester, 1998, p. 9.
20. *Co-operative Union Congress Report, Swansea*, Co-operative Union Ltd, Manchester, 1917, p. 552.
21. Rhodes, *Arsenal for Labour*, pp. 20–8.
22. Youngjohns, *Co-operation*, p. 72.
23. C. R. Fay, *Co-operation at Home and Abroad – A Description and Analysis*, P. S. King & Son Ltd, Westminster, 1939, p. 20.
24. *International Co-operative Alliance Congress Report, Delft*, The International Co-operative Alliance, London, 1897, pp. 25–39 and 40–3.
25. *International Co-operative Alliance Congress Report, Budapest*, The International Co-operative Alliance, 1904, pp. 111–27.
26. Denis Judd, *Empire – The British Imperial Experience from 1765 to the Present*, Harper Collins, London, 1996, p. 42.
27. Ibid., p. 43.
28. Deirdre McMahon, 'Ireland and the Empire–Commonwealth, 1900–1945', in J. Brown and W. R. Louis (eds), *The Oxford History of the British Empire – The Twentieth Century*, Vol. 4, Oxford University Press, Oxford, 1999, p. 138.
29. Ibid., p. 139.

30. Patrick Bolger, *The Irish Co-operative Movement – Its History and Development*, Institute of Public Administration, Dublin, 1977.
31. Jan Morris, *Pax Britannica – The Climax of Empire*, Faber and Faber, London, 1998, p. 461.
32. Bolger, *Irish Co-operative Movement*, pp. 51–3.
33. Patrick Bolger, 'Horace Plunkett – The Man', in C. Keating (ed.), *Plunkett and Co-operatives – Past, Present and Future*, UCC Bank of Ireland Centre for Co-operative Studies, 1983, p. 34.
34. Trevor West, 'The Development of Horace Plunkett's Thought', in ibid., p. 39.
35. Bolger, *Irish Co-operative Movement*, p. 112.
36. Ibid., p. 94.
37. Margaret Digby, *Horace Plunkett – An Anglo-American Irishman*, Basil Blackwell, Oxford, 1949, p. vi.
38. West, 'The Development', p. 42.
39. Digby, *Plunkett*, p. v.
40. Bolger, *Irish Co-operative Movement*, p. 61.
41. Ibid., pp. 62–3.
42. Ibid., p. 63.
43. Ibid., p. 69.
44. Ibid., p. 50.
45. Ibid., p. 72.
46. Ibid., pp. 72–3.
47. Ibid., p. 74.
48. Ibid., pp. 156–64.
49. Henry Wolff, *Agricultural Credit Societies*, P. S. King, London, 1895.
50. Bolger, *Irish Co-operative Movement*, p. 169.
51. Ibid., pp. 156–82.
52. Ibid., p.196.
53. Percy Redfern, *The Story of the C.W.S. – The Jubilee History of the Co-operative Wholesale Society Limited 1863–1913*, The Co-operative Wholesale Society Ltd, Manchester, 1913, p. 297.
54. Ibid., p. 198.
55. Bolger, *Irish Co-operative Movement*, pp. 196–7.
56. Redfern, *Jubilee History*, p. 298.
57. Bolger, *Irish Co-operative Movement*, p. 198.
58. Redfern, *Jubilee History*, p. 300.
59. Ibid., p. 295.
60. Ibid., p. 196.
61. Ibid., p. 299.
62. Bolger, *Irish Co-operative Movement*, p. 196.

CHAPTER 4

1. Denis Judd, *Empire – The British Imperial Experience from 1765 to the Present*, Phoenix Press Paperback, London, 2001, p. 52.
2. Ibid.
3. Ibid., p. 36.
4. Ibid., p. 37.
5. Ibid., p. 38.
6. Andrew Porter, *The Nineteenth Century – The Oxford History of the British Empire*, Oxford University Press, Oxford, 1999, p. 555.
7. Ibid., p. 573.
8. Ibid., p. 581.

9. Judd, *Empire*, p. 117.
10. Lawrence James, *The Rise and Fall of the British Empire*, Abacus, London, 1996, p. 251.
11. Willie Thompson, *Global Expansion – Britain and its Empire 1870–1914*, Pluto Press, London, 1999, pp. 62–3.
12. James, *Rise and Fall*, pp. 256–8.
13. Alan Palmer, *The Penguin Dictionary of Modern History 1789–1945*, 2nd edn, Penguin Books, 1983, p. 156.
14. Judd, *Empire*, p. 162.
15. Ibid.
16. Ibid., p. 165.
17. Jan Morris, *Pax Britannica – The Climax of an Empire*, Faber and Faber, London, 1998, pp. 67–8.
18. Ibid.
19. Ibid., p. 377.

CHAPTER 5

1. Niall Ferguson, *Empire – How Britain Made the World*, Allen Lane, Penguin Press, London, 2003, p. xxii.
2. ICA Archive: *Review of International Co-operation*, London, May 1931.
3. W. P. Watkins, *The International Co-operative Alliance 1895–1970*, The International Co-operative Alliance, London, 1970, p. 27.
4. Rita Rhodes and Dionysis Mavrogiannis, *Thematic Guide to ICA Congresses*, ICA, Geneva, 1996, pp. 1–18.
5. Henry Wolff, *Co-operation*, W. Thacker and Co., London, 1927; *People's Banks: A Record of Social and Economic Success*, 4th edn, P. S. King & Son Ltd, London, 1919; *Co-operative Banking: Its Principles and Practice*, P. S. King & Son Ltd, London, 1907; *A Co-operative Credit Handbook with Rules*, P. S. King & Son Ltd, London, 1910; *Co-operation in Agriculture*, 2nd edn, P. S. King & Son Ltd, London, 1917; *Co-operation for the United States*, The Macmillan Co., London, 1917; *The Future of our Agriculture*, P. S. King & Son Ltd, London, 1918; *Rural Reconstruction*, Selwyn & Blunt Ltd, London, 1921.
6. Co-operative Union Archive: *Report of the Co-operative Union Congress*, London, 1900, pp. 150–1.
7. Margaret Digby, *Digest of Co-operative Law at Home and Abroad*, P. S. King & Son Ltd, London, 1933, p. 81.
8. *Report of the Co-operative Union Congress*, Manchester, 1901, pp. 192–3.
9. Patrick Bolger, *The Irish Co-operative Movement – Its History and Development*, Institute of Public Administration, Dublin, 1977, p. 175.
10. Ibid., p. 166.
11. Ibid., p. 169.
12. Ibid., p. 177.
13. Ibid., p. 179.
14. Wolff, *Co-operation*, p. 44.
15. Margaret Woodhead, 'Nottinghamshire Co-operatives', *Nottingham Historian*, Autumn/Winter, 1996, pp. 11–12.
16. *Chambers Biographical Dictionary*, 1984, p. 87.
17. Durham University Library: Archive of fourth Earl Grey. Speech to Church Congress, Bradford, 1898.
18. Ibid.
19. Jan Morris, *Pax Britannica*, Faber and Faber Ltd, London, 1998, p. 89.
20. Ibid.

21. Ibid.
22. Durham University Library: Archive of fourth Earl Grey.
23. Ibid. Letter to 'My Dear Raleigh', who is believed to be joint secretary of the 'Chartered Company', the British South Africa Company, dated 27 August 1904.
24. Durham University Library: Archive of fourth Earl Grey. Letter to H. Fort, a Johannesburg politician, from Government House, Ottawa, dated 30 May 1905.
25. Durham University Library: Archive of fourth Earl Grey. Letter to Fort, c/o A. Bailey, Johannesburg, dated 21 January 1905.
26. Ibid. Letter to Sir John Willoughby, Bulawayo, dated 1 March 1905.
27. Durham University Library: Archive of fourth Earl Grey.
28. Ibid. Letter to Raleigh.
29. Co-operative Union Archive: Vaughan Nash,'The Encouragement of the Kaffir – A Question for Earl Grey', *Co-operative News*, 13 January 1900.
30. Ibid.
31. Bernard Porter, *The Absent-Minded Imperialists*, Oxford University Press, Oxford, 2004.
32. Digby, *Plunkett*, p. xii.
33. Bolger, *Irish Co-operatives*, p. 74.

CHAPTER 6

1. Hugh Bowen, '400 Years of the East India Company', *History Today*, July 2000, pp. 47–54.
2. Ake Eden, *East India Company's Indienpolitik Fore 1773 – Rapport 8*, Ekonomisk-historiska Institutionen Goteborg Universitet, 1994, opening page.
3. Laurence James, *Raj – The Making and Unmaking of British India*, Brown and Co., 1997, pp. 30–44.
4. William Dalrymple, *White Mughals*, Harper Perennial, London, 2003.
5. Fanny Parkes, *The Journal of Fanny Parkes*, Sickle Moon, London, 2002.
6. Laurence James, *The Rise and Fall of the British Empire*, ABACUS, London, 1995, p. 220.
7. Arnold Bonner, *British Co-operation*, Co-operative Union Ltd, Manchester, 1961, p. 66.
8. James, *Rise and Fall*, p. 13.
9. Ake Aden, 'The Remedy', in Hans-H. Muenkner, *100 Years Co-operative Credit Societies Act, India, 1904*, ICA, Asia and Pacific, New Delhi, 2005, pp. 217–25.
10. Ibid., p. 218.
11. Ake Aden, 'Oriental Economic Thoughts and Co-operative Development on the Pre-colonial Indian Subcontinent', in ibid., p. 23.
12. Jan Morris, *Pax Britannica*, Faber and Faber, London, 1998, p. 359.
13. Ibid., pp. 362–3.
14. Kusoom Vadgama, *India – British-Indian Campaigns in Britain for Indian Reforms, Justice and Freedom, 1831–1947*, Banyan Tree Publishing, London, 1997.
15. James, *Raj*, pp. 297–8.
16. Andrew Porter, *The Nineteenth Century – The Oxford History of the British Empire*, Vol. 3, Oxford University Press, Oxford, 1999, p. 429.
17. James, *Raj*, p. 293.
18. Henry Wolff, *Co-operation in India*, 2nd edn, W. Thacker & Co., London, 1927, p. 45.
19. James, *Raj*, p. 418.

20. Bolger, *Irish Co-operative Movement*, p. 167.
21. Wolff, *Co-operation*, p. 44.
22. Panchanandas Mukherji, *The Co-operative Movement in India*, Thacker, Spink & Co., Calcutta and Simla, 1923, p. 41.
23. James, *Raj*, p. 306.
24. B. G. Bhatnagar, *The Co-operative Organisation in British India*, Ram Narain Lal, Allahbad, 1927, p. 27.
25. Ibid., pp. 27–8.
26. Ibid., pp. 29–30.
27. Wolff, *Co-operation*, p. 41.
28. Bombay Co-operative Provincial Institute: *Fifty Years of Co-operation – Golden Jubilee Souvenir 1904–54*, Bombay, pp. 29–30.
29. Durham University Library: Archive of Fourth Earl Grey. *Report of the Committee on the Establishment of Co-operative Credit Societies in India*, HMSO, London, 1903, p. 5.
30. Ibid.
31. Wolff, *Co-operation*, p. 45.
32. Ibid., pp. 45–6.
33. Rita Rhodes and Dionysos Mavrogiannis, *Thematic Guide to ICA Congresse 1895–1995*, International Co-operative Alliance, Geneva, 1996, pp. 12–13.
34. Wolff, *Co-operation*, p. 47–8.
35. Rhodes and Mavrogiannis, *Thematic Guide*, pp. 19–24.
36. Wolff, *Co-operation*, pp. 48–50.
37. Ibid., p. 51.
38. Ibid., pp. 51–2.
39. Ibid., p. 58.
40. Aden, 'The Remedy', pp 269–80.
41. James, *Raj*, p. 422.
42. Ibbetson, Sir Denzil, 'Approach to Legislation on Co-operative Credit, 1904', in Muenkner, *100 Years Co-operative Credit.*
43. Ibid., p. 269.
44. Ibid., p. 271.
45. Ibid., p. 272.
46. Ibid., p. 274.
47. Ibid., p. 277.
48. H. Calvert, *The Law and Principles of Co-operation*, Thacker, Spink & Co., Calcutta, 1959.
49. Ibid., p. 52.
50. Ibid., p. 8.
51. Madhav v. Madane, 'A Century of Indian Co-operative Legislation – From State Control to Autonomy of State Partnership', in Muenkner, *100 Years Co-operative Credit*, p. 59.
52. Wolff, *Co-operation*, pp. 63–4.
53. Madane, 'A Century', p. 61.
54. Ibid., p. 57.
55. Madane, 'A Century', p. 58.
56. Margaret Digby, *Agricultural Co-operation in the Commonwealth*, Basil Blackwell, Oxford, 1956, p. 4.

CHAPTER 7

1. Jan Morris, *Pax Britannica*, Faber and Faber, London, 1998, pp. 243–4.
2. Plunkett Foundation Archive: Letter to Sir Horace Plunkett from Rider Haggard, 12 April 1911. We know much about Haggard's popular novels such

as *King Solomon's Mines* which had African settings, but he was also interested in co-operatives as his correspondence with Sir Horace Plunkett indicates.

3. Frank Welsh, *A History of South Africa*, Harper Collins, London, 2000, p. 311.
4. Thomas Pakenham, *The Scramble for Africa 1876–1912*, Weidenfield & Nicholson, London, 2001, p. 386.
5. Welsh, *History*, p. 315.
6. Ibid., pp. 315–16.
7. Ibid., p. 318.
8. Thomas Pakenham, *The Boer War*, Weidenfield & Nicholson, London, 1998, pp. 22–3.
9. Durham University Library: Archive of Fourth Earl Grey. Letter to Raleigh, 27 August 1904.
10. Ibid.
11. Durham University Library: Archive of Fourth Earl Grey. Letter from Grey to R. Fischer, Fischervale, Mashonaland, 12 May 1903.
12. Ibid.
13. Durham University Library: Archive of Fourth Earl Grey. Letter to Grey from Owen Thomas, 19 May 1903.
14. Durham University Library: Archive of Fourth Earl Grey. Reference to letter from F. E. Wienholt to Sir Lewis Mitchell.
15. Durham Unviersity Library: Archive of Fourth Earl Grey. Letter from Charles W. Boyd, joint secretary, Rhodes Trust, to the secretary, British South Africa Company, 19 January 1904.
16. Durham University Library: Archive of Fourth Earl Grey. Letter to Grey from Charles Bullock, 17 December 1903.
17. Durham University Library: Archive of Fourth Earl Grey. Letter from J. C. Gray, general secretary of the Co-operative Union Ltd, Manchester,15 May 1903.
18. Durham University Library: Archive of Fourth Earl Grey. Article from the *Rhodesian Agricultural Journal*, August 1903.
19. Patrick Bolger, *The Irish Co-operative Movement – Its History and Development*, Institute of Public Administration, Dublin, 1976, p. 375.
20. Plunkett Foundation Library: *Report of the Superintendent*, p. 5.
21. Ibid.
22. Ibid., p. 6.
23. Pakenham, *Scramble*, p. 216.
24. Ibid., p. 378.
25. Ibid., p. 379.
26. Botswana National Archives and Records: *Proclamation by His Excellency the High Commissioner, No.2. 1910*, 20 January 1910.
27. Margaret Digby, *Digest of Co-operative Law at Home and Abroad*, P. S. King and Son Ltd, London, 1933, p. 63.
28. Plunkett Foundation: *Agricultural Co-operation in its Application to Industry. The Business and the Life of the Farmer in the British Empire*, Routledge and Sons Ltd, London, 1925, p. 69.
29. Ibid., p. 69.
30. Digby, *Digest*, p. 58.
31. Ibid., p. 59.
32. Ibid., p. 60.
33. Ibid.
34. Ibid., p. 64.
35. Ibid., p. 70.
36. Ibid., pp. 70–1.
37. Ibid., p. 40.

CHAPTER 8

1. ICA: *Report of Thirteenth Congress, Vienna*, 1934, pp. 123–43.
2. Rita Rhodes and Dionysos Mavrogiannis, *Thematic Guide to ICA Congresses 1895–1995*, Studies and Report Series, ICA, Geneva, 1996.
3. Co-operative Union Ltd: *Report of Portsmouth Congress*, 1912, pp. 78–9.
4. Co-operative Union Ltd: *Report of the Bournemouth Congress*, 1931, p. 488.
5. Co-operative Union Ltd: *Report of the Cheltenham Congress*, 1927, p. 89.
6. Gary Lewis, *A Middle Way – Rochdale Co-operation in New South Wales 1859–1986*, Australian Association of Co-operatives Ltd, Sydney, p. 326.
7. Chapter 3, **pp. XX–XX**.
8. Lewis, *Middle Way*, p. 3.
9. Margaret Digby, *Agricultural Co-operation in the Commonwealth*, Basil Blackwell, Oxford, 1956, p. 51.
10. Jack Shaffer, *Historical Dictionary of the Co-operative Movement*, The Scarecrow Press, Lanham, MD and London, 1999, p. 152.
11. Digby, *Agricultural Co-operation*, pp. 51–3.
12. Lewis, *Middle Way*, p. 14.
13. Ibid., p. 326.
14. Arnold Bonner, *British Co-operation*, Co-operative Union Ltd, Manchester, 1961, p. 488.
15. Percy Redfern, *The Story of the CWS – The Jubilee History of the Co-operative Wholesale Society Limited 1863–1913*, The Co-operative Wholesale Society, Manchester, 1914, p. 376.
16. Ibid., p. 390.
17. Lewis, *Middle Way*, p. 41.
18. Redfern, *Story*, p. 387.
19. Bonner, *British Co-operation*, p. 488.
20. Lewis, *Middle Way*, p. 326.
21. Ibid., p. 326.
22. Ibid., pp. 326–7.
23. Ibid., p. 327.
24. Ibid.
25. Ibid., p. 264.
26. Ibid., p. 46.
27. Ibid., pp. 113–14.
28. Eric Hobsbawm, *The Age of Empire 1875–1914*, Abacus, London, 1994, p. 114.
29. C. R. Fay, *Co-operation at Home and Abroad*, Vol. 2, P. S. King & Son Ltd, London, 1939, pp. 349–50.
30. Plunkett Foundation Archive: *Report of 1924 Empire Conference, Wembley*, p. 65.
31. Shaffer, *Historical Dictionary*, p. 318.
32. Plunkett Foundation Archive: *Report 1924*, p. 65.
33. Ibid., p. 66.
34. Margaret Digby, *Digest of Co-operative Law at Home and Abroad*, P. S. King & Son Ltd, London, 1933, p. 56.
35. Ibid., p. 56.
36. Chapter 7.
37. Durham University Library: Archive of Fourth Earl Grey. Letter from Grey to Sir Lewis Harcourt, secretary of state for the colonies, dated 23 June 1911.
38. Ibid. Letter from Grey's secretary to Alphonse Desjardins, 22 February 1912.
39. Ibid. Letter from Grey to Sir Horace Plunkett, 27 December 1910.

40. Robert Bothwell, *The Penguin History of Canada*, Penguin Canada, Ontario, 2007, p. 212.
41. Margaret Digby, *Agricultural Co-operation in the Commonwealth*, Basil Blackwell, Oxford, 1956, p. 26.
42. Shaffer, *Historical Dictionary*, p. 173.
43. Digby, *Agricultural Co-operation*, p. 27.
44. W. B. Francis, *Canadian Co-operative Law*, The Carswell Co. Ltd, Toronto, 1959, pp. 4 and 7.
45. Ibid., pp. 7–8.
46. Plunkett Foundation Archive: *Report 1924*, p. 28.
47. Francis, *Canadian Co-operative Law*, pp. 9–10.
48. Plunkett Foundation Archive: *Report 1924*, pp. 33–4.
49. Ibid., p. 36.
50. B. N. Arnason, *It Was a Great Privilege*, British Institute of Co-operative Studies, London, 2004.
51. Durham University Library: Archive of Earl Grey. Letter from Earl Grey to Henry Wolff, 25 February 1905.
52. Ibid. Letter from Earl Grey to Henry Wolff, 15 March 1905.
53. Ibid., Report of the Special Committee, Canadian House of Commons, 1907, p. 89.
54. Ibid., p. 89.
55. Ibid., p. 91.
56. Ibid., pp. 91–3.
57. Ibid., p. 93.
58. Ibid., pp. 106–11.
59. Ibid., pp. 113–20.
60. Durham University Library: Archive of Earl Grey. Report of Special Committee, 1907, p. 70.
61. Ibid.
62. Ibid., pp. 73–4.
63. Ibid., p. 71.
64. Ibid., pp. 75–89.
65. Ibid., p. 79.
66. Ibid., pp. 53–67.
67. Brett Fairburn, Ian MacPherson and Nora Russell, *Canadian Co-operatives in the Year 2000*, University of Saskatchewan, Saskatoon, 2000, p. 44.
68. Ibid., p. 44.
69. Shaffer, *Historical Dictionary*, p. 278.
70. Durham University Library: Archive of Earl Grey. Letter to Sir Horace Plunkett, 7 December 1910.
71. Ibid. Letter from Plunkett to Grey, 6 January 1911.
72. Ibid. Letter from Grey's secretary to Alphonse Desjardins, 22 February 1912.

CHAPTER 9

1. Henry Wolff, *Co-operation in India*, 2nd edn, W. Thacker and Co., London, 1927.
2. Patrick Bolger, *The Irish Co-operative Movement – Its History and Development*, Institute of Public Administration, Dublin, 1977, p. 74.
3. Margaret Digby, *An Anglo-American Irishman*, Blackman, Oxford, 1949.
4. Bolger, *Irish Co-operative Movement*, p. 395.
5. Ibid., p. 396.
6. Plunkett Foundation Archives: Plunkett's Diaries.

7. Margaret Digby, *The Little Nut Tree – The Memoirs of Margaret Digby*, The Plunkett Foundation, Oxford, 1979, p. 58.
8. Bolger, *Irish Co-operative Movement*, p. 111.
9. Plunkett Foundation Archives: *Agricultural Co-operation – In its Application to the Industry, the Business and the Life of the Farmer in the British Empire*, George Routledge & Sons Ltd, London, 1925.
10. Digby, *Little Nut Tree*, pp 56–7.
11. Plunkett Foundation Archives: *Agricultural Co-operation*, p. 101.
12. Kusoom Vadgama, *India–British Campaigns in Britain for Indian Reforms, Justice and Freedom 1831–1947*, Banyan Tree Publishing, London, 1997, pp.82 and 155.
13. Denis Judd, *Empire – The British Imperial Experience from 1765 to the Present*, Phoenix Press, London, 1996, pp. 273–4.
14. Hans-H. Muenkner, *100 Years Co-operative Credit Societies Act, India, 1904*, ICA, Asia and Pacific, New Delhi, 2005, p. 65.
15. Plunkett Foundation Archives: *Agricultural Co-operation*, p. 127.
16. Ibid., pp. 131–3.
17. Ibid., p. 134.
18. Ibid., p. 169.
19. Ibid., p. 137.
20. Ibid., pp 165–6.
21. Ibid., p. 166.
22. Ibid., p. 167.
23. Ibid., p. 169.
24. Ibid.
25. Ibid., p. 171.
26. Ibid., p. 142.
27. Ibid., p 143.
28. Ibid., p. 127.
29. Ibid., p. 181.
30. Ibid., p. 222.
31. John Tilley, *Churchill's Favourite Socialist – A Life of A. V. Alexander*, Holyoake Books, Manchester, 1995.
32. Plunkett Foundation Archives: *Agricultural Co-operation*, 227–8.
33. Ibid., p. 229.
34. Ibid., p 231.
35. Digby, *Little Nut Tree – The Memoirs of Margaret Digby*, 1979, p. 56.
36. Ibid., p. 57.
37. Ibid., p. 59.
38. Ibid.
39. Ibid., p. 60.
40. Ibid., p. 61.
41. Ibid., pp. 139–58.

CHAPTER 10

1. Jan Morris, *Pax Britannica – The Climax of Empire*, Faber and Faber, London, 1998, pp. 185–6.
2. Ibid., p. 7.
3. Anthony Kirk-Green, *On Crown Service – A History of HM Colonial and Overseas Service, 1827–1997*, I. B. Tauris, London, 1999, pp. 20–2.
4. Ibid., p. 165.
5. Ibid., p. 167.
6. Ibid., p. 168.

7. Ibid., pp. 167–73.
8. T. Wainright, *Army and Navy Stores Limited Centenary Year*, Army and Navy Stores, London, 1971, p. 3.
9. Gary Lewis, *A Middle Way – Rochdale Co-operation in New South Wales 1859–1986*, Australian Association of Co-operatives Ltd, Sydney, 1992, p. 13.
10. Co-operative Wholesale Society Ltd: *The People's Year Book 1921*, Manchester,1921, p. 122.
11. ICA: *Report of Vienna Congress*, 1930, London, pp. 156–8.
12. ICA: *Report of London Congress*, 1934, London, p. 132.
13. Ibid., p. 155.
14. Ibid., pp. 150–1.
15. Ibid., p. 152.
16. Ibid., p. 153.
17. Ibid., p.156.
18. Ibid., p. 157.
19. ICA: *Report of ICA Paris Congress*, 1937, London, p. 145.
20. Plunkett Foundation Archives: *Select Bibliography of Co-operation* – reprinted from the *Plunkett Year Book of Agricultural Co-operation, 1954*.
21. C. R. Fay, *Co-operation at Home and Abroad*, Vol. 2, P. S. King & Son, London, 1939, p. 377.
22. Ibid., pp. 377–8.
23. Margaret Digby, *Agricultural Co-operation in the Commonwealth*, Basil Blackwell, Oxford, 1956, p. 3.
24. Margaret Digby, *The Little Nut Tree – The Memoirs of Margaret Digby*, The Plunkett Foundation, London, 1979, pp. 257–8.
25. Ibid., p. 69.
26. H. Calvert, *The Law and Principles of Co-operation*, ed. B. B. Mukherjee, 5th edn, Thacker Spink & Co. Ltd, London, 1959, p. xi.
27. B. J. Surridge and Margaret Digby, *A Manual of Co-operative Law and Practice*, The Plunkett Foundation of Co-operative Studies, Oxford, 1972.
28. Calvert, *The Law*, p. 10.
29. Ibid., p. 8.
30. Ibid., pp. 17–18.
31. Ibid., p. 18.
32. Ibid., p. 19.
33. Ibid., pp. 28–9.
34. Ibid., p. 27.
35. C. Strickland, *Co-operation for Africa*, Oxford University Press, London, 1933.
36. Morris, *Pax Britannica*, p. 243.
37. Ibid., p. 244.
38. Strickland, *Co-operation for Africa*, ppvi–vii.
39. Ibid., p. 30.
40. Ibid., p. 34.
41. Ibid., p. 38.
42. Ibid., p. 39.
43. Ibid., pp. 98–119.
44. Calvert, *The Law*, p. 25.
45. Madhav Madane, 'A Century of Indian Co-operative Legislation', in Hans-H. Muenkner (ed.), *100 Years Co-operative Credit Societies Act, India, 1904*, ICA, Asia and Pacific, New Delhi, 2005, p. 57.
46. Rita Rhodes, 'Paternalism in the Early British Co-operative Movement', in Ian MacPherson and Erin McLaughlin (eds), *Integrating Diversities within a Complex Heritage – Essays in the Field of Co-operative Studies*, New Rochdale Press, Victoria, BC, 2008, pp. 129–150.
47. Chapter 9.

CHAPTER 11

1. Glen Balfour-Paul, 'Britain's Informal Empire in the Middle East', in J. M. Brown and W. M. Roger Louis (eds), *Oxford History of the British Empire – The Twentieth Century*, Oxford University Press, Oxford, 1999, p. 494.
2. Roger Owen, *Lord Cromer: Victorian Imperialist*, Oxford University Press, Oxford, 2004.
3. Balfour-Paul, 'Britain's Informal Empire', pp. 494–6.
4. Balfour-Paul, 'Britain's Informal Empire', pp. 497–8.
5. Ibid., pp. 490–514.
6. Ibid., p. 497.
7. Henry Wolff, *Co-operation in India*, W. H. Thacker & Co., London, 1927, pp, 23–4.
8. Ibid., p. 22.
9. Ibid., p. 24.
10. Ibid.
11. C. F. Strickland, *Co-operation for Africa*, Oxford University Press, London, 1933, p. 47.
12. Ibid., pp. 47–8.
13. Jack Shaffer, *Historical Dictionary of the Cooperative Movement*, The Scarecrow Press, Inc., Lanham, MD and London, 1999, p. 294.
14. Strickland, *Co-operation*, p. 49.
15. Ibid., pp. 48–9.
16. International Co-operative Alliance: *Co-operation in the Colonies*, documentary reports prepared by the ICA Secretariat, Palestine Report, March 1942.
17. C. F. Strickland, *The Possibility of Introducing a System of Agricultural Co-operation in Palestine*, HMSO, London, 1930.
18. Plunkett Foundation Archive: *Year Book of Agricultural Co-operation 1936*, London, pp. 305–13.
19. Ibid., p. 307.
20. Ibid., pp. 307–8.
21. Ibid., p. 309.
22. ICA: *Co-operation.*
23. Plunkett Foundation Archive: *Year Book 1936*, p. 309.
24. Ibid., p. 310.
25. Ibid., p. 308.
26. Plunkett Foundation Archive: *Year Book of Agricultural Co-operation, 1947*, London, p. 181.
27. Margaret Nicholson, *Co-operation in the Colonies – Design for Study*, Co-operative Union Ltd, Education Department, Manchester, 1953, p. 61.
28. Plunkett Foundation Archive: *Year Book 1947*, p.180.
29. Ibid.
30. Ibid.
31. Ibid., p.181.
32. Ibid.
33. A. F. Laidlaw, *Co-operatives in the Year 2000, Studies and Reports*, No. 15, ICA, London, 1980, p. 10.

CHAPTER 12

1. Jan Morris, *Farewell the Trumpets – An Imperial Retreat*, Faber, London, 1998, p. 432.
2. Ibid., p. 435.

3. Ibid., p. 460.
4. Ibid., p. 435.
5. ICA Archives: Original typescript of article entitled 'The ICA and the Founding of the United Nations', appearing in the *Review of International Co-operation*, Vol. 76, No. 2, 1983, pp. 18–25 of original.
6. Howard Johnston, 'Demobilization to Constitutional Decolonization', in Judith M. Brown and W. Roger Louis (eds), *The Oxford History of the British Empire – The Twentieth Century*, Oxford University Press, Oxford, 1999, pp. 609–11.
7. *Co-operation in the Colonies*, a report from a special committee to the Fabian Colonial Bureau, George Allen and Unwin Ltd, London, 1945, p. 21.
8. Ibid., p. 612.
9. Rita Rhodes, *The International Co-operative Alliance during War and Peace 1910–1950*, The International Co-operative Alliance, Geneva, 1995, pp. 272–3, 278–9, 281.
10. Ibid., pp. 281–4.
11. Rhodes, *The International Co-operative Alliance*, p. 273.
12. Ibid., pp. 29–39, 49, 56, 81, 107–8, 139, 142, 179, 218, 256, 264.
13. W. P. Watkins, *The International Co-operative Alliance 1895–1950*, The International Co-operative Alliance, London, 1970, pp. 220–1.
14. *Co-operation in the Colonies*:, report from a special committee, pp. 22–3.
15. Ibid., p. 23.
16. Ibid.
17. Ibid., p. 1.
18. Ibid.
19. Ibid., p. 2.
20. Ibid., p. 19.
21. Ibid., p. 21.
22. Ibid.
23. Ibid., p. 26.
24. Ibid., p. 29.
25. Ibid., pp. 193–4.
26. Ibid., p. 195.
27. Ibid., p. 200.
28. Ibid., pp. 203–4.
29. Ibid., p. 204.
30. B. J. Surridge, 'Co-operative Advances', in Anthony Kirk-Greene (ed.), *Glimpses of Empire – A Corona Anthology*, I. B. Tauris, London, New York, 2001, pp. 142–5.
31. *Co-operation in the Colonies*, a report from a special committee, p. 202.
32. Brown and Louis, *The Oxford History*, p. 730.
33. Surridge, 'Co-operative Advances', p. 142.
34. Ibid., p. 143.
35. Ibid.
36. Ibid., pp. 143–4.
37. Arnold Bonner, *British Co-operation*, Co-operative Union Ltd, Manchester, 1961, p. 220.
38. Co-operative Union Ltd: *Report of Annual Co-operative Congress, Blackpool*, 1946, p. 68.
39. Co-operative Union Ltd: *Congress Report, Blackpool*, 1946, p. 95.
40. Ibid., p. 69.
41. E. M. Carr-Saunders, Florence P. Sargant and Robert Peers, *Consumers' Co operation in Great Britain*, 3rd edn, George Allen and Unwin Ltd, 1943, pp. 214–26.
42. Ibid., p. 225.

43. B. J. Surridge and Margaret Digby, *A Manual of Co-operative Law and Practice*, 3rd edn, The Plunkett Foundation, Oxford.
44. Taped interview with Dr Robert Marshall, 25 September 1998.
45. Co-operative Union Ltd: *Congress Report, Margate*, 1952, p. 63.
46. Co-operative Union Ltd: *Congress Report, Llandudno*, 1953, p. 46.

CHAPTER 13

1. Judith Brown and W. Roger Louis, *The Oxford History of the British Empire – The Twentieth Century*, Oxford University Press, Oxford, 1999, pp. 728–37.
2. Co-operative Union Ltd: *Congress Report, Blackpool, 1960*, Co-operative Union Ltd, Manchester, 1960, p. 204.
3. Archie Macintosh, Response to Questionnaire, 20 March 2000.
4. Ibid.
5. Ibid.
6. Trevor Bottomley, *Happy Highways*, ELSP, p. 112.
7. Basil Loveridge, *One Hundred Thousand Miles in the Kalahari*, published by Basil Loveridge, 2005, p. 32.
8. Bottomley, *Happy Highways*, pp. 118–19.
9. Hans-H. Munkner, *100 Years Co-operative Credit Societies Act, India, 1904*, ICA, Asia and Pacific, 2005, pp. 344–5.
10. Ibid., p. 345.
11. Ibid., p. 347.
12. E-mail from Trevor Bottomley to author, 30 April 2004.
13. Margaret Digby, *The Little Nut Tree – The Memoirs of Margaret Digby*, The Plunkett Foundation, Oxford, 1979, p. 178.
14. W. H. K. Campbell, *Practical Co-operation in Asia and Africa*, W. Heffer and Sons Ltd, London, 1955.
15. Munkner, *100 Years*, p. 245.
16. Ibid., p. 248.
17. Campbell, *Practical Co-operation.*
18. Munkner, *100 Years*, p. 249.
19. Loveridge, *One Hundred Thousand Miles*, p. 7.
20. Bottomley, *Happy Highways*, p. 125.
21. Loveridge, *One Hundred Thousand Miles*, p. 11.
22. Ibid., p. 69.
23. Ibid., p. 10.
24. Bottomley, *Happy Highways*, pp. 128–9.
25. Ibid., p.138.
26. Ibid., pp. 140–1.
27. Ibid., pp. 163–4.
28. Ibid., pp. 164–7.
29. Ibid., p. 160.

CHAPTER 14

1. Anthony Kirk-Greene, *On Crown Service – A History of HM Colonial and Overseas Civil Services, 1837–1997*, I. B. Tauris, London, 1999, p. 111.
2. Ibid.
3. Sheila Gorst, *Co-operative Organisation in Tropical Countries 1945–1960*, Plunkett Foundation for Co-operative Studies, Occasional Paper No. 26, London, 1965, p. 19.

4. Ibid., pp 39–40.
5. Ibid., p. 40.
6. J. Boyd, 'Malaya', in *Year Book of Agricultural Co-operation 1947*, Plunkett Foundation, London, 1947, pp. 174–5.
7. Ibid., p. 176.
8. J. G. Crawford, 'Malaya', in *Year Book of Agricultural Co-operation 1948*, Plunkett Foundation, London, 1948, p. 214.
9. Ibid., pp. 214–21.
10. Ibid., p. 221.
11. *Co-operation in the Colonies*, report of the special committee to the Fabian Colonial Bureau, Allen and Unwin Ltd, London, 1945, p. 84.
12. Jack Shaffer, *Historical Dictionary of the Co-operative Movement*, The Scarecrow Press Inc., Lanham, MD and London, 1999, p. 298.
13. *Co-operation in the Colonies*, p. 90.
14. Ibid., p. 40.
15. Ibid., p. 93.
16. Plunkett Foundation Archive: *Administration Report of the Working of Co-operative Societies from May 1, 1942 to April 30, 1945*, Ceylon Government Press, Colombo, 1946, p. 3.
17. Ibid.
18. Ibid., p. E19.
19. Ibid., p. E20.
20. Basil Loveridge, 'Meeting Famous Registrars – An Eye Witness Report', in Hans-H. Muenkner (ed.), *100 Years Co-operative Credit Societies Act, India, 1904*, ICA, Asia and Pacific, New Delhi, 2005, p. 249.
21. Plunkett Foundation Archive: *Administration Report 1945*, p. E9.
22. Plunkett Foundation Archive: *Report on the Ceylon Co-operative Movement for 1957*, Ceylon Government Press, Colombo, 1958, p. D19.
23. Plunkett Foundation Archive: *Administration Report 1945*, p. E5.
24. Ibid. p. E6.
25. Ibid.
26. Ibid., pp. E34–7.
27. Ibid., p. E35.
28. Plunkett Foundation Archive: *Administration Report on the Working of Co-operative Societies from May 1, 1945 to April 30, 1948*, Ceylon Government Press, Colombo, 1949, p. E45.
29. Ibid.
30. Plunkett Foundation Archive: *Report on the Ceylon Co-operative Movement for 1957*, p. D3.
31. Ibid., p. D5.
32. Ibid.
33. Ibid., p. D19.
34. Ibid., p. D21.
35. ibid., p. D26.
36. Plunkett Foundation Archive: *Administration Report 1948*, p. 45.
37. Plunkett Foundation Archive: *Report on the Ceylon Co-operative Movement for 1957*, p. D19.
38. Hans-H. Muenkner, *100 Years Co-operative Credit Societies Act, India, 1904*, ICA, Asia and Pacific, New Delhi, 2005, p. 246.
39. Shaffer, *Historical Dictionary*, p. 370.
40. Plunkett Foundation Archives: *Report on the Ceylon Co-operative Movement for 1957*, p. D68.
41. Ibid., p. D69.
42. *Co-operative Independent Commission Report*, Co-operative Union Ltd, Manchester, 1958.

CHAPTER 15

1. ICA: *Report of Nineteenth Congress, Paris, 1954*, ICA, London, 1954, p. 179.
2. Rita Rhodes, *The International Co-operative Alliance during War and Peace 1910–1950*, ICA, Geneva, 1995, pp. 279–84.
3. ICA: *Report of Nineteenth Congress, Paris, 1954*, p. 180.
4. Ibid., pp. 177–90.
5. Ibid., pp. 191–215.
6. Ibid., p. 177.
7. Ibid., p. 178.
8. Ibid., p. 180.
9. Ibid., p. 184.
10. Ibid., p. 185.
11. Ibid., p. 187.
12. Ibid., p. 189.
13. Ibid., p. 190.
14. Ibid., p. 196.
15. W. P. Watkins, *The International Co-operative Alliance 1895–1970*, ICA, London, 1970, pp. 284–5.
16. Ibid., p. 286.
17. ICA: *Report of Twentieth Congress, Stockholm, 1957*, ICA, London, 1957, pp. 147–52.
18. Ibid., pp. 162–72.
19. Ibid., pp. 153–61.
20. Ibid., p. 171.
21. Ibid., p. 153.
22. Ibid.
23. Ibid., p. 155.
24. Ibid., p. 157.
25. Ibid.
26. Ibid., pp. 153–4.
27. Ibid., pp. 197–8.
28. ICA: *Report of Twenty-first Congress, Lausanne, 1960*, ICA, London, 1960, pp. 149–61.
29. Ibid., pp. 162–9.
30. Ibid., pp. 170–6.
31. Watkins, *The International Co-operative Alliance 1895–1970*, p. 302.
32. Ibid., pp. 302–3.
33. Ibid., pp. 306–7.
34. Ibid., pp. 323–4.
35. Rita Rhodes and Dionysos Mavrogiannis, *Thematic Guide to ICA Congresses 1895–1995*, ICA, Geneva, Studies and Reports Series No. 30, 1995, p. 132.
36. Ibid., p. 159.
37. Watkins, *The International Co-operative Alliance 1895–1970*, p. 151.
38. Ibid., pp. 149–51.
39. Jack Shaffer, *Historical Co-operative Dictionary*, The Scarecrow Press, Inc., Lanham, MD and London, 1999, p. 186.
40. Anthony Kirk-Greene, *On Crown Service – A HistHHistory of HM Colonial and Overseas Civil Services, 1837–1997*, I. B. Tauris, London, 1999, pp. 74–5.
41. Department of Technical Co-operation: *Co-operatives Overseas Policy on the Recommendations of the Advisory Committee*, Cmnd. 2258, HMSO, London, 1964.
42. Ibid., pp. 3–4.
43. Ibid., p. 4.

44. Ibid., p. 5.
45. Ibid., p. 6.
46. Ibid., p. 7.
47. Ibid., p. 8.
48. Watkins, *The International Co-operative Alliance 1895–1970*, p. 284.
49. Patrick Bolger, *The Irish Co-operative Movement – Its History and Development* Institute of Public Administration, Dublin, 1977, p. 66.
50. W. H. K. Campbell, *Practical Co-operation in Asia and Africa*, W. Heffer & Sons Ltd, 1955, pp. 32–3.
51. Shaffer, *Historical Co-operative Dictionary*, p. 381.
52. Notes received from Archie Macintosh, dated 20 March 2000.
53. Jan Morris, *Pax Britannica – The Climax of Empire*, Faber and Faber, London, 1998, p. 15.

Index